S0-BZQ-320

The Archaeology and History of Glastonbury Abbey

ESSAYS IN HONOUR OF THE NINETIETH BIRTHDAY OF C. A. RALEGH RADFORD

Glastonbury Abbey is one of the great cultural centres of Anglo-Saxon and medieval England, with a history that touches on many of the most intriguing questions of the period: yet this is the first volume of scholarly essays to be devoted to the subject. Written in honour of one of Glastonbury's most distinguished investigators, C. A. Ralegh Radford, the first items naturally concern themselves with the physical remains of the abbey, ranging from the place of Glastonbury in the development of Christianity in Somerset to specific examinations of surviving monastic buildings. In the case of the Tribunal, this close examination shows how a piece of modern folklore evolved long after the dissolution of the monastery itself. The main body of the essays is concerned with the abbey's documents, its precious charters, the books from its library, the traditions – true or otherwise – contained in its histories. The earliest Anglo-Saxon period is discussed, and an attempt is made to present a coherent account of the pre-Conquest abbots. The links with the Celtic world, including a recently discovered fragment of what may be one of the Irish books mentioned in the Life of St Dunstan, are given their due place. The final section deals with the cultural life of the abbey, beginning with an essay which shows how imagination could reshape history when powerful claims, such as the authority of the bishop of Bath and Wells over the abbey, had to be challenged. In a wider context, Glastonbury's role in education is discussed, and the concluding essay touches on the most magical of all Glastonbury's legends, its link with Joseph of Arimathea and the Grail.

The Archaeology and History
of Glastonbury Abbey

ESSAYS IN HONOUR OF THE NINETIETH BIRTHDAY
OF C. A. RALEGH RADFORD

EDITED BY
Lesley Abrams AND James P. Carley

THE BOYDELL PRESS

© Contributors 1991

All Rights Reserved. Except as permitted under current legislation
no part of this work may be photocopied, stored in a retrieval system,
published, performed in public, adapted, broadcast,
transmitted, recorded or reproduced in any form or by any means,
without the prior permission of the copyright owner

DA
690
.G45
A78
1991

First published 1991 by The Boydell Press, Woodbridge

The Boydell Press is an imprint of Boydell & Brewer Ltd
PO Box 9, Woodbridge, Suffolk IP12 3DF
and of Boydell & Brewer Inc.
PO Box 41026, Rochester, NY 14604, USA

ISBN 0 85115 284 8

British Library Cataloguing in Publication Data
The archaeology and history of Glastonbury Abbey : essays in
 honour of the ninetieth birthday of C. A. Ralegh Radford.
 1. Somerset (England). Abbeys, history
 I. Abrams, Lesley 1952– II. Carley, James 1946– III. Radford,
 C. A. Ralegh (Courtenay Arthur Ralegh) 1900–
 942. 383
 ISBN 0–85115–284–8

Library of Congress Cataloging-in-Publication Data
The Archaeology and history of Glastonbury Abbey : essays in honour of
 the ninetieth birthday of C. A. Ralegh Radford / edited by Lesley
 Abrams and James Carley.
     p.   cm.
 Includes bibliographical references.
 ISBN 0–85115–284–8 (acid-free paper)
 1. Glastonbury Abbey. 2. Glastonbury (England) – Antiquities.
 3. Glastonbury (England) – Church history – Sources. 4. Excavations
 (Archaeology) – England – Glastonbury. I. Radford, Courtenay Arthur
 Ralegh, 1900– . II. Abrams, Lesley, 1952– . III. Carley, James P.
 DA690.G45A78 1991
 942.3'83–dc20   90–26578

This publication is printed on acid-free paper

Printed in Great Britain by
St Edmundsbury Press Ltd, Bury St Edmunds, Suffolk

CONTENTS

III. INTERPRETATIONS

ILLUSTRATIONS AND FIGURES

Dunning, *The Tribunal, Glastonbury, Somerset*

Abrams, *A Diploma of King Ine for Glastonbury*

Reproduced by permission of the Somerset Archaeological and Natural History Society. Photograph, British Library.

Carley and Dooley, *An Early Irish Fragment of Isidore of Seville's* Etymologiae

All the plates are of Longleat House, Marquess of Bath, NMR 10589, flyleaf.

Reproduced by permission of the Marquess of Bath, Longleat House, Warminster, Wiltshire.

PREFACE

I had worked for many years among documents concerning the history of Glastonbury Abbey – a place which always exercises a fascination on those who endeavour to explore its history, an exploration which in that place of legends so often leads to imaginative interpretations – when I first met Dr Ralegh Radford. I was, of course, well aware of his extremely distinguished career in archaeology, covering so much of England, Wales and Scotland, but I was not prepared for his totally genial presence.

Later, over a period of years, I was part of the Excavation Committee appointed by the Church of England and was thus privileged to be in close touch with Radford's excavations. There is no one who could explain more cogently or clearly the tasks he was undertaking; tasks which combined a thorough knowledge of the complex history of the place with exact historical expertise. Over luncheon and a refreshing drink in a nearby hotel Radford would explain in the simplest terms what had been done and what was next to be done. We all know that conversation with experts can confuse the uninitiated; this was never the case at Glastonbury.

Each year, exciting – and in many cases unexpected – finds occurred. There were the considerable remains of the *uallum monasterii*, dating from *ca* 700 at the very latest, a bank and ditch which surrounded the early monastic settlement and which, indeed, was part of a great complex separating the site from the outside world. Ponter's Ball, though probably a twelfth-century embankment on the road east of Glastonbury, seems to mark an external boundary of a monastic 'city' dating back to much earlier times. Post-holes at the abbey excavations showed wattled buildings and supported the chroniclers' statements that the *uetusta ecclesia* was so constructed. William of Malmesbury's account of how St Dunstan raised the ground level of the ancient burial site and walled it around was fully supported by the digs, and parts of his cloister (of a kind hardly known at that date north of the Alps) were discovered. There were also remains of a glass-works whose nearest parallels were at Constantinople.

It has been a great privilege to have known a scholar whose extreme competence is only equalled by his unassuming and courteous manner. Within the last few years – to take just one example – I discovered a Saxon stone on the outside of the church at Horsham St Faith's in Norfolk, and despite the demands on his time Dr Radford identified its character for me and wrote a thorough report. It was typical of him.

Aelred Watkin

ABBREVIATIONS

AD	*Adami de Domerham Historia de Rebus Gestis Glastoniensibus*, ed. Thomas Hearne, 2 vols (Oxford, 1727)
ASC	Anglo-Saxon Chronicle
The Chronicle of Glastonbury Abbey	*The Chronicle of Glastonbury Abbey. An Edition, Translation and Study of John of Glastonbury's 'Cronica sive Antiquitates Glastoniensis Ecclesie'*, ed. James P. Carley (Woodbridge, 1985)
Cronica	*Cronica siue antiquitates Glastoniensis ecclesie* of John of Glastonbury, in *The Chronicle of Glastonbury Abbey. An Edition, Translation and Study of John of Glastonbury's 'Cronica sive Antiquitates Glastoniensis Ecclesie'*, ed. James P. Carley (Woodbridge, 1985)
DA	*De antiquitate Glastonie ecclesie*, in *The Early History of Glastonbury. An Edition, Translation and Study of William of Malmesbury's 'De Antiquitate Glastonie Ecclesie'*, ed. John Scott (Woodbridge, 1981)
DB	Domesday Book
The Early History	*The Early History of Glastonbury. An Edition, Translation and Study of William of Malmesbury's 'De Antiquitate Glastonie Ecclesie'*, ed. John Scott (Woodbridge, 1981)
EETS	Early English Texts Society
es	extra series
IC	*Index chartarum* (Cambridge, Trinity College R. 5. 33, 77r–78v)
JG	*Johannis Confratris et Monachi Glastoniensis Chronica sive Historia de Rebus Glastoniensibus*, ed. Thomas Hearne, 2 vols (Oxford, 1726)
LT	*Liber terrarum*
MGH	Monumenta Germaniae Historica
NMR	North Muniment Room, Longleat House
ns	new series
os	old series
PRO	Public Record Office
PSANHS	*Proceedings of the Somerset Archaeological and Natural History Society*
RS	Rolls Series
S.	P. H. Sawyer, *Anglo-Saxon Charters. An Annotated List and Bibliography* (London, 1968). Cited by charter number.
SDNQ	*Notes and Queries for Somerset and Dorset*
Somerset	*Domesday Book*, gen. ed. John Morris, 35 vols in 40 (Chichester, 1975–86) VIII: *Somerset*, ed. Caroline and Frank Thorn (1980)
SRS	Somerset Record Society

I

BUILDINGS AND ARCHAEOLOGICAL SURVEYS

Pagan and Christian by the Severn Sea

PHILIP RAHTZ

INTRODUCTION

Sometimes by design, but more particularly by good fortune, a number of the excavations in which archaeologists have been involved in the old county of Somerset (see figure 1) have directly or indirectly proved relevant to our understanding of the late-Roman and post-Roman centuries in the upper reaches of the Bristol Channel.[1] Subsequent post-excavation research moreover has led to the consideration of issues which are wider than those immediately related to the data recovered, both thematically and spatially.

Somerset cannot be viewed in isolation in this period of history: two of its neighbouring counties, Gloucestershire to the north and Wiltshire to the east, should afford earlier evidence of Anglo-Saxon domination, even if archaeology has not yet been enlightening on this point;[2] Dorset, on another coast, shows evidence of a more positive Romanized background in the fourth century; Ralegh Radford's own county of Devon is a neglected but potentially rich area for these studies; and Cornwall, together with Scilly, has yielded much evidence to the spades and scholarship of Radford and of his disciple, Charles Thomas.

Research has led also to the other (northern) side of the Severn Sea,[3] and of course further west to Ireland.[4] An even more exotic element has been provided from the distant shores of the eastern and central Mediterranean, from Iberia and Gaul; from these places fine tableware and amphorae found their way onto our western seaboards.[5] Their presence in the west of Britain is an astonishing piece of good fortune for archaeology. The material provides at

[1]   P. A. Rahtz, 'The Dark Ages 400–700 AD', *The Archaeology of Somerset*, ed. M. Aston and I. Burrow (Taunton, 1982), pp. 99–108; and P. A. Rahtz, 'Post-Roman Avon', *The Archaeology of Avon*, ed. M. Aston and R. Iles (Bristol, 1987), pp. 73–82.

[2]   C. Heighway, 'Anglo-Saxon Gloucestershire', *The Archaeology of Gloucestershire*, ed. A. Saville (Cheltenham, 1984), pp. 225–47.

[3]   The Dark-Age archaeology of Wales has recently been freshly and neatly summarized; see *Early Medieval Settlements in Wales 400–1100*, ed. N. Edwards and A. Lane (Cardiff, 1988).

[4]   P. A. Rahtz, 'Irish Settlements in Somerset', *Proceedings of the Royal Irish Academy* 76 C (1976), 223–30.

[5]   Charles Thomas has recently suggested (in a letter to the author) that these ceramics were the scattered offloadings of a single merchant adventurer, the archaeologically more durable hold-fellows of more valuable silks and spices; such a ship would have sought a return cargo of tin, silver, and perhaps human merchandise

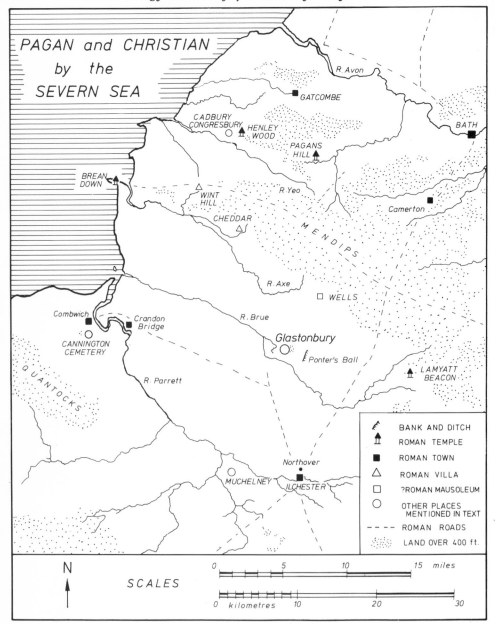

Figure 1 Pagan and Christian by the Severn Sea

once the dating evidence, together with some social and economic (if not also religious) context, for many sites in the west of Britain which are otherwise lacking in surviving material culture. It is still a matter of wonder to

from the princes of Dumnonia and Gwent. Thomas may be right; or these sherds may derive in contrast from *several* such voyages, or from intermediary sources.

find these ceramics on remote hilltops such as Glastonbury Tor, and to consider the history of their travels. They do of course come from areas which were Christian, and some carry Christian symbols; ideological concepts, and even missionaries, could have been carried by the same route.[6]

Spatially, then, the field of enquiry is wide. Thematically, the scope is also broad. Archaeologists of this period have tried to co-ordinate sparse and puzzling data relating to the environment,[7] the economy, crafts, industry, and trade; and to the defensive works and fortunes of the princely and military leaders, who are introduced to us also from the difficult sources of written history. Finally, and most problematically, we must consider the ideology of the period, the theme which has always been at the heart of Ralegh Radford's own research.

This last theme is the subject of this essay. I shall examine such evidence as we have for pagan and Christian religious beliefs and behaviour, principally from Somerset, but also occasionally from the other areas mentioned. The data come mainly from temples and shrines, cemeteries, hillforts and hilltops, and from other buildings or places we may believe to have been associated with Christianity. Looking for elements of indigenous survival,[8] my time-scale must include some recognition of the prehistoric and early Roman background. I am, however, concerned especially with the fourth century of Roman Britain, with western British independence in the fifth and sixth centuries, and with the seventh and eighth centuries, in which were laid the foundations of the English West (if not yet beyond the Tamar).

My first serious encounter with the Dark Ages (which is still, alas, an evocative and useful term) was at Pagans Hill – the very name drew me to the site – in the early 1950s.[9] It proved to be of outstanding interest from a religious point of view, illuminating the architectural and ideological significance of a great late-Roman temple complex. By the late 1960s, I was beginning to consider the wider implications of the data from excavations in Somerset. I gave a lecture in 1966 to the Cambrians in Shrewsbury on the relevance of these data to protohistoric Wales. One of my themes on that occasion, which I have pursued ever since, was that we should look at the late- and post-Roman period in the west of Britain holistically. This involves an attempt to examine all the environmental, social, economic, and ideological aspects of society objectively, in all their interacting complexity. In that lecture I stressed that we should not be influenced by epithets such as 'sub-Roman' or 'Dark-Age' (with their negative implications), 'Arthurian' (a term historically misleading and an example of the trivial personalization which

---

6   C. Thomas, 'East and West: Tintagel, Mediterranean Imports and the Early Insular Church', *The Early Church in Western Britain and Ireland*, ed. S. Pearce, BAR Brit. ser. 102 (Oxford, 1982), pp. 17–34.

7   Including the rise and fall of the Severn Sea itself.

8   P. A. Rahtz, 'Celtic Society in Somerset AD 400–700', *Bulletin of the Board of Celtic Studies* 30 (1982), 176–200.

9   See now P. A. Rahtz and L. Watts, 'Pagans Hill Revisited', *Archaeological Journal* 146 (1989), forthcoming. The place-name, which is a corruption of the name of a local family, the Paynes, has no religious connections.

bedevils history and historical archaeology) or 'Early-Christian'. This last term can lead to an undue emphasis on the ideological, specifically Christian, aspects of the period, influencing the choice of sites to be dug and the interpretation of the evidence recovered.[10]

On the occasion of that lecture, Ralegh Radford was in the front row. The proposal that we should discard the term 'Early-Christian' was not well received by him; with a very uncharacteristic passion, he came up to the rostrum afterwards and said, 'as to your last suggestion, Mr Rahtz: over my dead body!' I suspect that this is not the least reason why he is still so bonny a quarter of a century later!

THE PAGAN BACKGROUND

INDIGENOUS BELIEFS

This is no place to survey the panorama of prehistoric pagan belief, from the Neolithic or earlier to the infiltration of the Graeco-Roman pantheon. Whatever speculation there may have been about the religious beliefs associated with the great monuments of Avebury and Stonehenge and with chambered tombs and other impressive manifestations of ideology, it is only in the Iron Age that we can begin to fill in the background to the temples and shrines of the first four centuries of the Christian era.[11] We may discern in the equations made between the Mediterranean pantheon and the 'Celtic' deities – principally from epigraphic and sculptural evidence – something of the attributes of the late pre-Roman gods, and even something of their continuing importance in Roman times.[12] The classic example in Somerset is the iconographic and epigraphic primacy of Sul over Minerva at Bath, while in Gloucestershire the sole (if composite) deity of Nodens at Lydney can probably be equated with the god of the Severn Bore.[13]

This essay examines the culmination of this fusion of 'Celtic' and Roman religion in the fourth century,[14] by which time the indigenous culture was a dozen generations old.

ROMAN TEMPLES IN THE FOURTH CENTURY

Roman temples are a well-known feature of the late-Roman scene in Britain; and nowhere are there more than in Somerset, where no less than a dozen

10   Cf. Rahtz, 'The Dark Ages 400–700 AD', *passim.*
11   See P. J. Drury, 'Non-classical Religious Buildings in Iron Age and Roman Britain', *Temples, Churches and Religion*, ed. W. Rodwell, BAR Brit. ser. 77 (Oxford, 1980), pp. 45–78; and G. Wait, *Ritual and Religion in Iron Age Britain*, BAR Brit. ser. 149 (Oxford, 1986).
12   See A. Ross, *Pagan Celtic Britain* (London, 1967).
13   G. C. Boon, 'A Roman Sculpture Rehabilitated', *Britannia* 20 (1989), 201–17.
14   Whatever 'Celtic awareness' may have smouldered under the pseudo-classical infrastructure; see Rahtz, 'Celtic Society'.

examples are known from the fourth century and before.[15] Some, like Henley Wood,[16] have their origins in the first century, if not earlier. Such antiquity is matched in neighbouring counties by Nettleton Scrubb (in Wiltshire)[17] and, more remarkably, by Uley in Gloucestershire, with its origins in the Neolithic period.[18] Other Somerset sites such as Pagans Hill,[19] or Brean Down,[20] began only in the later third or earlier fourth century. The temples exhibit signs of change or even stress in the course of the fourth century. This may not be unrelated to the influence of Christianity, following the conversion of Constantine. We must envisage a co-existence (possibly uneasy) between the new religion and the pagan cults.

Anyone who had pinned their hopes on the new faith might have been disillusioned; this may have been at least one factor in the revival of pagan religion in Britain in the later fourth century. Archaeologically, *de novo* or renewed activity at Pagans Hill, at Maiden Castle in neighbouring Dorset,[21] and at Lydney in Gloucestershire[22] bears witness to this revival.

One problem is that the oscillating fortunes of late-Roman temples in the fourth century and later are difficult to define chronologically.[23] This is because of the absence of secure means of dating, following the demise of the money economy in the early fifth century. This and the stagnation of material culture means that any 'late-Roman' material found in temple or other sequences in the archaeology of this period in Britain provides no more than a *terminus post quem* of *ca* A.D. 400 at the latest. Hence, for instance, the pagan-Christian-pagan sequence postulated by W. J. Wedlake for Nettleton Scrubb may be interpreted as extending through decades or even centuries, rather than being concentrated in the later fourth-century *milieu* that the excavator depicted. Such an extended chronology is now demonstrable for Uley, where there is evidence for use of the site in the seventh or eighth

---

[15] P. A. Rahtz and L. Watts, 'The End of Roman Temples in the West of Britain', *The End of Roman Britain*, ed. P. J. Casey, BAR Brit. ser. 71 (Oxford, 1979), pp. 183–210.

[16] L. Watts and P. Leach, *The Roman Temples and Later Cemetery at Henley Wood*, forthcoming.

[17] W. J. Wedlake, *The Excavation of the Shrine of Apollo at Nettleton, Wiltshire, 1965–1971*, Research Report of the Society of Antiquaries 40 (London, 1982).

[18] A. Ellison, 'Excavations at West Hill, Uley . . .', *Temples, Churches and Religion*, ed. Rodwell, pp. 305–28; and A. Woodward and P. Leach, *Excavations at West Hill, Uley, Gloucestershire, 1976–79*, forthcoming.

[19] P. A. Rahtz, 'The Roman Temple at Pagans Hill, Chew Stoke, N. Somerset', *PSANHS* 96 (1951), 112–42, and now Rahtz and Watts, 'Pagans Hill Revisited' (see above, note 9).

[20] A. M. ApSimon, 'The Roman Temple on Brean Down, Somerset', *Proceedings of the University of Bristol Spelaeological Society* 10 (1965), 195–258.

[21] R. E. M. Wheeler, *Maiden Castle, Dorset*, Research Report of the Society of Antiquaries 12 (London, 1943).

[22] R. E. M. Wheeler and T. V. Wheeler, *Report on the Excavations at Lydney Park, Glos.*, Research Report of the Society of Antiquaries 9 (London, 1932), pp. 60–3.

[23] Rahtz and Watts, 'The End of Roman Temples'.

century; there are otherwise no datable finds later than the later fourth century.[24]

Pagan religion as manifested in these late-Roman temples is at least reasonably well understood from archaeological, epigraphic and written sources. The number of temples in Somerset might suggest that such pagan beliefs were especially strong there.[25]

ROMAN CHRISTIANITY IN SOMERSET

Charles Thomas, in his survey of Roman Christianity in Britain,[26] used a scoring system by which the extent of the faith might be measured.[27] Although Somerset was not in Thomas's lowest ranking,[28] the evidence he cited was sparse enough.

At Gatcombe, a chi-rho graffito on a pot was found in a building destroyed about 380.[29] At Wint Hill there was a Rhenish glass bowl carrying the inscription VIVAS CUM TUIS ('May you and yours have life'), together with the Graeco-Latin PIE Z (*pie zeses*).[30] At Bath (not strictly speaking now in Somerset) there is among the inscriptions one which can be interpreted as a reference to temple-wrecking by Christians.[31] There are also the sarcophagi and lead coffins found by Peter Leach in the Northover cemetery at Ilchester.[32] Finally, and most importantly, as this paper was going to press, a silver-alloy amulet cross, comprising a disc with short segmented arms, decorated with an equal-armed chi-rho punched onto the disc, probably of the later fourth century, was found by Peter Leach in a west-east grave in a newly discovered cemetery at Shepton Mallet. (See Plate I.)

Notably absent so far in Somerset are any structural remains that could be interpreted as churches: also missing are lead tanks with or without iconographic detail, mosaics with Christian attributes (such as those at Hinton St Mary and Frampton in Dorset);[33] villas such as Lullingstone with its Christian frescos, and Roman buildings which were built on, or were succeeded

---

24   See below, p. 16.
25   Martin Carver has, however, suggested that the large number of temples was, on the contrary, a reaction to the growing strength and threat of Christianity in the area; M. Carver, 'Sutton Hoo in Context', *Settimane di studio del Centro italiano di studi sull'alto medioevo* 32 (1986), 77–123.
26   C. Thomas, *Christianity in Roman Britain to AD 500* (London, 1981), pp. 96–142.
27   Also see W. Frend, 'Romano-British Christianity in the West: Comparison and Contrast', in *The Early Church*, ed. Pearce, pp. 5–17.
28   See Thomas, *Christianity*, fig. 16, p. 139.
29   *Ibid.* pp. 89–90, 108.
30   *Ibid.* pp. 129–30.
31   *Ibid.* pp. 126–7.
32   R. Morris, *Churches in the Landscape* (London, 1989), pp. 31–3 and fig. 10.
33   Thomas, *Christianity*, pp. 104–6.

Plate I Silver-alloy disc from Shepton Mallet

by, Christian churches of a later period.[34] The only possible exception is Cheddar.[35]

There has been a good deal of discussion about the fate of Romano-British Christianity.[36] W. H. C. Frend saw the destruction of an episcopally based

---

[34]   R. Morris and J. Roxan, 'Churches on Roman Buildings', in *Temples, Churches and Religion*, ed. Rodwell, pp. 175–209.

[35]   See P. A. Rahtz and S. M. Hirst, 'Cheddar Vicarage 1970', *PSANHS* 117 (1973), 65–96.

[36]   For example, Thomas, *Christianity*, pp. 240–74. For a more recent discussion see Morris, *Churches in the Landscape*, pp. 6–45.

framework as complete by *ca* 450,[37] brought on by the combination of civil disorder, alien raiding and the indifference or hostility of the rulers of the rising British kingdoms.

ROMAN CHRISTIAN CEMETERIES

The best evidence of a stratum of Christianity in Somerset society in the fourth or later centuries may prove to come from cemeteries, notably from the rural examples of Cannington and Henley Wood (see below) and the urban cemetery at Ilchester.[38] Ilchester, although so far explored only in a small sample, has attributes which link it to the cemetery of Poundbury, near Dorchester,[39] which is widely believed to have been a Christian cemetery in the fourth century. These attributes include lead and freestone coffins and, at Poundbury at least, slight epigraphic evidence; here there were also plaster-encased burials, and mausolea with personal portraiture painted on plaster. Both cemeteries are characterized by large numbers of west-east extended mixed inhumation burials in deep graves, with an orderly layout in rows; but these characteristics are not in themselves exclusively Christian. It may be significant that both Ilchester and Dorchester were the most urban Roman places in their respective counties.[40]

OTHER POSSIBLE CHRISTIAN STRUCTURES

Three other sites in Somerset may be Christian. The first is the remarkable stone and timber structure at Wells (Roman *Fontinetum*), which Warwick Rodwell interprets as a Roman mausoleum.[41] This was an important feature in what may have been an earlier and possibly originally pagan religious complex. Roman buildings, possibly belonging to a villa, were also found; these were aligned on the massive resurgence now known as St Andrew's spring, in the gardens of the bishop's palace. Unfortunately, any original interments in the mausoleum structure (possibly two lead coffins) had been removed, their place being taken by many other later bones, so there is no secure dating. The structure may be fifth-century or later. What is important is that the mausoleum became the nucleus of a Christian complex, which by A.D. 909 was the cathedral of a bishopric. There may have been a similar

---

37   Frend, 'Romano-British Christianity in the West', p. 11.

38   Morris, *Churches in the Landscape*, pp. 31–3 and fig. 10.

39   C. Sparey Green *et al.*, *Excavations at Poundbury. Vol. II: The Cemeteries*, forthcoming; C. Sparey Green, 'The Cemetery of a Romano-British Community at Poundbury, Dorchester, Dorset', in *The Early Church*, ed. Pearce, pp. 61–76.

40   Leaving aside Bath, which is a special case.

41   W. Rodwell, 'From Mausoleum to Minster: The Early Development of Wells Cathedral', in *The Early Church*, ed. Pearce, pp. 49–60; or, conveniently, M. Aston and I. Burrow, 'The Early Christian Centres 600–1000 AD', *Archaeology of Somerset*, ed. Aston and Burrow, pp. 119–22.

sequence at Bath, from the great Roman temple and baths complex to the Anglo-Saxon minster.[42]

The other two possibly Christian structures are smaller features, orientated west-east. These were excavated very close to the late-Roman temples of Brean Down and Lamyatt Beacon (which were themselves *not* west-east). At the former site,[43] a small rectangular building was built using part of the semi-ruined temple; it was apparently securely dated by numerous coins, predominantly Theodosian issues of the end of the fourth century. The excavator considered, but rejected, the possibility that this structure was Christian. Roger Leech, however, following his discovery of a similar but undated building at Lamyatt Beacon (associated with some fifteen west-east graves), claimed both small buildings as Christian.[44] He compared them to Irish or other chapels of similar size and shape associated with early monastic sites. If he is right, these small buildings would be, in their remote and windswept localities, of eremetic character; and if indeed they date from the latest Roman phases, or even the fifth century, they would be by far the earliest monastic remains known in the west of Britain, except possibly those on Lundy Island.

PAGANISM AND CHRISTIANITY

CONFLICT?

I have discussed the evidence for paganism and Christianity in late-Roman Somerset as if they were two irreconcilable belief-systems which must always have been in conflict, competing for adherents within a given society. This is certainly the impression we get from the early writers on the Church. But a more objective view might look for elements of syncretism: pagan deities, sites or mosaic motifs acquiring Christian attributes, or, in reverse, early Christianity being 'contaminated' by absorbing pagan practice. This would have been inescapable, if a policy of peaceful integration was practised.[45] Such a fusion is neatly exemplified in the Water Newton treasure, where Christian motifs appear on votive plaques of characteristically pagan form.[46]

Another more recent example is the remarkable figured plaque from a fourth-century context at Uley. This plaque has four panels, which are interpreted by Martin Henig as two scenes from the Old Testament (Jonah and the whale, and Abraham and Isaac) and two from the New Testament (Christ

---

[42]   Rodwell, 'From Mausoleum to Minster', p. 49; see also Morris, *Churches in the Landscape*, p. 33 and fig. 11.

[43]   ApSimon, 'The Roman Temple on Brean Down'.

[44]   R. Leech, 'The Excavation of a Romano-Celtic Temple and a Later Cemetery on Lamyatt Beacon, Somerset', *Britannia* 17 (1986), 259–328.

[45]   Frend, 'Romano-British Christianity in the West', p. 8; Morris, *Churches in the Landscape*, pp. 6–92.

[46]   K. S. Painter, *The Water Newton Early Christian Silver* (London, 1977).

and the centurion, and the healing of the blind man).[47] The plaque was carefully folded, as though to 'kill' it or 'render it appropriate for deposition in a pit for the reception of sacred items no longer needed but still dedicated to the deity'[48] (in this case Mercury). The plaque is probably from a casket.

If there *was* conflict between religions, it might be traceable archaeologically in damage to pagan structures or statues.[49] Violent action has been tentatively suggested as a possible reason for such damage at Pagans Hill.[50] Here the late third- or early fourth-century temple, possibly dedicated to Apollo, was apparently vandalized in the middle of the fourth century, temple sculpture being broken and architectural débris being thrown down the well. The well is itself on the temple axis and is assumed to have initially had a religious significance. The deposition of architectural débris in the well was followed by what might be interpreted as profanation, in the form of the dumping of domestic débris. There was, however, a revival, presumably of a pagan cult, in the later years of the fourth century or afterwards. This did not extend to the use of the well or the domestic areas, but only to the temple and ceremonial buildings to the east. Christian activities on other temple sites may explain their ultimate destruction, but the evidence is usually difficult to date.[51]

Finally, we must admit the possibility that some temples may themselves have been converted to Christian use, even if there is no direct evidence in the archaeology. Wedlake believed that the octagonal temple of Apollo at Nettleton Scrubb was converted to a cruciform plan for Christian use, though there was subsequently a reversion to paganism.[52] The structure at Pagans Hill could also conceivably have been used as a church at any time after its initial pagan phase;[53] its architectural form was at least appropriate for a religious building.[54]

47   M. Henig, in *Britannia*, forthcoming.
48   Ellison, 'Excavations at West Hill, Uley', pp. 305–28; and Woodward and Leach, *Excavations at West Hill, Uley*, forthcoming.
49   As in the case of the pulling-down in the sixth century of a statue of Diana by a 'saint' in Gaul, recounted by Gregory of Tours; cf. Morris, *Churches in the Landscape*, pp. 48–51.
50   Rahtz and Watts, 'Pagans Hill Revisited' (see above, note 9); and Boon, 'A Roman Sculpture', pp. 201–17.
51   The only possible example in our area is Brean Down, in or before the late fourth or early fifth century, as discussed above, p. 11.
52   Wedlake, *The Excavation of the Shrine of Apollo at Nettleton*, pp. 61 and 79.
53   It was indeed with early centrally planned and dome-vaulted churches in the Eastern Mediterranean that Ralegh Radford compared the temple, in his percipient notes on the architectural reconstruction (in Rahtz, 'The Roman Temple at Pagans Hill', pp. 123–6).
54   The double octagon was of a diameter and height similar to the octagonal chapter houses of Wells and Salisbury cathedrals.

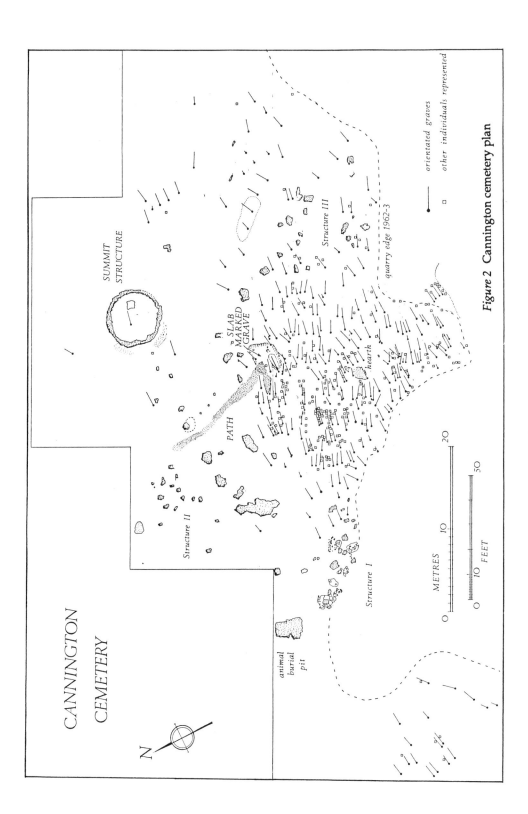

Figure 2 Cannington cemetery plan

LATE- AND POST-ROMAN RURAL CEMETERIES

There exists in the west of Britain a class of rural cemetery which is not 'Roman' in any conventional sense, nor pagan Anglo-Saxon, nor associated with churches or chapels.[55] The type-site of this class is Cannington, near the mouth of the Parrett in western Somerset (see figure 2);[56] Henley Wood is the only similar cemetery to be extensively excavated in modern times.[57] Both are characterized by extended inhumations in rock-cut graves, orientated west-east (with heads to the west), in a relatively orderly layout, mostly in rows; the population was mixed (male, female, adult, juvenile, and infant). The cemeteries were probably multi-nuclear, divided into kin-group or other areas.

At Cannington, a hilltop structure has been interpreted as a late-Roman shrine, temple or mausoleum, with only a few graves in the vicinity. The cemetery, which may originally have numbered at least a thousand graves, developed on the southern slopes of the hill. All the graves were orientated within the northern and southern limits of sunrise or sunset. Dating evidence consisting of finds and radio-carbon determinations indicates that the cemetery was in use from the fourth century to the seventh or early eighth. In its latest elements, Cannington has much in common with the 'final-phase' cemeteries of eastern England.[58]

An important nucleus of the cemetery consisted of a special burial of a juvenile.[59] The rock-cut grave was covered by a low mound (the 'slab-marked grave' on figure 2), on the surface of which was set a box-like structure of stone slabs, aligned on the grave below; at the east end of this was a possible post-setting of stones; one stone was decorated with a circular motif and possible runes. A well-defined path showed this slab-marked grave mound to have been the object of frequent visits; the mound was itself cut into by other graves, as was eventually the path itself.

The community burying here may have come from a wider area of dispersed settlement, but at least part of the population probably lived in or around the neighbouring hillfort of Cannington Camp. Settlement shift, possibly to Cannington itself, was presumably the cause of the ultimate

---

55   P. A. Rahtz, 'Late Roman Cemeteries and Beyond', *Burial in the Roman World*, ed. R. Reece, CBA Research Report 22 (London, 1977), pp. 53–64.

56   P. A. Rahtz, S. M. Hirst and S. M. Wright, *Excavations at Cannington Cemetery 1962–3*, forthcoming.

57   Watts and Leach, *The Roman Temples and Later Cemetery at Henley Wood*, forthcoming.

58   This does not imply the presence of Germanic elements in the population, though there may have been some Germanic infiltration into south-west Somerset during the course of the seventh century. Richard Morris has compiled a list of final-phase cemeteries; see his *The Church in British Archaeology*, CBA Research Report 47 (London, 1983), table IV, pp. 55–6.

59   The skeleton has now been reburied in the parish church at Cannington under a slab decorated with a chi-rho and the inscription, 'The name is known to God'; a wooden statue representing the child stands nearby.

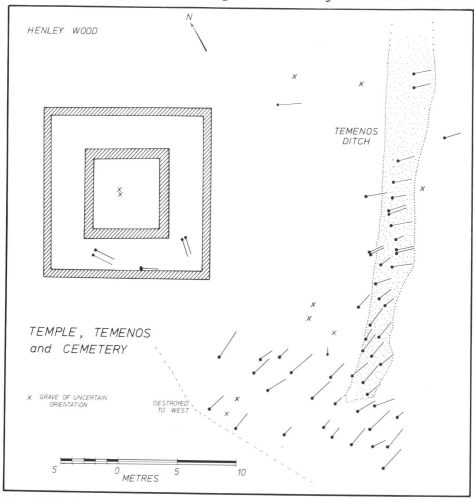

Figure 3 Henley Wood temple, temenos and cemetery plan

abandonment of the hillfort and the cemetery. There may have been a regular Christian burial ground and church in the village by the eighth century.

It is possible that the excavated cemetery at Cannington was Christian from the start, in late-Roman times; alternatively it may have begun as a pagan burial site, associated with the hilltop shrine, temple or mausoleum, which was gradually Christianized. It is not hard to find Christian analogues for the specially marked grave and for evidence of a strong desire to be buried near a focal burial.

At Henley Wood, over fifty graves were excavated on the site of the Roman temple already mentioned (see figure 3). A few graves of the latest phase of the site were cut through the temple floors. Most of the graves were laid out in rows to the east and south-east of the temple, especially in the filled-up *temenos* ditch. There were no certain grave goods or other distinctive grave attributes; the date (based on radio-carbon determinations) centred on the fifth to seventh centuries.

The site of the temple and cemetery at Henley Wood is, like Cannington, close to a hillfort (Cadbury Congresbury) which was occupied by a high-status group in the later fifth or the sixth century;[60] the Henley Wood graves may be at least in part those of this hillfort community.

ROMAN TEMPLES IN THE POST-ROMAN CENTURIES

In a previous paper,[61] I discussed evidence for the continuation of Roman temple sites into the fifth and later centuries in the west of Britain. At Uley, on the Cotswolds, Ann Woodward and Peter Leach have since excavated with meticulous care a Roman temple of several phases dedicated to Mercury.[62] In the final phases (late fourth-century and later), there was a remarkable series of buildings, ending, Woodward argues, with a small Christian church.[63]

Pieces of window or decorative glass were found, unfortunately not directly associated with the church.[64] The glass is important, as it is comparable to that known from Anglo-Saxon ecclesiastical contexts in such classic sites as Monkwearmouth, Jarrow and Repton. These sites are associated with the monastic or missionary activity of the English Church in the Midlands and North-east in the later seventh and eighth centuries.

Another remarkable example in Somerset of such continuing use of temple sites, or of their revival, is again at Pagans Hill. The seventh-century evidence came not from any buildings of the temple complex, but from the partly filled well.[65] Water was drawn from this by an iron pail, which, with animal bones and other finds, later found its way into the well. Amongst these finds was a remarkable blue glass jar.[66] It has recently been suggested

60 See below, pp. 18–19.
61 Rahtz and Watts, 'The End of Roman Temples'.
62 Woodward and Leach, *Excavations at West Hill, Uley* (see above, note 18).
63 In one of the intermediary phases, a stone head of Mercury (one of the finest pieces of Romano-British sculpture ever to be found in Britain) was specially kept, and possibly revered, before its final careful burial. Could it have been equated with Christ? See A. Ellison and M. Henig, 'Head of Mercury from Uley, Glos.', *Antiquity* 55 (1981), 43–4 and frontispiece. As a possible parallel, there may have been a timber church at Cadbury-Camelot, inside (and presumably earlier than) the late-Saxon cruciform church there; see L. Alcock, 'Cadbury-Camelot: A Fifteen Year Perspective', *Proceedings of the British Academy* 68 (1982), 355–88, n. 1.
64 Information from A. Woodward (personal communication).
65 P. A. Rahtz *et al.*, 'Three Post-Roman Finds from the Temple Well at Pagans Hill, Somerset', *Medieval Archaeology* 2 (1958), 104–11.
66 This belongs to the class of squat jars which are among about 200 forms of glass vessel of this period known from Britain; the squat jars are nearly all from rich Anglo-Saxon graves of the sixth and seventh centuries, mostly from Kent. Some, including possibly the Pagans Hill glass, may have been made in the south-east, though the majority are more likely to have been imports from the Rhineland. See Evison in Rahtz and Watts, 'Pagans Hill Revisited' (see above, note 9).

by E. Campbell that blue glass vessels of this squat-jar type were being made or imported under the aegis of the Kentish kings.[67] The jars were, he has suggested, distributed as gifts or trade items to other kings or princes in neighbouring kingdoms. The jars also travelled further afield, to high-status individuals in the North and the British West. The implication is that at Pagans Hill (or nearby) there was someone important enough to be the recipient of such an object – either a British chieftain or a recently settled high-status Anglo-Saxon, a person who had a connection with, or even control over, the temple site and buildings. A Christian context for the use of the temple in the seventh century is perhaps at least as likely as a pagan one; and the glass itself, a rare and costly object, may have been used in ritual observance.[68]

POST-ROMAN PAGANISM

WHICH PANTHEON?

Some confusion is apparent in any discussion of the topic of post-Roman paganism, even in contemporary Early-Christian writings such as those of Bede. The precise nature of the pagan beliefs that Christianity encountered and had to supplant is obscure. Enduring pagan beliefs of the classical world were of course manifest, for example, in the surviving statue of Diana in Gaul mentioned by Gregory of Tours.[69] Doubtless, residues of indigenous and Graeco-Roman faiths were still encountered beyond the fourth century by Christian missionaries in Britain. These residues may however have little to do with the paganism which appears in the pages of Bede. But our knowledge is unfortunately limited, for Bede was not interested in describing the deities worshipped, nor the idols which represented them.[70]

We should bear in mind that in Somerset during the late fifth, sixth and seventh centuries there were Germanic settlers only a hundred or so kilome-

---

[67]   E. Campbell, 'A Blue Glass Squat Jar from Dinas Powys, South Wales', *Bulletin of the Board of Celtic Studies*, forthcoming, and 'Glass Vessels or Cullet? A Taphonomic Study of the Dinas Powys Glass', *Bulletin of the Board of Celtic Studies*, forthcoming.

[68]   Rahtz and Watts, 'Pagans Hill Revisited' (see above, note 9). It may be observed that, like the temple, the glass has eight sides, a number not without significance in Christian belief, stressing the association with resurrection (on the eighth day; see S. McKillop, 'A Romano-British Baptismal Liturgy', in *The Early Church*, ed. Pearce, pp. 35–48, esp. 46). The fourth- or fifth-century baptisteries at the Lateran and S. Tecla, Milan, were of this form.

[69]   See above, note 49. Roger Leech ('Religion and Burials in South Somerset and North Dorset', in *Temples, Churches and Religion*, ed. Rodwell, pp. 321–66, at 335) has hinted at a late survival of the cult of the horned god *Cernunnos*; see also Ross, *Pagan Celtic Britain*, pp. 140, 143 and 186–7. This survival is, in Leech's view, suggested by the finds of pieces of antler in several post-Roman temples, some in what may be religious contexts (cf. Watts and Leach, *The Roman Temples and Later Cemetery at Henley Wood*, as in note 16 above).

[70]   For a recent discussion of pagan English temples, cults, practices and idols, see Morris, *Churches in the Landscape*, pp. 57 ff.

tres to the east; they may have been (even if only for a short time) devotees of the northern pantheon. Expression of their beliefs is likely to be found principally in cemeteries, though the direct links between mortuary behaviour and religious belief are by no means clear.

The only early Anglo-Saxon cemeteries or graves in Somerset (as conventionally defined) are from the end of the period and are found on the eastern fringes of the county.[71] It has been suggested that these 'final-phase' cemeteries, broadly of the seventh century, may belong to a time when pagan and Christian beliefs were merging; alternatively, they could be interpreted as the burial grounds of people who were by that time Christian, in spite of the sometimes quite rich grave goods found.[72] Those cemeteries which are on a new site, replacing an earlier cemetery at another location, may mark a sharp transition from pagan to Christian belief, even if there is no associated church. For the present purpose it is enough to say that changes in mortuary behaviour in areas further to the east may have affected those in Somerset, irrespective of any movements in population or racial mix; new behaviour could have included Christian elements, even if only half understood.[73]

By the end of the seventh century or in the earlier eighth, due to political domination by both Anglo-Saxon rulers and prelates, we may expect to find an amalgam of indigenous, Roman and northern pagan beliefs gradually fusing with, and ultimately being replaced by, Christianity, leading to an increase in burial in churchyards.[74]

HILLFORTS – PAGAN OR CHRISTIAN?

The topic of hillforts is not exclusive from that of temples and shrines,[75] since the sites discussed are themselves largely on hilltops or on promontories in inland or coastal landscapes, such as Pagans Hill or Brean Down.

At Cadbury Congresbury,[76] there is evidence of a fifth- and sixth-century earthwork enclosure and of a high-status community whose *floruit* is dated by imported ceramics from the Mediterranean, Gaul and Cornwall. Secular activities and structures are represented by débris from jewellery-making,

71   P. A. Rahtz and P. J. Fowler, 'Somerset AD 400–700', in *Archaeology and the Land-scape*, ed. P. J. Fowler (London, 1972), pp. 187–221.

72   A. L. Meaney and S. C. Hawkes, *Two Anglo-Saxon Cemeteries at Winnall*, Society for Medieval Archaeology Monograph 4 (London, 1970); Morris, *Churches in the Landscape*, table IV, pp. 55–6.

73   Cf. R. Cramp, 'Northumbria: The Archaeological Evidence', in *Power and Politics in Early Medieval Britain and Ireland*, ed. S. Driscoll and M. Nieke (Edinburgh, 1988), pp. 69–77.

74   This mixture and transition may well be illustrated by the later phase and ultimate abandonment of Cannington.

75   I. Burrow, *Hillfort and Hill-top Settlement in Somerset in the First to Eighth Centuries AD*, BAR Brit. ser. 91 (Oxford, 1981).

76   P. J. Fowler, K. S. Gardner and P. A. Rahtz, *Cadbury Congresbury, Somerset, 1968* (Bristol, 1970); Burrow, *Hillfort and Hill-top Settlement*, pp. 91–110; Rahtz, 'The Dark Ages 400–700', pp. 104–7. A full report is forthcoming in P. A. Rahtz *et al.*, *Excavations at Cadbury Congresbury, 1968–73*.

including copper alloy, glass, enamel and gold. There is also evidence of religious belief.[77] In one part of the site fragments of weathered human skulls, divorced from other parts of the skeleton, attest to a skull cult in the post-Roman centuries.[78] Whatever objects or structures were associated with the skulls were destroyed and incorporated in the make-up for a setting for a wooden receptacle or a major standing post.[79] This could in a Christian context have been a water tank or a cross. There was certainly a change at Cadbury Congresbury, which could of course be interpreted as representing either two pagan phases or a transition from pagan to Christian use.

Further up the shallow northern slope of the hillfort interior, prominent inside the excavated entrance into the post-Roman enclosure earthworks, was a circular timber structure. The distribution of finds suggests that this was not a secular but a religious building,[80] in some ways similar to the hilltop temple or shrine at Cannington.

GLASTONBURY

Glastonbury, as a topographical entity, consists of a west-facing promontory (see figure 4). In periods of severe flooding, or when the sea-level was relatively high, reaching up to 7.6m (25 ft) above Ordnance datum (OD), there would have been water on three sides. A neck of land links the promontory to the higher ground to the east. Glastonbury can never have been an island in historic times.[81] The area would nevertheless have been particularly prominent when the sea-level was high, when boats might have approached the westerly end at Beckery, or penetrated up the River Brue. Two high areas dominate the promontory – the ridge of Wirral Hill rising to over 61m (200 ft) close to the western approaches by water, and the remarkable eminence of the Tor, rising sharply to over 150m (500 ft) above OD. For travellers by land, access was either across a bridge or causeway across the Brue, now linking

[77] Independent of the possibly contemporary cemetery at nearby Henley Wood, discussed above.

[78] The skulls were found near an entrance, on the side of the hillfort facing Henley Wood.

[79] Whatever was in this setting either decayed or was removed. As excavated, the feature was a shallow cylindrical pit defined among the stones which acted as a surround for the tub, post, or cross. In the dark soil fill of this pit was a remarkable group of finds, among which are represented almost every date and class of artefact found on the site. These finds are interpreted as votive offerings of ordinary domestic character, similar to those still found associated with rural Irish holy wells and caves (Rahtz and Watts, 'The End of Roman Temples', pp. 205–10). For a possible parallel, see the incident from the *Vita Samsonis*, recounted in Morris, *Churches in the Landscape*, p. 84; Samson had some troubles with a hilltop *simulacrum* (a stone image) in Cornwall.

[80] There were a few possibly votive finds associated with this structure. These included two handles from Mediterranean amphorae and two bone head-dress or necklet leaves, similar to those found in Roman temples.

[81] This would require a sea-level of over 12m (40 ft) above OD.

Plate II Aerial photograph of Glastonbury Tor, looking ENE.
Crown copyright/RAF photograph

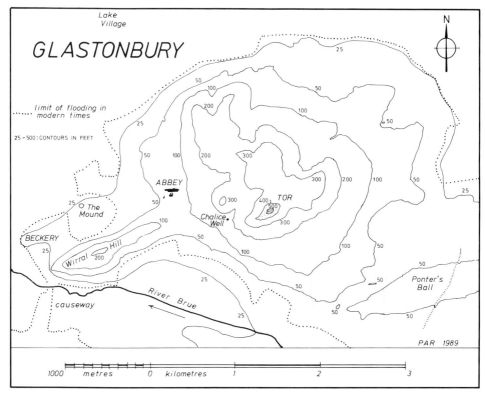

Figure 4 Glastonbury: contour plan of promontory

Glastonbury to Street (and possibly, as the latter name may suggest, of Roman origin), or from the east. Here the connecting neck of land is crossed by Ponter's Ball (*pontis uallum?*), an earthwork with a ditch on its eastern side.[82]

The whole area is one of high economic potential – a point of some importance in considering the wealth of the abbey's estates – and includes a number of important sites (see figure 4).[83] Chalice Well is a buried medieval

[82] Although there have been small excavations at Ponter's Ball, none has been properly executed or published, and the date of the earthwork – whether prehistoric, Roman, Dark-Age or medieval – is still a matter of debate; see P. A. Rahtz, 'Excavations on Glastonbury Tor', *Archaeological Journal* 127 (1971), 1–81, at 4, n. 11. The ends merge into alluvial deposits, where there should be good preservation of dating and environmental evidence.

[83] In the surrounding Levels, this potential was realized as early as the fifth millennium B.C.; this is the date of the earliest of a series of wooden trackways found in peat-cutting, the subject of extensive research by John Coles and Bryony Coles in recent years. For the pre-Roman centuries, there is the very rich archaeological material from the lake- or marsh-villages to the north of Glastonbury. There are also a number of Roman sites in the area. Some of these – consisting of no more than scatters of Roman finds – are on the promontory. There is at present no evidence of any structure of the Roman period nor of any contemporary pagan or Christian site (see R. Dunning, 'The Middle Ages', in *Christianity in Somerset*, ed. R. Dunning [Taunton,

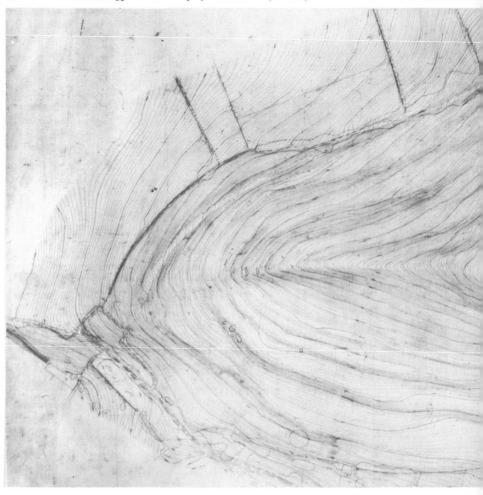

Plate III   Glastonbury Tor: contour plan at one-foot intervals (1964)

well-house.[84] There are also early prehistoric and Roman finds from the vicinity of this major spring, which doubtless provided the principal water supply for the Dark-Age and later buildings on the Tor, as it did for the medieval abbey. The Mound is a medieval earthwork, though a few Dark-

1976], pp. 1–28, at 1–2). It should be emphasized that although Roman material (such as sherds) *has* been found in excavations within the abbey precinct, the finds were all in soil moved in medieval times; so far no Roman finds have been recovered *in situ*. A few Roman sherds and tile fragments were found on the Tor, but these are all likely to be residual in Dark-Age levels (Rahtz, 'Excavations on Glastonbury Tor', p. 11).

84   P. A. Rahtz, 'Excavations at Chalice Well, Glastonbury', *PSANHS* 108 (1964), 143–63.

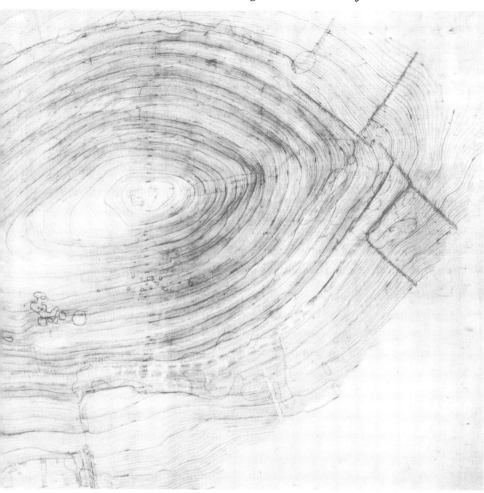

Age imported sherds have been found there.[85] The Tor, the abbey, and Beckery will be discussed further below.

The earliest structures known from the Glastonbury promontory were found on the Tor, the summit and shoulder of which were extensively excavated in 1964–6.[86] Plates II and III and figure 5 illustrate the precipitous topography of the Tor. The contours have been redrawn (figure 5) from an unpublished aerial photogrammetric survey commissioned in 1964 by the late Geoffrey Russell in an attempt to validate his hypothesis that the Tor

[85]   J. Carr, 'Excavations on the Mound, Glastonbury, Somerset, 1971', *PSANHS* 129 (1985), 37–62.

[86]   Rahtz, 'Excavations on Glastonbury Tor', pp. 1–81.

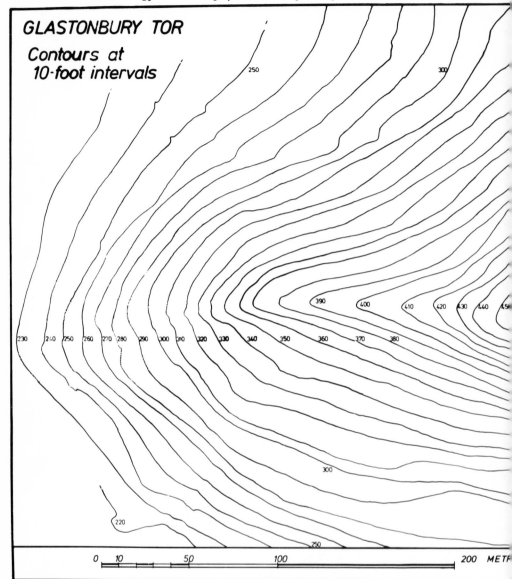

Figure 5 Glastonbury Tor: contours at ten-foot intervals

slopes had been engineered into a gigantic three-dimensional maze of the classic pattern best known from its delineation in the floor of the cathedral of Chartres (see figure 6 and Plate II).[87] The contours of the higher area are shown on figure 7, which illustrates the inaccessibility of the top, relevant in either a military or a religious context.

[87]   *Ibid.* pp. 6–7.

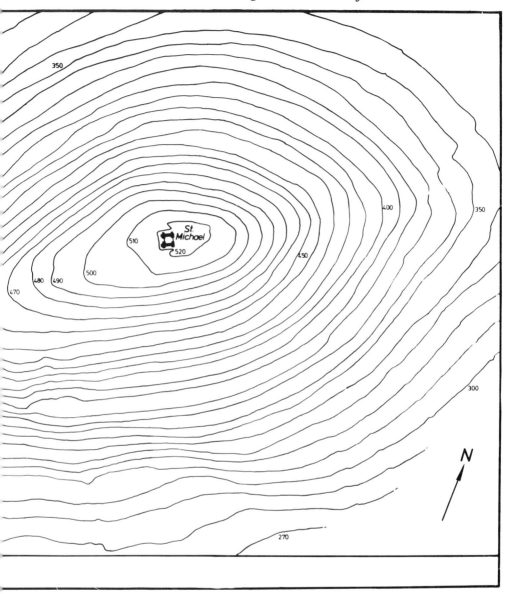

Three main phases – of Dark-Age, later Anglo-Saxon, and medieval date – were defined in the areas excavated, culminating in the erection of the church of St Michael, whose tower is such a splendid landmark on the already prominent Tor.[88] The earliest phase (Areas A–D on figure 8, and figures 9–12) was dated to the later fifth or sixth century by a dozen or so

[88] The significance of the dedication is discussed by Morris, *Churches in the Landscape*, pp. 52–6; see also his figs. 15–16.

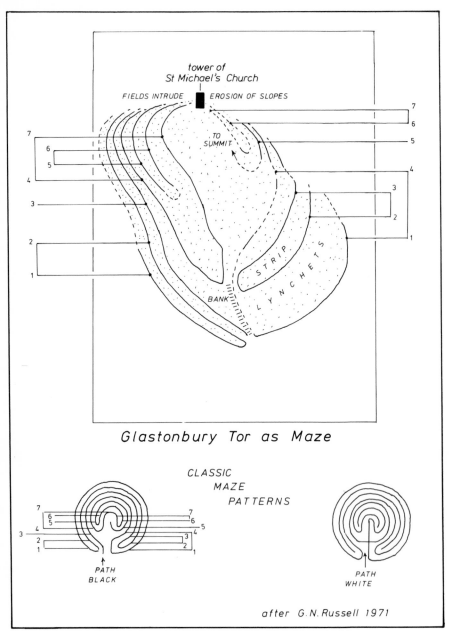

Figure 6 Glastonbury Tor as a maze (after G. Russell)

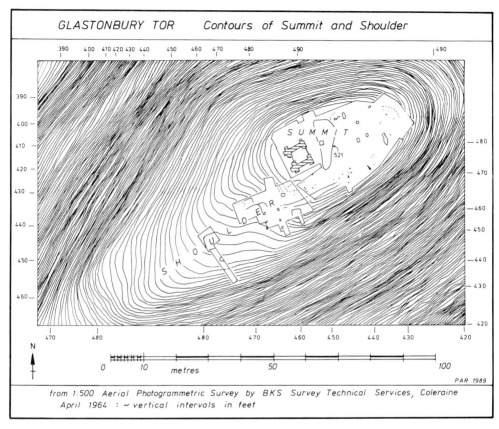

Figure 7 Glastonbury Tor: contours of summit and shoulder

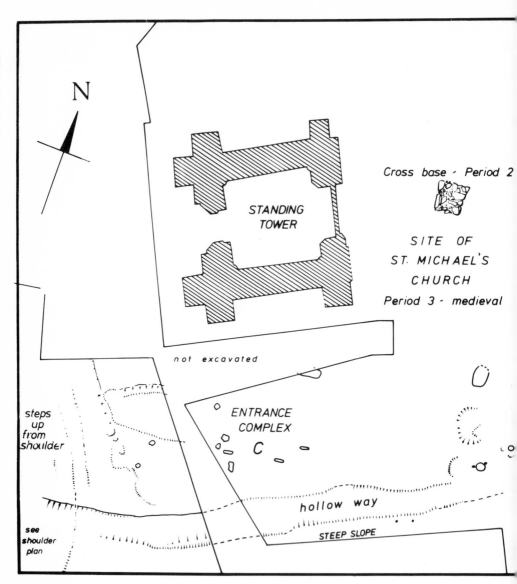

Figure 8 Glastonbury Tor: summit

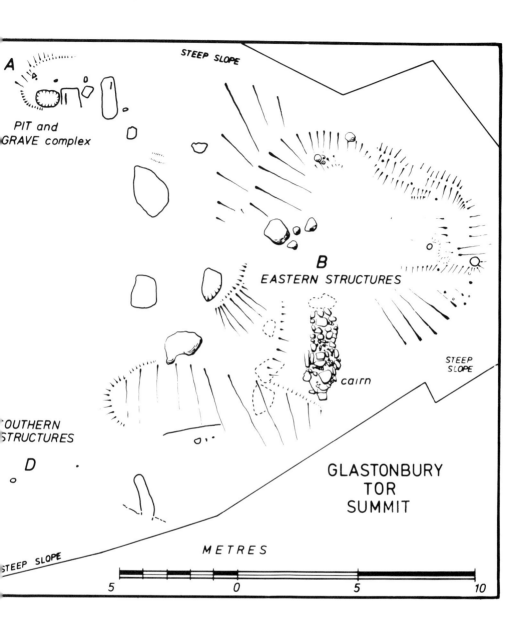

A

STEEP SLOPE

PIT and
GRAVE complex

B
EASTERN STRUCTURES

cairn

STEEP
SLOPE

SOUTHERN
STRUCTURES

D

GLASTONBURY
TOR
SUMMIT

STEEP SLOPE

METRES

5   0   5   10

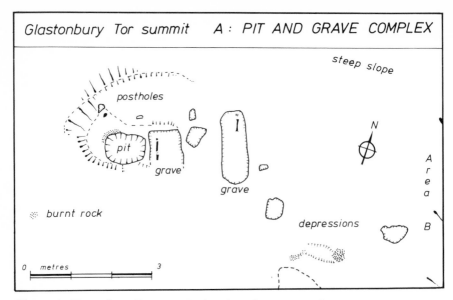

Figure 9 Glastonbury Tor summit: A – pit and grave complex
Figure 10 Glastonbury Tor summit: B – eastern structures

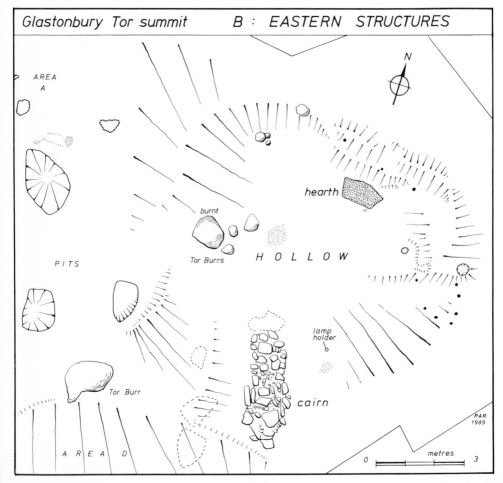

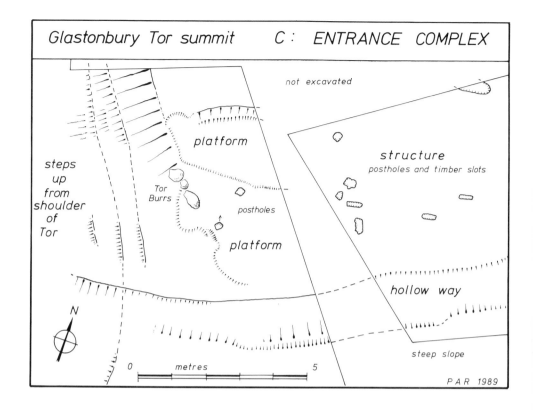

Figure 11 Glastonbury Tor summit: C – entrance complex
Figure 12 Glastonbury Tor summit: D – southern structures

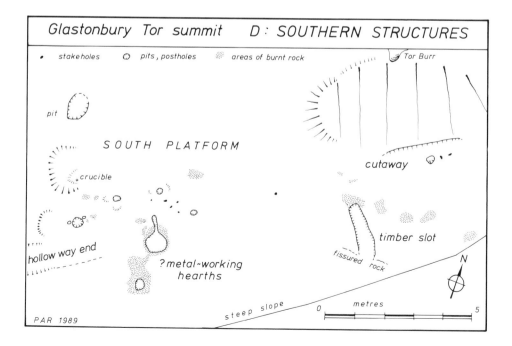

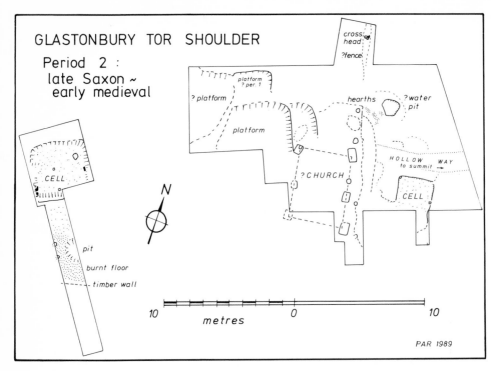

GLASTONBURY TOR SHOULDER

Period 2 :
late Saxon ~
early medieval

cross
head
?fence

platform
? per. 1

? platform

? platform

platform

hearths

?water
pit

N

HOLLOW   WAY
to summit

? CHURCH

CELL

CELL

pit

burnt floor

timber wall

10   0   10

metres

PAR 1989

Figure 13 Glastonbury Tor shoulder, period 2: Late Saxon/Early Medieval

sherds of imported amphorae. Associated with these were post-holes and other features of timber structures,[89] with much animal bone and evidence of non-ferrous metalworking. The evidence is ambiguous: were these features and finds those of a secular eyrie-like stronghold of some local chieftain,[90] or could they belong to an early eremitic monastic site, for which this remote 'desert' location and the craft evidence would be equally appropriate?

Eighteen years ago, when the work on the Tor was published,[91] I was influenced towards an interpretation of the site as a secular stronghold by the presence of two possibly contemporary graves that were north-south rather than west-east (see figure 9), and by the large numbers of animal bones representing prime cuts of meat brought to the site. These did not at the time seem to be consistent with Christian affiliations or with an ascetic lifestyle. Since then the significance of the presence of the bones has been rather undermined by the finding of extensive evidence for meat-eating at no less a place than Iona,[92] and also at Whithorn.[93] It seems probable that

89   Redrawn here more clearly than in the original report.
90   'A bone-strewn redoubt' in Frend's words; Frend, 'Romano-British Christianity in the West', p. 11.
91   See above, note 82.
92   R. Reece, *Excavations on Iona 1964–1974* (London, 1981), p. 38.
93   Information from Peter Hill (personal communication).

traditional views of ascetic early monasticism in western Britain have been based on written sources rather than archaeological evidence. It is therefore at least equally possible that the later fifth- or sixth-century hilltop settlement on the Tor was monastic and eremitic. It would not have been the kind of monastery where high-level secular elements merged inextricably with monastic ones, as later at Glastonbury Abbey, where kings and prelates were equally in evidence.

A monastic interpretation of the site on the Tor may also be considered more likely inasmuch as the second phase of the site, in the middle- to late-Saxon period, included rock-cut cells and a rectangular building, possibly a timber church, on the shoulder of the summit (figure 13). The site was by then under the control of the abbey. On the summit itself was a stone foundation, probably supporting a cross (figure 8); part of a wheel-headed stone cross-head of tenth- or eleventh-century date was found nearby; and it was on the summit that the church of St Michael was eventually founded.

Continuity of religious foundation on the Tor from the sixth century to medieval times is thus more likely than the replacement of a secular stronghold by a monastic complex, especially bearing in mind the later importance of Glastonbury Abbey. The Tor could in this case be seen as the earliest Christian monastic site in the west of Britain, with Lundy Island.[94] Cadbury Congresbury must also be considered in this light and, as we have seen, the two small structures on Brean Down and Lamyatt Beacon. With all these must be considered the difficult evidence of dedications of Celtic saints.[95]

Such a monastic foundation in the sixth century as the remains on the Tor may imply would have been due to the influence of early missionaries of the Western British Church in Wales and/or Ireland,[96] in no way connected with those of the English Church. We may hardly believe the latter to have been effective in this area before the later seventh or eighth century.

The antiquity of the abbey site has been the subject of massive and continuing debate. There has been no published archaeological evidence to suggest that the abbey site was established before the eighth century, though – as must be emphasized – excavation there has been on a very small scale. However, relatively recently an East Mediterranean cast censer of copper alloy of late sixth- or seventh-century date and Byzantine origin has been found, not through controlled excavation, apparently in the area of the northern edge of the abbey precinct.[97]

---

[94] Now that Tintagel has been interpreted as a secular site; see C. Thomas, 'Tintagel Castle', *Antiquity* 62 (1988), 421–34.

[95] Burrow, *Hillfort and Hill-top Settlement*, pp. 47–63.

[96] Morris, *Churches in the Landscape*, pp. 46–92.

[97] The British Museum acquired this object in 1986 from a dealer who had been told that it had been found five or six years previously, during the digging of a service trench. It has been suggested (by Warwick Rodwell, personal communication) that the censer may have been found while road works in the Silver Street car park, which cuts off the northern edge of the abbey precinct, were in progress in 1978; these works, however, antedate the (unfortunately vague) stated date of discovery by several years, and it is not impossible that its discovery is to be associated with

Notably absent from the abbey site are imported sherds such as those found nearby on the Tor. The present writer's view, as an archaeologist, is that the Tor was the pre-Saxon Christian nucleus of Glastonbury, of such repute ultimately as to attract major support from the incoming rulers of Wessex; that the inconvenience of access to the Tor and its restricted space necessitated expansion on a new site; and that this was found in the flatter area where the abbey now stands.[98]

THE ENGLISH CHURCH

The seventh century in Somerset as elsewhere was a crucial transition period between the new Western British societies that arose from the residues of late-Roman Britain and the increasingly dominant English settlement. This transition must be considered not only in relation to secular society, with which this essay has not been concerned, but to ideology, including the fate of what Charles Thomas has called 'undeveloped' cemeteries (those not surviving long enough to have a church or chapel).[99] It is relevant also to the major changes evident in temples, and to the development of possible Christian elements on their sites, and also to the (by this time historically attested) relationships between Western British monasticism and the establishment and take-over of the English Church.[100]

Mention has already been made of some structures or sites where, by the eighth century (if not sooner), a Christian presence may be confidently assumed.[101] These include the earlier elements of cathedrals or other superior churches (at Wells, at Bath,[102] and at Exeter),[103] Glastonbury Abbey itself, and the second phase of the Tor (figures 8 and 13). To these should be added Beckery, a monastic complex on the edge of the Glastonbury peninsula.[104]

subsequent building works in the vicinity of Silver Street (Humphrey Wood, personal communication to Leslie Webster). If from the car park, however, it may have some connection with the corner of an early precinct ditch (the *uallum monasterii?*) that was sectioned at that time (see P. Ellis, 'Excavations at Silver Street, Glastonbury, 1978', *PSANHS* 126 [1982], 17–31). Three radio-carbon determinations from stakes in the base of this ditch centred on the late sixth and seventh centuries A.D. (*ibid.* p. 17); and in a layer above was an eighth-century *sceatta* (*ibid.* pp. 20 and 30). A photograph and brief description of the censer have appeared in Rosemary Cramp, *Anglo-Saxon Connections* (Durham, 1989), p. 32 (no. 49); see also the forthcoming article by C. J. S. Entwistle and L. Webster.

98   Further work in the abbey area is described by P. Ellis, 'Excavations in Glastonbury 1978 and 1979', *PSANHS* 126 (1982), 33–8, and by I. Burrow, 'Earthworks in the South-eastern Part of the Abbey Precinct, Glastonbury', *PSANHS* 126 (1982), 39–42.

99   Thomas, *Christianity*, pp. 253–6.

100   Morris, *Churches in the Landscape*, pp. 46–92 and *passim*.

101   Cf. S. Pearce, 'Estates and Church Sites in Dorset and Gloucestershire: The Emergence of a Christian Society', in *The Early Church*, ed. Pearce, pp. 117–38.

102   Rodwell, 'From Mausoleum to Minster', p. 49.

103   C. G. Henderson and P. T. Bidwell, 'The Saxon Minster at Exeter', in *The Early Church*, ed. Pearce, pp. 145–76.

104   P. A. Rahtz and S. M. Hirst, *Beckery Chapel 1967–8* (Glastonbury, 1974).

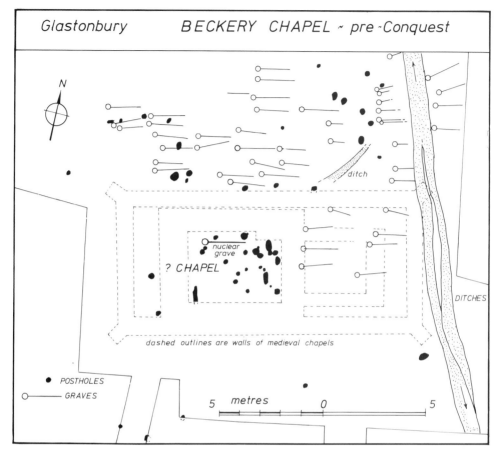

Figure 14 Glastonbury, Beckery Chapel: Pre-Conquest

This began as a cemetery of the middle- to late-Saxon period, almost exclusively of adult males, centred on a nuclear male grave within a timber setting (figure 14). On this was grafted a timber and later a stone chapel, developing into a substantial medieval complex. Like the Tor's second phase, this must, together with other unexcavated chapels around Glastonbury (such as Nyland), be seen as a satellite or daughter foundation of the Anglo-Saxon abbey itself.

Anglo-Saxon churches and sculpture are not well represented in Somerset by surviving architectural remains; those that do survive are late in the sequence, by comparison with those in Kent or Northumbria.[105] The evidence for many more must lie beneath the numerous later medieval

105 For the churches, see H. M. and J. Taylor, *Anglo-Saxon Architecture*, 3 vols (Cambridge, 1965–78), esp. vols I and II; for the sculpture see Sally Foster, 'A Gazetteer of the Anglo-Saxon Sculpture in Historic Somerset', *PSANHS* 131 (1987), 49–80.

churches or under open sites like Beckery, abandoned in Tudor times. Only the churches of Glastonbury Abbey, Muchelney, Beckery, Wells, and Cheddar have been excavated.[106]

CONCLUSION

By the eighth century, Christianity was well established by the Severn Sea.[107] Beliefs or practices that had their origins in indigenous prehistoric, Roman or Germanic paganism survived (as they do today) only in folk custom, largely absorbed into Christianity.[108] Evidence for paganism in the Anglo-Saxon period rests largely on the surviving prohibitions of the Church, implying that pagan practices were still current. Apart from these residual beliefs and practices, all that remained of the pagan past were the ruins of the temples themselves or the earthworks of their former sites.[109]

Much more remains to be discovered about all the topics discussed in this paper; it is hoped that it will act as a stimulus to further research and as a comparison for further work, especially in Devon, notably that planned in Exeter.

This essay has tried to summarize the archaeological evidence for religious practices from late pre-Roman times to the fully historic period which saw the establishment of the English Church. Such evidence does not always lend itself to the kind of interpretations that historians may look for in archaeology (usually in vain). Such evidence as there is must stand on its own, providing a basis for discussion for both archaeologists and historians. It is best seen within an anthropological framework rather than an historical one, as illustrated in the following diagram.[110]

Late Iron Age	*Roman*	*Dark Age*	*English Christian*
Pagan organized religion:	Pagan organized religion:	?	Organized religion:
Natural deities	Pantheon		Triple-identity deity
Specialists (druids)	Priests		Priests

---

[106] Glastonbury and Muchelney are sorely in need of re-evaluation and dating. The church excavated at Cheddar was a royal chapel of the tenth-century palace; see P. A. Rahtz, *The Saxon and Medieval Palaces at Cheddar*, BAR Brit. ser. 65 (Oxford, 1979), and P. A. Rahtz and S. M. Hirst, 'The Chapel of St Columbanus at Cheddar', *PSANHS* 131 (1987), 157–61.

[107] Dunning, 'The Middle Ages', pp. 1–28.

[108] Now fully discussed by Morris, *Churches in the Landscape*, pp. 46–92.

[109] Pagans Hill was still apparently standing as a roofed structure in the earlier medieval period. One plastered and purple-painted wall of Apollo's temple at Nettleton stood visible in a wood to a height of two metres when excavations began in the 1950s (personal observation).

[110] After Ellison; see Rahtz, 'Celtic Society in Somerset', pp. 187–8.

Late Iron Age	Roman	Dark Age	English Christian
Elements of witchcraft and totemism	Elements of magic		Hints of magic; integration of indigenous cults and symbols
Shrines and holy places	Shrines and temples		Shrines, chapels, churches
Holy men on islands			Hermits, monasticism

This scheme deliberately leaves a gap in the Dark Ages, to emphasize that religious practice in this period cannot be so readily pigeon-holed as that of earlier or later times. The simple dichotomy pagan/Christian created by historians and/or Christians is misleadingly clear-cut.[111]

---

[111] I am indebted to Richard Morris, Lorna Watts, Ann Woodward, James Carley and Lesley Abrams for valuable comments on earlier drafts of this text.

Some Evidence for New Settlements and Field Systems in Late Anglo-Saxon Somerset[1]

MICHAEL D. COSTEN

The chronology of village settlement in Somerset is vague in the extreme. Although we have extensive references to settlements in the Anglo-Saxon charters of the county they tell us of the existence of estates but very little about their internal arrangements. Nor does archaeology help us very much. Excavations covering sites in the county which were in use between 658 and 1066 have been very few and they have been confined to major sites such as Glastonbury Abbey and its environs, Wells Cathedral, Cadbury Castle, and the Saxon palace at Cheddar.[2] To this might be added rescue work in towns and villages, such as Taunton and Lyng.[3] No settlement site of the Anglo-Saxon period has been excavated and we know very little about village origins.

However, some attempts at constructing a pattern of settlement in the county have begun, using the hypothesis that the pattern of settlement of the earliest Anglo-Saxon dwellers was based upon the multiple estate and that the origin of Somerset's later settlements is to be found in the break-up of that pattern in the ninth and the tenth centuries.[4]

This essay is an attempt to link the appearance of open-field agriculture with the growth of village settlements, developments which produced the nucleated villages with open fields which were such a common feature of medieval and early modern North and Central Somerset. It seeks to give a

[1] Lizzie Induni drew the maps from my sketches. I am grateful to my colleague and friend Michael Aston for much helpful discussion. The errors are my own.
[2] C. A. R. Radford, 'Glastonbury Abbey Before 1184: Interim Report on the Excavations, 1908–64', *Medieval Art and Architecture at Wells and Glastonbury*, British Archaeological Association Conference Transactions 4 (London, 1981), pp. 110–34; W. Rodwell, 'The Lady Chapel by the Cloister at Wells and the Site of the Anglo-Saxon Cathedral', *Medieval Art and Architecture at Wells and Glastonbury*, pp. 1–15; L. Alcock, '*By South Cadbury is that Camelot'. . . The Excavation of Cadbury Castle 1966–70* (London, 1972); P. A. Rahtz, *The Saxon and Medieval Palaces at Cheddar*, BAR Brit. ser. 65 (Oxford, 1979).
[3] *The Archaeology of Taunton*, ed. P. J. Leach, Western Archaeological Trust 8 (Bristol, 1984), p. 75; P. J. Leach, 'Excavations at East Lyng, Somerset 1975', *PSANHS* 120 (1976), 29–38.
[4] M. D. Costen, 'The Late Saxon Landscape: The Evidence from Charters and Place-Names', *Aspects of the Medieval Landscape of Somerset*, ed. M. Aston (Taunton, 1988), pp. 33–48.

partial answer to the question, how did the early landscape of Anglo-Saxon Somerset grow into the pattern upon which our present-day landscape is still largely based?

The controversy about open-field farming in the Anglo-Saxon period has continued for many years and there have been many fine contributions to the evidence. The debate and the interest it arouses spring from an appreciation of the importance of the method of cultivation employed by the Anglo-Saxons. An understanding of the system in use at any one time can produce interpretations of the social structure, of the changes in the relative positions of social groups and of the pressures on society from economic constraints. In 1981 David Hall pointed to the antiquity of ridge and furrow and suggested that strip cultivation had occurred in the East Midlands by later Anglo-Saxon times.[5] Much earlier, Fowler and Thomas had produced evidence for pre-Conquest ridge and furrow at Gwithian, and Barker and Lawson did the same for Hen Domen.[6]

Since they contain so much information about the landscape the boundary clauses of the Anglo-Saxon charters form an obvious starting-point for any search for evidence. Their evidence is generally against the early existence of open-field agriculture, with some exceptions. It is not possible to be certain about the date of every set of bounds attached to the charters of Somerset, but some of the clauses are of pre-Conquest date.

The Anglo-Saxon estate of Rimpton was the property of Brihtric Grim, who left the land and the two charters, S.441 of 938 and S.571 of 956, to the Old Minster at Winchester. His will, S.1512 of 964x980, has also survived and in it Brihtric Grim stated that he had left Rimpton to the minster, *mid þere hide þe he syþþan begeat into þan lande.*[7] I have shown that the existing parish boundaries are not the same as the bounds in the charter.[8] Instead, an additional piece of land exists inside the parish, but outside the charter bounds, which must clearly be the extra land mentioned in the will. Thus the two sets of bounds must be older than the will and must certainly represent two different surveys, both of which describe the same boundary.

The charter S.236 of 681 relating to West Pennard has been discussed by Heather Edwards.[9] Although this is a charter of a very early date it contains a boundary clause which must be much later, since it is a detailed boundary in Old English, rather than a simple Latin boundary clause, characteristic of the early period. This is one of the few Glastonbury Abbey documents which

[5]   D. Hall, 'The Origins of Open-field Agriculture – The Archaeological Fieldwork Evidence', *The Origins of Open-Field Agriculture*, ed. T. Rowley (London, 1981), pp. 22–38.
[6]   P. J. Fowler and A. C. Thomas, 'Arable Fields of the Pre-Norman Period at Gwithian, Cornwall', *Cornish Archaeology* 1 (1962), 61–84; P. A. Barker and J. Lawson, 'A Pre-Norman Field System at Hen Domen', *Medieval Archaeology* 15 (1971), 58–72.
[7]   *Anglo-Saxon Wills*, ed. D. Whitelock (Cambridge, 1930), p. 18, no. 7.
[8]   M. D. Costen, 'Rimpton in Somerset – a late Saxon Estate', *Southern History* 7 (1985), 13–24.
[9]   H. Edwards, *The Charters of the Early West Saxon Kingdom*, BAR Brit. ser. 198 (Oxford, 1988), pp. 11–15.

survive in a pre-Conquest copy and the existing manuscript was considered by J. Armitage Robinson to be of tenth-century date.[10] The bound is therefore of tenth-century origin at the latest.

Surrounding West Pennard, to which the charter bounds belong, are two other estates, East Pennard and Pilton. In the case of S.563 of 955 for East Pennard, a single sheet which includes the boundary clause exists and again dates from the tenth century.[11] S.247, dated 705, is a text which survives in the Great Cartulary and covers the estate of Pilton. Edwards considered that it represented a charter with an authentic basis, though not of the date claimed.[12] The boundary clause describes an estate which includes settlements which became independent units and separate ancient parishes. By 1086 Pilton had already begun to break up into those units as a result of sub-infeudation of its lands by the abbey.[13]

There are a small number of words which regularly appear in the bounds of charters which are descriptive of agricultural activity. Among them is *feld*, which has the primary meaning 'a stretch of open ground',[14] but it is possible that in the tenth century it was already being used to mean something like the later 'open field'. *Furlang*, the modern 'furlong', a piece of land the length of a furrow and by extension a division within the open field,[15] is clearly of great importance and so too is *æcer*, which was used as a measure of land, but also as a description of a plot of ground which was under cultivation.[16] Della Hooke has shown that there are references to what seems to be open-field agriculture in the charters of Anglo-Saxon Gloucestershire.[17] In the bounds for Adlestrop there is a reference to *Rahulfes furlung quae est in campo de Euenlode*, while open-field agriculture at Cudley is also suggested by the expression *xxx æcra on þæm twæm feldan dal landes wiðutan*.[18] Hooke has also suggested that the term *furh*, 'a furrow', is consistently associated with known later open-field systems, often as a bounding ditch.[19] There are many references to divided hides, to leases of individual acres and to divisions of lands by the acre in northeast Gloucestershire and in the central River Avon area, with a concentration around Worcester.[20] Hooke has concluded that divided arable land, a feature of open-field systems, was certainly in exist-

---

[10]   Longleat House, Marquess of Bath, NMR 10564; see J. Armitage Robinson, *Somerset Historical Essays* (London, 1921), p. 30, n. 2.

[11]   Longleat House, Marquess of Bath, NMR 10565.

[12]   Edwards, *The Charters*, pp. 33–40.

[13]   DB, I, 90rb; *Somerset*, 8.20.

[14]   A. H. Smith, *English Place-Name Elements*, 2 vols, English Place-Name Society 25–6 (Cambridge, 1956) I, 167–9.

[15]   *Ibid.* I, 189–90.

[16]   *Ibid.* I, 2.

[17]   D. Hooke, *Anglo-Saxon Landscapes of the West Midlands: The Charter Evidence*, BAR Brit. ser. 95 (Oxford, 1981).

[18]   S.1548 (bounds only, no date); S.1329 of 974.

[19]   Hooke, *Anglo-Saxon Landscapes of the West Midlands*, p. 195.

[20]   D. Hooke, 'Village Development in the West Midlands', *Medieval Villages: A Review of Current Work*, ed. D. Hooke (Oxford, 1985), pp. 125–54.

ence in Warwickshire and Worcestershire by the tenth century.[21] In Wiltshire, a charter of 963 (S.719) describes land at Avon Farm at Durnford as *singulis iugeribus mixtum in communi rere huc illacque dispersis*. Elsewhere in Wiltshire, if the Latin bounds of S.1580 for Dauntsey are actually tenth-century, the reference to *locum qui appellatur heuedakerhende* suggests a reference to a pre-Conquest open-field layout of some kind. References to furlongs in Wiltshire are unequivocal. S.449 of 939, for East Overton, has *þæs furlanges west heafde*. S.492 of 943, for South Newton, has *ðæs furlanges up ende*. Detailed analysis of Wiltshire must wait for another occasion, but the evidence points towards open-field agriculture in operation by the middle of the tenth century.

The evidence in Somerset is of two kinds: the first from the boundary clauses of Anglo-Saxon charters, the second from landscape study, which deals with evidence from maps and from a study of the physical remains on the ground.

There are nine examples of the use of *feld* in the Somerset charters. From the charter for Weston, near Bath (S.508 of 946), comes *clænan feldan*, 'the bare field'. At Batcombe, near Bruton, the charter S.462 of 940 has *of þere mede over þan feld to þa wode*, 'from the meadow across the field to the wood'. The charter for Compton Bishop, near Axbridge, has *ut on þone fold*, 'out over the field'.[22] The great Taunton charter, S.311 of 854, has been criticized as spurious, however the boundary clause contains much information about the area and there is nothing in the clause which is inconsistent with a date prior to the Norman Conquest; in any case it cannot be later than the date of the twelfth-century manuscript in which it occurs.[23] It contains *campum qui oxenafeld dicitur*, 'the field called Oxenafeld' (the oxen's field). This site is also mentioned in one of the Pitminster charters where it reads *of ðære greatan lindam on oxenafeld*, 'from the big lime tree to the oxen's field'.[24] S.380 of 899x909, the charter for Lydeard and district, has a reference to *fasingafeld*, 'the field of Fasa's men'. At Isle Abbots, near Ilminster, in S.740 of 966 we have *þeodnesfeld*, 'the lord's field'. At Rimpton in S.571 of 956 we have *suþ on feld*, 'south along the field'. From S.593 of 956, for Corston, near Bath, we have *ofer feld on ða riht land gemære*, 'over the field straight along the boundary'.

Few of these *feld*s are ready candidates for open-field status. The 'bare field' at Weston looks as if it was a pasture of some kind; the term *clæn* contrasts the land with scrubland or woodland and is used again in the modern 'clean moor' in Milverton parish in the west of the county. At Batcombe the *feld* lay near a wood, on the edge of the estate. It was not open field at a later date, but probably pasture land. The Compton Bishop refer-

[21]   Hooke, *Anglo-Saxon Landscapes of the West Midlands*, p. 205.
[22]   Wells, Cathedral Library, Liber Albus II (R. III), 246v. See the *Calendar of the Manuscripts of the Dean and Chapter of Wells*, ed. W. H. B. Bird, 2 vols, Historical Manuscripts Commission 12.2–3 (London, 1907–14) I, 431; printed by F. H. Dickinson, 'The Banwell Charters', *PSANHS* 23 (1877), 49–64, at 55–8. This charter is not catalogued in Sawyer. It is dated 1067.
[23]   London, British Library, Add. 15350.
[24]   S.1006 of 1044.

ence is to ground on the top of the Mendips, now in Cheddar parish and at some distance from Compton Bishop, close to where King Edmund is supposed to have had his near accident in *ca* 943.[25] This was almost certainly pasture ground then, since the Mendips tops remained open waste until the late eighteenth century.[26] At Pitminster, the *oxenafeld*, which also appears in the Taunton charter, lay on a steep rough hillside and as its name implies was a grazing ground for oxen. An examination of the landscape described in the boundary clause for S.380, for Lydeard, suggests that the ground lay on a hillside on the western slope of the Quantocks, on land which was too steep for use as arable. The 'lord's field' at Isle Abbots lay close to the river and might have been grazing ground. At Rimpton the *feld* was probably a contrast to the *scaga*, a thick hedge or small copse, along which the boundary still runs.[27] This *feld* might have been cultivated land, and was within a later area of open field. At Corston, near Bath, the boundary ran straight across an area which was open fields on both sides, in the estates of Corston and Stanton Prior. Both belonged to St Peter's Abbey in Bath from the tenth century. The later boundary as defined in the tithe map is not quite straight, but makes several small turns around the ends of individual strips, although these are very modest deviations from the straight line.[28] Here if anywhere it is possible that we are dealing with an early open field of some kind, but the evidence is hardly conclusive.

The word *æcer* was used to describe a plot of ground and also as a unit of measurement.[29] References to *æcers* in the Somerset charters are again quite sparse, considering the size of the body of material available. In S.508 of 946, for Weston, near Bath, there are several occurrences of this term. The first is *Ðis synd þa land gemæru þa viiii æceras þe Æþelere ahte*, 'these are the bounds of the nine acres Æthelhere has'. These nine acres probably lay in Langridge, nearby and not inside Weston. The points around this small area are *oden æcre*, 'the threshing acre', *anan ænne æcer innan wudu*, 'a single acre in the wood', *sclæt æcere*, 'the acre by the sheep slait' and *þam iii æcere*, 'the three acres'. At Clifton, near Bath, in S.777 of 970, there is a *crundel æcer*, a 'quarry acre'. At Marksbury, also near Bath, S.431 of 936 has *foure acres by northan dych*, 'four acres on the northern side of the [Wans]dyke'. At Wrington there are *winter acres* in S.371 of 904. In S.791 of 973, for High Ham, there are *xxx acres þis kingis*, 'thirty acres belonging to the king', and at Creech (S.345 of 882) there are *nigon æceras*, 'nine acres'. The most striking feature of these references is that they nearly all occur in the north of the county around Bath. Perhaps arable agriculture was more extensive around the town, or the abbey of St Peter in Bath, as landlord, demanded a high output of arable crops for its own use. The references all seem to be to isolated plots of land.

[25]   B., *Vita S. Dunstani*, ch. 14 (*Memorials of St Dunstan*, ed. W. Stubbs, RS 63 [London, 1874], pp. 23–5).

[26]   M. Williams, 'Mendip Farming, the Last Three Centuries', *Mendip: A New Study*, ed. R. Atthill (Newton Abbot, 1976), pp. 102–25.

[27]   Costen, 'Rimpton in Somerset', pp. 13–24.

[28]   Tithe map for Stanton Prior, Somerset Record Office, D/D/Rt 358.

[29]   Smith, *English Place-Name Elements*, I, 2–3.

Most cannot now be identified with certainty, but the thirty acres belonging to the king seem to have been in Wearne, inside the later manor of Huish Episcopi, and are represented now by a piece of that parish which is isolated across a stream, making a salient which pokes into High Ham. The ground is still partly arable.

The only reference to *furlong* is in the charter for Marksbury, S.431 of 936. However, I have suggested elsewhere that the bounds of this charter are probably of the twelfth century, or modified at that time, and cannot be relied upon as pre-Conquest evidence.[30] The absence of the word *furlong* in Somerset charters is in stark contrast to Wiltshire, where there are six references in charter bounds.

Furh, 'a furrow', is completely absent from the Somerset charters, in contrast to Wiltshire where there are at least eleven examples.

The charter evidence for open-field agriculture in Somerset is very sparse and at the best ambiguous. Field archaeology may provide rather more. The first site to be considered consists of the three ancient parishes of East, West and Middle Chinnock, situated just southwest of Yeovil (see map 1).[31] It is immediately apparent that there was once a time when there was only one Chinnock estate, bounded by natural features. To the north the boundary is formed by a hill crest and to the west and south by streams. Only on the east is it less well determined. The estate of Chinnock is mentioned in the will of Wynflæd of *ca* 950.[32] It is unclear whether the will refers to a part or the whole of the estate. We do know that Chinnock had been divided before the Norman Conquest, because it appears as three units in the Domesday Book.[33] Edmer Ator, a major landholder in Somerset prior to the Conquest, held East Chinnock as a seven-hide unit in 1066. Middle and West Chinnock were each held by an anonymous thegn as three-hide and four-hide estates respectively. The original fourteen-hide unit had been split into three unequal parts. It is possible that the estate was first divided into two seven-hide units and then one of the new units was divided again. This would explain why the East Field of West Chinnock lay to the east of Middle Chinnock. The division between the two major portions of the estate is not a straight line. There is a salt spring in the western part of East Chinnock and that has clearly been left in the eastern estate, since it would have been a valuable asset. Also left in the east was a probable area of woodland. This suggests that East Chinnock was the most important part of the unit when the division took place. The two western estates were most intimately connected. As we have seen already the East Field of West Chinnock lies detached, inside Middle Chinnock, suggesting that its position was fixed by an outside authority. Furthermore the boundary between these two estates runs

[30] M. Costen, 'Stantonbury and District in the Tenth Century', *Bristol and Avon Archaeology* 2 (1983), pp. 25–34.
[31] This plan is reconstructed from the tithe maps for the three parishes in the Somerset Record Office, D/D/Rt 347 for West Chinnock, D/D/Rt 456 for East Chinnock and D/D/Rt 350 for Middle Chinnock.
[32] S.1539; *Wills*, ed. Whitelock, pp. 10–15, no. 3.
[33] DB, I, 92va; *Somerset*, 19.44, 19.48 and 19.49.

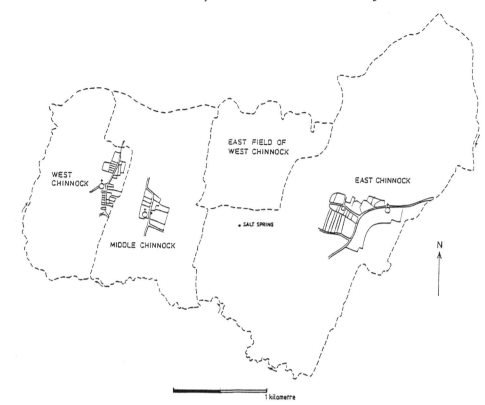

Map 1 East, West and Middle Chinnock

close between the villages, which appear to have been laid out more or less parallel to it. Clearly their field systems were designed to take account of the existing boundaries, and the villages seem to be sited in relation to those boundaries, in a way that East Chinnock is not. I would suggest that both Middle and West Chinnock and their field systems were laid out at the same time.

We have seen that the three settlements were in independent existence by 1066. What cannot be accurately determined is when the division occurred. By the time of the Domesday survey both of the smaller manors were held by thegns in parage, suggesting that they had been divided at least long enough for heirs to succeed to them.[34] The last Anglo-Saxon owner of East Chinnock had been Edmer Ator, a thegn with holdings in Devon which passed to the Count of Mortain, as did the three Chinnocks and Edmer's other Somerset holdings at Odcombe and Camerton. The thegns in Middle and West Chinnock may have been the men of Edmer, since he was clearly important enough to have vassals of his own. Since the division of the three estates predates 1066, it seems inherently unlikely that the villages and fields of Middle and West Chinnock were laid out after the Norman Conquest. The

---

[34] *Somerset*, notes to 19.48–50 and 19.52, p. 322.

obvious occasion for such planning would have been at the time that the estates were divided, not at a much later date. Both West and Middle Chinnock were smaller than East Chinnock and this suggests that they were estates for dependants. In Somerset there is a noticeable correlation between the size of the estate and the status of the holder in 1066. The rather lowly status of the holders at Middle and West Chinnock in the mid-eleventh century suggests that their predecessors had been dependants of the lord of the major estate and not holders-in-chief themselves. The new estates might then have been created to accommodate men whose primary function as thegns was to be retainers and military servants of their lord.

The next site to be considered includes the ancient parishes of East and West Lydford. The first reference to either of the Lydfords is in the Glastonbury charter S.1410, dated 744, when 10 *cassati* were granted in Lydford and Lottisham. In the Domesday survey Lydford appeared as two separate estates, East and West Lydford. In 1066 East Lydford was held by the thegn Ælfweard who 'could not be separated from the church' of Glastonbury,[35] a phrase probably indicating that he was a leaseholder for life, in return for service. He held an estate of 4 hides. West Lydford, an estate of 9 hides, was in the hands of Ælfric in 1086 and had been held by his father, 'Brictric', in 1066.[36] Ælfric was one of the 'king's thegns' in Domesday Book, and so must be regarded as an independent landholder. We do not know when his ancestors became owners of the estate, or the process by which they obtained it. What is clear is that a physical division of the estate had taken place. The major division was formed by the Fosse Way, which was the boundary between the two later parishes, but with some important anomalies (see map 2).[37] The first of these was that the East Field of West Lydford lay on the east side of the Fosse Way, divided from East Lydford by the River Brue to the south. East Lydford also had a detached portion, on the west side of the Fosse Way, to the north of West Lydford, which was actually a piece of woodland taken out of a larger area of wood which formed the northern part of West Lydford and ran over into Baltonsborough. The most reasonable explanation of this arrangement is that East Lydford was split off from the main estate; since it had no woodland of its own, it was given a share in the woods which formed a major portion of the lands of the main estate. It would also be reasonable to assume that the field systems of the two estates were laid out at the same time. The land on the east of the Fosse Way provided a good level area for the East Field of the major settlement, while the secondary settlement of East Lydford was easily defined as that part of the major estate to the south of the Brue and east of the Fosse. Its fields must surely post-date such a division. It seems likely that the settlements were laid out at the time of the division, or at least that their positions were fixed at

[35]   DB, I, 90ra; *Somerset*, 8.4.
[36]   DB, I, 99ra; *Somerset*, 47.21.
[37]   The boundaries of the two ancient parishes are best seen on the tithe map for East Lydford in the Somerset Record Office: D/D/Rt 114; for West Lydford, which lacks a tithe map, see Q/R/De 87 of 1827, an enclosure award map.

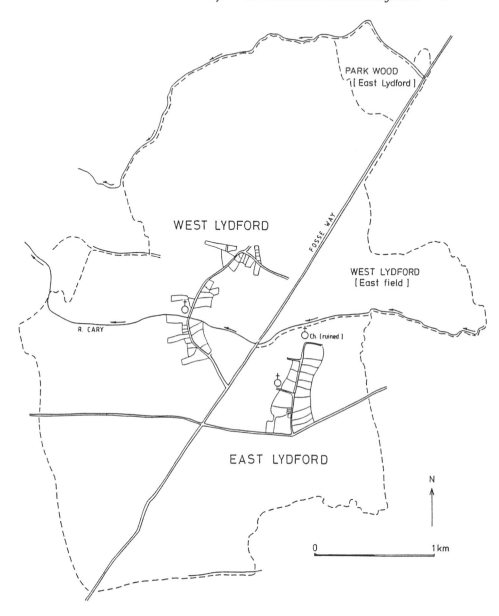

Map 2 East and West Lydford

that time. Both settlements were provided with churches which were close to
the river. In the case of West Lydford there is some evidence to suggest that
the medieval settlement lay close to the church, where there are signs of
house platforms; the village has become more dispersed in recent times. At
East Lydford, the medieval church lay near the river, and the post-division
settlement may have lain around this church site, which was finally abandoned in the nineteenth century in favour of a new church in the village,

which had moved away from the river, possibly to avoid flooding.[38] Since East and West Lydford were separately owned by 1066 and existed as distinct units by that date, we must assume that the division and the fields were pre-Conquest and were the work of a single authority, which could have divided up the land as it saw fit. In this case the authority must have been the abbey of Glastonbury and the likely time would be the second half of the tenth century, when the refounded abbey might be expected to be concerned with the reorganization of its estates.

Shapwick was an estate which was probably in the hands of the abbey of Glastonbury from the early eighth century onwards.[39] The initial grant was of a block of land which may have covered most of the western end of the Polden Hills; the Domesday survey shows that Shapwick in 1086 included the present villages of Sutton Mallet, Edington, Chilton Polden, Catcott and Woolavington, although they were enumerated as separate units. Shapwick itself was part of the demesne of the abbey, while Sutton, Edington, Chilton and Catcott had been held from the abbey by a group of fourteen thegns in 1066.[40] The village of Shapwick has been described by Nicholas Corcos, who argued that it was a part of a multiple estate which had broken up, possibly in the tenth century.[41] Certainly, the bound of Shapwick in the charter S.253 of 729 describes the estate in terms of simple natural boundaries, taking in all the surrounding lands which were later independent manors. Corcos also pointed out that the village and the surrounding fields were part of a plan, as were the other villages of Sutton, Edington, Chilton and Catcott (see map 3). The regular pattern of each village and its relationship to the open fields around it suggest that they were all laid out at the same time. Corcos suggested that the planning dated from the time of the refoundation of Glastonbury Abbey and should be associated with St Dunstan. It is unlikely that the abbey of Glastonbury, which was in decline in the late ninth century and in a state of collapse during the early tenth century, could have achieved any kind of estate planning during that period.[42] The position of the village church at Shapwick prior to 1331 argues against late medieval planning. It stood outside the village, actually surrounded by the East Field.[43] Clearly this

---

[38]   *A History of the County of Somerset*, ed. R. W. Dunning, Victoria County History 3 (London, 1974), p. 121.

[39]   See S.253 of 729.

[40]   DB, I, 90ra; *Somerset*, 8.5.

[41]   N. Corcos, 'Early Estates on the Poldens and the Origin of the Settlement at Shapwick', *PSANHS* 127 (1982/3), 47–54.

[42]   D. Knowles (*The Monastic Order in England*, 2nd ed. [London, 1963], pp. 695–6) discussed the state of Glastonbury in the mid-tenth century. He made the point that the first thing that Dunstan did after becoming abbot was to build his new community monastic buildings. He suggested that Dunstan's first biographer, the priest 'B.', described a community which was no more than a group of clerks. William of Malmesbury, admittedly writing much later, described the site as 'desolatus' before Dunstan's arrival; see *Gesta pontificum Anglorum*, ch. 91 (*Willelmi Malmesbiriensis Monachi de Gestis Pontificum Anglorum*, ed. N. E. S. A. Hamilton, RS 52 [London, 1870], p. 196).

[43]   The church was moved to its present site in the village. The licence to move the

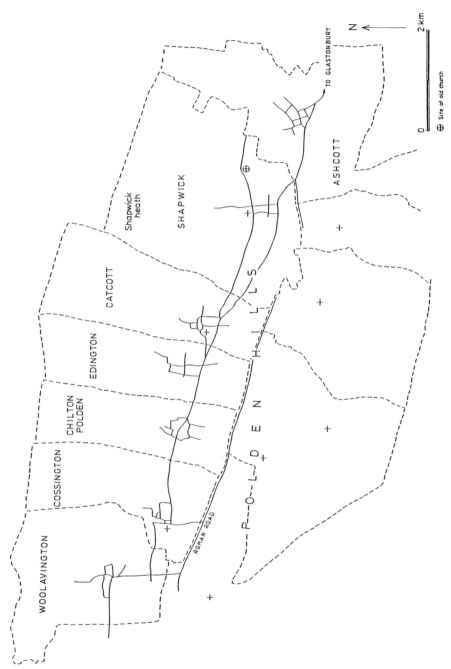

WOOLAVINGTON
COSSINGTON
CHILTON POLDEN
EDINGTON
CATCOTT
Shapwick heath
SHAPWICK
ASHCOTT
P O L D E N   H I L L S
ROMAN ROAD
TO GLASTONBURY

N

0   2 km

⊕ Site of old church

Map 3 The Polden Hills

church must predate the village plan and the fields. It was probably a minster for the earlier multiple estate, built next to the estate headquarters and serving a wide area: in the later Middle Ages it was still the mother church of a number of the settlements in the immediate district.[44] The Life of St Indract associated the saint with Shapwick in the eighth century, although the Life as it survives may have been prepared from a late Old English original.[45] If the traditional first burial place for Indract and his followers was Shapwick, this might suggest that a tenth-century church stood there at the time the Life was being prepared. Settlement replanning left it stranded outside the village, in the middle of the open fields. It seems inherently unlikely that the estate was divided at a different time from the planned layout of the fields and village. Among the estates along the Poldens, all the property of Glastonbury Abbey, the regular divisions between estates and the regular field systems within each estate again point to a common date and authority for the division and planning; the need to provide estates for retainers would provide an explanation of the division of the estate, and the existence of the fourteen thegns holding the outlying part of the Shapwick estate in 1086 supports this suggestion.

Shapwick and its dependencies and East and West Lydford were part of the vast estates of the abbey of Glastonbury. The Chinnocks were certainly property held by members of the royal family of Wessex in the mid-tenth century. Further north evidence comes from estates which were probably part of the royal holding at Wedmore, although it is not clear if the king still held the whole Isle of Wedmore in the tenth century. Alston Sutton was an estate of 4½ hides held in 1066 by two thegns.[46] Although within the ecclesiastical parish of Upper Weare, it has its own tithe map.[47] In 1548 the Free Chapel was described as 'utterly decayed',[48] and nothing now stands, although field-name evidence enables us to identify the site.[49] It is clear that Alston Sutton had a church which was not the parish church and had no burial rights, but still had its own tithes attached to it. This is one of only nine examples in Somerset. It is unlikely that it was simply a chapel of ease. That

church was granted on 28 January 1329 (*The Register of Ralph of Shrewsbury, Bishop of Bath and Wells, 1329–1363*, ed. T. S. Holmes, 2 vols, SRS 9–10 [1896] I, 27). The church was newly constructed in October 1331 (*ibid.* p. 73). The old church site has been positively identified by aerial survey by M. Aston in 1989 and by field-work by M. Aston and M. Costen in the same year. It lies 500 m to the east of the present church.

[44]   In the sixteenth century the rectory of Shapwick still owned the tithes of Edington, Moorlinch, Sutton Mallet, Chilton Polden, Catcott and Stawell, while the vicar of Shapwick was the owner of the great tithes of Ashcott; see Somerset Record Office, DD/SG 12 of 1599.

[45]   M. Lapidge, 'The Cult of St Indract at Glastonbury', *Ireland in Early Mediaeval Europe: Studies in Memory of Kathleen Hughes*, ed. D. Whitelock, R. McKitterick and D. Dumville (Cambridge, 1982), pp. 179–212, at 186.

[46]   DB, I, 95ra; *Somerset*, 24.14.

[47]   Somerset Record Office, D/D/Rt 92.

[48]   *Calendar of Somerset Chantry Grants, 1548–1603*, ed. G. H. Woodward, SRS 77 (1982), p. 58.

[49]   'Chapel Close' stands next to 'Court Close', both in the shrunken village.

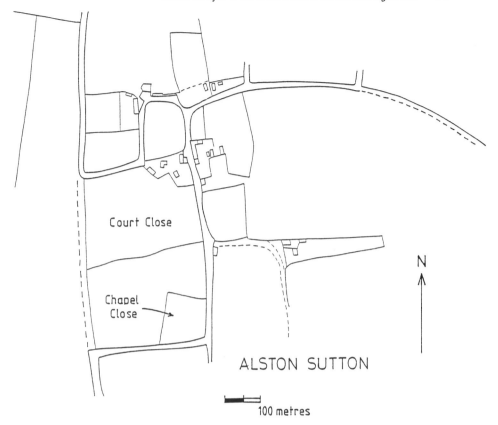

Court Close

Chapel
Close

N

ALSTON SUTTON

100 metres

Map 4 Alston Sutton

it had its own tithes suggests that the chapel was in existence before *ca* 1150, when Gregorian reforms of tithes began to affect English churches and their lay landlords. It is very difficult to envisage the vicar of Weare permitting the dispersal of part of his revenues to a chapel, on a permanent footing. He certainly did not allow it for the chapel of ease which existed in Lower Weare, a founded medieval new town. The chapel at Alston Sutton may have been founded prior to the Norman Conquest, or just after it. If it was built before the Norman Conquest it could have been contemporary with the village as a unit, built as a sign of status by a thegn who first held the newly created estates. This chapel would fit the description in the laws of Edgar (promulgated 959–63) which state that 'If anyone has a church with which there is no graveyard he is then to pay to his priest from the nine parts what he chooses'.[50]

Alston Sutton shows some physical signs of planning. It is today a single farm, with half a dozen houses (see map 4). It seems to have been laid out as a very small planned settlement, in a grid shape. The farm lies close to the

[50] *English Historical Documents, c. 500–1042*, ed. D. Whitelock, Eng. Hist. Documents 1, 2nd ed. (London, 1979), p. 395.

manorial boundary and beside a track which was once a local road. Alston Sutton was an open-field village, with two fields, a common practice in medieval Somerset. If church and village do predate the Norman Conquest, then so do the fields, since they are clearly a unit. It was probably a unit taken out of the larger estate of Weare which already had a church with a graveyard, with the result that the proprietary church at Alston Sutton could not have a graveyard of its own.

The final example of planned settlement concerns the two estates of North and South Barrow. Here also a single unit has clearly been divided (see map 5). The original area has neat continuous boundaries, formed of streams and a very substantial hedge bank. By 1066 the two estates were in existence as two units, with quite different secular holders, although their common origin is betrayed by the single name they share in the survey.[51] Each estate was of five hides. The tithe maps show that the division was made across the middle of the original unit.[52] I think that, as with the previous examples, we must presume that the settlement sites were chosen at the time of the division and that the field systems were laid out at the same time, when a single lord had control over the two parts of the estate. It is difficult to see how the two field systems, which seem to fit together so closely, could have emerged unless this were so.

The evidence from the charters which survive for Somerset suggests that the growth of open-field agriculture had not proceeded very far by the time most of the bounds for the Somerset charters were written. Most of the surviving charters describe large estates which belonged to monastic or episcopal owners. Even if they were open-field units at the time that the bounds were surveyed, it is possible that such agricultural systems would not show on the periphery of the estate. But what happened on the estates used here as examples was part of a conscious process of foundation by township splitting.[53] The setting-out of open fields was an integral part of the process by which smaller estates were created. I have used a few examples where I think we can begin to discern a pattern emerging. A lord divided up an estate which he held into smaller units. His authority forced the peasants to accept a new pattern of agriculture and a new settlement, either for those already on the land, or for people who were transferred from elsewhere as colonists. By this process settlement expanded, and open-field agriculture emerged as the result of this expansion of settlement in the tenth century. Somerset saw the emergence of a number of small new towns in the tenth century. Towns such as Axbridge, Bruton, Crewkerne and South Petherton would have had no chance of survival had there not been an expansion of population in the countryside. Although small in 1086 these settlements and others in Somerset survived to become important market centres in the eleventh century and are still towns today.

[51]   DB, I, 92vb and 95rb; *Somerset*, 19.62 and 24.20.
[52]   Somerset Record Office, D/D/Rt 442 and D/D/Rt 290.
[53]   For further argument about township splitting see R. A. Dodgshon, *The Origins of the British Field Systems: An Interpretation* (London, 1980), pp. 137–50.

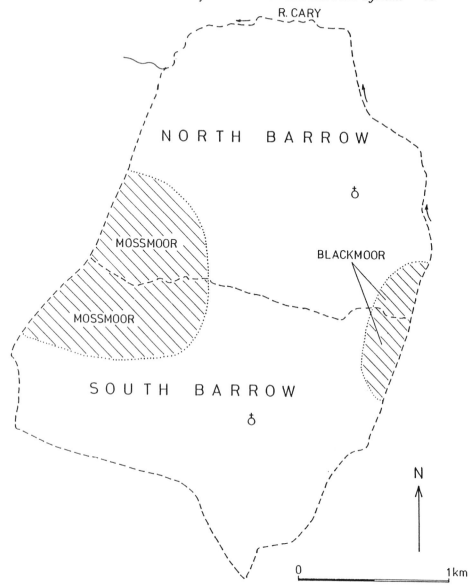

Map 5 North and South Barrow

The tenth-century growth of population which supported the towns was made possible by the success of the Anglo-Saxon monarchy after the Danish wars, and the growth of founded villages, as with royal founded market towns, was a consequence of the desire of the nobility to keep control of the surpluses available. The driving force for the social and economic change which the foundation of villages must represent came from the needs of the lords, not the peasantry, who, left to themselves, would have divided small-holdings between heirs and assarted in a random way as opportunity arose.

The needs of the lords were expressed as a desire to provide estates for retainers who could fulfil military obligations for the lord, whether lay or secular, under pressure from the tenth-century kings who demanded such services.[54]

Some of the examples cited in this paper involve the lands of the abbey of Glastonbury. The monastic revival of the tenth century was based upon the resumption and the acquisition of land by the monks. The amount of land given to them was astonishing, and they probably relied more than other landowners upon extension of their estates (rather than intensification of cultivation) for the growth in income they needed to build and beautify their monasteries. By 1086 Glastonbury had a holding of 410 hides in Somerset alone. But the monks were landlords, like other men, and did the same things. Like the great secular lords they also had retainers to support and military obligations to meet. By 1066 Glastonbury Abbey had 181 hides in Somerset held by sub-tenants with some 80 retainers on the land. Some of these men were relatively important, but most were not named in the Domesday Book and were simply referred to as *taini*. They often held less than a hide of land. In many cases whole estates had been granted to sub-tenants. In addition to the examples of East and West Lydford and Shapwick it is likely that the estate at Pilton had also been divided in a similar manner. The charter S.247 clearly does not have bounds of its purported date of 705, but the boundary clause describes the Pilton estate as it was before it broke up, showing that Shepton Mallet, Croscombe and Pylle were inside it. Their existence as named settlements with a separate survey, although included for the purposes of the Domesday Book within the Pilton estate, suggests that they too were creations of the tenth century. The burden of retainers, probably military, was new to the monastic world in the tenth century. The division of estates, and their parcelling-out to the men who figure as thegns in the Domesday Book, went on whether the lord was an abbot, a king's thegn or an earl. For the abbey of Glastonbury it is likely that the need to endow retainers was the driving force behind the reorganization of settlement and farming. Once created as small units the pattern of open-field agriculture would have been forced upon estate holders by the need to be as nearly as possible self-sufficient on each estate, as well as the need to compensate for the loss of revenue, men and supplies from those lands now held by retainers. The insertion of this non-productive group into the countryside would have been a further incentive to increased production. Only in the case of a monastery such as Glastonbury is the existence of these dependent thegns clear because of the way in which the Domesday survey treated the lands of the Church, probably reflecting the form in which the information of the survey was supplied to the inquisitors by the monastery itself. The impetus behind the expansion of open-field agriculture was the growth of a militarized, landed class which needed to intensify exploitation of the land in order to pay for its way of life. Once begun, wherever the right sort of

[54] P. Abels, *Lordship and Military Obligation in Anglo-Saxon England* (London, 1988), pp. 116–31.

landscape existed the process spread because of the advantages it offered the lord, not the peasant.

NOTE

In the Life of St Indract recorded by John of Glastonbury in his *Cronica siue antiquitates Glastoniensis ecclesie*,[55] Shapwick is mentioned as the site of the martyrdom of St Indract and his companions. An alternative account printed by Michael Lapidge from the Digby manuscript speaks of the martyrdom as occurring at *Hywisc*.[56] Both versions, Lapidge has suggested, derived ultimately from a tenth-century or early eleventh-century original in Old English.[57] I would like to suggest that the two conflicting accounts may be reconciled as follows. The *Hywisc* of the Digby manuscript may be a lost *hiwisc* which was part of the estate of Shapwick. The 1327 extent of the lands of Glastonbury abbey referred to a discrete area of land called *Wythes*, which included within it a *hywysch*.[58] This area can be positively identified from the tithe map as a detached portion of Shapwick, lying about 10 kilometres to the west, just to the north of the Polden Hills. It is now represented by Wythy Farm in Huntspill civil parish. I would suggest that the author of the lost Life located his murder at this *hywysch* in the marshes, intending to take his pilgrims to the mouth of the river to take ship across the Bristol Channel, perhaps from Combwich. Ine was at his royal estate at North Petherton (like South Petherton part of the ancient demesne in 1066),[59] which was about 12 kilometres distant to the south. John of Glastonbury may have assumed, perhaps from his source, that the bodies were first buried at Shapwick and then moved to Glastonbury. I would suggest that the geography seems plausible for a tenth-century origin, with the hagiographer having in mind an estate which belonged to Glastonbury and a well-known major route for the pilgrims to follow, directly from the monastery to a place where they might reasonably have taken ship.

---

[55] *Cronica*, chs 50–1 (ed. Carley, pp. 100–5).
[56] Lapidge, 'The Cult of St Indract', pp. 179–212, at 186.
[57] *Ibid.* pp. 194–7.
[58] London, British Library, Egerton 3321, fol. 61.
[59] DB, I, 86rb; *Somerset*, 1.3 and 1.4.

The Somerset Barns of Glastonbury Abbey

C. J. BOND AND J. B. WELLER

INTRODUCTION

The recording of monastic barns has engaged the attention of many architectural historians, especially since the mid-1950s.[1] Barns are the commonest extant monastic farm buildings, their comparatively high survival rate being at least partly related to their sheer scale and the care lavished upon their construction. At the same time, monastic estates of various kinds have been subjected to extensive investigation by economic historians and historical geographers, who have tended to concentrate upon their distribution and the processes of their acquisition, internal administration and economic exploitation.[2] These two fields of study have tended to remain curiously separate. Platt's study of the monastic grange, published in 1969, was the first systematic attempt to examine the domestic and agricultural buildings from which monastic demesnes were worked, and still stands alone as a general synthesis.[3] There have been few attempts to relate monastic farm buildings to their estate context, and on the limited number of occasions where this has occurred, the objectives have usually been restricted to fairly basic identification and recording.[4] While many surviving barns have been recorded in some detail, the surveys have rarely been integrated with archaeological and documentary evidence relating to the barton or steading, let alone the entire

[1] See R. B. Wood-Jones, 'The Rectorial Barn at Church Enstone', *Oxoniensia* 21 (1956), 43–7; W. Horn, 'The Great Tithe Barn of Cholsey, Berkshire', *Journal of the Society of Architectural Historians* 22 (1963), 13–23; W. Horn and E. Born, *The Barns of the Abbey of Beaulieu at its Granges of Great Coxwell and Beaulieu St Leonards* (Berkeley and Los Angeles, 1965); W. Horn and F. W. B. Charles, 'The Cruck-Built Barn of Middle Littleton in Worcestershire, England', *Journal of the Society of Architectural Historians* 25 (1966), 221–39; P. L. Heyworth, 'A Lost Cistercian Barn at Shilton', *Oxoniensia* 36 (1971), 52–4; F. W. B. Charles and W. Horn, 'The Cruck-Built Barn of Leigh Court, Worcestershire, England', *Journal of the Society of Architectural Historians* 32 (1973), 5–29; F. W. B. Charles and W. Horn, 'The Cruck-Built Barn of Frocester Court Farm, Gloucestershire', *Journal of the Society of Architectural Historians* 42 (1983), 211–37.
[2] For a recent review, see S. Moorhouse, 'Monastic Estates: Their Composition and Development', in *The Archaeology of Rural Monasteries*, ed. R. Gilchrist and H. Mytum, BAR, Brit. ser. 203 (Oxford, 1989), 29–81.
[3] C. Platt, *The Monastic Grange in Medieval England: A Reassessment* (London, 1969).
[4] See, for example, C. J. Bond, 'The Estates of Evesham Abbey: A Preliminary Survey of their Medieval Topography', *Vale of Evesham Historical Society Research Papers* 4 (1973), 1–62; C. J. Bond, 'The Reconstruction of the Medieval Landscape: The Estates of Abingdon Abbey', *Landscape History* 1 (1979), 59–75.

monastic estate. There is scope for a much fuller investigation of monastic farm buildings, their relationship to the monastic demesnes, the resources used to build and maintain them, and their precise functions with respect to the abbey's agrarian management. Barns, as a reflection of arable farming, are concerned with only one component of the monastic economy, and should not be studied in isolation. However, they do demand special consideration over other farm buildings because of their more widespread survival.

The following brief discussion is a prelude to a long-term project which aims at a comprehensive examination of Glastonbury Abbey's four surviving Somerset barns and their relationship to their bartons, to their manors and to the abbey estate as a whole. In turn this may pave the way for comparisons with building investment within other monastic estates. Our purpose here is merely to open the debate and to raise some of the questions to which we hope to find answers in due course.

Before turning to the barns themselves, we should provide a brief summary of the historical background of the Glastonbury estate. Like many of the ancient Benedictine abbeys of southern and midland England, Glastonbury Abbey was endowed with extensive estates at least from the tenth-century reform period, if not necessarily from the time of its first foundation.[5] Those landed endowments, often concentrated in well-settled vale areas but also including less-developed tracts of upland, woodland or marshland, provided support for the monastery through produce and revenues from the demesnes, through services and rents from tenants, and through tithes and other income from appropriated churches.

By 1086 Glastonbury Abbey held 442 hides in fifty-six different named vills in Somerset alone, holding twenty-three of those vills in demesne; this comprised something like one-eighth of the land in the county. It also held 258 hides in fourteen named vills in Wiltshire, fifty-eight hides in six named vills in Dorset, and single vills in Berkshire, Gloucestershire, Hampshire and Devon.[6] Its gross income in 1086 was £827 18s. 8d., and it was already the richest monastery in England.[7] When its revenues were assessed for Pope Nicholas IV's ecclesiastical taxation of 1291, £1,355 out of a total of £1,406 1s. 8d. was derived from temporalities: landed properties, demesne manors, rents, arable lands, livestock, mills, dovecotes and other agricultural resources.[8] Aspects of Glastonbury's economic organization and administration

5   S. C. Morland, 'Glaston Twelve Hides', *PSANHS* 128 (1983–4), 35–54; S. C. Morland, 'The Glastonbury Manors and their Saxon Charters', *PSANHS* 130 (1986), 61–105.
6   T. S. Holmes, 'The Abbey of Glastonbury', in the *Victoria History of Somerset*, ed. W. Page (London, 1911) II, 82–99, at 85 and 97–8.
7   Domesday incomes are tabulated by D. Knowles, *The Monastic Order in England* (Cambridge, 1963), pp. 702–3.
8   *Taxatio Ecclesiastica Angliae et Walliae, Auctoritate Papae Nicholae IV, Circa A.D. 1291*, ed. S. Ayscough and J. Caley (London, 1802); the totals are given by Holmes, 'The Abbey of Glastonbury', p. 98.

after the Norman Conquest have been explored by various authors.[9] Glastonbury retained its pre-eminence to the Dissolution; the *Valor ecclesiasticus* of 1535 estimated its annual revenues at £3,311 7s. 4d., but the final survey following the surrender in 1539 increased this figure to £4,085 6s. 8d.[10]

Four barns which belonged to Glastonbury Abbey survive. Two (Doulting and West Pennard) are still used by farmers, one (at Glastonbury itself) is now part of the Somerset Rural Life Museum, and the other (Pilton) has been roofless since a fire in 1963. How representative are the survivors, either in capacity or in character, of the many other barns which once stood within other manors and bartons on the abbey's estate? Repairs following a great storm in 1274/5 were recorded in one set of accounts which provide some insight into the number of Glastonbury barns and other farm buildings which have been lost: investigation of the contemporary manorial *compoti* by S. D. Hobbs has yielded references to 'granges', which may refer to barns rather than entire steadings (especially, perhaps, in south-west England, where 'barton' so often means 'steading'). There were granges at Glastonbury itself, at Walton and at Zoy (Middlezoy, Westonzoyland or Othery). Elsewhere, the references to barns seem specific: at Batcombe a quarter of the larger barn was rethatched; a new barn was recorded at Brent; a roofer was at work on the barn roof at Glastonbury itself; timbers were acquired for the door of the barn at Marksbury; the barn roof at Pennard was completely repaired; work took place on the barn roof at Pilton; the barn roof at Shapwick was repaired, following wind damage; at Street there was work on the barn roof, and its door was repaired; at Walton the barn roof was repaired, following wind damage; at Wrington two barns were rethatched and a carpenter made and fitted doorposts to the small barn there; and at Zoy a thatcher spent four days on the roof of the main barn.[11]

It is clear that in the last quarter of the thirteenth century Glastonbury possessed many barns; indeed, at least three places had more than one. The surviving barns thus represent a small proportion of those which once existed (figure 1). For comparison, on the Evesham estates the building of at

9   M. M. Postan, 'Glastonbury Estates in the Twelfth Century', *Economic History Review* 2nd ser. 5 (1952–3), 358–67; R. Lennard, 'The Demesnes of Glastonbury Abbey in the Eleventh and Twelfth Centuries', *Economic History Review* 2nd ser. 8 (1955–6), 355–63; M. M. Postan, 'Glastonbury Estates in the Twelfth Century: A Reply', *Economic History Review* 2nd ser. 9 (1956–7), 106–18; I. J. Keil, 'The Estates of Glastonbury Abbey in the Later Middle Ages' (unpublished PhD dissertation, Bristol University, 1964). For examinations of more specific themes, see I. J. Keil, 'The Granger of Glastonbury Abbey, 1361–62', *SDNQ* 28 (1961–7), 86–90; I. J. Keil, 'Mills on the Estates of Glastonbury Abbey in the Later Middle Ages', *SDNQ* 28 (1961–7), 181–4; R. Holt, 'Whose Were the Profits of Corn Milling? The Abbots of Glastonbury and their Tenants, 1086–1350', *Past & Present* 116 (1987), 3–23.

10   *Valor Ecclesiasticus, temp. Henr. VIII, Auctoritate Regia Institutus*, ed. J. Caley and J. Hunter, 6 vols (London, 1810–34) I, 142–8. The 1539 survey is printed in W. Dugdale, *Monasticon Anglicanum*, ed. J. Caley, H. Ellis and B. Bandinel, 6 vols in 8 (London, 1817–30) I, 10–21. The total values from both are given by Holmes, 'The Abbey of Glastonbury', p. 98.

11   We are grateful to S. D. Hobbs for this information. The original *compoti* are at Longleat House.

least fourteen barns is documented, only one of which can now be recognized, while a second, apparently undocumented, barn also survives. On the Abingdon estates the rather less satisfactory written sources attest to a minimum of six barns, but no documentation has been found for any of the three surviving buildings.[12]

THE MANORS

All four of the extant barns lay on properties which had been held by Glastonbury Abbey since before the Norman Conquest.[13] The early history of these properties cannot be followed here, but some of the main references for their management, extent and yields after the Conquest are summarized below.

In 1086 the abbey's geld-free land in Glastonbury amounted to twelve hides; there were five ploughs on the abbey's demesne and five ploughs worked by the villeins and bordars.[14] In 1252–61 the abbey's demesne estate included 524 acres of arable.[15]

The Domesday Survey records that the abbey had paid geld for twenty hides at *Doltin* (Doulting) in Edward the Confessor's time. In 1086 the abbey still held twelve hides in demesne; the abbot had two ploughs there and his villeins, bordars and cottars had six ploughs between them.[16] A survey made during the time of Bishop Savaric, *ca* 1198–9, included Doulting among the nineteen manors then still directly managed by the abbey.[17] However, from the evidence of plough oxen recorded in manorial surveys, Postan detected some evidence here, as elsewhere, for a slow contraction in the demesne during the twelfth century.[18] In 1266 the abbey received licence to appropriate the church of Doulting,[19] and in 1291 the temporalities of Doulting

---

12   Bond, 'Estates of Evesham Abbey', pp. 13–19; Bond, 'Estates of Abingdon Abbey', pp. 64–8.

13   For the charter evidence see H. Edwards, *The Charters of the Early West Saxon Kingdom*, BAR Brit. ser. 198 (Oxford, 1988), pp. 1–78; H. P. R. Finberg, *The Early Charters of Wessex* (Leicester, 1964); G. B. Grundy, *The Saxon Charters and Field-Names of Somerset* (Taunton, 1935); Morland, 'The Glastonbury Manors'; P. H. Sawyer, *Anglo-Saxon Charters. An Annotated List and Bibliography* (London, 1968); *The Great Chartulary of Glastonbury*, ed. A. Watkin, 3 vols, SRS 59, 63–4 (1947–56).

14   DB, I, 90ra; E. H. Bates, 'Text of the Somerset Domesday', in the *Victoria History of Somerset*, ed. W. Page (London, 1906) I, 434–526, at 460. The translation provided by Bates is in certain respects preferable to that of the more recent editions.

15   *Rentalia et Custumaria Michaelis de Ambresbury, 1235–1252, et Rogeri de Ford, 1252–1261, Abbatum Monasterii Beatae Mariae Glastoniae*, ed. C. J. Elton and E. Hobhouse, SRS 5 (1891), pp. 180–1.

16   DB, I, 90va; Bates, 'Somerset Domesday', p. 464.

17   Savaric's survey, quoted by Postan, 'Glastonbury Estates in the Twelfth Century', pp. 360–2, and 'Glastonbury Estates: A Reply', pp. 114–15, is on 116Ar/v of Cambridge, Trinity College R. 5. 33.

18   Postan, 'Glastonbury Estates in the Twelfth Century', pp. 360–2.

19   Dugdale, *Monasticon Anglicanum*, ed. Caley *et al.*, I, 32.

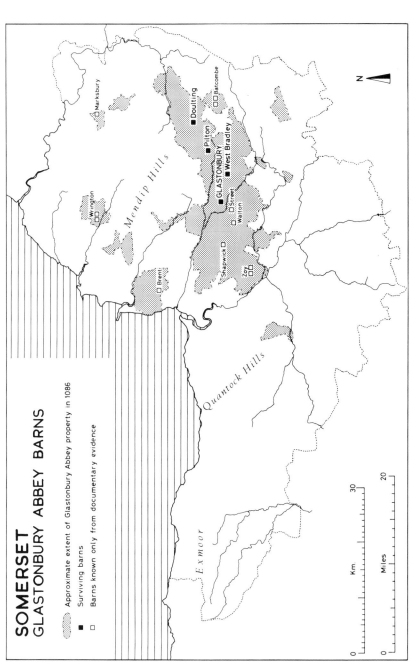

Figure 1 Glastonbury Abbey barns in Somerset

yielded £21 2s., and the tithes thereof £2 2s.[20] The granger's account of 1361–2 recorded 43 quarters, 2 bushels and 1 peck of wheat, 37 quarters, 5 bushels of barley, 120 quarters of oats and 11 quarters, 5 bushels of mixtillion or maslin from Doulting.[21] Clearly Doulting remained one of the abbey's more important sources of arable produce. A fourteenth-century extent records 357 acres of arable, 30 acres of meadow and 118 acres of pasture, the whole manor being valued at £48 7s. 4½d. annually.[22] By 1539 the demesne and tithes were both let out to farm, the demesne yielding £10 annually and the tithes of the whole parish £18 13s. 4d.[23] John Horner, lessee of the tithes and the barn before the Dissolution, negotiated a reissue of his lease, confirmed on 15 March 1540.[24]

In the time of Edward the Confessor, Abbot 'Alnod' (Æthelnoth) paid geld for twenty hides at Pilton. The Domesday Book records land for thirty ploughs, with the abbot holding land for a further twenty ploughs which had never paid geld. The abbot had ten ploughs on his demesne, and his villeins and bordars had ten ploughs on the ungeldable land. Roger de Courcelles held lands in Croscombe and Shepton as part of this manor.[25] The rectory of Pilton was granted to the bishop of Bath and Wells in 1173.[26] Otherwise, the 1198–9 survey shows Pilton as one of the manors which the abbey preferred to keep in its own hands.[27] However, Postan's discussion of the contracting demesne of the abbey is illustrated here perhaps better than anywhere by the declining number of ploughteams: ten demesne teams in 1086, six in *ca* 1135, three in 1176 and two in 1201.[28] The rental of Abbot Ford (1252–61) gives details of 763 acres of demesne arable at Pilton,[29] and in 1291 the abbot's possessions here were rated at £42.[30] A manorial extent of the time of Abbot Geoffrey Fromond (1303–22) describes the manorial buildings standing in a court and garden extending to seventeen acres; there were 687 acres of arable land, 107½ acres of meadow and further pastures, woodland and moor, in addition to two dovecotes and a watermill. The demesne alone was worth £60 18s. 7d. a year.[31] The granger's account of 1361–2 records 30

20   *Taxatio Ecclesiastica*, ed. Ayscough and Caley, pp. 203b, 205b.
21   Keil, 'The Granger of Glastonbury Abbey', p. 87.
22   London, British Library, Egerton 3321, fols 175–6, quoted in Platt, *The Monastic Grange*, p. 202.
23   London, P. R. O. Ministers' Accounts SC6/Henry VIII/3163, m. 42, quoted in Platt, *The Monastic Grange*, p. 202.
24   *Letters and Papers, Foreign and Domestic, of the Reign of Henry VIII*, ed. J. Gairdner and R. H. Brodie, 21 vols in 33 (London, 1862–1910) XV, 172.
25   DB, I, 90rb/va; Bates, 'Somerset Domesday', p. 464.
26   J. Collinson, *The History and Antiquities of the County of Somerset*, 3 vols (Bath, 1791) III, 481–2.
27   Postan, 'Glastonbury Estates in the Twelfth Century', pp. 359–66.
28   *Ibid*. p. 361
29   *Rentalia et Custumaria*, ed. Elton and Hobhouse, pp. 208–9.
30   *Taxatio Ecclesiastica*, ed. Ayscough and Caley, p. 203b.
31   BL Egerton 3321, fols 280–2, quoted in Platt, *The Monastic Grange*, p. 227.

quarters and 4 bushels of wheat from Pilton, but no barley or oats.[32] In September 1539 the demesne lands of Pilton were held by Thomas Whiting, presumably a relative of the last abbot, Richard Whiting. A survey of the abbey properties carried out after Abbot Whiting's attainder describes the park and house at Pilton in some detail; the premises then included a barn (presumably the building now existing) and sheepcote, together served by a close of pasture containing one acre, worth 12d. yearly.[33] The demesne as a whole was let out and valued at £15 per annum.[34]

At West Bradley the Court Barn lies just 100 metres within the modern parish of that name, but it has often been described under the name of West Pennard, the adjoining parish, which the abbey retained for much longer as a demesne vill. It is probable that West Bradley was originally part of the Pennard estate, and the barn certainly lay within the bounds of the Glastonbury Twelve Hides, as described in *ca* 1263 and again in 1503–10.[35] The charter evidence suggests that West Bradley may have been included within Pennard Minster (East Pennard).[36] This is described in 1086 as a former ten-hide vill recently increased to twenty hides. West Bradley may be identifiable with the hide of thegnland in *Pennarminstre* held from the abbey by 'Ailmar' (Æthelmær) in the time of Edward the Confessor and by Serlo of Burcy in 1086.[37]

The whole of the tithes of the estate at Glastonbury, including West Pennard, were appropriated by Bishop Savaric to the sacristan's office;[38] East Pennard church with its chapelry of West Bradley was also appropriated to Glastonbury Abbey by 1291, when the temporalities of Pennard as a whole yielded £18 8s. 8d. and the tithes thereof £1 16s.[39] It is possible, therefore, that the existing barn was built specifically as a tithe barn, and was not intended to house the products of the demesne. The granger's account of 1361–2 records yields of 62 quarters and 2 bushels of wheat, 2 quarters, 4 bushels of barley, 14 quarters of oats and 1 quarter, 4 bushels of dredge from Pennard.[40]

---

[32]   Keil, 'The Granger of Glastonbury Abbey', p. 87.
[33]   London, P. R. O. Ministers' Accounts SC6/Henry VIII/3163, m. 13d; P. R. O. Augmentation Office Miscellaneous Books E315/420, 39v; both quoted in Platt, *The Monastic Grange*, p. 227.
[34]   Dugdale, *Monasticon Anglicanum*, ed. Caley *et al.*, I, 12.
[35]   Morland, 'Glaston Twelve Hides', pp. 44, 50.
[36]   S.563; see Grundy, *Saxon Charters*, pp. 65–71, 233–4, and Morland, 'The Glastonbury Manors', pp. 76–7.
[37]   DB, I, 90va; Bates, 'Somerset Domesday', p. 464.
[38]   *Rentalia et Custumaria*, ed. Elton and Hobhouse, p. xxii.
[39]   Collinson, *History and Antiquities of Somerset*, III, 478–9; *Taxatio Ecclesiastica*, ed. Ayscough and Caley, pp. 203b, 205b.
[40]   Keil, 'The Granger of Glastonbury Abbey', p. 88.

SITING AND LAYOUT

If the precise relationship of the four extant barns to the estates is still unclear, adequate archaeological and documentary evidence for their relationship to their bartons is almost wholly lacking. None is known to have had an associated granary prior to 1389–90, when there is a reference to one adjoining the Abbey Barn in Glastonbury itself.[41]

From the 1274–5 records of repairs, we know that Glastonbury had a barton plus a barn with an oast house at one end; Pilton had a barn, stable and two other buildings; whilst West Bradley had a barn, cattle-house and oxherd's house. (No repairs at Doulting were mentioned.) It is a matter of surmise whether any of these buildings survived until the barns we know today had been built. Indeed, within each manor, we do not know whether there might have been more than one steading, more than one place for crop storage. It is no more than an assumption that the 1274–5 account and later repair references do relate to bartons where the extant barns stand. Today, with the possible exception of Pilton and the attached dovecote at West Bradley, the four sites have no medieval remains other than the barns themselves. An examination of each site raises questions for further study (see figures 2 and 3).

The home farm of Glastonbury Abbey lay immediately outside the south-east corner of the walled monastic precinct. The present Abbey Farm has traces from *ca* 1800, but house and steading are mainly Victorian, and the barn is the only surviving medieval structure. Its position, on the margins of the precinct, is broadly comparable with that of other Benedictine abbeys, including Abbotsbury, Ely, Eynsham and Evesham. The home farm of Sherborne Abbey lay within its outer precinct, and at Christ Church, Canterbury, it abutted the outer precinct. Glastonbury's barn is unexceptional in terms of its position with respect to the precinct buildings. It does, however, display several peculiarities. For a predominantly non-arable area it is large. Its workmanship is of exceptional quality. Its whole character advertises its high status, and it also acts as a focal point. Yet its alignment both to Bere Lane and to the south-eastern approach to the abbey, let alone to the known precinct entrances, is awkward. Moreover, it is set into a level terrace formed by the laborious excavation of some 1.5m depth of subsoil from its north-eastern end. Its recession into this gradient of about 1 in 15 considerably reduces its visual impact. While other barns elsewhere were excavated into banks, they were normally aligned parallel with the contour, as at Pilton, Abbotsbury, Bradford-on-Avon and even some of the Canterbury timber barns such as Godmersham. In each case the dominant entrance is from the lower flank, and the retaining walls either have no entrance or a ramped drive down to a lesser porch or doorway. At Glastonbury the siting seems perverse (only in later times was the ground ramped away from the walls) and its orientation conforms neither with that of the precinct, nor of the other

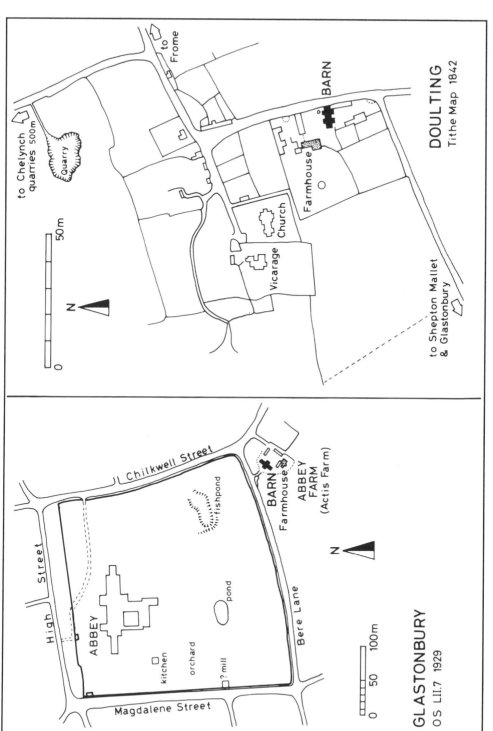

Figure 2 Barn location plans: Glastonbury and Doulting (by courtesy of Somerset Record Office and HMSO)

barns. Possibly its position was dictated by an earlier barton: did it, perhaps, replace the barn with an attached oasthouse, where roof repairs were recorded in 1274–5? Is the present instability of its south-east porch, described below, due to its being built over disturbed ground?

At Pilton the church, the abbot's manor-house (on the site of the present Manor Farm, a largely Georgian building incorporating some medieval fragments) with its *curia*, including a dovecote, and the village clustered on the higher land northwards, all lie on a south-facing slope overlooking the River Whitelake. This is now only a brook, but was once capable of accommodating small barges from the River Brue and the Bristol Channel. The demesne barton (now known as Cumhill) lay in full view of the manor-house, on the north-facing slopes across the Whitelake, reached over a medieval bridge. The barn stands at the highest point of the present (and possibly also of the original) barton, parallel to the contour and cut some 0.75m into the slope. From the manor-house its full length can be seen, and it is surely for this reason that its north facade and porch are more ostentatious than their southern counterparts. Contrary to normal steadings, the stockyards are now, and probably were in the Middle Ages, north of the barn. Due to the fall of the land, this arrangement protected the yards from the prevailing winds sweeping over the arable open fields to the south. To the north-east, off the entrance track, at the lowest level, is the farmhouse. Though fenestration and detail are much altered, both walls and roof appear partly medieval, possibly contemporary with the barn. The position suggests that it might have been a reeve's house; otherwise its scale would not be inappropriate for a granary.

Doulting, by contrast, is a village barton at a road junction, and lies hard by the church and vicarage. The abbot's acquisition of the rectory in 1266 could have provided the occasion for building investment. No repairs were noted here in 1274–5, possibly because it lay far enough east to avoid the worst of the great storm. The east gable of the barn abuts the road and now, as possibly when first built, the porches serve a dirty stockyard to the south and a clean entrance yard to the north. The house, offset to the latter, is difficult to date; it appears to be either of *ca* 1620 or *ca* 1680, but shows alterations, probably of the same century. At right angles to the house, opposite the barn, is an implement and general store of seventeenth- or eighteenth-century date. To the north is another stockyard and, on the 1842 map, a shape which may represent a further barn, now demolished; also, west of the house, the map marks a circular structure, possibly a dovecote. The barn is aligned along the contour, its porches spanning a fall of some 0.5m from south to north without apparent levelling-up. The structure of the building, though apparently symmetrical, poses other problems, discussed below.

At West Bradley the barn and its attached dovecote stand alone within a paddock of only 0.12ha, at the western edge of the parish. Unsupervised grain storage adjoining a dovecote seems an improbable practice. There is a small cottage immediately south-east of the barn paddock, while beyond the field to the north is Court Barn Farm, the steading for which is across the boundary in West Pennard; all of these buildings are modern and none

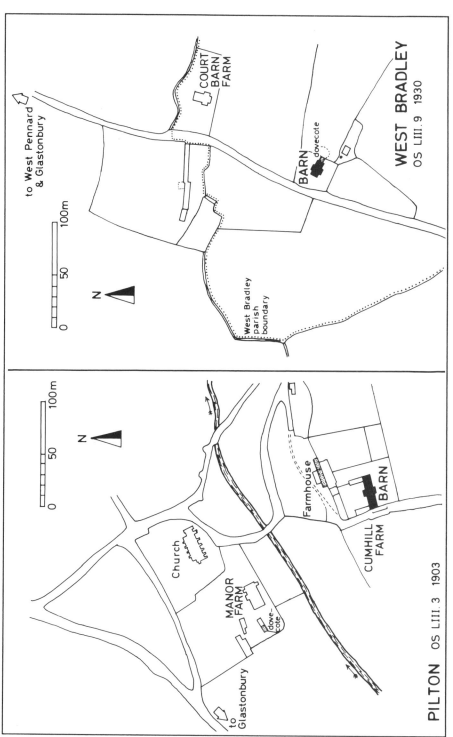

Figure 3 Barn location plans: Pilton and West Bradley (by courtesy of Somerset Record Office and HMSO)

appear to have any relevance to monastic management. Nonetheless, the 'Court' name implies the former existence nearby of a building more important than any of the modest structures now standing. There are indistinct earthworks in the paddock immediately east of the barn, which warrant fuller investigation.

ARCHITECTURAL DESCRIPTIONS (figure 4)

GLASTONBURY ABBEY BARN

The barn is of seven bays, its long axis orientated from north-east to south-west (for the sake of simplicity it will be treated below as if its alignment were east-west). Opposed cart porches project outwards from the central bay, with waggon entrances in their gable walls and arched pedestrian doorways in each of their side walls (figure 5).

The builders employed stone from several sources, yellow-grey Jurassic limestones being predominant. The walling is mainly of neatly coursed limestone rubble. In places courses of orange-brown marlstone were laid to form bands of darker colour, but no attempt was made to follow any consistent pattern. The buttresses, window dressings, gateway jambs, voussoirs and ornamental details are of a high-quality hard grey Jurassic limestone ashlar, the source of which is unknown; recent examination has suggested that it is probably not from Doulting, as had been assumed.[42] Blue lias slabs were used quite deliberately to provide a contrast of colour and texture immediately over the two waggon-gate arches. Contrary to the high quality of masonry everywhere else in the barn, the rubble used in the south porch gable wall is very mixed, including dressed blocks of grey limestone and material from the Yeovil Sands series, marlstone and blue lias in no regular pattern. Subsidence has affected the western flank of this porch, causing the lateral buttress to list two degrees out of vertical, the resulting tension causing several of the voussoirs over the waggon doorway to drop and dislocating the framework and mullion of the window above. This subsidence is probably a long-term problem, and the somewhat makeshift appearance of the masonry above the arch may well be the result of an earlier emergency repair.[43] The roof is of graduated stone slates.

At the apex of each main gable is a traceried window of three small trefoiled lights within a two-centred pointed-arched frame moulded like the porch windows, and of a typical Decorated style. There are three buttresses to each gable end, of which the central one is taller and of two stages. Close to their top stage the central buttresses are flanked by two slit vents in the form of a cross pommée. Lower down in each gable-end wall, roughly midway between the central and side buttresses, are two tall slit vents, chamfered externally and deeply splayed within. There are similar slit vents in the

---

[42]   We owe this identification to Dennis Parsons.
[43]   C. J. Bond, 'Glastonbury Abbey Barn: The South-East Porch', *PSANHS* 132 (1988), 251–6.

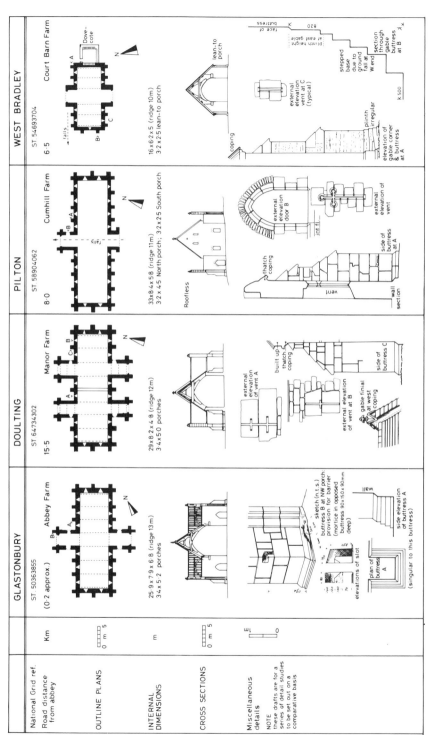

Figure 4 Comparative architectural descriptions

middle of each bay of the side walls. All the remaining buttresses of the end and side walls and the front buttresses of the two porches are single-stage with plinths. The lateral buttresses of the porches are capped by a continuation of the porch gable coping with a fleur-de-lys section at the top, and are stepped high up to the rear, i.e. facing the main body of the barn.

From the evidence of the masonry bonding, the porches are clearly coeval with the main body of the barn. The waggon doors in the porches are set in four-centred arches with two plain 45-degree chamfers separated by a step and stopped with half-pyramids. At each side of each porch is a two-centred arched pedestrian doorway, of which the rear-arch is segmental. In each porch gable is a window of two lights with cusped ogee arches in a square frame with reserved chamfers combined with hollow mouldings; the mullions have a roll and frontal fillet flanked by two hollow mouldings. A scroll dripmould extends almost the full depth of both windows.

Immediately below the windows in the main gables and above those in the porches the emblems of the four evangelists are carved within quatrefoil frames: St Mark, a winged lion, on the south; St Luke, a winged bull, on the north; St John, an eagle, on the west; and St Matthew, a winged man, on the east. These appear to be *in situ*, and it is curious that two earlier sources indicate quatrefoil openings in their place.[44] Pugin's drawings of 1834 include illustrations of all four of the evangelists' panels and show them in their present positions,[45] and it seems extremely unlikely that he would have failed to recognize them as recent insertions, had this been the case. A human head is carved on the kneelers of each of the main gables which are topped by half-sized statues, that at the west of a bishop, that at the east of the Virgin Mary. Both porch gables terminate in fleur-de-lys finials, and unidentified animals stand astride the side buttresses on the north porch, but are missing from the south.

The roof structure has been discussed by previous authors.[46] It consists of eight raised base-cruck trusses set on horizontal timber baulks halfway up the walls and carrying a superstructure of upper crucks. An upper and lower row of purlins are tenoned into the upper and base crucks respectively, a typical medieval arrangement; between these are roof plates of heavier section, not in the slope of the roof, which are carried on the ends of the ties. Surprisingly, these plates are not secured in any way to the ties, nor are they trapped by the upper crucks to resist tilting moments due to thrust from the common rafters; nevertheless, they show no signs of displacement. They are

[44]   Engraving by C. Hollis from a drawing by J. Buckler in R. Warner, *History of the Abbey of Glaston and the Town of Glastonbury* (Bath, 1826), plate VIII; W. Phelps, *The History and Antiquities of Somersetshire*, 2 vols (London, 1839) I, 551.

[45]   A. Pugin and A. W. Pugin, *Examples of Gothic Architecture Selected from Various Antient Edifices in England*, 2 vols (London, 1836) II, facing p. 56; we owe this reference to David Bromwich.

[46]   The fullest and most recent description, which has provided the basis for the account here, is by E. H. D. Williams and R. G. Gilson, 'Base Crucks in Somerset, Part i: Glastonbury Abbey Barn and the Priory of St John, Wells', *PSANHS* 121 (1977), 55–66, at 59–62.

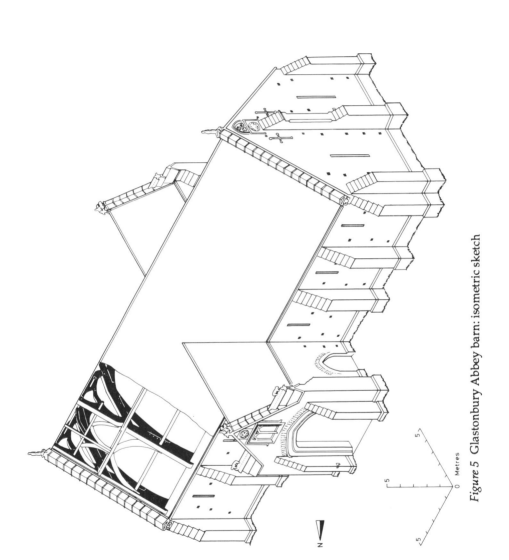

Figure 5 Glastonbury Abbey barn: isometric sketch

in bay lengths with tongued joints above the ties. The common rafters, in separate lengths of timber above and below the roof plates, have in the past been replaced and are now supported in their apices by a small ridge purlin, but the latter is an addition, and originally each pair would have been joined by a side-lapped joint at the apex. There are intermediate trusses carried on the roof plates midway between the main trusses, with the upper purlins clasped by the collars. No carpenters' marks have been found here or on the other abbey barns.

The completely new roofs built on the porches in 1976–7 are exact copies of their predecessors, but these themselves were probably nineteenth-century replacements in a style showing no affinities with the main roof. The slots in the walls carrying small vertical posts under the inner lower princi-pal rafters imply that originally the porches were roofed with small cruck trusses, as at Doulting. The lower ends of the common rafters of the main roof are supported over the porch entrances on large timbers tenoned into the adjacent main cruck blades at wall-top level, but otherwise there are no wall-plates. Other than the loss of the porch roofs and the addition of the ridge purlin, original features have not been materially altered either by the extensive past repairs or those of 1976–7, during which several complete cruck blades and other timbers were replaced.

The dating of the barn has been bedevilled by a myth about the presence of the arms of Abbot Beere on the building,[47] which has led other authors to ascribe to it a sixteenth-century date.[48] Beere's arms cannot now be located on the building, and the original source of this statement cannot be identi-fied. Ralegh Radford elected for a much earlier date, ascribing it to the fourteenth century in one of the popular guides to the abbey.[49] This view has been supported by E. H. D. Williams and R. G. Gilson who, on the basis of typological evidence, suggested that the roof structure was probably of late fourteenth-century date, although the gable windows and carvings could be somewhat earlier.[50]

The principal documentary references have been summarized by M. Bridge and R. W. Dunning.[51] The surviving manorial accounts record fre-quent repairs to a thatched barn at Glastonbury between 1302–3 and 1364–5. It had a porch which was also thatched in 1330–1. In 1333–4 it is said to have had both a 'little entry' and a 'great entry' where a new *flaellum* (an iron swivel bar for closing the double doors)[52] was fastened, the latter housing the threshing floor. The 'little entry' had a door, the bolt of which was removed

---

[47]   N. Pevsner, *The Buildings of England: South and West Somerset* (Harmondsworth, 1958), p. 177.

[48]   For example, J. T. Smith, 'Cruck Construction: A Survey of the Problems', *Medieval Archaeology* 8 (1964), 119–51, at 147.

[49]   C. A. R. Radford, *Glastonbury Abbey, the Isle of Avalon* (London, 1973), p. 18.

[50]   Williams and Gilson, 'Base Crucks in Somerset, Part i', p. 62.

[51]   M. Bridge and R. W. Dunning, 'The Abbey Barn, Glastonbury', *PSANHS* 125 (1981), 120.

[52]   Cf. L. F. Salzman, *Building in England Down to 1540: A Documentary History* (Oxford, 1952), p. 301.

and repaired. There is then a gap in the accounts from 1365 to 1389. The last surviving fourteenth-century roll, for 1389–90, reveals that the character of the building had changed in the interim, or that an entirely new barn had been built. Two tilers were paid for roofing the barn and an adjoining granary and oxshed using stone tiles. The work took the two men nine days and involved moving a stack of unthreshed corn inside from one part of the building to another, as work progressed. This presumably involved at least the replacement of the roof timbers to carry the heavier weight, if not a major reconstruction of the whole building. Bridge and Dunning pointed out that no record of barn construction at Glastonbury appears in the Obituary of Abbot Walter de Monington, which purports to record all major building works carried out during his abbacy (1342–75).[53] The presumption is that any major reconstruction must therefore have occurred during the period 1375–89, though it remains possible that the replacement of the roof alone might have occurred in Monington's time after 1365 without special record.

The firmest dating evidence has come from the dendrochronological examination of samples from the barn's roof timbers. Examination by Martin Bridge of Portsmouth Polytechnic has shown that fifteen samples may be cross-matched one to another, and that the site master curve constructed from these samples may be dated against several existing reference chronologies. This evidence suggests that the trees used for the timbers of the roof were possibly felled during the period 1343–61, and that the roof construction took place fairly soon after that.[54]

DOULTING BARN

The most curious feature of the Doulting barn (figure 6) is the presence of two full-scale cart porches on either side. Numerous other monastic barns have two cart entrances along their side walls which would also serve as threshing-floors, but other recorded examples are all appreciably longer: Abbotsbury (82.9m), Bradford-on-Avon (51.2m), Leigh (42.9m) and Middle Littleton (41m). The possible advantages of being able to unload two waggons into the barn simultaneously and of having two threshing-floors must be balanced against the loss of storage space; and the shorter the barn, the more considerable the latter drawback becomes. At Doulting the effect of the two porches is to limit storage space to only 75 per cent of its volume, compared with 81 per cent at Littleton or 91 per cent at Abbotsbury. Most of

---

[53] Bridge and Dunning, 'The Abbey Barn, Glastonbury', p. 120.
[54] J. Fletcher, M. Bridge and J. Hillam, 'Tree-Ring Dates for Buildings with Oak Timber', *Vernacular Architecture* 12 (1981), 38–40; Bridge and Dunning, 'The Abbey Barn, Glastonbury', p. 120. Despite their apparent architectural contemporaneity, eight of the fifteen samples revealed an end date between *ca* 1250 and 1300. Such anomalies are not uncommon, and several possible reasons, including the reuse of older timbers, are put forward by M. C. Bridge, 'The Dendrochronological Dating of Buildings in Southern England', *Medieval Archaeology* 32 (1988), 166–74; however, the possibility of a building period earlier in the century with a period of repair after 1343 cannot entirely be discarded.

the other barns possessing two entries within their long axis also have full-scale cart porches only on the one side, with much shallower projections on the other; indeed, Leigh has porches only on its southern side, the north wall being wholly blank.

The Doulting barn is also divided internally midway along its length by an inserted wall, the precise date of which is unclear. However, while this is not structurally an original feature, it is conceivable that some such division was always intended, in view of the double porches. Possibly half of the barn housed the produce of the abbey's own demesne and the other half that of its tenants; a barn built in 1505–6 at Headstone Manor, Harrow, comprised three bays used by the archbishop of Canterbury, separated by a dividing wall from the seven bays used by his tenant, each of the two sections having a waggon porch.[55]

The barn is of good-quality Doulting stone masonry, but the architecture is simpler than that of the barns at Glastonbury and Pilton. The vents are smaller. The gable-end walls are each supported by a massive central buttress of three stages flanked by two single-stage buttresses. The side walls are supported by buttresses with a short, shallow upper stage. The two north porches have side buttresses with a short upper stage and front single-stage buttresses, while the south porches have single-stage buttresses to both front and side. The moulding of the doorways is of two orders, chamfered at 45 degrees, with an intervening step, similar to that of Glastonbury's barn, but without chamfer-stops at the base. The doorway arches are segmental rather than four-centred as at Glastonbury. Decorative carving is limited to crocketed finials at the gables. There are cusped triangular apertures over three of the doorways (the west porch on the north side has a tall rectangular light instead) and at the main gable ends flanking the top of each central buttress. The present roof is of graduated stone slates; however, the existence of a cornice, one course below roof-eaves level round the side walls of the main building and porches, together with the fact that the pitch of the main gable copings is steeper than the present roof pitch, suggests that there may have been an earlier thatched roof.

The medieval timber roof survives substantially intact in both the main body of the barn and its porches, and has been described previously by Williams and Gilson.[56] The main roof is carried on nine trusses, all of which were originally arch-braced raised base-crucks. The two end trusses survive, of thinner section than the others. Trusses III, IV and V, numbered from the east, also survive in their original form, the inserted dividing wall filling the space up to the arch-brace of Truss V. Truss II has been replaced below the tie-beam by short straight principals, with a lower tie supported by a round stone pillar inserted at wall-top level. A wall-top tie supported on a square

55   P. A. Clarke, 'The Great Barn at Headstone Manor, Middx.: a Dated Building', *Vernacular Architecture Group Newsletter* 17 (1989), 4–5.
56   E. H. D. Williams and R. G. Gilson, 'Base Crucks in Somerset, Part ii', *PSANHS* 123 (1979), 27–53, at 27–32; this account has also provided the basis for the description of the roof of the West Bradley barn, which follows.

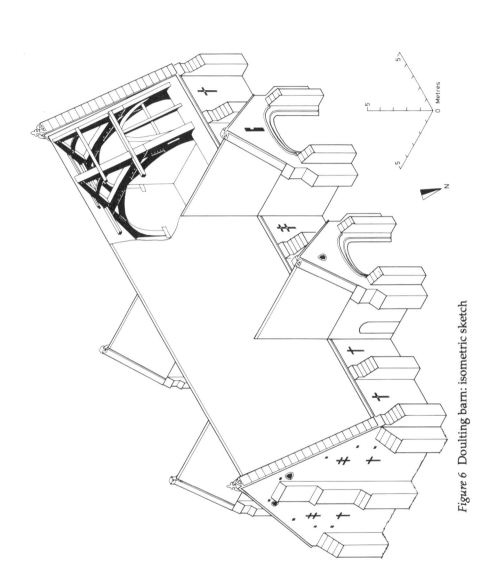

Figure 6 Doulting barn: isometric sketch

stone pillar has also been added to Truss VI, with radial struts rising to the original upper tie. Truss VII has been replaced entirely by a tie-beam truss supported by a central square stone pillar, with struts between the tie- and collar-beams. Truss VIII has been strengthened by the addition of a wall-top tie and other timbers, but there is no inserted pillar. Square-set roof-plates originally rested on top of the ties; some sections remain, others have been replaced. Horizontal angle-braces, some of which still survive, were pegged between the roof-plates and tie-beams. Curved wind-braces, many of which are now missing, rise from below the lower purlins to the roof-plate, the purlins being tenoned into the wind-braces rather than into the cruck blades. Some of the original purlins have been replaced. The upper principals are notched over the side of the roof-plates; all taper towards the roof apex, some are straight, others have a distinct concave profile on the underside, but there are no genuine upper crucks such as occur at Glastonbury. The upper purlins are trenched rather than tenoned. A ridge-purlin has been inserted. Between the principal trusses there were originally intermediate trusses, taking the form of slightly curved principals set into the top of the wall and rising to the roof-plate.

The porches all retain their original roof trusses, consisting of curved principals arch-braced to tenoned collars. The single purlins are tenoned into the principals and supported by wind-braces. The feet of the inner porch trusses rest upon upright posts set into the wall of the building; the feet of these posts are tenoned into the baulks upon which the cruck blades of the main building rest, and their tops are also tied to the main blades by short horizontal timbers, so that the porch structure is firmly bound with that of the main body of the barn. The only significant modifications to the porches have been the insertion of ridge-purlins and the replacement of the original common rafters.

The character of the Doulting barn, plainer and more massive than the others, suggests that it antedates them. J. H. Parker suggested a mid-fourteenth-century date,[57] and more recent writers have placed it in the fifteenth century,[58] but there seems no reason why the barn should not date back to the period immediately after the appropriation of the church in 1266.

PILTON, CUMHILL BARN

Parker regarded the Pilton barn (figure 7) as one of the finest barns in the country, and commented on the quality of its ornamentation.[59] The similarities to the Glastonbury barn are immediately evident, and there can be little doubt that the same masons were involved.

---

[57] J. H. Parker's exposition of the Doulting barn is reported in 'The Excursion', *PSANHS* 13 (1865–6), pt i, 12–14, at 14.
[58] For example, Platt, *The Monastic Grange*, p. 202; Pevsner, *South and West Somerset*, p. 181.
[59] J. H. Parker's exposition of the Pilton barn is reported in 'Second Day: Excursion', *PSANHS* 13 (1865–6), pt i, 21–6, at 22.

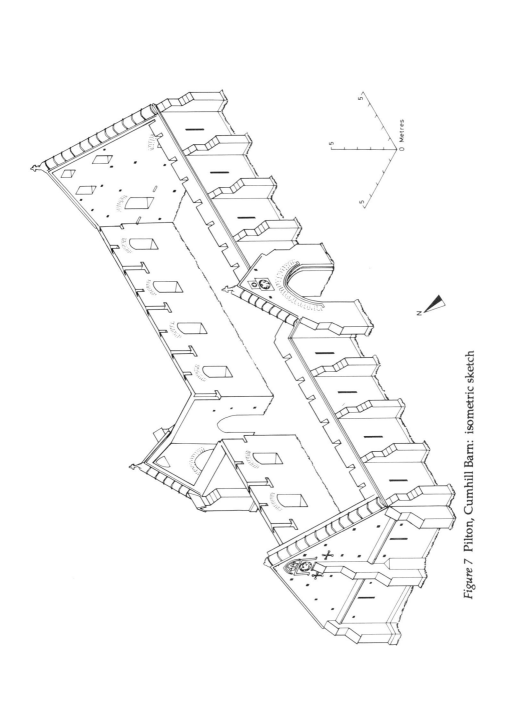

Figure 7 Pilton, Cumhill Barn: isometric sketch

The Pilton barn is of nine bays, its long axis aligned roughly east-west, the central bay with opposed single porches. It is of coursed liassic rubble with limestone ashlar buttresses and dressings. The long side walls have two-stage buttresses with plinths. The intervening vents on the north wall are unusually elaborate, taking the form of an elongated cross pommée, but those on the south are simple slits similar to those of Glastonbury, all chamfered externally with deep internal splays. Both gable-end walls are supported by three buttresses, the tallest central one of three stages, the flanking pair of two stages. There is a string-course below roof-eaves level, with the wall above set back slightly. At the gable ends there are two slit-vents in the lower stage, chamfered externally and splayed internally with a chamfered rear-arch; and, above the string-course and close to the top of the central buttress, two small cross-pommée vents, larger at the east end than at the west. There are medallions of the four evangelists on the gables, very similar to those at Glastonbury. At each gable end the evangelist's motif is protected by a dripstone continued down either side to make three sides of a square outline. They are set immediately above the central buttress, and above them in turn, immediately below the peak of the gable, is a small window of two cusped lights with linked pointed hood-moulds, all within a single semi-circular dripstone. The porches contain shallow-arched cart entries with projecting labels. The north porch has a contemporary pointed-arched doorway in the east wall, two-stage plinthed frontal buttresses and more complex flanking buttresses, similar to those of Glastonbury though less grand; the south porch has two-stage flanking buttresses but no frontal buttresses. Above each cart entry is the evangelist's symbol, here with no dripstone. Immediately above each symbol is a small quatrefoil light within a roundel, also cut out of a single limestone block; and above that, in the peak of the gable itself, a stone with a rose-like motif in low relief. The gable copings all have ruined crocketed finials. There are three inserted doorways, two in the north wall, one in the south, all now blocked; that towards the east end of the north wall truncates one of the vents, and from its external moulding appears to be of Tudor date.

The medieval roof was unfortunately destroyed by fire in 1963, but the slots in the masonry, formerly occupied by the feet of the ten principal trusses and the eight intermediate mid-bay trusses, survive. The two end trusses were close to the gables, a feature common to all the surviving barns of Glastonbury Abbey. Internal photographs taken before the loss of the roof provide some evidence for its structure, and a section-drawing showing a raised base-cruck, arch-braced to the tie-beam, has been reconstructed by Stuart Rigold.[60] There was a set of lower purlins, but it is not clear how these were linked to the cruck-blades. Above the tie-beam straight rafters of somewhat slender scantling rested upon roof-plates, with upper purlins clasped by the collars. There were also intermediate trusses.

Parker placed the Pilton barn in the latter part of the fourteenth century, a

---

[60]   R. de Z. Hall, 'A Preliminary Catalogue of Cruck-Roofed Buildings in Somerset', *PSANHS* 114 (1970), 48–63, at 52–5.

date followed by Platt,[61] and a date of *ca* 1375 would seem entirely reasonable.

WEST BRADLEY, COURT BARN

The Court Barn at West Bradley (figure 8) is the smallest of the surviving barns of Glastonbury Abbey. It is of five bays, the central bay half a metre longer to accommodate opposed shallow porches. The west gable wall is supported by a pair of high two-stage buttresses, and four lower two-stage buttresses support each of the side walls in line with the principal trusses, where these are not set into the porch structure. The walls are pierced by four narrow slits in either side wall, chamfered externally and deeply splayed internally, a similar vent in the west end wall, and a more ornamental vent in the form of a cross pommée high up at either gable end. Each gable has a stone coping with a fleur-de-lys finial. The porches are much simpler than on the other three barns: they are unbuttressed, with no independent roof structure, merely an extension of the main roof-line down towards the doorway lintel. The walls are of coursed blue lias rubble, with quoins, dressings and porches of better-quality oolitic ashlar, probably from Doulting. The roof was comprehensively relaid by the National Trust in the 1930s using red clay tiles, but the bottom course is of stone slates, probably the original material.

Like those of Glastonbury, Doulting and Pilton, the roof is of arch-braced base-cruck form. Of the six principal trusses, those at the west end, I and II, have been substantially replaced, though the feet of the crucks remain. The remaining trusses and upper principals are original, though all are now reinforced. Mortices for wind-braces are evident in the crucks, though no wind-braces survive. All of the common rafters and trenched purlins are replacements. A drawing made by J. B. M. Macgregor in 1932 shows roof-plates set square above the tie-beam.[62] These have been replaced by an additional intermediate set of purlins set in the slope of the roof in the triangular space left by the removal of the original roof-plates. Over the entrances a fourth small low purlin has been morticed into the cruck-blades at wall-top level to support the principal rafters. The feet of the crucks rest upon transversely laid baulks *ca* 0.25m square, set high in the walls. Some of the blades were formed from timbers of inadequate section, and in order to give a full bearing-surface on the baulks their base has been widened by 'filler-pieces' secured by a face-peg and slip-tenon. The upper principals are tapered and their feet are trimmed vertically on the outer face to accommodate the now-vanished roof-plate, giving a misleading superficial resemblance to small upper crucks.

The barn has few architectural embellishments to provide secure dating evidence, but a late fourteenth-century date seems likely. Adjoining the barn to the east are the remains of a square dovecote, the construction of which is

---

61 'Second Day: Excursion', p. 22; Platt, *The Monastic Grange*, p. 226.
62 Referred to by Williams and Gilson, 'Base Crucks in Somerset, Part ii', p. 53, n. 3.

of considerable interest in its own right; this requires a fuller discussion than is possible here.

BUILDING MATERIALS

No specific documentation for the source of building materials for any of the extant barns has yet been located. However, all of the identified building stone is from various Jurassic beds, all available reasonably nearby on the abbey's own estates. The blue lias outcrops on Pennard Hill, at Pylle, and further south along the Polden Hills. It was being exploited long before the Norman Conquest; some of the earliest stonework at the abbey itself is of this material, and tenth-century boundary perambulations attached to the charters of East and West Pennard mention a stone-quarry, located near the present Hill Farm, which would have been a source of blue lias.[63] It remained in use throughout the Middle Ages, although it was not a building material of the highest quality. The middle liassic marlstone was also available from parts of Pennard Hill and from Glastonbury itself. The Yeovil sands of the upper lias outcrop near Glastonbury and Doulting. Neither the marlstone nor the Yeovil sands were exploited on a major scale locally, but both appear in the Glastonbury barn. The inferior oolites outcrop along the eastern fringes of the central block of Glastonbury estates, and include the Doulting stone, the finest material available to the abbey. Doulting stone belongs to the middle part of the upper inferior oolite, and is a distinctive coarse-grained limestone, weathering to a brownish-grey colour, very largely formed from crinoid detritus from the Carboniferous series, cemented by calcite. It does not appear to have been exploited on any significant scale before the last quarter of the twelfth century, but was then widely used in numerous local churches, including Glastonbury Abbey itself. Wells Cathedral also was permitted stone from Doulting after 1352, and was renting quarries there after 1381.[64] The quarries remained a source of considerable profit to the abbey up to the Dissolution. Stone roofing slates were also available from the oolitic limestones.

Roofing timber is also likely to have come from the abbey's own estates. Glastonbury Abbey had woodlands at Pilton and on many of the islands in the Levels, including Glastonbury itself, Meare, Northload and Nyland. However, it is likely that the most massive oak timbers for the base-cruck blades would have come, not from managed woodland, but from the abbey's parks, where outsized trees are most likely to have survived. The surveys carried out by Richard Pollard and Thomas Moyle in 1539, immediately after the attainder of Abbot Whiting, show that even some of the park woodlands

[63]   S.236 and S.563; see Grundy, *Saxon Charters*, pp. 68, 76.
[64]   C. H. Vellacott and E. M. Hewitt, 'Building Stone', in the *Victoria History of Somerset*, ed. Page, II, 393–8; see also *The Calendar of the Manuscripts of the Dean and Chapter of Wells*, ed. W. H. B. Bird, Historical Manuscripts Commission 12.2–3, 2 vols (London, 1907–14) I, 290–1; II, 20, 86–8, 100.

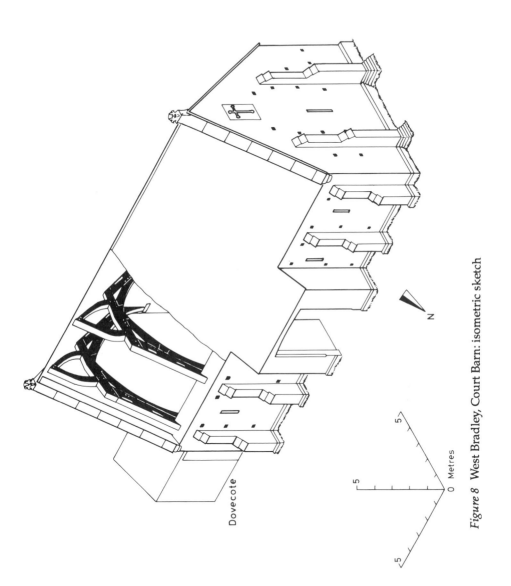

Dovecote

N

5

5

5

0 Metres

Figure 8 West Bradley, Court Barn: isometric sketch

were coppiced by that date; but Wearyall Park still included 60 acres of fair timber of an estimated value of £290 10s., and Sharpham Park still contained 200 oaks fit for timber, valued at 2s. each.[65]

DISTINCTIVE CHARACTERISTICS

To what extent do the four extant barns share common design charac-teristics? Can we speak of a Glastonbury 'house-style' for barns? The use of base-crucks with upper principals of one kind or another is common to all four of the barns, but this appears to be part of a regional building tradition in south-western England as a whole.[66] Roofs such as those of the barns of Bradford-on-Avon and Glastonbury itself, where the base-cruck is combined with an upper-cruck to bridge a wide span, have been acclaimed as repre-senting the crowning achievement of the cruck tradition.[67] The use of inter-mediate trusses, as at Glastonbury, Doulting and Pilton, is also a regional characteristic. Although these features are distinctive, they were not re-stricted to the Glastonbury estates.

In terms of planning and design, all four barns are comparatively elabor-ate, with generous buttressing, gable coping at both ends of the building, and full-scale cart porches on both sides. The quality of the masonry is also generally high, and one is left with the clear impression that the barns were designed to impress as well as to perform their function efficiently, and that expense was not spared.

Some decorative features which are repeated on more than one of Glas-tonbury Abbey's barns are not known elsewhere. The most distinctive are the motifs of the four evangelists, which are carved with great delicacy and detail, and appear both at Glastonbury itself and at Pilton. Cross-pommée lights appear at Glastonbury, Pilton and West Bradley. It is in the architectu-ral embellishment of its barns, rather than in their basic structure, that the distinctive hand of the abbey can be most clearly seen.

In England generally there is little evidence of any major monastic invest-ment in barns before the twelfth century, but a widespread programme of barn construction seems to begin soon after 1200, continuing into the fif-teenth century. Documentary references suggest that the building of substan-tial barns may have begun early on the Glastonbury estates; there was certainly a sizeable building at Wrington by 1189.[68] So far as the existing buildings are concerned, it can tentatively be suggested that the main peri-ods of building activity were *ca* 1275 (represented by Doulting) and *ca* 1375 (represented by Glastonbury, Pilton and West Bradley).

---

[65]   Dugdale, *Monasticon Anglicanum*, ed. Caley *et al.*, I, 10.
[66]   N. W. Alcock and M. W. Barley, 'Medieval Roofs with Base-Crucks and Short Principals', *Antiquaries Journal* 52 (1972), 132–65.
[67]   Smith, 'Cruck Construction', p. 129.
[68]   *Liber Henrici de Soliaco, Abbatis Glaston. An Inquisition of the Manors of Glastonbury Abbey*, ed. J. E. Jackson (London, 1882), p. 94.

Although we have no way of knowing how representative the four survivors are of Glastonbury Abbey's barns as a whole, the fact that three of them appear to post-date the difficult years of the early to mid-fourteenth century is of some interest. Why was Glastonbury investing considerable sums of money in barn construction on some of its properties at a time when demesne farming was everywhere in retreat ? The answers can only come with further work, but we can postulate that, alongside extensive leasing, a policy of selective retention of some demesnes was being pursued. Income from leasing provided ready cash for new building projects on those manors which remained in the abbey's hands, and certain of the manor-houses, including Doulting and Pilton, were developed as luxurious country residences for the abbot. Resistance to the leasing of the home demesne may account for the investment at Glastonbury itself, while the building of the Pilton barn may be seen as part of a policy of enhancement of those properties kept in hand for residential purposes. It may, indeed, be the most elaborate and well-constructed barns built during this period of retreating demesne farming which stood the best chance of survival, while the earlier, more strictly functional structures have generally disappeared.

CONCLUSION

What remains to be considered is precisely how the barns were used and what relationship they bore to the individual demesne estates of the abbey. Any attempt to find solutions to these questions is fraught with difficulties, and demands a much wider consideration of medieval agricultural techniques and estate management practices than is possible here. Nonetheless, it is worth exploring some of the factors involved in order to formulate further questions.

The size of each barn is a fundamental consideration. Even the smallest of them represented a considerable capital investment, and it is a reasonable supposition that their capacity was fairly carefully calculated to ensure that they would provide adequate storage and processing space for whatever goods they were expected to accommodate.

Medieval monastic barns span a wide spectrum of sizes, and do not lend themselves to rigid classification. However, it is suggested that an arbitrary threefold classification can be adopted: 'large barns' are defined as those over 40m in length and over 9m in width, and would include Abbotsbury, Beaulieu St Leonards, Tisbury, Frocester, Bradford-on-Avon, Great Coxwell, Leigh and Middle Littleton; 'medium-sized barns' are between 25m and 40m in length and between 8m and 9m in width; 'small barns' are less than 25m long by 8m wide (all dimensions are internal). None of the surviving barns of Glastonbury Abbey falls into the 'large' category. Glastonbury, Pilton and Doulting all fall within the 'medium' range. West Bradley is amongst the smallest known monastic barns, comparable with Enstone (21.9m x 7.9m) or Shippon (17.5m x 5.6m). This considerable size range surely reflects some variation in function, land exploitation or estate organization. This presumption in turn, however, prompts a series of supplementary questions.

(i) What commodities were stored in the barns? It is a reasonable enough assumption that all medieval barns were used primarily for the storage and processing of unthreshed grain, but on some estates different cereal crops were stored in separate barns. At least two barns are recorded in the home barton of Evesham Abbey, and one of these, built in the time of Abbot Brokehampton (1282–1316), was specifically said to be for barley.[69] The Merton College manor of Cuxham, during the later thirteenth and early fourteenth centuries, included two barns, one for wheat, one for spring-corn, and a new wheat-barn was built between 1324 and 1327, one of the two old barns continuing in use for spring-corn.[70] By contrast, at least one of Glastonbury Abbey's lost barns, that at Wrington, was certainly used for multiple crop storage, including wheat, oats and beans, in the twelfth century.[71] The extent to which barns were used for the storage of other non-cereal commodities, such as hay or pulses, would have depended very largely on what other storage buildings were provided on that particular manor. Storage of the hay crop, likely to have been considerable in Somerset, must have been as vital as corn storage. Unfortunately, we usually lack information on the smaller storage buildings, which hardly ever survive.

(ii) How was the produce actually stacked and processed within the barn? Contemporary manuscript illuminations appear to show a range of harvesting practices current in western Europe during the Middle Ages. The corn could be cut by sickle fairly close below the heads, leaving a long stubble which could then be cut separately for thatch, forage or litter.[72] This method is said to have been normal in medieval England.[73] An alternative practice is depicted in the Luttrell Psalter of *ca* 1340, where the corn is being reaped by two women leaning forward to use their sickles close to the ground. Stalks could also be cut at midway point, leaving some stubble for the cattle.[74] Since a good medieval cereal crop might be expected to be one metre tall, the choice of harvesting method had considerable implications for the amount of barn storage space required.

The assumption is that, once in the barn, the sheaves were stacked up from floor to eaves level, leaving clear only the bays within the cart porches. These bays served as threshing-floors, where grain could be threshed throughout the winter, whenever it was required for bread-making, brewing, animal feed or seed-corn. The space between the eaves and the roof-ridge,

---

[69] Bond, 'Estates of Evesham Abbey', p. 13.

[70] P. D. A. Harvey, *A Medieval Oxfordshire Village: Cuxham, 1240 to 1400* (Oxford, 1965), p. 35.

[71] *Liber Henrici*, ed. Jackson, p. 94.

[72] See, for example, a thirteenth-century French illustration reproduced in J. Chapelot and R. Fossier, *The Village and House in the Middle Ages* (London, 1985), p. 152.

[73] Lord Ernle, *English Farming, Past and Present* (London, 1961), p. 12.

[74] Cf. *Les Tres Riches Heures du Duc de Berry*, ed. E. Pognon (Geneva, 1979), pp. 28–9; and Dijon, Bibliothèque Municipale, 170, 75v, reproduced in G. Zarnecki, *The Monastic Achievement* (London, 1972), p. 83.

and the cross-passages themselves, would provide overflow capacity for good years, when waggons might be overwintered in the porches.

Direct evidence for the contents and manner of loading of one of Glastonbury Abbey's barns comes from a manorial survey drawn up when Henry of Sully became abbot in 1189.[75] The passage concerns the now-vanished Wrington barn; the use of the term *furcae* has been quoted as a possible piece of contemporary documentary evidence for crucks,[76] but the evidence which it provides for the use of the space within the barn is even more valuable, and is worth quoting in full:

> Ibi est una grangia. in aquilonali parte cuius debet esse unum tas durans usque ad proximum hostium aquiloni. et debet esse plenum usque ad festum. Inter duo hostia est unum aliud tas durans ab hostio aquilonali usque ad furcas proximas hostio australi. Illud tas debet esse in altum equale muro. Et implementum frumenti ibi est rationabiliter. In australi parte est unum tas auene durans ad furcas. in longum. In altitudine durans ad trabem furcarum. Ante illud tas est unum aliud tas auene durans fere ad hostium. uacuitas inter tas et hostium continet duos pedes. De hoc tas desunt duo pedes in altum. Et ibidem debent esse tres carucate fabarum. Extra grangiam debet esse unum tas trium carrearum. modo est tantum quantum debet esse. Ibi debent esse duo . . . [at this point the entry breaks off abruptly].

> There is a barn, in the northern part of which should be a stack extending as far as the nearest doorway on the north, and should be full up to the ridge. Between the two doorways is another stack extending from the northern doorway to the 'forks' (? crucks) next the southern doorway. This stack should be as high as the wall. Such a loading of wheat there is reasonable. On the southern side is a stack of oats extending to the forks in length and in height to the collar-beam (?) of the 'forks'. In front of this stack is another stack of oats reaching nearly to the doorway, and the space between the stack and the doorway is two feet. From this stack there are lacking two feet in height, and thereon should be three loads of beans. Outside the barn should be a stack of three cartloads, built up in the proper manner. There should be two. . . .[77]

Calculations of the amount of grain which a barn might contain are, therefore, fraught with difficulty, though formulae for estimations are given in several medieval sources: for example, one treatise in Gloucester Cathedral Library includes a memorandum stating that one stack of wheat in a barn 30 feet (9.1m) broad between a bay of crucks (*furcae*) 15 feet (4.6m) long and 10 feet (3m) high should contain 40 quarters.[78]

[75] The *Liber Henrici de Soliaco*; see above, note 68.
[76] C. F. Innocent, *The Development of English Building Construction* (London, 1916), p. 20; N. W. Alcock and R. de Z. Hall, 'Documentary Evidence for Crucks', in *Cruck Construction: An Introduction and Catalogue*, ed. N. W. Alcock, CBA Research Report 42 (1981), pp. 28–36, at 32.
[77] *Liber Henrici*, ed. Jackson, p. 94; translated by R. de Z. Hall, 'A Twelfth-Century Barn of Glastonbury Abbey', *SDNQ* 29 (1970), 138–9.
[78] Gloucester, Dean and Chapter Library, 33, published in D. Oschinsky, *Walter of*

(iii) What was the hinterland from which produce actually came to the barn, and what arable acreage did each barn serve? Here practices may have varied enormously from estate to estate. Monasteries whose landed estates were not particularly extensive might have elected to have a single large barn in their own outer court instead of numerous outlying barns on their granges or manors, thereby centralizing the storage of grain from all their properties. This might account for the enormous size of the barn at Abbotsbury. Even where there were barns on the outlying estates, there were often also one or more barns on the home grange, which might have served more than just the home demesne. On the extensive Glastonbury estates it seems to have been the practice to have a barn on most, if not all, of the principal demesnes. However, produce from other more scattered properties may also have found its way into the nearest convenient abbey barn.

(iv) What proportion of the crops produced within the manor or catchment area of any given barn were actually stored there? How does the barn capacity relate to corn consumption at the abbey, or within the manor, or to local markets? Was the barn reserved strictly for the produce of the abbey's own demesne lands? Did it also house grain from rents paid in kind? Where the abbey had appropriated the parish church, as was the case at Doulting, did the barn also house the tithes? Were the smaller barns such as West Bradley intended solely for the storage of tithes and nothing else? The Shippon barn on the Abingdon estate appears to have housed the tithes destined for the abbey kitchener's office, and Winchcombe Abbey's barn at Enstone was built just seventy-five years after the abbey's appropriation of the valuable living, following a petition from the local bailiff.[79]

(v) The position may be further complicated by the internal administration of the abbey. Were some barns designed to house produce destined specifically for the abbot, or for certain of the obedientiaries, as appears to have been the case at Bury St Edmunds?

(vi) Finally, can any relationship be detected between the cubic capacity of the barn, the expected volume of the annual harvest and the arable acreage of the estates they served? Since so many variable factors are involved, it would be naive to hope for some simple, universally applicable formula. Nonetheless, on manors such as Doulting and Pilton, which form comparatively discrete parts of the Glastonbury estates, barn capacities and demesne acreages are known, and the possibilities of examining the relationship further do exist.

The quality of the surviving barns of Glastonbury Abbey pays lasting testimony to the importance accorded to crop storage and to its vital role in the maintenance of a great abbey in the Middle Ages. However, much more investigation of how the barns worked is needed if we are ever to bridge the

Henley and Other Treatises on Estate Management and Accounting (Oxford, 1971), pp. 469–75, at 475.
[79] *Accounts of the Obedientiars of Abingdon Abbey*, ed. R. E. G. Kirk, Camden Society ns 51 (London, 1892), p. 35; Wood-Jones, 'The Rectorial Barn at Church Enstone', p. 43.

gulf between the economic historian studying estates and the architectural historian studying buildings. The formulation of questions such as those raised here is an essential preliminary step towards a fuller understanding.

ACKNOWLEDGEMENTS

JBW has held a Leverhulme fellowship to research tithe barns and has also received assistance from the Eric Fletcher fund; we have both benefited from grants from the Maltwood Fund of the R. S. A. We owe a considerable debt to the authors of previous descriptions of the barns and of the other published works mentioned in the footnotes below. We would like to thank D. Bromwich and S. D. Hobbs for their advice and assistance with sources. Finally, we would like to express our gratitude to the owners of the four barns, who have willingly allowed access for study.

The Tribunal, Glastonbury, Somerset

ROBERT W. DUNNING

In the Parliament of 1554 'Mr Sydnam', probably Sir John Sydenham of Brympton, proposed that Glastonbury should become the county town of Somerset.[1] The failure of the proposal undoubtedly ensured both that the town changed little in size for at least two centuries, and also that the town centre was not rebuilt. Several interesting medieval buildings still stood in the High Street in the earlier nineteenth century,[2] but increased prosperity by the 1880s inevitably brought destruction. The 'unashamedly neo-Gothic'[3] structures which now grace the street are, for some tastes, over-conscious reminders of the genuine medieval buildings which they replaced. Two among the few survivors are the George and Pilgrim Hotel, rebuilt in the mid-fifteenth century by Abbot John Selwood, and what has come to be known as the Tribunal. The Tribunal is a two-storied, L-shaped structure on the north side of the High Street with a two-storied addition in the rear, including a kitchen. The front range, according to the current guide leaflet, is 'not older than 1400', although the street frontage was inserted between earlier gable walls in the early years of the sixteenth century. The rear wing has details of the fifteenth century and its open roofs are of the same period. The building has been interpreted as containing the court room and the lodging for the justices who administered the judicial franchise of the abbots of Glastonbury known as the Twelve Hides. The royal arms above the entrance have been seen as supporting the claim.[4]

The name Tribunal is of relatively recent origin. The property was evidently one of many in the street of similar character, of no particular antiquarian interest to the parish administrators of the earlier years of the nineteenth century; and it was regarded as an ordinary dwelling for rating purposes. It has, in consequence, so far proved impossible to identify its ownership with certainty before 1796.[5] From that time onwards the house was occupied by a succession of tenants, and was distinguishable only by its rateable value.

Richard Warner, writing in 1826, was unable to discover when the name

[1]   S. W. Bates-Harbin, *Members of Parliament for the County of Somerset* (Taunton, 1939), pp. 122–3.

[2]   Taunton Castle, Somerset Archaeological Society, wash drawings dated 1825 and 1846 in the Pigott and Braikenridge collections.

[3]   N. Pevsner, *South and West Somerset* (Hardmondsworth, 1958), p. 181.

[4]   C. A. Ralegh Radford, *Glastonbury Tribunal* (HMSO, 1977, 1984).

[5]   Somerset Record Office, Tithe Map and Award; Somerset Record Office, D/P/gla.j 4/1/56–58; 13/1/3–5.

Tribunal came to be attached to it, but noted that it had formerly been 'a residence of much respectability' and the home of one of Glastonbury's eighteenth-century incumbents. He published at the same time an illustration, in which the house seems to have been occupied by a commercial school for young gentlemen, while the garden and perhaps the rear wing were let to a nurseryman (see Plate I).[6]

The name Tribunal actually seems to have been first used in print by John Collinson in 1791. Collinson gave no source for the name nor claimed it had been a court house of any kind,[7] but he may have been influenced, as others before him, by a version of a terrier compiled by Abbot Beere which he himself printed, using as his source Hearne's edition of John of Glastonbury's *Cronica siue antiquitates Glastoniensis ecclesie*, by that time well known to antiquarians.[8] The terrier included a description of the abbey court house,[9] which probably led the surveyor who drew a map of Glastonbury before 1778 to identify the building on the north side of the High Street as 'formerly the judgement hall belonging to the abbot'. That surveyor was probably Richard Locke of Burnham, an associate of Edmund Rack, from whose projected antiquarian survey of the county Collinson drew much of his material.[10] Earlier visitors did not notice the building. A Mr Savage in 1677 mentioned only the George Inn;[11] Charles Eyston in 1716 recorded 'a small old building of stone', possibly this building, in the High Street which he called 'Beere's Hospital'. He enquired locally what it was 'but none upon the spot could inform me; so I knew not what to make of it'. Further down the street he identified the present George and Pilgrim Hotel as 'The Pilgrims' Hospital'.[12]

Abbot Beere's Terrier, as printed by Hearne, has thus, it seems, provided the temptation to identify the surviving building in the High Street as the abbot's court house. An examination of the original manuscript of the terrier and of an earlier description of the manor of Glastonbury suggests a rather different story.

The first reference to the 'County Hall' is said to occur in the thirteenth century,[13] but in fact there is no such certainty. The place where William de Fortibus paid homage to Abbot Roger of Ford in 1255 was simply *in aula Glastonie*,[14] which surely is more likely to have been the abbot's hall within

---

6   R. Warner, *A History of the Abbey of Glaston and of the Town of Glastonbury* (Bath, 1826), p. lxxi and plate XV.
7   J. Collinson, *The History and Antiquities of the County of Somerset*, 3 vols (Bath, 1791) II, 263.
8   The terrier is found in London, British Library, Egerton 3034; it was printed in *JG*, ed. Hearne, II, 287–357.
9   *Ibid*. II, 306.
10   Somerset Record Office, DD/SAS C/1461.
11   Bristol Record Office, Ashton Court 36074, fol. 88.
12   Warner, *A History of the Abbey of Glaston*, Appendix, p. xxxv.
13   Radford, *Glastonbury Tribunal*.
14   *Rentalia et Custumaria Michaelis de Ambresbury, 1235–1252, et Rogeri de Ford, 1252–1261, Abbatum Monasterii Beatae Mariae Glastoniae*, ed. C. J. Elton and E. Hobhouse, SRS 5 (1891), p. 233.

the monastic precinct than a hall used for common sessions. In 1325, the third year of the rule of Abbot Adam of Sodbury, an extent of the abbey estates was drawn up.[15] Almost forty folios cover the town and manor of Glastonbury, beginning with the various sources of income of a medieval lord – perquisites, fines and tolls from courts, fairs, markets. The first entry records a certain hall for holding tourns and courts (*tournis et comitatibus*) of the sheriff and justices. Under this hall was a gaol for holding prisoners, five stalls or shops (*seldi*), together paying rent of 30s., and a little stall or shop for receiving tolls at the time of the fairs, worth 6d.[16] The stalls, and especially the tolsey, suggest a position near the centre of the town, and an agreement made between Abbot Sodbury and Robert de Brent in 1333, while not exactly defining the site, indicates its location a little more precisely. That agreement referred to a plot of land on the north part of the High Street opposite (*ex opposito*) the building then called the court hall (*aule comitatus*).[17] That same plot of land was referred to in John of Glastonbury's chronicle as 'opposite' the hall.[18] Abbot Sodbury's court hall was thus on the south side of the street.

Nearly two centuries later the survey known to later generations as Abbot Beere's Terrier was compiled.[19] Laid out with Abbot Sodbury's extent as a model, the record of the town begins again with the court hall for tourns and sessions and courts of the sheriff and justices of the peace within the liberties of the Twelve Hides. Under the hall, as before, was a gaol for holding and keeping prisoners, but there is no mention of stalls or shops there; and there is a further significant phrase. The hall was newly built (*nouiter constructa*)[20] by Abbot Beere, abbot from 1493, and thus joins a long list of buildings credited to him.[21] The phrase 'newly built' could, of course, be interpreted as a reconstruction of an earlier hall but for a hitherto unnoticed entry later in the terrier. Among the tenements in the High Street belonging to the abbey were three, standing side by side and occupied respectively by Augustine Sadeler, Thomas Towker and William Corye.[22] They, too, were described as having been newly built by Abbot Beere, and were said to be on the site of the ancient hall. Each tenement was 45 feet deep and 22 feet broad, and thus the three together occupied a street frontage of some 66 feet – reasonable space for gaol, stalls and tolsey beneath a hall, standing in the centre of town where the abbot's power would be most visible and effective.

Abbot Beere's hall, a room covering a gaol but not stalls, seems to have been more modest in size than that of Abbot Sodbury, a possible explanation

[15]   London, British Library, Egerton 3321.
[16]   BL Egerton 3321, fol. 1.
[17]   *The Great Chartulary of Glastonbury*, ed. Aelred Watkin, 3 vols, SRS 59, 63–4 (1947–56) II, 334.
[18]   *Cronica*, ch. 139 (ed. Carley, pp. 264–5) – where the phrase *aule comitatus* is rendered 'hall of the Earl'.
[19]   See note 8.
[20]   BL Egerton 3034, fol. 9.
[21]   *The Itinerary of John Leland*, ed. Lucy Toulmin Smith, 5 vols (London, 1906–10) I, 289–90.
[22]   BL Egerton 3034, 16v–17r.

for its failure to survive in so-far recognizable form. As the outward and visible sign of the abbot's power, it may have been an early target for destruction. What at present may be asserted with confidence is that Abbot Sodbury's court hall, a large building with gaol and space for stalls on the ground floor and sessions room above, stood on the south side of the High Street until some time during the period 1493–1503, the period when Richard Beere was abbot. It was subsequently demolished and three tenements were built on the site. A new hall was built elsewhere, providing a gaol on the ground floor and a sessions room above. The site of this second hall has not yet been identified, but it was evidently a building with its principal room on the first floor, over a gaol. By no stretch of the imagination can the obviously domestic rooms on the ground floor of the present modest house on the north side of the High Street, called the Tribunal, have ever been a gaol, for there is a fine, original window facing the street, and others overlooking the burgage plot in the rear. The rooms on the first floor are similarly domestic in character. The dwelling may well have been reconstructed during the abbacy of Richard Beere, and Collinson noted that still at the end of the eighteenth century the glass in the principal window bore the coats of arms of abbots and kings.[23] He made no mention, however, of the royal arms in stone, at present over the entrance, and they, like many specimens of carved stone-work throughout the town, are not necessarily in their original position. Without the pressure to identify the building as the court hall of the abbots of Glastonbury and quarters for the abbot's justices, the 'Tribunal' can surely be seen as the sole surviving example in Glastonbury of a substantial merchant's house, and its name the result of misplaced antiquarian enthusiasm of the late eighteenth century.

---

[23]   Collinson, *The History and Antiquities of Somerset*, II, 263.

Plate I Medieval house in High Street, Glastonbury, now called the Tribunal

II

MANUSCRIPTS AND TEXTS

A Single-Sheet Facsimile of a Diploma of King Ine for Glastonbury

LESLEY ABRAMS

INTRODUCTION

Fifteen texts of diplomas purportedly issued by Ine, king of Wessex (688–726), survive today, as well as notices of at least a further eight grants whose texts are lost. It is noteworthy that more than half of these twenty-three grants are associated with the religious house at Glastonbury;[1] the remainder were preserved at Abingdon, Malmesbury, Muchelney, Sherborne and Winchester.[2] Although the foundation of the ecclesiastical community at

[1]   Record survives of thirteen grants by Ine to Glastonbury. These have been variously preserved. There are six extant texts, which (with the exception of the single sheet under discussion) survive in the two fourteenth-century cartularies, Longleat House, Marquess of Bath 39 (printed as *The Great Chartulary of Glastonbury*, ed. A. Watkin, 3 vols, SRS 59, 63–4 [1947–56] [hereafter *GC*]), and its copy, the *Secretum Domini*, Oxford, Bodleian Library, Wood empt. 1 (*S. C.* 8589). A contents-list of an earlier lost cartulary, the *Liber terrarum* (hereafter *LT*), preserves notices but not texts of further grants by Ine in its lengthy register of pre-Conquest charters, as does a list of single sheets, the *Index chartarum* (hereafter *IC*) (both of these, dated 1247/8, in Cambridge, Trinity College R. 5. 33 [724], at 77r–78v; see Julia Crick's discussion and description of this manuscript elsewhere in this volume). A register compiled in the early fifteenth century, Longleat House, Marquess of Bath 39A, lists the charters held in the archive at that time. Finally, the narrative histories of Glastonbury Abbey, the *De antiquitate Glastonie ecclesie* begun by William of Malmesbury and the *Cronica siue antiquitates Glastoniensis ecclesie* of John of Glastonbury, give fuller, though not necessarily trustworthy, accounts of these transactions (summarized in *DA*, ch. 69; ed. Scott, pp. 140–5). Grants recorded only in the histories were not listed in Peter Sawyer's *Anglo-Saxon Charters. An Annotated List and Bibliography* (London, 1968), but were numbered in H. P. R. Finberg's *The Early Charters of Wessex* (Leicester, 1964) (hereafter *ECW*). Glastonbury's thirteen grants by Ine are: S.238, S.245 (although no longer extant in the abbey's archive, this was no. 2 and no. 135 in the *Liber terrarum*), S.246, S.247, S.248, S.250, S.251, S.1670 (*IC* A6), S.1671 (= S.238?; *LT* 20), S.1672 (= S.247; *LT* 9), S.1673 (*LT* 12), *ECW* 373 (*DA*, ch. 40; ed. Scott, p. 94), and *ECW* 377 (*DA*, chs 40 and ?69; ed. Scott, pp. 94 and 140).
[2]   Abingdon – S.239, S.241 and S.252; Malmesbury – S.243 and S.245 (possibly suspicious content, but diplomatically unobjectionable; on this privilege for the Wessex diocese as a whole, see H. Edwards, 'Two Documents from Aldhelm's Malmesbury', *Bulletin of the Institute of Historical Research* 59 [1986], 1–19, and *The Charters of the Early West Saxon Kingdom*, BAR Brit. ser. 198 [Oxford, 1988], pp. 107–14); Muchelney – S.240, S.244 and S.249; Sherborne – *ECW* 372, now lost (*Charters of Sherborne*, ed. M. A. O'Donovan, Anglo-Saxon Charters 3 [London, 1988], p. 81); and

Glastonbury seems to have predated his reign, in some medieval sources Ine was identified as the founder of the house,[3] and it is doubtless no coincidence that this comparatively large corpus of charters in his name has survived there. The status of the diplomas of Ine in favour of other religious houses is almost uniformly suspect (if based on genuine elements, they have been extensively manipulated at later dates), and Glastonbury's six surviving texts of Ine's grants typically include several clearly spurious diplomas as well as others with some claim to authenticity.[4]

One diploma, however, stands out: no. 248 in Sawyer's handlist of Anglo-Saxon charters records the gift of four estates in Somerset to Abbot Berwald, dated June 705, the fourth indiction.[5] This charter survives only in a single sheet, apparently written by a scribe seeking to imitate as far as possible a rather current early medieval Insular hand (see Plate I). On the evidence of the script, this single sheet is almost certainly not an original, but it may nevertheless represent a unique survival. No original charters of Ine are known to have been preserved, and all other diplomas in his name survive merely as transmitted texts which were recorded, in most cases, in late medieval cartularies. If, however, the exemplar of the extant single sheet from Glastonbury was an authentic original of the early eighth century, the surviving copy could preserve the sole record of a charter of Ine whose text has not undergone subsequent alteration; it could also represent the earliest West Saxon diploma about which physical details of layout and script can be known.[6] As we shall see, the palaeographical, orthographic, and diplomatic evidence appears to support the existence of a genuine exemplar. In addition, various factors – especially the script, which preserves so closely so many early features, and the old-fashioned formulation of the grant, which reveals no interest in updating – recommend this as a facsimile-copy, not a

---

Winchester – S.242 and *ECW* 1, now lost (*Annales Monastici*, ed. H. R. Luard, 5 vols, RS 36 [London, 1864–9] II, 6; see Edwards, *The Charters*, pp. 137–8 and 162–4).

[3]   William of Malmesbury (although he had changed his mind by the time he began the *De antiquitate*) attributed Glastonbury's foundation to Ine in his *Gesta pontificum Anglorum*, ch. 91; see *Willelmi Malmesbiriensis Monachi de Gestis Pontificum Anglorum*, ed. N. E. S. A. Hamilton, RS 52 (London, 1870), p. 196. See also the A and G texts of the Anglo-Saxon Chronicle, s.a. 688, and the West Saxon genealogies in London, British Library, Cotton Tiberius B. v, part 1 (23r), and the *Textus Roffensis* (Rochester, Cathedral Library, A. 3. 5, 104r). The Glastonbury reference in the genealogies is discussed by D. N. Dumville in 'The Anglian Collection of Royal Genealogies and Regnal Lists', *Anglo-Saxon England* 5 (1976), 23–50, at 26. See also the entry in the Annals of St Neots, s.a. 726: *The Annals of St Neots with Vita Prima Sancti Neoti*, ed. D. Dumville and M. Lapidge, The AS Chronicle: A Collaborative Edition, gen. ed. D. Dumville and S. Keynes 17 (Cambridge, 1985), pp. xviii, xxxvi–xxxvii, lxix and 29.

[4]   See Edwards, *The Charters*, pp. 23–40.

[5]   The charter was not known to Kemble; it is no. 113 in *Cartularium Saxonicum*, ed. W. de G. Birch, 3 vols (London, 1885–93) (hereafter B.). There is a description by Edwards in *The Charters*, pp. 27–33.

[6]   The first king of Wessex for whom a number of originals survive is Æthelwulf (A.D. 839–58) (S.287, S.293, S.296, S.298 and S.316).

Plate 1 Diploma of King Ine, S.248 (Taunton, Somerset Record Office, DD/SAS PR 501 c/795) (By permission of the Somerset Archaeological and Natural History Society. Photograph, British Library.)

forgery, although it (or its exemplar) came to be used as the basis of a later 'improved' version.[7]

Formerly kept at the Taunton Museum, the single sheet is now housed at the Somerset Record Office in Taunton and is the property of the Somerset Archaeological and Natural History Society.[8] The Society acquired the document from one of its members, the Reverend Hill Dawe Wickham (1807–74), who deposited it in 1849, the Society's inaugural year.[9] The circumstances of Wickham's ownership of the document are obscure, and its previous history is, unfortunately, unknown. Most of the surviving estate records from Glastonbury were preserved in the archive of the Thynne family, owners of a substantial number of Glastonbury's estates after the Dissolution. Their collection at Longleat is thus one possible source of stray Glastonbury material. It is perhaps more likely, however, that the charter escaped instead from the Horner archive at Mells: the Horners were long-standing abbey tenants who also acquired lands and estate records, including two surviving documents for Doulting: a court roll of 1337 and a terrier of 1515/6.[10] Two endorsements on the extant single sheet of S.248 indicate that it was identified with Doulting by the late fourteenth or fifteenth century, and it may thus have gone to Mells as documentation for one of the 'plums' enjoyed at the Dissolution by 'Jack' Horner and his brother Thomas.[11] This possibility is strengthened by the connection between the Horners and the Wickhams, the latter being stewards at Mells in the late eighteenth century; there is even some suggestion that the Wickhams took documents home with them from Mells.[12] Hill Dawe Wickham, however, like many of his family, was an antiquary and a collector, and may have bought the charter, simply because of his interest in historical records. The links between the two families (and between Mells and Doulting) are highly suggestive, but as the early history of Mells's muniments is unknown and the dissemination of Glastonbury's estate records is very rarely recorded, a post-Dissolution Mells provenance for the single sheet of S.248 cannot definitely be proved.

Even the medieval history of this charter is obscure, for there is no explicit mention of it in any of the surviving administrative records of Glastonbury Abbey.[13] The transaction recorded in S.248 does appear, however – though in a somewhat different form – in the history of the abbey begun by William of

7   See below, pp. 121–2.
8   Taunton, Somerset Record Office, DD/SAS PR 501 c/795.
9   A graduate of Exeter College, Oxford (MA, 1831), Wickham became rector of Horsington, the seventh successive member of his family to do so since 1686. Other Wickhams were solicitors at Frome from the late seventeenth century to 1885. I am grateful to Michael McGarvie for his detailed information on the Wickham family and their activities (personal communication). For the deposition of the charter in the Society's new museum, see 'First Annual Meeting', *PSANHS* 1 (1849–50), part i, 3–26, at 25.
10   Mells, Horner 8 and 36. There is a copy of the catalogue of Horner manuscripts at Mells in the Somerset Record Office (SRO DD/X/HNR).
11   I am indebted to Robert Dunning for this suggestion (personal communication).
12   Michael McGarvie, personal communication.
13   Listed in note 1.

Malmesbury in the early twelfth century, the *De antiquitate Glastonie ecclesie*, and in the fourteenth-century history by John of Glastonbury, the *Cronica siue antiquitates Glastoniensis ecclesie*.[14] In this respect S.248 is unusual, since only a few of Glastonbury's pre-Conquest grants have the histories as their sole witness, most transactions also being recorded in the abbey's cartularies, lists and registers. S.248 alone seems to appear exclusively in the histories and as a single sheet. Multiple grants must have been difficult to catalogue, however, and in lists of charters they could be concealed under the name of only one of the estates granted. Nevertheless, the apparent invisibility of S.248 and its relative isolation within Glastonbury's surviving archive is, as we shall see, only one way in which this diploma defies expectation and, perhaps, explanation.

DESCRIPTION

At the time of the Ordnance Survey facsimile-reproduction of this charter (published in 1881),[15] the dorse of the single sheet was completely covered with cloth. This was removed in the course of repair in the late 1980s, when a parchment backing (exposing the endorsements) was attached; the charter was then mounted on board.[16] The parchment measures approximately 410x190 mm., with margins of approximately 20 mm. and 60 mm. (at the top and bottom, respectively) and approximately 35 mm. and 40 mm. (on the left and right). The writing runs along the long side of the sheet, which has three discernible folds vertically across the script; the medial fold had been reused at some time after the application of the cloth backing. No ruling is visible. The surface of the parchment, which is flaking in parts, is dry, leathery and rough. Though generally legible, the charter has not worn as well as Glastonbury's tenth-century single sheets preserved at Longleat (S.236 and S.563)[17] and has suffered from damp, especially in the area of the central fold.

The facsimile-reproduction in the Ordnance Survey volume gives the impression of a rather soft, blurred script. This misrepresents the appearance of the charter and is caused by a most curious feature. A large part of the written text is now scored very deeply into the parchment, exhibiting grooves or narrow channels, oddly reminiscent of incisions in a stone surface, in the exact shapes of the letter-forms (see Plate II); under a microscope the brown ink can be seen lying at the bottom of these grooves, which have

---

[14]   *DA*, chs 40 and 69 (ed. Scott, pp. 94 and 140–2); *Cronica*, chs 16 and 47 (ed. Carley, pp. 40 and 92). For the treatment of Glastonbury's Anglo-Saxon grants in these two texts, see below, pp. 119–22, and Sarah Foot, 'Glastonbury's Early Abbots', in this volume.

[15]   *Facsimiles of Anglo-Saxon Manuscripts*, ed. W. B. Sanders, 3 vols (Southampton, 1878–84) II, Taunton.

[16]   I am grateful to Steven Hobbs, then of the Somerset Record Office, for information on this repair and for his assistance throughout the writing of this article.

[17]   Longleat House, Marquess of Bath, NMR 10564 and 10565.

Plate II Diploma of King Ine, S.248. Extract from Plate I: detail of central section.

perfect, not frayed, edges.[18] I have seen no other manuscript displaying exactly this feature. Although ordinary photographs are unreliable indicators of its presence, perusal of E. A. Lowe's *Codices latini antiquiores* has revealed a small number of possible parallels: in *CLA* IV, 436a and b, entire lines of text have dissolved, demonstrably beginning with the dissolution of individual letters; this, however, is a purple manuscript with silver ink.[19] More relevant instances of black or brown ink acting in a similar fashion may be found in the early eighth-century uncials of *CLA* IV, 488, visually the closest parallel in *CLA* to the sunken letters of our charter, or in *CLA* X, 1539, a fourth- or fifth-century parchment folio with holes, originally in the form of its rustic capitals but now spread into larger areas, which Lowe identified as 'eaten through by the ink'.[20] A possible explanation of the unusual aspect of the Glastonbury charter, therefore, lies in a faulty preparation of the ink, for an excess of acid in an iron-gall mixture could have caused corrosion, burning into the parchment.[21] The straight edges of the sunken letters of the charter are, however, difficult to reconcile with the more random and uncontrolled effect which one would expect if corrosion due to the chemical properties of the ink were solely to blame; nor is the damage as radical as the perforations in the manuscripts cited. It is unclear, therefore, whether the grooved letters of the single sheet of S.248 are simply a less advanced case of the same phenomenon or whether they are attributable to a different cause. The presence of gum arabic in the ink has been suggested as an alternative explanation: under certain conditions, as the gum arabic hardens and the parchment softens, ink with this binding ingredient can press into the parchment, with various pernicious results.[22] Whether this is of any relevance to the Glastonbury charter, however, will remain uncertain unless a full chemical analysis of its ink is undertaken.[23] In any event, the fact that the far left quarter of the single sheet is largely unaffected should probably lead us to seek a more complex, possibly multi-phased, cause.

[18]   I should like to thank Tony Parker of the British Library for his help with the technical examination of the charter.

[19]   E. A. Lowe, *Codices Latini Antiquiores*, 11 vols and supplement (Oxford, 1934–71) (henceforth *CLA*). The seventh-century display capitals of *CLA* S, 1808, once filled with green, are also now mainly transparent.

[20]   The fifth-century primary script of *CLA* III, 345 (retraced in the seventh century) exhibits similar damage.

[21]   As Humphry Davy commented, 'in some old parchments, the ink of which must have contained much free acid, the letters have, as it were, eaten through the skin, the effect always being most violent on the side of the parchment containing no animal oil'; see 'Some Observations and Experiments on the Papyri Found in the Ruins of Herculaneum', *Philosophical Transactions of the Royal Society of London* (1821), 191–208, at 205. It has been suggested that such destructive acidity was mostly produced by sulphuric acid in the ink's ferrous sulphate, but that the acetic acid in vinegar (a common ingredient of ink) could have been another possible cause: see R. Reed, *Ancient Skins, Parchments and Leathers* (London, 1972), p. 219. On ink in general see M. Zerdoun Bat-Yehouda, *Les Encres noires au moyen age* (Paris, 1983), esp. pp. 144–213.

[22]   I should like to thank Michelle Brown of the British Library for this suggestion.

[23]   Examination with infra-red light does suggest the absence of carbon, but the chemical composition of the ink has not yet been determined.

Unfortunately, other explanations which came to mind have had to be discarded. If the letters had been incised with a sharp pen, the effect would not be limited to the right-hand three-quarters of the charter. Writing on wet parchment might possibly produce such indentations, but under those circumstances the ink would no doubt be blurred. Faulty preparation of the parchment – at the unhairing stage, or in the application of oil varnishes, other fats, dressings of vegetable tannin, or parchment finishes[24] – could perhaps lead to localized rather than uniform damage. The application of a reagent is another possible cause, but there is none of the familiar evidence of this. In fact, close examination of the charter shows that, if they go hand-in-hand with the damage caused by mould, the grooves developed after the document was folded. This is suggested by the mirror-image of damp patches on both sides of the central fold and, more significantly, by a lighter but identical pattern of stains on the outer edge of the far right quarter as well; in the far left quarter (where the letters are not sunken) only very faint damp stains are visible,[25] indicating that this quarter formed the outer flap of a document that had been folded in half and then in half again, leaving the middle quarters together on the bottom and the outer quarters on top, with the left one outermost.[26] Whatever the specific cause, the sunken letters thus appear to have developed during storage, as a result of a chemical reaction induced by damp to which the outer left quarter was not so seriously exposed. Scientific analysis of the parchment, as well as the ink, might explain this unusual aspect of the charter; it might also contribute some evidence to the difficult question of its date.

The sheet carries thirteen lines of text on its face. The subscriptions, in the same script as the body of the text, are arranged in two parallel columns of four witnesses; the attestation of the ninth witness, Daniel, is recorded alone on the second line of a third column. Punctuation by the single raised point is most common, with instances of groups of three points. The text begins with a simple cross outside the written area, following which there is a slight diminuendo effect in the opening letters, as the first word (*IN*) is capitalized. The crosses of the first (vertical) row of subscriptions are also placed outside the writing area.

Three endorsements read *Carta Ine regis* (in a hand of the late fourteenth or early fifteenth century), *Dultyng* (in a fifteenth-century hand?) and ?*Dulltyng uykary* (in a later, possibly early sixteenth-century, hand).[27]

---

[24]   See Reed, *Ancient Skins*, especially pp. 118–73.
[25]   These stains do not show up well on the accompanying photographs (Plates I and II taken with oblique fibre-optic illumination), which instead deliberately emphasize the grooving of the letters.
[26]   Two of the three endorsements are indeed on the back of this quarter.
[27]   Edwards mentioned only two endorsements; I disagree with her reading of the second (my third) as ?*Iny carta* (*The Charters*, p. 27). I should like to thank the staff of the Somerset Record Office and Tony Parker of the British Library for their assistance in examining these endorsements; I am also grateful to Robert Dunning and Diana Greenway for offering their opinions on the dates of the scripts.

PALAEOGRAPHY

The script of the single sheet appears to be an extraordinarily careful imitation of an early exemplar.[28] Abbreviations are not numerous: four *nomina sacra*;[29] the Insular compendium for *autem*; simple suspension of *m* following *a*; and, in the witness-list, a variety of technical or capricious suspensions of *episcopus* and *subscripsi*.[30]

Ligatures are frequent: especially of tall *e*, open and closed, with *c*, *g*, *i*, *m*, *n*, *o*, *p*, *r*, *s*, *t* and *x*, but also of *t* with a following letter; tall *c* and *s* each ligature with following *t*;[31] *ffi* (*sufficeret*, line 2) and *ro* (*propter*, line 2) are notable individual forms; *a* + *e* is found, as in *uitæ* (line 7). Subscript ligatures *ci* and *ti* each occur in varying forms.

Of individual letter-forms, Insular pointed and round *a* are accompanied by the ultimately Uncial, so-called 'Caroline', form; *c* is often tall; *d* is round-backed; the epsilon form of *e* (ε) is sometimes found; split *f* and *s* occur; a tall Insular *g* is a notable feature of this script; *i*-longa occurs frequently; underslung *l* is common and joins the next-but-one letter from below; *p* is open and with a right-curving finish to the second stroke; Insular *r* is here a rapid letter-form, with the second member raised well above the line; *t* is often tall and swept over the surrounding letters, or else the upper stroke sweeps down from top left (often to join another letter, as in *partem*, line 7); in numbers, *u* is found, not *v*.

If, as it seems, the extant single sheet is a facsimile-copy, it can be said that the features of its exemplar are so helpfully reproduced here as to leave no room for doubt that it was written in Insular cursive minuscule: on the face of it, there appears to be no compelling palaeographical reason why the exemplar should not have been a product of the early eighth century.[32] The important question of the date of the production of the facsimile, however, is one that stubbornly resists an answer, for the evidence offered by the script is not of the sort to lead directly to a single conclusion.[33] A summary of the palaeographical complexities should serve to illustrate the problems involved.

Heather Edwards's description of the script of the charter included an

---

[28]   I should like to thank David Dumville and Julia Crick for their helpful discussions on the script.

[29]   *Dñi, Dī, Ihū, Xp̄ī* (line 1).

[30]   *ēp, ēps, epī, archiepīs*; the seven instances of *sūb* and *sūbs* vary visually.

[31]   In *dicitur* (line 5), tall *c* ligatures with the next-but-one letter, *t*; in *duluting* (also line 5), the *t* joins the *g* by passing over two letters.

[32]   *CLA* II, 189, *CLA* VIII, 1196, *CLA* S, 1806, and *Chartae Latinæ Antiquiores*, ed. A. Bruckner and R. Marichal (Olten and Zurich, 1954–) III, 185, though written in a more cursive script, reveal significant points of comparison, as do *CLA* II, 139, *CLA* VII, 1140, and *CLA* S, 1803.

[33]   I should like to thank the many people who have shown interest in and offered opinions on this question: in particular, Michelle Brown, Julia Crick, David Dumville, Robert Dunning, Diana Greenway and Tessa Webber.

account by Julian Brown of certain intrusive features (inconsistent with an early origin) which could, said Brown, date the execution of the copy to 'as late as the sixteenth century'.[34] Brown, working from the Ordnance Survey reproduction only, not the original, found the 'hairline approach strokes' of the letters *m*, *n* and *u* and the final strokes of *h*, *m*, *n* and *u* – strong, upward curves – anachronistic; my own investigation of eighth-century Insular minuscule has confirmed that in that script these letters do indeed consistently begin with a more wedged, tapered, stroke and terminate in either blunt minims, ending on the line, or pointed ones, often descending below it. Other letters in the single sheet reveal further – slight – deviations from eighth-century norms in addition to those noted by Brown: a single bifurcated *b* and *l* (forms which appeared in the eleventh century in Old English manuscripts and which are a common feature of twelfth- and thirteenth-century documentary script) in *sub'* (line 13) and *sedulis* (line 2), a misunderstanding of the reverse ductus of the *g* (as in *pertingentes*, line 5) and an *et*-ligature (as in *licet*, line 1) of a sort unusual in eighth-century examples but commonly found in tenth-century Square minuscule.[35]

The quality of the Insular minuscule is nevertheless strikingly good, and the four apparently post-medieval letters cited by Julian Brown thus particularly demand explanation. Foot-serifs of a quite different sort – very small movements of the pen – are considered a diagnostic feature of canonical Insular hybrid minuscule before A.D. 850;[36] these, however, are distinguished from the end-strokes of *h*, *m*, *n* and *u* in the Glastonbury single sheet not only by their size and shape but by the fact that they are found on every minim of the letter, not just the final stroke.[37] Similarly, foot-serifs or upturns on all minims of *m*, *n* and *u* are a feature of tenth- and eleventh-century English scripts – Square minuscule and Caroline – with the same slight rounded upwards movements, small horizontal bars, or light sharply angled strokes. This range of end-strokes can be found on *h* in the tenth and eleventh centuries, especially, but not exclusively, in Old English texts, although *h* appears most commonly to have been finished with a stroke curving down and back, in the opposite direction, which helped to distinguish it from *li*.[38] These late Anglo-Saxon serifs or upturns are all quite different from

---

34   Edwards, *The Charters*, pp. 27–8.
35   With the top of the *e* curving back to meet the cross-bar of the *t* at its leftmost extent, not crossing it in the middle as is frequently the case in eighth-century examples. This feature (and its significance) was pointed out to me by Julia Crick.
36   See T. J. Brown, 'The Irish Element in the Insular System of Scripts to circa A. D. 850', in *Die Iren und Europa im früheren Mittelalter*, ed. H. Löwe, 2 vols (Stuttgart, 1982) I, 101–19, especially 101 and 109.
37   Although the *h* in the single sheet, with upturns on both its strokes, is different from the other letters in this respect.
38   Serifs or upward curves on *h* occur (with other forms) in Latin texts in Cambridge, Corpus Christi College 153, part 2 (Phase II Square minuscule of the early tenth century; see the facsimile in T. A. M. Bishop, 'The Corpus Martianus Capella', *Transactions of the Cambridge Bibliographical Society* 4 [1964–8], 257–75, plate XXI[b]), and CCCC 57 (hand 2), a late Square minuscule; it appears in Latin too in essentially Caroline manuscripts such as London, Lambeth Palace 200, part 1 (of the second half

the strong terminal curves of the four letters in the charter. From the twelfth century until the end of the Middle Ages, more rounded initial and terminal strokes appeared on *m*, *n* and *u* in English manuscripts, but *h* was almost universally finished with the reverse curve. Not until the sixteenth century was a rounded upturned end-stroke comparable to that of this single sheet commonly found on *h* (as well as *m*, *n* and *u*), but there the ascender was frequently looped or hooked, and the separate minims forming the letters had generally lost their identity – an identity still present in the charter's script – and had merged to produce an altogether different kind of letter.[39]

English examples of *h* with a serif or small upturned end-stroke can be supported with more from tenth- and eleventh-century France.[40] This fact becomes more significant when the anachronistic opening and closing strokes of *m*, *n* and *u* in the charter are compared with continental manuscripts. Suddenly the script of the single sheet no longer has a post-medieval look, but bears a striking resemblance (in those three specific letter-forms, that is) to continental examples: from late tenth-century Cluny, for instance, or eleventh-century Tournai.[41] When we then look at manuscripts written in England, but with strong suggestions of continental involvement, we may perhaps have found a plausible context for this script. A sacramentary written at Winchcombe in ?985x1009 and taken to France (991x1009), possibly by 'un transfuge de S. Benoit refugié en Angleterre',[42] for example, or S.1028, a

of the tenth century; see E. M. Thompson, *Introduction to Greek and Latin Palaeography* [Oxford, 1912], p. 431 [no. 171]), and Oxford, Bodleian Library, Auct. F. 4. 32 (*S. C.* 2176) (St Dunstan's Classbook). Bishop called one form of *h* found in the latter manuscript (with a serif) 'Insular': T. A. M. Bishop, *English Caroline Minuscule* (Oxford, 1971), p. 1, with reference to plate I. When it became fashionable to distinguish between Old English and Latin by different letter-forms, *h* with a serif or upturn was reserved for Old English; see, for example, London, British Library, Cotton Tiberius B. v, part 1, 23v, where the final strokes of *h* turn up in the Old English names in the list of abbots, but down in the adjacent Latin text: see *An Eleventh-Century Anglo-Saxon Illustrated Miscellany*, ed. P. McGurk *et al.*, Early English Manuscripts in Facsimile 21 (Copenhagen, 1983).

[39] See, for example, John Leland's hand in *English Literary Autographs, 1550–1650*, ed. W. W. Greg *et al.*, 2 vols (Oxford, 1925–32) II, Appendix, plate CI.
[40] See, for example, Troyes, Bibliothèque Municipale, 960 (from Brittany, A.D. 909; see F. Wormald and J. Alexander, *An Early Breton Gospel Book* [Cambridge, 1977], p. 14, n. 3), and Orléans, Bibliothèque Municipale, 229 (200) (from Fleury, 1080x1087): *Catalogue des manuscrits en ecriture latine portant des indications de date de lieu ou de copyiste*, ed. C. Samaran and R. Marichal (Paris, 1959–) V, plate IV, and VII, plate XXV. For the latter, see also M. Mostert, *The Library of Fleury. A Provisional List of Manuscripts* (Hilversum, 1989), BF704 (p. 156).
[41] Paris, Bibliothèque Nationale, nouv. acq. lat. 1438 (Cluny, 979x994): *Catalogue des manuscrits en ecriture latine*, ed. Samaran and Marichal, IV, pt i, plate VIII; Tournai, Bibliothèque du Séminaire, 1 (Tournai, 1084): *Manuscrits datés conservés en Belgique*, ed. F. Masai and M. Wittek, 4 vols (Brussels, 1968–82) I, plate VII.
[42] Orléans, Bibliothèque Municipale, 127 (105): *Catalogue des manuscrits en ecriture latine*, ed. Samaran and Marichal, VII, 219 and plate IX. See also D. Gremont and fr. Donnat, 'Fleury, le Mont Saint-Michel et l'Angleterre à la fin du Xᵉ et au début du XIᵉ siècle à propos du manuscrit d'Orléans no. 127 (105)', in *Millénaire monastique du Mont*

charter of King Edward the Confessor for Saint Denis (A.D. 1059),[43] both have curved opening strokes and strong upturns (on the final strokes only) of *m*, *n* and *u*, as in the Glastonbury charter. It is thus tempting to associate the copyist of that document with the late tenth or the eleventh century, and with some kind of continental training or influence. The letter *h* remains problematic, as it generally ends with a blunt stroke or (most commonly) a reverse curve in tenth- or eleventh-century script in English (Latin) and continental manuscripts (even those with strong rounded upturns on the other three letters), but contemporary examples of slightly rounded and upturned *h* at least do show that an alternative to the reverse curve existed, both in England and on the Continent.[44]

The persistence throughout the document of the forms not of eighth-century date is striking, but their significance is not instantly apparent when we attempt to draw conclusions. These forms have so far offered only clues, not answers, to the question of the date of composition of the extant single sheet, for the fact remains that I have as yet found no other script that parallels all the features of this charter's. Several possible interpretations, considering only palaeographical arguments for the moment, can be suggested, none of which entirely succeeds in resolving the tensions in the dating evidence.

First, the script of the extant single sheet could be not a copy but an early example of Insular minuscule, with a consistently eccentric formation of the letters *h*, *m*, *n* and *u*, but otherwise conforming in the main to the canon of letter-forms. Given the small number of early eighth-century West Saxon minuscule manuscripts that survives for comparison (and, more specifically, the small number of early charter specimens), and given our ignorance of the contemporary practices of the Glastonbury scriptorium, we should beware of identifying something as imitative rather than original on the basis of selective deviations. The striking continental parallels for *m*, *n* and *u* could, alternatively, suggest careful copying in the later Anglo-Saxon period: one feature of the script reminiscent of early Square minuscule (the *et*-ligature) recalls the tenth century, although other elements (the *g* with its almost closed tail and the bifurcated *b* and *l*) might point more to the eleventh. The possibility must also be considered of the charter having been copied later in the Middle Ages by a talented scribe – by now far removed from the Insular

Saint-Michel, ed. J. Laporte *et al.*, 4 vols (Paris, 1966–71) I, 751–93, and Mostert, *The Library of Fleury*, BF538 (p. 131).

[43] S.1028 survives in a single sheet, probably the original which Bishop Wulfwig was given permission (in a surviving writ) to draw up; on the date of the charter, see *Facsimiles of English Royal Writs to A.D. 1100*, ed. T. A. M. Bishop and P. Chaplais (Oxford, 1957), facing plate XVIII, and F. Harmer, *Anglo-Saxon Writs*, 2nd ed. (Stamford, 1989), p. 36. Bishop and Chaplais considered that the writ now attached to the charter could have been written by Baldwin, a monk of Saint Denis and later abbot of Bury St Edmunds (1065–1097/9). For a reproduction of the charter, see S. D. Keynes, *Facsimiles of Anglo-Saxon Charters*, Anglo-Saxon Charters Supplementary Volume 1 (Oxford, 1991), no. 21.

[44] See notes 38 and 40.

tradition – who for some reason was unable or did not feel the need to reproduce exactly throughout his copy the form of four letters of his exemplar. This is no less bizarre a suggestion than the next (which follows from Julian Brown's analysis), that the document may have been the product of an antiquarian environment, written by a scribe who repeatedly allowed only the same few elements of his usual handwriting to mar an otherwise credible rendition of an early exemplar.

All these suggestions are more or less unsatisfactory. In the first case, the evident pressure towards canonical conformity in early medieval script argues against accepting the oddities of this example as those of a capricious original: I know of no parallel in the eighth century for such fidelity to a canonical norm combined with such limited, consistent, eccentricity. In addition, though in general very convincing, there is something not quite right about the final effect of the charter – due, perhaps, to the spacing of the letters on the page, which is unlike the compression typical of most early specimens of Insular minuscule. The later Anglo-Saxon period might, alternatively, provide a plausible context, since exact parallels to three of the 'intrusive' forms identified by Brown can be discovered without difficulty in tenth- and eleventh-century manuscripts if we widen our sphere to include the Continent; but it is not easy to understand why a late Anglo-Saxon copyist, otherwise so successful in his facsimile, would not have taken more care with those letter-forms, consistently 'wrong' for 705/6. Meanwhile, the charter's letter *h* remains a renegade, without close parallel until the sixteenth century. The script betrays so few flaws and exhibits such confidence, however, that it is difficult to justify placing it outside the medieval scribal tradition; even in the late Middle Ages it would have been very difficult to produce such an excellent copy without making more mistakes or importing an even more anachronistic aspect. Thomas Elmham, for example, described by Michael Hunter as having an 'elementary palaeographical awareness such as was rare in his period',[45] included facsimile-copies of early Kentish charters, with transcripts, in his history of St Augustine's, Canterbury, written *ca* 1414. These are well observed and carefully done, but the facsimiles of the two minuscule charters, in particular, are unconvincing.[46] In fact, I know of no late medieval facsimiles of a quality to approach this single sheet, nor of any comparable early modern parallels. The sixteenth century certainly does not advertise itself in this facsimile as it does in the 'Anglo-Saxon' hands of antiquaries such as John Jocelyn and Laurence Nowell,[47] for example, or in the imitative replacement-leaves in a host of Parkerian manu-

---

[45] M. Hunter, 'The Facsimiles in Thomas Elmham's History of St Augustine's, Canterbury', *The Library* 5th ser. 28 (1973), 215–26, at 217.

[46] Cambridge, Trinity Hall 1, 21v, 22r and 23rv; see *Historia monasterii S. Augustini Cantuarensis*, ed. C. Hardwick, RS 8 (London, 1858), pp. xxix–xxxii. Three of the four charter-facsimiles were reproduced by Hunter in 'The Facsimiles', plates I–III. All four charters, S.2, S.3, S.4 and S.1244, are forgeries, and the date of the script of the lost originals is uncertain.

[47] Illustrated, for example, by C. E. Wright, 'The Dispersal of the Monastic Libraries and the Beginnings of Anglo-Saxon Studies. Matthew Parker and his Circle: A Pre-

scripts,[48] or as the seventeenth century does, say, in the Ballidon charter of King Edgar or in Dugdale's facsimiles of early Chester charters.[49] It seems that not until Thomas Astle's studies, in the late eighteenth century, was early medieval script so accurately reproduced.[50]

The question of the date of composition of the single sheet must therefore remain open, as the evidence of the script is not decisive. What can be said is that a copyist appears to have made a very creditable attempt to imitate the script of his exemplar – an exercise that could range in date from the eighth to the eighteenth century, but which, at this stage of the analysis, perhaps sits most comfortably in a tenth- or eleventh-century context. These were obviously significant times at Glastonbury, spanning Dunstan's return to the abbacy from exile in Ghent, the upheavals of a reform inspired from across the Channel, and the increasing penetration of continental culture throughout the eleventh century, culminating in the installation of a Norman abbot in *ca* 1077/8. No doubt a profusion of otherwise unknown contacts produced a late Anglo-Saxon multiculturalism which we might hold responsible for this document's eclectic script. More light – or further gloom – may be cast on the question of its date when we come to examine the production of Glastonbury's charters in more detail.

SPELLING

Returning first to the question of the date and authenticity of the exemplar of S.248, rather than the extant copy, the few Old English spellings do not contradict a date contemporary with the transaction recorded.[51] In *Ini* and *Tyrctil*, the preservation of the unstressed *i* suggests an origin before the later

liminary Study', *Transactions of the Cambridge Bibliographical Society* 1 (1949–53), 208–37, at 234–5.
[48] In order to provide complete texts, Archbishop Parker's scribes copied missing portions into the Anglo-Saxon manuscripts in his library in scripts imitative of their exemplars: for example, CCCC 178, pp. 31–2; CCCC 188, pp. 1–2 and 317–22; CCCC 302, pp. 233–42; CCCC 383, pp. C–H and 42 ff. (unnumbered); and CCCC 449, fols 1–41.
[49] Stafford, Staffordshire Record Office, Temporary Deposit 140; see N. Brooks, M. Gelling and D. Johnson, 'A New Charter of King Edgar', *Anglo-Saxon England* 13 (1984), 137–55 and plate XIV. Examples of Dugdale's facsimiles can be found in Oxford, Bodleian Library, Dugdale 13 and 17 (p. 268 and fol. 55, respectively); see *The Charters of the Anglo-Norman Earls of Chester c. 1071–1237*, ed. G. Barraclough, Record Society of Lancashire and Cheshire 126 (Gloucester, 1988), pp. 74 and 148.
[50] See, for example, T. Astle, *The Origin and Progress of Writing* (London, 1784), tables XX and XXI, facing p. 112; a late seventh-century original charter from Kent was also reproduced in *The Antiquarian Repository: A Miscellaneous Assemblage of Topography, History, Biography, Customs and Manners*, ed. F. Grose and T. Astle, 4 vols (London, 1807–9) I, facing p. 25. An eighteenth-century facsimile of S.236 by James Bowen is kept with the original (Marquess of Bath, NMR 10564) at Longleat House.
[51] I am indebted to the late Ashley Amos of the Dictionary of Old English, University of Toronto, who gave me her opinion of these name-forms in June 1989.

eighth century.[52] In *Beruualdo, Bercuualdus, Uualdarius, Egguuinus* and *Eluui-nus*, the use of *uu* rather than wynn represents, in southern England, the earlier spelling.[53] *Ct* for *ht* (*Tyrctil*) is similarly an early feature, universal in the mid-eighth-century Moore Bede, for example.[54] Even earlier, *gg* (as found here in *Egguuinus*), had been largely replaced by *cg* (though *gg* could occasionally recur).[55] In our text, the *a* in *Beruualdo, Bercuualdus, Uualdarius* and *Aldhelmus* is retracted (not broken), a feature restricted to the early phases of West Saxon and Kentish (although found in Anglian texts of all dates).[56]

The place-names *Tan, Duluting* and *Corregescumb* likewise appear to be acceptable spellings for the early eighth century.[57] The case of *Pouelt* is more complex. The name, now obsolete, appears in various forms in texts ranging widely in date, whose sequence of development has not been satisfactorily explained. Ekwall found the meaning of the first element, *Po(u)*, obscure.[58] A. G. C. Turner's interpretation, that the name developed from a British form, **bouo-gelt-*, meaning 'cow-pasture', was based on the assumption that one of the forms found in the surviving manuscripts of the *De antiquitate* (*Bouelt*) was the earliest spelling; but *Bouelt* and *Rouelt* (which also occurs) are clearly scribal errors, deriving presumably from an exemplar in which the initial letter of the place-name was incorrect, difficult to read, or even missing.[59] It has been suggested instead that the name derives from other Celtic elements, possibly *pow* (Old Cornish *pou*), meaning 'region', and **elt*, the plural of **alt* (Welsh *allt*, Middle Welsh plural *eillt*), meaning 'cliff' or 'hill-slope'.[60] 'The region of hill-slopes' would certainly be a fitting meaning in view of the topography of the area.

Although the spellings *Pouholt* and *Poholt* appear in two further eighth-century grants of this estate recorded in other (later) Glastonbury documents,[61] the *Pouelt* of the extant single sheet of S.248 is more likely to represent the original spelling (and thus a genuinely early exemplar). *Pouholt* can be supposed to have developed by the addition of unpronounced *h*

---

[52]   A. Campbell, *Old English Grammar* (Oxford, 1959), ch. 369 (pp. 153–4); K. Luick, *Historische Grammatik der englischen Sprache*, 1 vol. in 2 (Leipzig, 1914; rev. imp. Oxford, 1964) I, ch. 350 (pp. 320–2).

[53]   Campbell, *Old English Grammar*, ch. 60 (p. 26).

[54]   *Ibid.* ch. 57.3 (p. 24).

[55]   *Ibid.* ch. 64 (p. 27).

[56]   *Ibid.* ch. 143 (pp. 55–6).

[57]   I am very grateful to Margaret Gelling for her comments on these place-names.

[58]   E. Ekwall, *Concise Oxford Dictionary of Place-Names*, 4th ed. (Oxford, 1960), s.n. Polden.

[59]   A. G. C. Turner, 'Some Somerset Place-Names Containing Celtic Elements', *Bulletin of the Board of Celtic Studies* 14 (1950–2), 113–19, at 117. For *Bouelt* and *Rouelt*, see *DA*, chs 40 and 69 (ed. Scott, pp. 94 and 140). All manuscripts of John of Glastonbury's *Cronica* use the spelling *Rouelt* for this grant: *Cronica*, chs 16 and 47 (ed. Carley, pp. 40 and 92, though Carley incorrectly printed *Pouelt* for the latter).

[60]   I am indebted to Oliver Padel for this suggestion and for his advice on the development of the name-form. For *als* (the later Cornish form of *alt*) and *pow*, see O. J. Padel, *Cornish Place-Name Elements*, English Place-Name Society 56/57 (Nottingham, 1985), pp. 4 and 193.

[61]   S.253 and S.1680. See below, pp. 124–6.

between syllables, with *e* changing to *o* either by scribal error due to similarity or by reinterpretation as Old English *holt*, 'wood'. As the *De antiquitate*,
the *Cronica* and the facsimile alone preserve the form *[P]ouelt*, it is possible
that William and the copyist of the single sheet worked from the same
exemplar (or, indeed, that this copy was William's exemplar). Two references
to *Poelt* in a forged privilege in the name of King Ine (S.250) appear to retain
a variant of the earlier spelling,[62] but *Poholt* is the form that predominates in
other grants in the *De antiquitate* and the *Cronica* relating to this estate. The
boundary clause of S.251, which cites a feature *on Poholte*, may provide
evidence of the existence of this later form already by the tenth or eleventh
century (the probable date of the bounds),[63] but as this is preserved only in a
fourteenth-century cartulary, the spelling there might have been modernized
in recopying. The name *Pouelt/Poholt*, however, may have gone out of use
even before the compilation of the cartulary, since it is not found among the
rubricated headings of the Great Cartulary or the *Secretum Domini*, and the
one text in those collections relating to the estate (S.253) is placed at the head
of the group of charters for the manor of Shapwick.[64] No *Pouelt* or *Poholt*
appears in Domesday Book, suggesting that even by 1086 the name may
have been obsolete, at least for official purposes.

DIPLOMATIC

The judgement in favour of an early date for the document's exemplar, based
so far on script and spelling, is supported by the diplomatic evidence.[65]
Although early Anglo-Saxon charters are not susceptible to the same rigorous criticism that can be applied to tenth-century diplomas, it is possible at
least to assess the genuineness of dubious early texts by comparing them
with others of established authenticity. An analysis of this sort indicates that
parallels to the individual features of S.248 can indeed be found in genuine
contemporary documents.

The invocation ('In nomine Domini Dei nostri Iesu Christi saluatoris')
appears in the records of early councils (Hertford, A.D. 672/3, and Hatfield,
A.D. 679)[66] and (with some omissions and variations in word order) in

---

[62]   This is the spelling in the earliest extant text of this privilege (in London, British
Library, Royal 13. D. ii [at 10v–11v], a twelfth-century manuscript of William of
Malmesbury's *Gesta regum Anglorum*). Later manuscripts exhibit a range of forms,
from *Poelt* and *Pohelt* to *Poeldun*.

[63]   I am indebted to Peter Kitson, here and below, for allowing me to see the results of
his unpublished work on the boundary clauses of pre-Conquest charters.

[64]   S.253, a grant by Æthelheard, although printed in the edition of the Great Cartulary by Watkin (GC, II, 372), does not actually appear in any of the Shapwick sections
of that manuscript. It is, however, at the head of the Shapwick grants in the *Secretum
Domini*, the abbot's contemporary copy of the Great Cartulary (Wood empt. 1, 152r).

[65]   I should like to thank Susan Kelly for her comments on my diplomatic analysis of
this charter.

[66]   Bede, *Historia ecclesiastica*, IV.5 and IV.17 (*Bede's Ecclesiastical History of the English*

several of the earliest authentic Anglo-Saxon charters from a number of different kingdoms.[67] It is also found in the continental models on which the first surviving English diplomas were based: in particular, in the influential charter of Gregory the Great for his monastery of St Andrew in Rome, in Roman synodal decrees, and in the *Liber diurnus*.[68] Other early texts from Wessex also begin with a version of this invocation.[69] The majority of these are not authentic as they stand, being a mixture of spurious material and early formulae, but two, S.255 and S.1164, are nevertheless acceptable as examples of genuine early eighth-century texts.

The proem of S.248 ('ea quæ secundum decreta canonum tractata fuerint, licet sermo tantum ad testimonium sufficeret, tamen pro incerta futuri temporis fortuna cirographorum s<c>edulis sunt roboranda') expresses a common theme of the English diploma's sixth- and seventh-century continental models, the need to give actions and statements strength through documentation. This theme was inevitably a commonplace of charter formulation, and not just in the early period, but a number of close parallels to the form of its expression in S.248 occur in the early Anglo-Saxon corpus,[70] although none exactly duplicates its phrasing here.

The king's superscription, *regnante Domino rex*, is found in a number of early grants preserved in the Malmesbury archive.[71] The dispositive section is brief, without elaboration. It begins 'ego Ini . . . lxv casatos pro remedio animæ meæ Beruualdo abbati uideor contulisse'. The formula 'pro remedio animæ meæ' has a respectable continental pedigree and frequently appears in early English charters.[72] The failure to specify the monastery of the reci-

---

People, ed. B. Colgrave and R. A. B. Mynors [Oxford, 1969]) (hereafter *HE*), pp. 348–52 and 384–6.

[67] S.8, S.10 and S.13 (from Kent), S.45 (from Sussex), S.71 and S.73 (from Mercia), and S.1171, S.1784 and S.1787 (from Essex).

[68] See W. H. Stevenson, 'Trinoda Necessitas', *English Historical Review* 29 (1914), 689–703, at 702–3; W. Levison, *England and the Continent in the Eighth Century* (Oxford, 1946), pp. 229–30; P. Wormald, 'Bede and the Conversion of England: The Charter Evidence', Jarrow Lecture, 1984, p. 4.

[69] S.241 (from Abingdon); S.255 (from Crediton/Exeter); S.246, S.247, S.250 and S.257 (from Glastonbury); S.234, S.243, S.245 and S.1170 (from Malmesbury); S.1164 (from Shaftesbury); and S.235 (from Winchester).

[70] S.65 and S.1787 (by contemporary kings of Essex), S.241 (a spurious grant to Abingdon in the name of Ine with early elements), S.247 (the later, revised version of S.248), S.1164 (a probably authentic charter of 670x676 in the Shaftesbury cartulary), S.1169 (a Malmesbury forgery with some early formulae) and S.1248 (a late seventh-century grant probably originally to Barking, preserved at Westminster, probably authentic).

[71] S.245 (the record of privileges granted by Ine to the West Saxon diocese; see above, note 2); S.243 (another grant by Ine to Malmesbury, with *Saxonum* added after *rex*); S.231 and S.234 (two probably spurious charters in Cædwalla's name in favour of Malmesbury); and S.1169 (an interpolated charter, also for Malmesbury, in the name of Berhtwald).

[72] Levison, *England and the Continent*, p. 225; it is found, for example, in S.65, S.243, S.1164 and S.1169.

pient of the grant is similarly an early feature.[73] The grant is of not one estate, but four. The extensive lands are defined in Latin, in the most general of terms, with reference to local topography: 'his locorum limitibus <terram> designatam: iuxta flumen quod appellatur Tan xx casatos, et alibi in loco qui dicitur Pouelt xx manentes, necnon ex utroque margine fluminis cuius uocabulum est Duluting xx casatos pertingentes usque ad conuallem qui dicitur Corregescumb, ex occidentali uero plaga eiusdem uallis quinque casatos.' There are no Old English bounds. All of these characteristics of the formulation of the grant suit an early stage of charter production and can be paralleled in authentic texts predating the diplomatic developments of the early tenth century.

The blessing and anathema do not take the extremist line that characterizes many later examples, but are simple and straightforward: 'Si quis hanc donationis cartulam augere et amplificare uoluerit, auget et amplificet Deus partem eius in libro uitæ; si quis frangere aut inrita facere tirannica potestate temtauerit, sciat se coram Christo et angelis eius rationem redditurum.' Similarities can be found in the blessings of other early charters with genuine elements;[74] several sanctions likewise exhibit parallels.[75]

The form of the dating clause, which makes use of the month, the indiction and the incarnational year, compares with S.241 and S.1248 (from Abingdon and Barking, respectively). The appearance of the *annus Domini* at this early date, before the composition of Bede's *Historia ecclesiastica* (which has traditionally been seen as the means of its introduction into English letters) need not prejudice us against the charter. Kenneth Harrison has suggested that, from the late seventh century, the incarnational year was used in documents recording the conveyance of land, although it was not until Bede that it achieved a wider and more imaginative application in historical writing. Harrison has argued persuasively that the Easter tables of Dionysius Exiguus, which contained columns identifying the indiction and the year of the incarnation, had been brought to England from Rome by Wilfrid and had been adopted at the Northumbrian Synod of Whitby in 664.[76] These tables could have been easily and swiftly circulated, and Harrison has suggested that it would not be farfetched to imagine them in Wessex by 670,[77] especially given the presence of the West Saxon bishop, Agilbert, at Whitby. Patrick Sims-Williams has pursued the question by scrutinizing two late seventh-

---

[73]   See, for example, S.10, S.11 and S.18 (from Kent) and S.233, S.234 and S.238 (from Wessex).

[74]   For example, S.65 (from Essex), S.71 (the closest example, from Malmesbury) and S.1248 (from Barking via Westminster).

[75]   Such as those of S.65, S.71 and S.1248 (see note above), as well as S.238 (from Glastonbury), S.245 (the Malmesbury privilege), S.234, S.1170 and S.1176 (interpolated texts from Malmesbury) and S.244 (from Muchelney).

[76]   K. Harrison, *The Framework of Anglo-Saxon History to A.D. 900* (Cambridge, 1976), pp. 52–75 and 97–8; 'The *Annus Domini* in Some Early Charters', *Journal of the Society of Archivists* 4 (1970–3), 551–7; and 'The Synod of Whitby and the Beginning of the Christian Era in England', *Yorkshire Archaeological Journal* 45 (1973), 108–14.

[77]   Harrison, *The Framework*, p. 135.

century charters bearing the incarnational year (S.51 and S.52).[78] His analysis has supported Harrison's judgement on the authenticity of these charters and has, in addition, emphasized their association – and that of the A.D. date – with Wilfrid. Sims-Williams's arguments can allow us to accept with greater confidence that the multiple dating formula of S.248 may be a legitimate original feature, but it should be noted that the Glastonbury charter breaks the link he proposed, having no evident association with Wilfrid. It is of course also possible, if the exemplar was not written when it claims to have been but at a later date, that the incarnational year was added at that time, or (less likely) when the facsimile-copy was made.[79]

To turn to the witness-list, it is composed of nine names, all of which are acceptable for the stated date of the charter: after Archbishop Berhtwald (692–731) come Headda, bishop of Lichfield and Leicester (691–716x727), Æcce, bishop of Dunwich (672x716), Tyrhtel, bishop of Hereford (688–705x710), Waldhere, bishop of London (693–705x716), Ecgwine, bishop of Worcester (693x717), *Eluuinus* (?possibly Æthelwine, bishop of Lindsey *ca* 680x716),[80] and Aldhelm, bishop of Sherborne (705/6–709/10). The attestation of Daniel (the bishop of Winchester *ca* 705–44) comes last, in the most junior position, and exhibits a degree of originality consistent with his style in a number of other charters.[81] He is not given the title of bishop but is referred to as *ministrans plebi Dei*. Could this indicate that the decision to split the diocese of Wessex had not yet been made? Alternatively, this humility formula might, as suggested by Sims-Williams and Edwards, identify Daniel as the drafter of the charter.[82] Neither Berwald, the abbot of Glastonbury to whom the estates were granted,[83] nor the king appears among the witnesses.

[78] P. Sims-Williams, 'St Wilfrid and Two Charters Dated AD 676 and 680', *Journal of Ecclesiastical History* 39 (1988), 163–83.

[79] See below, p. 118.

[80] J. B. Davidson, 'On the Charters of King Ine', *PSANHS* 30 (1884), 1–31, at 10, suggested the identification with Æthelwine. Edwards has tentatively identified *Eluuinus* with Ealdwine, also known as Worr, who succeeded Headda as bishop of Lichfield (*The Charters*, pp. 30–1). Worr appears with Headda in S.22, a ninth-century Kentish forgery incorporating a genuine early eighth-century witness-list: see Edwards, *ibid.*, and N. Brooks, *The Early History of the Church of Canterbury. Christ Church from 597 to 1066* (Leicester, 1984), p. 195, n. 65.

[81] For example, S.93, S.239, S.250, S.253 and S.256.

[82] Sims-Williams, 'St Wilfrid and Two Charters', p. 166; Edwards, *The Charters*, p. 31.

[83] The exact dates of Berwald's abbacy are unknown. He acted as a witness to S.245 (dated 704) and was mentioned as active *ca* 710 in Willibald's Life of St Boniface (ch. 4); see *Vitae Sancti Bonifatii Archiepiscopi Moguntini*, ed. W. Levison, MGH Scriptores rerum germanicarum in usum scholarum (Hanover, 1905), p. 14. Some time after 709/10, Berhtwald, archbishop of Canterbury (692–731), wrote to Forthhere, bishop of Sherborne (709/10–37), asking the bishop to exert pressure on Berwald to release a Kentish captive; see *Councils and Ecclesiastical Documents Relating to Great Britain and Ireland*, ed. A. W. Haddan and W. Stubbs, 3 vols (Oxford, 1869–78) III, 284. See also J. Armitage Robinson, *Somerset Historical Essays* (London, 1921), pp. 31–2, and J. P. Carley, *Glastonbury Abbey. The Holy House at the Head of the Moors Adventurous* (Woodbridge, 1988), p. 6. For the unfortunate confusion of Berwald and Berhtwald, see Sarah Foot's discussion in 'Glastonbury's Early Abbots', pp. 171–2 in this volume.

From this summary, we can conclude – while acknowledging that before the tenth century the production of Anglo-Saxon charters was undoubtedly less systematic than it became and that the results were therefore more varied – that S.248 appears to be diplomatically sound, all the formal elements being paralleled in genuine early texts.[84] The vocabulary (in particular the terms *cirographum* and *singrapha*) likewise can support (but not prove) an early date for the exemplar.[85] The witness-list would have been almost impossible to construct duplicitously at a later period, although it could, of course, have been lifted from an authentic original that no longer survives; a cut-and-paste job of this sort could have been performed at any time after the original list was recorded.[86] The consistency of the other diplomatic elements, however, and the absence of suspicious features argue against such a possibility. Nothing in the spellings, the place-names, or the formulation of the grant is out of character for an authentic early eighth-century exemplar. This consistency and, most particularly, the vagueness of the dispositive details also speak strongly against the charter being a forgery based on a genuine early text.

DATE: 705 OR 706?

The question of the date of the grant itself bears further examination. The indiction and the incarnational year given in the charter do not correspond. The choice between A.D. 705 and the fourth indiction (706) is, however, a difficult one, as it raises the question of the date of the accession of Aldhelm (called *episcopus* in this witness-list) to the see of Sherborne. This date hinges, of course, on that of the death of Aldhelm's predecessor, Hædde, which is calculated from the information – not very specific – given by Bede concerning the death of Aldfrith, king of Northumbria.[87] The year of Aldfrith's death

---

[84]   The king's superscription is the least strongly authenticated: apart from S.245, whose genuineness is debatable, none of the other examples are found in charters which are authentic in their surviving form.

[85]   For *cirographum*, see *Dictionary of Medieval Latin from British Sources*, fascicule II, under *chirographum*. The term has later as well as early occurrences. *Syngrapha* appears in a number of early Anglo-Saxon charters (S.241, S.245, S.246, S.269, S.1174 and S.1787, all ostensibly eighth-century in date but including some forgeries), but it is also attested in the tenth and eleventh centuries (for example, in S.460, S.469, S.473, S.496, S.687, S.926 and S.1004. Of these, S.473 is an authentic alliterative charter of King Edmund from the Glastonbury archive.) I am grateful to Richard Sharpe for searching the files of the Dictionary of Medieval Latin from British Sources for occurrences of *syngrapha*.

[86]   Cf. S.22 for an Anglo-Saxon example of this process (above, note 80); and S.553 for a probably post-Conquest forgery with an authentic pre-Conquest witness-list (see L. Abrams, ' "Lucid Intervals": A Rediscovered Anglo-Saxon Diploma from Glastonbury Abbey', *Journal of the Society of Archivists* 10 [1989], 43–56, at 51–3).

[87]   Bede (*HE* V.18; ed. Colgrave and Mynors, p. 512) stated that Aldfrith died in 705, having reigned nearly twenty years, and that Hædde died at the beginning of the reign of the succeeding king, Osred. The 'northern recension' of the Anglo-Saxon Chronicle (written 970x1030) is more specific. See Harrison, *The Framework*, pp. 89–91,

has been variously interpreted, with the result that 705 and 706 have both been put forward for the start of Aldhelm's episcopacy.[88] Since these are the two options offered by S.248, the contradiction in the charter's dating clause merely perpetuates the existing uncertainty about Aldhelm's promotion.

Composed entirely of ecclesiastics, the witness-list of S.248 must derive from a provincial council of the Southumbrian Church.[89] If the list could be linked to a known and dated synod, it could perhaps resolve the question of the date of the grant. If the attestations have not been tampered with (and Aldhelm promoted retroactively), this is not the council at which Aldhelm was ordered to write against the British Easter, often dated 705, for there, it seems, he was still simply an abbot and not yet raised to the see. There has, however, been disagreement over the date of this synod. Michael Lapidge and Michael Herren have argued that Aldhelm was given his task at the council of Hertford in 672, although this predates the usual dates for Aldhelm's abbacy, 675–705.[90] Bede gave no date for Aldhelm's discourse against the British; he said that it was a book, not a letter, that Aldhelm had written, and that he was ordered to do so at a synod *suae gentis* (which has been taken to mean a West Saxon council) before he became bishop.[91] Faricius, in his *Vita S. Aldhelmi*, written in the early twelfth century, stated that Aldhelm, still only an abbot, was asked to write against the Britons at a council of the West Saxons convoked in 706;[92] the value of Faricius's information has been questioned, however, on the grounds that it may have been based solely on the authority of Bede.[93] But, unlike Bede, Faricius supplied a year for this synod, although his date of 706 contradicts the traditional one of Aldhelm's accession to Sherborne (705).[94] Meanwhile, the testimony of

97, and *Aldhelm. The Prose Works*, trans. M. Lapidge and M. Herren (Ipswich, 1979), p. 10.

[88] R. L. Poole, *Studies in Chronology and History* (Oxford, 1934), p. 80, and Levison, *England and the Continent*, p. 274, argued that Aldfrith died in 704. Harrison, *The Framework*, pp. 85–91, especially 89–91, corrected this to 705, which was supported by Lapidge and Herren (*Aldhelm. The Prose Works*, p. 10), who thereby adjusted the year of Aldhelm's promotion from 705 to 706; D. P. Kirby, 'Bede, Eddius Stephanus and the "Life of Wilfrid"', *English Historical Review* 98 (1983), 101–14, especially 113, has followed Levison and Poole in accepting 704 for Aldfrith's death, and 705, therefore, for Aldhelm's promotion to bishop.

[89] It is listed in the appendix of C. R. E. Cubitt, 'Anglo-Saxon Church Councils, *c*.650–*c*.850' (unpublished PhD dissertation, University of Cambridge, 1990), p. 449, where the choice of dates is incorrectly given as 704 or 705.

[90] *Aldhelm. The Prose Works*, trans. Lapidge and Herren, pp. 140–3. The council that led to Aldhelm's letter was dated 675x705 by Simon Keynes in 'Anglo-Saxon Church Councils', *Handbook of British Chronology*, ed. E. B. Fryde *et al.*, 3rd ed. (London, 1986), pp. 583–9, at 587.

[91] *HE* V.18 (ed. Colgrave and Mynors, p. 514).

[92] *Vita S. Aldhelmi*, ch. 2, in *Vita quorundum Anglo-Saxonum* [sic], ed. J. A. Giles (London, 1854), p. 131.

[93] See *Aldhelm. The Prose Works*, trans. Lapidge and Herren, p. 198, n. 10, where Faricius was reported to have given the date 705 for the council.

[94] As in *Venerabilis Baedae Opera Historica*, ed. C. Plummer, 2 vols (Oxford, 1896) II, 309.

Aldhelm himself fails to clarify the question. His letter to Gerent on the subject of British religious practices survives, but bears no date;[95] in it Aldhelm seems to imply a provincial rather than a local synod and styled himself abbot. None of these authorities, therefore, can fix this synod's date or context and thereby allow – or dismiss – an association with the gathering represented by the witness-list of S.248.

Can this witness-list be associated instead with any other council? It may, in fact, support a reference in a letter in charter form from Aldhelm to his monasteries at Malmesbury, Frome and Bradford, said to have been written after he had become bishop and to have been sanctioned at a council on the *Noodr* (thought to be the River Nadder, in Wiltshire).[96] The text is dated A.D. 705, in the third indiction (which, unlike the indiction of S.248, corresponds correctly with the incarnational year), and bears only three names: Daniel (called *episcopus*), Ine, and Æthelfrith, *patricius*. Although the aim of this charter – to ensure freedom of abbatial election – and its anachronistic diplomatic features mark it as a forgery, it could, despite its spurious intentions, preserve evidence of a real, otherwise unrecorded, event. Edwards has suggested that the forger based his charter on Bede's account of the council on the River Nidd in 705.[97] Since Ine, who appears as a witness in B. 114, is unlikely to have attended a church council in Northumbria, Edwards seems to have assumed that the forger spliced Northumbrian material into a document which is otherwise West Saxon in context. Is it not equally likely, however, that the attestations and the geographical location go together, that the *Noodr* is indeed the Nadder, not the Nidd, and that Ine and Aldhelm and Æthelfrith (who attests S.239 and S.245) were there in 705 for the same council as produced S.248?

The equation of the witness-list of S.248 with the bishops attending this putative council in Wiltshire in 705 succeeds, of course, only if the incarnational date of S.248 – rather than its indiction – is correct. If, on the other hand, the indiction is correct, this charter would be evidence of an otherwise unrecorded council in 706.

This choice between indiction and incarnational date, as we have seen, cannot be resolved by reference to Aldhelmian chronology, but other considerations may allow us to suggest which of the two dating formulae – if they were both original – is most likely to have introduced the disagreement.

[95]   *Aldhelmi Opera Omnia*, ed. R. Ehwald, MGH Auctores antiquissimi 15 (Berlin, 1913–19), pp. 480–6 (Letter no. 4).

[96]   B. 114 (no Sawyer number). This is Ehwald's Charter no. 5 (*ibid.* pp. 514–16), which Lapidge and Herren have called 'patently spurious' (*Aldhelm. The Prose Works*, trans. Lapidge and Herren, p. 204). It is preserved in three texts: in William of Malmesbury's *Gesta pontificum Anglorum*, ch. 225 (ed. Hamilton, p. 379), in ch. 22 of the thirteenth-century Malmesbury Register, the *Registrum Malmesburiense*, ed. J. S. Brewer, 2 vols, RS 72 (London, 1879–90) I, 228–9, and in London, British Library, Lansdowne 417 (fol. 4), a late fourteenth- or fifteenth-century cartulary from Malmesbury (G. R. C. Davis, *Medieval Cartularies of Great Britain. A Short Catalogue* [London, 1958], no. 645).

[97]   Edwards, *The Charters*, pp. 115–16.

There is more scope for error in both dates as we have them in Roman numerals than if they had been written out in words: an extra minim could have been added to *iii* in the indiction by mistake when the facsimile was copied, which would make the correct date 705 not 706. The evidence of the *De antiquitate*, which gives the year A.D. 705 (*DCCV*) (no indiction), would support this case, but only equivocally, since the date appears at the head of a summary of several grants, and cannot therefore certainly be applied to this particular gift of the four estates of S.248. It is also quite possible, if the extant single sheet predates the 1120s, that William of Malmesbury took his information from this very document, in which case the *De antiquitate* corroborates nothing.[98] Alternatively, a minim could have been omitted from the year and *dccu* written in the copy where *dccui* was intended, making 706, not 705, the correct date. If there had been an intermediate stage of copying between the original and the facsimile (in the later eighth or the ninth century, for example), this could have been the occasion for the introduction into the text of an incorrect reading, but there are no definite palaeographical indicators of this (which would, admittedly, be difficult to detect). The incarnational date, once the strongest argument for an intermediate copy or against a genuine exemplar for the extant facsimile, cannot, as we have seen, now serve as proof of either of those possibilities.

As there is no longer a need to insist on a single form of date in the original text, the indiction (indicating 706) cannot be preferred automatically, with a discordant A.D. date blamed on incompetent calculation by a later copier. Technical considerations (of minims added or dropped) weigh no more heavily on one side than the other. This leaves only the highly dubious and unsatisfactory evidence of the *De antiquitate* and one interpretation of Aldhelm's ambiguous dates to argue for the year 705. As with so many aspects of this charter, close examination of the question, rather than providing a definite answer, instead encourages uncertainty.

WILLIAM OF MALMESBURY AND THE GLASTONBURY ARCHIVE

As with its date, the history of the transmission of S.248 is complicated rather than clarified by its appearance in the *De antiquitate*, a complication shared by most of Glastonbury's other pre-Conquest grants.[99] Although the narrative of the *De antiquitate* is the earliest and (in some ways) most extensive account of Glastonbury's Anglo-Saxon endowment to survive, it is not a contemporary source, and confusion and error, not to mention deception, had no doubt already crept in. Worse still, we know little about William of Malmesbury's method. If we ask ourselves what he used as a source for his information on Ine's grant of the four estates, for example, we are faced immediately with difficulties. William claimed to have obtained his informa-

---

[98] *DA*, ch. 40 (ed. Scott, p. 94). See below, pp. 119–22, for further discussion of William of Malmesbury.
[99] As was recognized by Davidson, 'On the Charters of King Ine', p. 3.

tion on grants to Glastonbury from old documents ('sicut per cartulas ueteres apparet'),[100] and often seems to quote verbatim from texts (shifting into the first person, for example, when recording a grant). If the extant facsimile is indeed a pre-Conquest product, *it* could have been William's source, but because it has proved so difficult to place in context, we cannot even be sure of this. Possibly both the facsimile and its exemplar were in the archive in the 1120s. Although he has enjoyed a (perhaps exaggerated) reputation as a careful and sensible historian, how far William's method conformed to our ideas of historical integrity is not clear, and we cannot be certain of the extent to which he altered his original sources, 'improving' and adding touches of his own. To complicate the question further, interpolations intruded into the text in the later twelfth and thirteenth centuries cannot always be distinguished from William's work. A comparison of the text of the single sheet of S.248 with the summary of Ine's grants that appears in the *De antiquitate* reveals some interesting differences:

> Anno ab incarnacione Domini DCCV Ina Berwaldo abbati dedit xx hidas iuxta Tamer et xx hidas in loco qui dicitur Bouelt, Soei xii hidas, Corregs v hidas, Escford dimidiam hidam cum captura piscium, Dulting xx hidas. Ego Aldelmus hanc scedulam scripsi. Dedit eciam Ina rex Pilton xx hidas.

> In A.D. 705 Ine gave Abbot Berwald 20 hides on the Tamar, 20 hides at the place called *Pouelt*, 12 hides at *Sowy*, 5 hides at *Corregs*, half a hide and fishing rights at *Escford*, and 20 hides at Doulting. I, Aldhelm, wrote this document. King Ine also gave 20 hides at Pilton.[101]

The first and most obvious divergence between this summary and the record in S.248 is the inclusion of three additional grants, those of *Sowy*, *Escford* and Pilton.[102] Possibly the most interesting variation, however, lies in the sentence, 'Ego Aldelmus hanc scedulam scripsi'. The single sheet bears no such claim, although Aldhelm is, of course, one of the nine witnesses ('ego Aldhelmus episcopus subscripsi').

This attribution to Aldhelm prompts some speculation about William's method in the *De antiquitate*. With the original charter (or the facsimile) in front of him he could simply have added the sentence in Aldhelm's words (but not his style) as a flourish, to give greater authority to the transaction. Alternatively, conflating several of Ine's charters in these lines, William could have been quoting Aldhelm's attestation from a text other than that of S.248. In that case, his exemplar was not likely to have been the *Sowy* grant, for the

---

[100] *DA*, ch. 70 (ed. Scott, p. 144).

[101] *Ibid.* ch. 40, p. 94 (but my translation). In Trinity College R. 5. 33, 8v, *scilicet Linis* is written above the line, over *Tamer*. Above the *v hidas* of the *Corregs* grant is added *uel I*.

[102] The grant of *Sowy* (S.251), dated 725, exists independently in the Great Cartulary (GC, II, 495), and was still extant in 1247 (*IC* A7). No grant of *Escford* appears in the Great Cartulary or in any of the other surviving administrative records, although a charter of King Edmund for *Escford*, now lost, was recorded in the *Liber terrarum* (*LT* 58). For Pilton, see below, pp. 127–9.

surviving text of that gift of Ine's contains no such statement; Aldhelm, in fact, does not appear among its witnesses (although the list, like so many of Glastonbury's witness-lists, could have been abbreviated). The only possible source of this statement among the grants of Ine mentioned, therefore, is that of *Escford*, but as no text of this grant survives, this suggestion is unverifiable. There is, however, a candidate for William's model in a supposedly earlier charter – S.237, dated A.D. 682, in the name of Centwine – which bears almost the same wording: 'Ego Aldhelm hanc scedulam scripsi et subscripsi'.[103] William may thus have taken liberties with his text and lifted this formula from a copy of the grant in the name of one of Ine's predecessors. Borrowings of this nature – in support of both fraudulent and legitimate claims – cannot have been unusual and no doubt helped contribute to the corruption of those early texts preserved in chronicles or cartulary copies. Rhetorical retouching as well as inefficient copying and falsification may account for a number of other examples of differences in detail between the texts of surviving charters and their summaries in the *De antiquitate*.

Alternatively, William might have had before him a different text of Ine's multiple grant from the surviving single sheet or its exemplar. This raises some fundamental questions – for which (as usual) we have no ready answers – about archival organization and documentary survival at Glastonbury; we know that pre-Conquest single sheets were indeed available for copying there as late as the fifteenth century, although no document clearly identifiable with S.248 makes an appearance in the abbey's surviving lists of *cartae* or in its extant cartularies and registers. Could there have been several original copies of this multiple grant? Might there have been a charter for each of the four estates granted?[104] If so, it is hard to imagine that their formulaic elements would have differed, but we have little to go on for purposes of comparison.[105] It is also possible that a later copy or a redraft in a different form (which has failed to survive) could have had interpolated some such statement about Aldhelm, which William then copied. The circumstances of the production of early diplomas is so obscure that we are limited here to speculation. We are fortunate, however, to have preserved in the Great Cartulary the text of a diploma, S.247, which throws some light on the question and testifies to some interesting archival manipulation.

It appears that the original charter of S.248, or more specifically, the grant of the twenty hides on the River *Duluting* (the third unit of land), was found to be insufficient at a later date (presumably some time in the later tenth

[103] The text of this charter, which survives only in a very late collection (Longleat House, Marquess of Bath, NMR 10586), is not authentic in its current form, but contains genuinely early elements. William appears to quote from it directly in the *De antiquitate* (ch. 37; ed. Scott, p. 90).

[104] S. C. Morland, 'The Glastonbury Manors and their Charters', *PSANHS* 130 (1986), 61–105, at 63, expressed the belief that William ignored Ine's charter and quoted from four separate diplomas granting the same properties.

[105] S.41 (A.D. 805x807) survives in two original copies; the text of the grant is essentially the same in both single sheets, but the second contains an additional section in Old English relating to the arrangements by the recipient for the land after his death.

century, the probable date of the added bounds of S.247),[106] and another diploma was then created to provide more specific (retroactive) documentation, possibly to resolve a dispute or strengthen a claim.[107] The model of S.248, adapted to apply to the grant of one estate, not four, was followed closely, but, in addition to the few insignificant abridgements, there are some amplifications in the text. The most important – the provision of detailed Old English bounds – has already been mentioned. In addition, Abbot Berwald's monastery was identified ('ad sanctum monasterium Glastingaburgh'), and the king, missing from the witness-list of S.248, was intruded ('ego Iny signaui salutifero signo') while most of the other witnesses were omitted. In other words, the drafter of S.247 took care to remedy all the weaknesses of S.248, thereby bringing it into line with more up-to-date administrative practice. This, it should be noted, is exactly what the copyist of the extant facsimile did not do. Revised charters in Ine's name for the three other pieces of land granted in S.248 may also have been written at this (or any other) time, but if Glastonbury's possession of the estates was secure, such documents might not have been needed.[108] In the *De antiquitate*, the grant rewritten as S.247 appears as an additional gift by King Ine, bearing the later place-name of what was probably the same twenty hides:[109] without the survival of S.248 we might (unwisely) have accepted William's seemingly straightforward evidence at face value, at the expense of a rather more complex (and still very obscure) truth.

The only other account of S.248, which is preserved in John of Glastonbury's *Cronica*, does not constitute evidence independent of the *De antiquitate*. John, according to his editor, 'showed a great reluctance to write anything in his own words, or even to paraphrase other authors'.[110] His testimony, on the Anglo-Saxon period at least, thus appears to have added nothing to what he found in his source.

THE ESTATES

S.248 records the grant of four parcels of land totalling sixty-five hides. Extant diplomas from the archive have been thought to represent other transactions involving these four estates, but on close examination these identifications prove to be problematic. The estates forming the early phase of Glastonbury's endowment are particularly difficult to identify, as the only

---

[106] I am again grateful to Peter Kitson for information on the dating of these bounds.
[107] The retrieval of the estate at Doulting, which had been lost, and its grant by King Eadred (946–55) may have provided the occasion for the creation of this charter; see *LT* 32 and *DA*, chs 57 and 69 (ed. Scott, pp. 118 and 142–4).
[108] There is slight and inconclusive evidence for another rewritten charter, for the estate at Doulting: *IC* A5 ('[Yna rex] de Dulting') and Marquess of Bath 39A, 25v ('Carta Ine regis de Doultyng'). These could, however, refer either to S.247 (for land on the River *Duluting*) (i.e., Pilton) or indeed to S.248, which mentions the same river.
[109] *DA*, chs 40 and 69 (ed. Scott, pp. 94 and 140); see below, pp. 127–8.
[110] *The Chronicle of Glastonbury Abbey*, ed. Carley, p. xxxv.

contemporary documentary evidence to survive is unhelpfully imprecise; nor is there much from the middle centuries of the Anglo-Saxon period to illustrate developments. The significantly later testimony of Old English bounds or Domesday Book is often drawn into the analysis by default – it is sometimes all there is – but this method has its dangers, for an exact correspondence between the boundaries of estates in the eighth century and those of the later Anglo-Saxon period should not be assumed. As a result, the estates granted in S.248, even though they probably formed a substantial part of the core of Glastonbury's ancient endowment, are extremely difficult, perhaps impossible, to identify with certainty from the documentary evidence.

The first grant, of twenty hides on the River Tone, was thought by James Davidson to be a confirmation of the gift of land on both sides of the Tone near Quantock Wood granted to Glastonbury in S.237, a diploma of King Centwine dated 682.[111] The *Liber terrarum* entry, the boundaries attached to Centwine's grant, and the rubric in a late Glastonbury register all identify S.237 as recording the gift of the estate of West Monkton, near Taunton.[112] However, Ine's grant of land near the Tone in S.248, less than fifteen years later, is not cast in the form of a confirmation, and its twenty hides do not correspond to Centwine's twenty-three. Differences in hidage can often be argued away,[113] and to account for the need to regrant the same estate after such a short interval one could speculate about political turmoil and the difficulty of holding on to property in the late seventh century,[114] but given the vagueness of the locative attribution, the equation of Ine's twenty hides in S.248 with West Monkton may simply be wishful thinking.[115] Their identification is thus doubtful, although one further piece of evidence may be cited.

In the version of Ine's grant preserved in the Trinity manuscript of the *De antiquitate*, these first twenty hides are described as *iuxta Tamer, scilicet Linis*

---

[111] Davidson, 'On the Charters of King Ine', p. 11; see also F. H. Dickinson, 'West Monkton Charter', *PSANHS* 28 (1882), 89–98, especially 92, n. 3, and Morland, 'The Glastonbury Manors', p. 76.

[112] *LT* 8 ('Kenwinus de Cantucwudu .s. Munekaton'. G'). The boundaries are found with the text in Marquess of Bath, NMR 10586. The grant is mentioned in the register, Marquess of Bath 39A, at 70r. The *De antiquitate* specified that the estate consisted of twenty hides at Cary and three hides south of the river at Creech (chs 37 and 69; ed. Scott, pp. 90 and 140). G. B. Grundy experienced some difficulty in identifying the bounds: see 'West Monkton. Revised Notes of its Charter', *PSANHS* 84 (1938), 104–6, modifying his analysis in *The Saxon Charters and Field Names of Somerset* (Taunton, 1935), pp. 51–4. (This book was originally published in instalments as appendices in *PSANHS* 73–80 [1927–34]; the pagination remained the same.)

[113] If, with Morland ('The Glastonbury Manors', p. 76), we trust the account in the *De antiquitate* (see note above), for example, we could say that Ine's grant applied to the twenty hides north of the river only. The text of Centwine's charter, however, appears to refer to twenty-three hides north of the river and a further three to the south.

[114] Edwards, *The Charters*, p. 31.

[115] Edwards also made this point; *ibid.* p. 32.

(later *Linig*).[116] This intrusion of the River Tamar in error for the Tone misled Finberg into attributing to Glastonbury the possession of an estate in the far south-west, from which he drew false conclusions about the extent of King Ine's advance into Dumnonia.[117] This evidence of confusion in R. 5. 33 does not inspire confidence in the accuracy of geographical knowledge about its early endowment at thirteenth-century Glastonbury; it suggests instead that *scilicet Linis*, a marginal note, may represent an attempt by a much later writer to make sense of what was already an obscure description. Factors other than ignorance could have been involved, and further study may prove enlightening, but the error (Tamar for Tone) must raise doubts about the usefulness to us of the annotation in the *De antiquitate* in considering the question of the site of the eighth-century estate. Its location accordingly remains a matter for speculation.[118]

The second grant, of *Pouelt*, is the earliest of three (possibly four) known eighth-century transactions involving this estate. Although the combined evidence of the sources is generous in comparison with that for the hides on the Tone, it affords us only a fragmentary picture of *Pouelt*'s history. In chronological order (and it is by no means certain that this is the order in which the grants were composed), this gift by Ine in S.248 – a grant of twenty hides – is followed by a charter of 729 (S.253) in which King Æthelheard granted sixty hides at *Poholt* to Abbot Coengils. King Sigeberht is said to have sold twenty-two hides at *Poolt* to *Tica* (for Tyccea), abbot of Glastonbury, for fifty *solidi* in 756 (S.1680). The sale for another fifty shillings of a further six hides 'in occidentali parte illius' (presumably also *Poolt*) by Sigeberht to Tyccea probably represents a fourth transaction involving this estate. It is typical of the complexity of the Glastonbury archive that the evidence for these four grants was preserved – generally without overlap – in four different sources: the first (omitted from the cartularies) in this single-sheet copy; the second in the *Secretum Domini*, the contemporary copy of the fourteenth-century Great Cartulary;[119] the third in the lost early cartulary, the *Liber terrarum* (but not in the later, extant, collections);[120] and the fourth in the *De antiquitate* (and the *Cronica*) alone.[121] No charters for these grants are listed in the 1247 *Index chartarum*, although at least one (S.253) must still have been in the archive at that date, and another (S.248) probably remained there as well. Curiously, none of the grants appears in the Great Cartulary. The one

---

[116] R. 5. 33, 8v and 15r: *DA*, ch. 40 (ed. Scott, p. 94, note z), and ch. 69, p. 140 (*Lining* misprinted for *Linig*); for a discussion of *Linig* and the substitution of the Tamar for the Tone, see O. J. Padel, 'Glastonbury's Cornish Connections', in this volume, pp. 250–2.

[117] H. P. R. Finberg, 'Sherborne, Glastonbury, and the Expansion of Wessex', in his *Lucerna. Studies of Some Problems in the Early History of England* (London, 1964), pp. 95–115, especially 100–4.

[118] For example, see Padel, 'Glastonbury's Cornish Connections', p. 252.

[119] Wood empt. 1, 152r; it is also *LT* 15. See above, note 64.

[120] *LT* 63.

[121] *DA*, ch. 47 (ed. Scott, p. 104); *Cronica*, ch. 53 (ed. Carley, p. 106).

source that records all four, the *De antiquitate* (followed by the *Cronica*)[122] is, as we have seen, not necessarily the most reliable.

These transactions involving *Pouelt* are not easy to reconcile with one another. Successive grants in 705/6, 729 and 756 are difficult to account for. The hidages of the grants do not agree, and the exact location of the lands to which they referred is far from clear. The short Latin bounds of Æthelheard's grant of *Pouelt* invite diverse interpretation: but his charter (S.253) appears in the *Secretum Domini* under the heading 'Schapwik', and its sixty hides have been taken to represent the Domesday manors of Shapwick and Walton, each assessed at thirty hides.[123] Which part of this area might be represented by the twenty hides of S.248 is probably impossible to determine. The marginal note (*id est Grenton*) above the name *Poelt* in the Trinity manuscript's text of the spurious privilege S.250,[124] may again, like its identification of Glastonbury's hides on the Tamar/Tone as *Linig*, be too late to be useful in identifying the eighth-century location of this estate.[125] The discrepancy in the number of hides of the grants – twenty, sixty, and twenty-two (plus six) – raises the possibility that they referred to different parts of a large land-unit, parts which later acquired individual names.[126] It also raises the possibility of interference with the documents. The text of S.1680 has been lost and therefore cannot be tested diplomatically (although the fact that it records a sale rather than a gift might count against its being a complete invention); S.248 seems to be sound; could S.253 be spurious? Edwards has argued in favour of the authenticity of this last grant on the grounds – among others – that a later forger would have included details corresponding to those in Domesday Book.[127] Certainly it is unlikely that a post-Conquest forger would have fabricated S.253 or changed the number of hides granted without at least replacing the place-name, which (as we have seen above) was possibly already obsolete, with more contemporary and specific ones. This argument does not, however, rule out an early forgery. It is also weakened by the fact

---

[122] S.248 appears twice in the *De antiquitate* (chs 40 and 69; ed. Scott, pp. 94 and 140–2) and John of Glastonbury's *Cronica*, chs 16 and 47 (ed. Carley, pp. 40 and 92); S.253 is recorded in the *De antiquitate* in chs 44 and 69 (pp. 102 and 142) and in John's *Cronica* in ch. 52 (p. 104); S.1680 is in the *De antiquitate* in chs 47 and 69 (pp. 104 and 142) and in ch. 53 of the *Cronica* (pp. 104–6).

[123] Wood empt. 1, 152r; S. C. Morland, 'The Saxon Charters for Sowy and Pouholt and the Course of the River Cary', *SDNQ* 31 (1982), 233–4, at 234, pointed out that Grundy, 'misled by the title, omitted the Walton group [of villages] and did not look for the first landmark in the right place'; see Grundy, *The Saxon Charters*, pp. 114–16; further discussion by Morland can be found in 'Hidation on the Glastonbury Estates: A Study in Tax Evasion', *PSANHS* 114 (1970), 74–90, at 78–9, and in 'The Glastonbury Manors', pp. 78–9; for Shapwick and Walton in Domesday Book, see DB, I, 90ra and 90rb (*Somerset*, 8.5 and 8.11).

[124] R. 5. 33, 9v; *DA*, ch. 42 (ed. Scott, p. 100).

[125] Greinton was indeed a Glastonbury possession, but in 1086 it was a small unit of two and a half hides forming part of the Walton estate (DB, I, 90rb; *Somerset*, 8.15).

[126] Morland ('Hidation on the Glastonbury Estates', pp. 78–9, and 'The Glastonbury Manors', p. 79) attempted to identify these parts, but his explanation did not resolve all the difficulties, especially those raised by Ine's twenty hides.

[127] Edwards, *The Charters*, pp. 40–1.

that S.250, a blatantly spurious grant of privileges (designed to restrict the power of the bishop of Wells) which dates probably from the early twelfth century, twice cited the early name *Poelt*, once in a list of past grants, and again in identifying one of the two estates in Glastonbury territory at which the bishop was allowed to stay overnight.[128] The status of S.253 – despite its many acceptable diplomatic features – should thus remain open, leaving unresolved the question of the relationship of the three eighth-century grants. No further transactions involving this estate (by this name, that is) are recorded.

A related place-name, however, apparently derived from *Pouelt*, occurs in the perambulations of Glastonbury's Twelve Hides which are interpolated into the *De antiquitate*.[129] This name (spelt *Poldune* and *Poldon'*) is evidently the precursor of the modern name (Polden) for the hills to the south-west of Glastonbury. However, the perambulations and a small number of further references indicate that an estate, not a range of hills, was intended.[130] Could this be the *Pouelt* of the pre-Conquest grants? The earliest attestation of the form *Poldone*, in the Trinity manuscript where it appears as a sub-heading for Æthelheard's grant of *Pouelt*,[131] seems to support the identity of the two, as does the entry in the contents-list of the *Liber terrarum* (in the same manuscript): 'Poolt, id est Poldon''(*LT* 15). It is nevertheless unlikely on linguistic grounds that Polden is simply the later form of *Pouelt* (as Watkin implied and Scott seems to have accepted in their respective editions of the Great Cartulary and the *De antiquitate*);[132] it appears rather to consist of the older name *Pouelt* with the addition of OE *dun*, 'hill', here 'range of hills' – 'the range at or near *Pouelt*'. How the name of the larger area came to be applied back to an estate is unclear, but it seems that by the thirteenth century, at least, *Poldone* could be used to refer to *Pouelt* (the estate granted by Ine) and to a contemporary estate on the Poldens, possibly Shapwick.[133] The absence of any associated name from Domesday Book is puzzling. Its omission from the Great Cartulary and other late administrative records suggests that *Poldone*

---

[128] See note 62. Was the use of this ancient form in the twelfth century simply antiquarian showing-off, or could it have been the Glastonbury forger's idea of a joke to allow the bishop of Wells this privilege at an estate which he would not be able to identify?

[129] *DA*, chs 72 and 73 (ed. Scott, pp. 148–52; see also pp. 208–9); also in John's *Cronica*, chs 3 and 4 (ed. Carley, pp. 12–16).

[130] *Cronica*, chs 16 and 33 (ed. Carley, pp. 38 and 74), where *Poldune* was said to have been granted by King Arthur; and *Rentalia et Custumaria Michaelis de Ambresbury, 1235–52, et Rogeri de Ford, 1252–1261, Abbatum Monasterii Beatae Mariae Glastoniae*, ed. C. J. Elton and E. Hobhouse, SRS 5 (1891), p. 2, where two tenants held twelve knights' fees *apud Septone et Poweldun*.

[131] R. 5. 33, 9v; *DA*, ch. 44 (ed. Scott, p. 102, which omits the heading).

[132] GC, II, cxxi; *The Early History*, ed. Scott, p. 94, n. 87, and p. 102, n. 94, for example. See also the index in the latter.

[133] Which may be the *Poldune* of the perambulations of the Twelve Hides; see the text and map in S. C. Morland, 'Glaston Twelve Hides', *PSANHS* 128 (1984), 35–55, especially 49, 53 and 55.

had gone out of use as an estate-name by the mid-fourteenth century, although it survived as the name of the range of hills.

Nicholas Corcos has proposed a tentative history for *Pouelt* in his study of Shapwick.[134] Originally a multiple estate, possibly of Roman origin, *Pouelt* consisted of at least sixty hides, perhaps more, in the early Anglo-Saxon period. It was made up of specialized constituent members, including the pastoral unit of Shapwick. The multiple estate fragmented and disappeared, probably in the mid- to late tenth century, with the conversion to open-field agriculture and nuclear settlement (the shift to arable from pastoral being prompted by economic motives and a drive for efficiency). According to Corcos, the original *Pouelt* covered approximately the same area as the modern Polden Hills – a very large tract of land. Once it had broken up, the monks were faced with the problem of how to classify the estate's documentation, and S.253, the surviving charter of Æthelheard for sixty hides at *Pouholt*, although it appears to have been omitted from the Great Cartulary, was placed in the *Secretum Domini* under Shapwick because that manor may have been remembered as the estate centre. It is unfortunate that this picture of the changing landscape is flawed by Corcos's omission of S.248 from the analysis, beginning the Anglo-Saxon history of *Pouelt* as he does with the questionable charter of Æthelheard dated 729. If instead we include Ine's charter and acknowledge that the earliest known grant of *Pouelt* consisted of only twenty hides, Corcos's identification of *Pouelt* as a large multiple estate, possibly co-terminous with the Polden Hills, is somewhat undermined. It could be, on the other hand, that Ine's twenty hides at *Pouelt* were only a part of the estate by that name and that the subsequent eighth-century grants (if genuine) continued the process of transferring this putative very large estate to Glastonbury in portions. This raises the question of how estates were identified and how names were applied: might a multiple estate be called after one of its parts? What, exactly, did a name refer to? Can we detect how its frame of reference changed over time? Until we have clearer answers to these important questions, it is not surprising that the exact location of the twenty hides at *Pouelt* granted by Ine remains a matter for debate.[135]

The third unit of land granted in S.248, twenty hides on both sides of the River *Duluting* (now the Sheppey, according to Ekwall),[136] was recognized by Davidson as the same twenty hides to be found in S.247, the revised version

---

[134] N. J. Corcos, 'Early Estates on the Poldens and the Origin of Settlement at Shapwick', *PSANHS* 127 (1983), 47–54.

[135] A further reference to the estate (*on Poholte*) appears in the bounds of S.251 for *Sowy*, dated by Kitson to the tenth or eleventh century. Davidson identified this *Poholt* as 'a point on the "King's Sedge Drain" . . . where the three parishes of Othery, Aller and Greinton meet'; see Davidson, 'On the Charters of King Ine', p. 11. Finberg took this to mean that this 'point' also represented the *Pouelt* of S.248 (*ECW*, p. 112). Morland has since pointed out that 'it seems improbable that the estate covering a number of villages on the Poldens took its name from a copse on Sedgemoor' ('The Saxon Charters for Sowy and Pouholt', p. 234), and Gelling has suggested (personal communication) that *on Poholte* in S.251 qualifies *Hamelondsmere* (which can thus be interpreted as a feature located on the boundary of the *Pouelt* estate).

[136] Ekwall, *Concise Oxford Dictionary of Place-Names*, s.n. Doulting.

of S.248 which was, as we have seen, written probably in the later tenth century.[137] The twenty hides of S.247 are also described as on both sides of the Sheppey, but can be more precisely located, thanks to the addition of a set of Old English bounds. Davidson mapped this perambulation, which included Pilton, Croscombe, and Shepton Mallet west of the Fosse.[138] S.247 was entered in the Great Cartulary under Pilton and was there attributed to King Ine and the year 705 (no indiction).[139] A second copy of the same text (attributed likewise to Ine and specifically to the fourth indiction, but misdated 702) was inserted in the Great Cartulary under the name of another Glastonbury estate, Doulting, with the implication that it represented a separate grant of this latter estate by Ine.[140] This does not appear to have been the case, for the boundaries are identical; the misunderstanding (deliberate or not) arose from the confusion of the river-name, *Duluting*, with the name of the estate (in which the source of the river is to be found).[141] According to Davidson, the bounds of S.247 did not extend across the Fosse from Pilton into Doulting, its neighbour. The charter may therefore have been copied into the cartulary at this point to provide a title deed for an estate which otherwise lacked pre-Conquest documentation.[142]

---

[137] Davidson, 'On the Charters of King Ine', p. 12. Davidson (pp. 13 and 18) also recognized other crucial similarities between S.247 and S.248. See above, pp. 121–2.

[138] *Ibid.* Grundy also analysed these bounds in *The Saxon Charters*, pp. 79–84. See also Morland, 'The Glastonbury Manors', pp. 77–8. A fresh analysis on the ground might prove productive.

[139] GC, II, 433. It is also recorded as *LT* 9 (for Pilton) and in *DA*, chs 40 and 69 (ed. Scott, pp. 94 and 140) (also Pilton; Morland considered this an interpolation: 'The Glastonbury Manors', pp. 64 and 77). It may also have been listed in the 1247 *Index chartarum* (*IC* A5, for Doulting); but see notes 108 and 142. Sawyer catalogued *LT* 9, Ine's grant of Pilton, as a lost charter (S.1672), although he raised the possibility (correctly, it seems) that *LT* 9 (S.1672) might be S.247.

[140] GC, II, 450.

[141] In his *Gesta pontificum Anglorum*, William of Malmesbury stated that the *uilla* of *Dulting* had been given to Glastonbury by Aldhelm (ch. 228; ed. Hamilton, p. 382); no record of this survives in Glastonbury's archive. In the *De antiquitate*, it is recorded that 'Doulting' (the future estate of that name? or the estate that came to be called Pilton?) was restored to the abbey in 851, when twenty hides (the future Doulting? or perhaps Pilton?) were added to it by King Æthelwulf; *DA*, ch. 53 (ed. Scott, p. 113). Since, according to the *Liber terrarum* (*LT* 32; S.1742), 'Doulting' was restored to Glastonbury by King Eadred, some part, at least, of this estate seems to have been lost in the intervening century. Whether Eadred's restoration applied to both Pilton and Doulting is uncertain. In 1086, Glastonbury held twenty hides at Pilton and twenty hides at Doulting (DB, I, 90rb and 90va; *Somerset*, 8.20 and 8.23). It is unclear how Morland's assertion that Pilton 'originally' had ten hides should fit into this sequence ('Hidation on the Glastonbury Estates', p. 78). I am grateful to Simon Keynes for his help in deciphering the history of these grants.

[142] Sawyer gave no number for a lost charter of Ine for Doulting; he did not include or consider two important references. The entries in the *Index chartarum* (A5: '[Yna rex] de Dulting') and in Marquess of Bath 39A, 25v ('Carta Ini regis de Doultyng') could provide evidence that a separate single sheet was written for Doulting (and lost). Alternatively, these entries could refer to S.247 (Pilton's hides on the *Duluting*); or they could even apply to S.248, given the facsimile's two late medieval endorsements for Doulting, which suggest that this single sheet came to represent the Doul-

With the bounds of S.247 we encounter a difficulty common to all early charters with later boundary clauses attached: the time lag between the original grant and the creation of the extant survey. Davidson's assumption that the twenty hides on the Sheppey of the eighth-century grant in S.248 were exactly reproduced in the tenth-century decription of Pilton in S.247 ignores the question – a fundamental one, and a major stumbling block – of what developments are concealed in the gap between the first known grant of a piece of land and the first description of its extent. In Pilton's case, the sparse late evidence – the bounds and Domesday Book – testifies against a static estate unit, for Pilton increased its area (but not its assessment) between the tenth and the late eleventh century. There is no reason to believe that changes of this sort, now invisible, could not have taken place in the early period as well.[143]

The last area granted, five hides on the western side of the valley called *Corregescumb*,[144] was identified by Davidson as the estate of North Wootton, which lies between Glastonbury and Shepton Mallet.[145] According to the *De antiquitate*, King Cynewulf gave five hides at *Wudeton* to Abbot Guba in 760; this may be confirmed by an incomplete statement in the *Liber terrarum*.[146] Another *Liber terrarum* entry records a grant of *Wodeton'* to Heregyth by King Æthelwulf in 855x860.[147] Finally, a charter of 946 in the name of King Edmund (S.509) appears to represent a lease of a five-hide estate there, with annual renders to Glastonbury.[148] Again, we are faced with a succession of grants that imply a phenomenon of constantly shifting property ownership, or confusion of identity, or unreliable and possibly fabricated documentation, or a combination of all the above. The complexities of the estate history of North Wootton may, however, be outside the purview of S.248, for the identification of that estate with the five *Corregescumb* hides, though possible, is not certain; it appears to be based on the agreement in hidage and on the fact that North Wootton lies beside the tenth-century Pilton estate. Davidson and Grundy found some coincidences in the bounds of S.509 (North Wootton) and S.247 (Pilton), which would confirm a shared boundary,[149] but this does not necessarily locate *Corregescumb*. In any event, as those

---

ting estate in the archive (although those endorsements are both later than the *Index chartarum*). The note in Marquess of Bath 39A, 25v, indicating that there were two copies of this mystery charter for Doulting extant in the fifteenth century, just complicates the question.

[143] See below, pp. 130–2.

[144] The summary of grants in the *De antiquitate* (*DA*, ch. 69; ed. Scott, pp. 140–4) fails to include this fourth grant of S.248, although it does appear in the main entry on Ine (ch. 40; ed. Scott, p. 94), where an interlinear correction in the Trinity manuscript changed the amount from five to six hides (see above, n. 101).

[145] Davidson, 'On the Charters of King Ine', pp. 12–13.

[146] *DA*, chs 48 and 69 (ed. Scott, pp. 106 and 142); *LT* 27: 'Cynewlfus de .u. hidis. G.'.

[147] *LT* 64.

[148] *GC*, II, 447; also in the *Liber terrarum* (*LT* 131).

[149] Davidson, 'On the Charters of King Ine', pp. 18–23; Grundy, *The Saxon Charters*, pp. 94–7.

bounds date at the earliest from the late Anglo-Saxon period, they should not be assumed to represent the extent and shape of the estates in Ine's day.

Is there any other evidence for North Wootton that might bear on its identification with the *Corregescumb* hides? North Wootton is in Domesday Book as a five-hide unit belonging to Glastonbury, not an independent unit, however, but a component of Pilton. Pilton is supposedly represented in S.248 by its third grant (of the twenty hides on the Sheppey), which should therefore also include North Wootton; but thanks to the survival of the late Anglo-Saxon bounds of Pilton in S.247, Davidson could determine that when the bounds were written, Pilton, unlike its Domesday successor, did not include the sub-unit of North Wootton. We have no evidence to indicate whether or not the twenty hides on the Sheppey excluded North Wootton in the eighth century as well. If they did, North Wootton would indeed be a candidate for the *Corregescumb* hides.

Is there another? The description of the single sheet of S.248 when it was deposited at the Taunton Museum in 1849 suggests that, at least in the nineteenth century, the charter was particularly linked to Croscombe, another village on the Sheppey,[150] whose modern name does suggest an identification with Ine's hides in the valley called *Corregescumb*.[151] Croscombe, however, also formed part of the Pilton estate, not only in Domesday Book,[152] but (unlike North Wootton) in the tenth century as well, if Davidson's analysis of the bounds is sound.[153] Whether this inclusion in Pilton's twenty hides extended back to the eighth century, we cannot say.

This insistence on the possible difference between Glastonbury's estates in, say, 705 and 975 appears to be resisting the accumulating evidence for continuity which has been put forward since the 1950s by students of landscape history. In his seminal article on Withington in Gloucestershire, for example, H. P. R. Finberg argued that the Roman villa-estate there had not disintegrated in the fifth century, hitherto seen as a cataclysmic break with the past, but was identical to the Anglo-Saxon estate granted in the late seventh century for the endowment of a minster.[154] That a unit of land could maintain its shape and integrity while political and social systems changed around it was a radical, and very influential, idea. Desmond Bonney's subsequent work in Wessex confirmed the Roman date of a number of medieval boundaries there; some were pushed even further back, into the Iron Age.[155]

---

[150] 'A charter of King Ina (702) [*sic*] relating to property at Croscombe'; see 'First Annual Meeting', as in note 9 above.

[151] Morland seems recently to have supported this identification: 'The Glastonbury Manors', p. 71.

[152] DB, I, 90rb and 90va; *Somerset*, 8.20, where it was assessed for only three, not five, hides.

[153] Davidson, 'On the Charters of King Ine', pp. 18–23.

[154] H. P. R. Finberg, *Roman and Saxon Withington: A Study in Continuity* (Leicester, 1955); reprinted in his *Lucerna*, pp. 21–65.

[155] D. Bonney, 'Early Boundaries in Wessex', in *Archaeology in the Landscape. Essays for L. V. Grinsell*, ed. P. J. Fowler (London, 1972), pp. 168–86; and 'Early Boundaries and Estates in Southern England', in *Medieval Settlement: Continuity and Change*, ed. P. H. Sawyer (London, 1976), pp. 72–82.

These discoveries prompted more, and the possibility of continuity became widely accepted. An unfortunate side-effect, however, where continuity could be demonstrated, was the implication of a static landscape: but there is a difference between the continuity of a boundary over a period of time and the immutability of an estate, and neither Finberg nor Bonney had argued that Anglo-Saxon estates with ancient boundaries reached the later Middle Ages, or even 1066, unchanged. Withington, for example, experienced an amalgamation of two units some time before the late eighth century, and subsequent expansion increased its area further.[156] Bonney argued, similarly, that some of the large multiple estates visible in Anglo-Saxon charters had resulted from the amalgamation of small units, which later separated.[157]

The recognition of these sub-units has been only one of the significant contributions of Della Hooke's in-depth study of the boundary clauses of pre-Conquest charters.[158] Her work, following on from that of Glanville Jones,[159] has brought into focus the patchwork nature of the multiple estates of early Anglo-Saxon England and the processes of fragmentation and amalgamation which can be glimpsed through the documents, in the place-names, and on the land.[160] Hooke identified an 'intricate pattern of minor boundaries' marking out internal divisions.[161] These consisted of clearly defined and significant sub-units within estates, recognizing the separate and enduring identity of the parts that made up the whole. Although some estates stabilized early, in many cases sub-units were grouped and re-grouped, influenced no doubt by a variety of factors, including developments in the local economy and in lordship. The *longue durée* of agricultural life must have been interrupted by the changes brought on, for example, by the fragmentation of large multiple estates such as that envisaged on the Poldens, and the developments in land-use and settlement patterns that followed. More minor manoeuvrings in response to changing local conditions were no doubt commonplace. These regroupings are difficult to trace, as they did not necessarily result in changes of assessment, which, if recorded, would help alert us to possible differences in size and shape.

There is thus a danger in assuming that the silence of the documents conceals a static landscape and that late testimony can be taken as a reflection of the early reality. What little documentary evidence there is argues for a dynamic situation: charters imply that estates passed in and out of Glaston-

---

[156] Finberg, *Lucerna*, pp. 21–2.
[157] Bonney, 'Early Boundaries and Estates', pp. 78–81.
[158] D. Hooke, *Anglo-Saxon Landscapes of the West Midlands: The Charter Evidence*, BAR Brit. ser. 95 (Oxford, 1981), and *The Landscape of Anglo-Saxon Staffordshire: The Charter Evidence* (Keele, 1983).
[159] Cf. G. R. J. Jones, 'Multiple Estates and Early Settlement', in *Medieval Settlement*, ed. Sawyer, pp. 15–40.
[160] See further, D. Hooke, 'Pre-Conquest Estates in the West Midlands: Preliminary Thoughts', *Journal of Historical Geography* 8 (1982), 227–44, and 'Village Development in the West Midlands', in *Medieval Villages. A Review of Current Work*, ed. D. Hooke, Oxford University Committee for Archaeology 5 (Oxford, 1985), pp. 125–54.
[161] Hooke, 'Pre-Conquest Estates', p. 242.

bury's hands, and that their areas were not fixed. When they returned they were sometimes larger, sometimes smaller, than when they had left. Many phenomena were no doubt at work: some estates, for example, apparently extended their boundaries to reduce their fiscal assessments.[162] We are largely ignorant of the developments that transformed the earliest endowment into the landscape of Domesday Book, but it is likely that the paucity of documentation masks a complex situation of change and adjustment to change.

In summary, the vagueness of the estate locations in early grants such as S.248 – and the long delay before most estates were specifically described – leaves us in doubt about their identification. As we have seen, this seems already to have been a problem in the tenth century. The original versions of many of the very early grants (if they existed in written form) were by that time probably of limited value, lacking as they did up-to-date identification of the estates and clear definitions of their limits. The provision of boundary clauses was one obvious solution to this problem; another was apparently the reconstruction or redrafting of early grants, as in the case of S.247. S.236 for Pennard, which survives as a tenth-century single sheet dated 681, is probably another example from the Glastonbury corpus. There need have been no criminal intent in this process, although the reconstitution of authentic early grants would have provided an excellent opportunity for the infiltration of fabrications into the collection, and several of Glastonbury's spurious charters may date from this period. Exactly when this putative recasting of the archive could have taken place, and how systematically, is not yet clear. But we can perhaps envisage a spring-cleaning of the archives in the second half of the tenth century, following on from a reorganization or at the least a review of Glastonbury's estates paralleling the well-documented activity at reformed Ely under Æthelwold.[163] We can only imagine the kind of administrative activity that would have been required over the centuries to keep the archive up to date with developments on the land.

How this should affect our thoughts concerning the facsimile-copy of S.248 is unclear. The seeming absence of all notice of this grant from the administrative records of Glastonbury may be due to the fact that, after such a reorganization and rewriting of the documents, the original charter had become redundant, even obsolete, especially after an updated version had been produced. Yet someone took the trouble to make a facsimile, possibly at the time of the putative archival reorganization, or possibly when documents were being collected for the production of proof of possession for the new Norman lords; and this facsimile was not destroyed, although its exemplar failed to survive. The original of S.248 – or its copy, or both – was used by the drafter of S.247, perhaps as early as the tenth century; one or the other (or, again, both) was still at Glastonbury in the early twelfth century, when

---

[162] Morland, 'Hidation on the Glastonbury Estates', pp. 77–80.
[163] As documented in the *Libellus Æthelwoldi*, ed. S. Keynes and A. Kennedy, forthcoming.

William of Malmesbury seems to have used it for his history. Small but significant distinctions (especially in the dating clause) between the two texts of S.247 in the Great Cartulary might suggest that S.248, although excluded from the collection, had been consulted during its compilation. Finally, later endorsements testify to the continuing use of the facsimile in the last centuries of the Middle Ages, after which we may be able to detect it playing a bit part in the largely unrecorded drama of the dispersal of Glastonbury's documents at the Dissolution.

Despite our uncertainty over the age of the surviving copy of S.248, it is clear that either it or its exemplar has shown remarkable staying power, belying its appearance of obsolescence. Obstinately different, the extant single sheet at least conforms to Glastonbury type by raising more questions than it answers. While remaining a very enigmatic document, it repays study by casting a rare though feeble light into areas of otherwise persistent obscurity.

DIPLOMA OF KING INE (S.248)[1]

+In nomine Domini Dei nostri Iesu Christi saluatoris, ea quæ secundum decreta canonum tractata fuerint, licet sermo tantum ad testimonium sufficeret, tamen pro incerta futuri temporis fortuna cirographorum sedulis[2] sunt roboranda. [3]Quæ propter[3] ego Ini regnante domino rex .lxv. casatos pro remedio animæ meæ Beruualdo abbati uideor contulisse his locorum limitibus <terram> designatam: iuxta flumen quod appellatur Tan .xx. casatos; et alibi in loco qui dicitur Pouelt .xx. manentes; necnon ex utroque margine fluminis cuius uocabulum est Duluting .xx. casatos pertingentes usque ad conuallem qui dicitur Corregescumb; ex occidentali uero plaga eiusdem uallis quinque casatos. Si quis hanc donationis cartulam augere et amplificare uoluerit, auget et amplificet Deus partem eius in libro uitæ; si quis frangere aut inrita facere tirannica potestate temtauerit, sciat se coram Christo et angelis eius rationem redditurum. Scripta est autem haec singrapha indictione .iiii., mense Iunio, anno ab incarnatione Domini .d.cc.v.

+Ego Bercuualdus archiepiscopus consentiens subscripsi.
+Ego Headda episcopus subscripsi.
+Ego Ecce episcopus subscripsi.
+Ego Tyrctil episcopus subscripsi.
+Ego Uualdarius episcopus subscripsi.
+Ego Egguuinus episcopus subscripsi.
+Ego Eluuinus episcopus subscripsi.
+Ego Aldhelmus episcopus subscripsi.
+Ego Daniel, plebi Dei ministrans, subscripsi.

[1]   A diplomatic text of this diploma will be provided, not here, but in the edition of the entire corpus of Glastonbury's charters in the British Academy's Anglo-Saxon Charter series (in preparation).

[2]   *leg.* scedulis.

[3...3] *leg.* quapropter.

An Early Irish Fragment of Isidore of Seville's Etymologiae*

JAMES P. CARLEY AND ANN DOOLEY

The question of the first arrival and subsequent circulation of the works of Isidore of Seville in Ireland is one which has engendered considerable scholarly debate.[1] The earliest surviving manuscript of any portion of the *Etymologiae* – Sankt Gallen, Stiftsbibliothek, 1399 a 1 (*CLA* VII, 995) – is Irish: that is, it may have been written either in Ireland or in an Irish centre on the Continent.[2] In Irish computistical circles, moreover, Isidore's writings seem to

*Although this article is a collaborative effort AD is responsible for the material on Old Irish and JPC made the journeys to Longleat House to examine the fragments *in situ*. In this latter endeavour he was aided by a Faculty of Arts Research Grant from York University, Toronto. Various scholars have read the typescript and we thank them here: Michelle Brown, David Dumville, Michael Herren, Michael Lapidge, Jennifer Morrish. Malcolm Parkes and Bernhard Bischoff provided important palaeographical judgements and Peter Baker and Dáibhí Ó Cróinín helped us to interpret the dating clauses. Ann M. Hutchison spent many hours poring over the badly rubbed boxed area under ultraviolet light and solved a variety of problems with readings. Aelred Watkin first suggested that the fragment needed re-examination. The Marquess of Bath, Longleat House, Warminster, Wiltshire, kindly gave permission to reproduce photographs of the fragments.

1   On Irish knowledge of Isidore from the earliest period see J. N. Hillgarth, 'Ireland and Spain in the Seventh Century', *Peritia* 3 (1984), 1–16, at 8–10, 15–16. M. Herren ('On the Earliest Irish Acquaintance with Isidore of Seville', in *Visigothic Spain: New Approaches*, ed. Edward James [Oxford, 1980], pp. 243–50) observed (p. 250): 'In the case of the *Etymologies*, it is at least possible that the work reached Ireland before the middle of the seventh century.' For a more cautious approach see Marina Smyth, 'Isidore of Seville and Early Irish Cosmography', *Cambridge Medieval Celtic Studies* 14 (1987), 69–102; it should be noted, however, that Smyth restricted her evidence to reflections of Isidore's scientific doctrines in Hiberno-Latin texts. On the influence of the Spanish liturgy and the use of Isidorian collects in the liturgy of Bangor in the seventh century see M. Curran, *The Antiphonary of Bangor* (Dublin, 1984), pp. 121–2, 135, 179–81. On the early transmission of Isidore see B. Bischoff, 'Die europäische Verbreitung der Werke Isidors von Sevilla', in his *Mittelalterliche Studien. Ausgewählte Aufsätze zur Schriftkunde und Literaturgeschichte*, 3 vols (Stuttgart, 1966–81) I, 171–94, and especially 180–7 on the importance of Irish transmission at the very earliest discernible stage of dissemination.

2   See A. Dold and J. Duft, *Die älteste irische Handschriften-Reliquie der Stiftsbibliothek St. Gallen mit Texten aus Isidors Etymologien*, Texte und Arbeiten 31 (Beuron, 1955); also Bischoff, 'Die europäische Verbreitung', pp. 180–1, who is of the opinion that it was written in Ireland. On dating see Bischoff, 'Eine verschollene Einteilung der Wissenschaften', in *Mittelalterliche Studien*, I, 273–88, at 285, n. 43. See also T. J. Brown, 'The

have been known from the middle of the seventh century and may even have been in circulation in Ireland before his death in 636.[3] The manuscript fragment of the *Etymologiae* which we present and discuss in this paper provides additional evidence which may serve to expand current understanding on this important question.

Longleat House, Marquess of Bath, NMR 10589 comprises an examination of Glastonbury Abbey properties compiled at the time of Henry of Sully's election as abbot in 1189.[4] The volume remains in its medieval parchment wrapper marked (in a fifteenth-century hand) 'liber henrici de solia/co Abbatis Glaston. /Et uocatur. A.' Underneath, a large 'A' has been written.[5] It is one of a large number of Glastonbury records to be found at Longleat House.[6] Presumably these came when Sir John Thynne (d. 1580), the builder of Longleat House, acquired property from the dissolved monastery. Longleat House, Marquess of Bath, NMR 10580 contains a letter, dated from the Court 20 February 1554/5, addressed to Sir John Thynne from William Paulet, Marquis of Winchester (Lord Treasurer), requiring Thynne to hand over to 'Nicholas Halfwell gentleman the king and quenes majesties Stuard of londes in the Com. of Somerset all suche bookes, munimentes, transcriptes and writinges as youe had oute of the house of Glastonburie. . . .' One can only assume that this request was ignored.[7]

As J. E. Jackson noted, the manuscript has flyleaves taken from an older manuscript.[8] Jackson took as his authority concerning these leaves the opinion of E. A. Bond, Keeper of Manuscripts at the British Museum, who had seen the volume in 1875 and who had concluded from the script (Insular minuscule) that 'The MS is contemporaneous. The fly-leaves are part of

Irish Element in the Insular System of Scripts to circa A.D. 850', in *Die Iren und Europa im früheren Mittelalter*, ed. H. Löwe, 2 vols (Stuttgart, 1982) I, 101–9, at 104.

3   For the extensive Irish use of a variety of Isidorian texts including the *Etymologiae* see *Cummian's Letter 'De Controversia Paschali'. Together with a Related Irish Computistical Tract, 'De Ratione conputandi'*, ed. and trans. M. Walsh and D. Ó Cróinín (Toronto, 1988). See also D. Ó Cróinín, 'A Seventh-Century Irish Computus from the Circle of Cummianus', *Proceedings of the Royal Irish Academy* 82 C (1982), 405–30, esp. 421–5.

4   See *Liber Henrici de Soliaco, Abbatis Glaston: An Inquisition of the Manors of Glastonbury Abbey*, ed. J. E. Jackson (London, 1882). On Sully's abbacy (1189–93) see *Cronica*, chs 98–101 (ed. Carley, pp. 180–9, 297).

5   Presumably the 'A' is part of a cataloguing system; another Glastonbury book (Longleat House, Marquess of Bath, NMR 10592) has 'Liber R' written on the cover.

6   On this topic see G. R. C. Davis, *Medieval Cartularies of Great Britain. A Short Catalogue* (London, 1958), pp. 49–51. No catalogue of the Longleat/Glastonbury documents has been published, although one will soon be forthcoming, so it is still necessary for the individual scholar to work his way through the card index at Longleat itself.

7   We owe this reference to Kate Harris, Librarian and Archivist to the Marquess of Bath. The request came during the reign of Queen Mary and it is tempting to link it with an abortive plan to restore the abbey – on which see J. P. Carley, *Glastonbury Abbey. The Holy House at the Head of the Moors Adventurous* (Woodbridge, 1988), pp. 170–1.

8   *Liber Henrici*, ed. Jackson, p. xii.

Isidore's Origines, written in English [*sic*] probably early in the 9th cent.'[9] Here the matter has rested ever since.

At some point, as it appears, two leaves must have been removed from an older manuscript (of much larger proportions) and folded along the width to create wrappers for Henry of Sully's book. In the fifteenth century, when the manuscript was rebound, these were retained as flyleaves. Each original leaf thus forms a front and back flyleaf. One flyleaf from the outer pair – the one which would have formed the back flyleaf of the Sully manuscript – has been lost, but that at the front (which we have labelled fol. 1) remains and measures 214 x 149 mm. Folio 2 (at the front of the book) and folio 3 (at the back of the book) measure 215 x 154 mm. and 179 x 153 mm. respectively; they are conjoint and suggest an original volume measuring a little in excess of 315 x 240 mm., although one must allow for some clipping of original margins. Folio 3r is the top part of a page which is concluded on 2v. The outer leaves (1r and 3v) have been badly damaged during the passage of the centuries and, although it is possible to make a partial transcription of 3v, 1r is more or less illegible. It does, however, have a repeat of the 'A' of the wrapper in a fifteenth-century hand and 'Glaston' written under this.

The ruling is dry-point and runs across the page; sometimes it has scored the parchment so heavily that there are now breakages along the ruling. The text is written in two columns with capitals projecting into the left margins. Prickings are evident down the left side of the page and also on the right margin of the only surviving pages with a right margin intact (i.e., 1v, 2v and 3r). The parchment itself has some original defects, most significant of which is the uneven edge at the top right of 3r (top left of 3v), to which the text has been accommodated. The ink is now a faded brown colour, but seems originally to have been black; certain areas (in particular, 2vb) seem less faded than others. Capital letters are surrounded by dots of a yellowish hue, a characteristic of early Insular manuscripts.[10]

As we have already pointed out, Bond asserted that the hand was English and dated from the ninth century. Given the fact that the manuscript could be traced to an English monastery in the late twelfth century, the English character of the script would seem a logical assumption. There are, however, a certain number of features – palaeographical and other – which suggest Ireland rather than England as the area of origin and which may also argue for a late seventh- or early eighth-century date rather than a ninth-century one. In the following analysis the characteristically Irish features will be signalled.

The punctuation includes the use of single and double dots as well as medial points. There seem to be two types of capitalization employed: full-

[9]   Handwritten note kept with volume at Longleat House.
[10]   Michelle Brown has kindly supplied the following analysis of the pigments: 'Iron ink – a suspension of black organic salt of iron mixed with other salts in solution – fades from black to brown. The orange/yellow tone may be due to the strength and duration of roasting – white lead turns yellow and then into orange tetroxide of lead. Those which fade back to yellow probably underwent a lesser roasting process.'

Plate I Longleat House, Marquess of Bath, NMR 10589, flyleaf, 3r

Plate II Longleat House, Marquess of Bath, NMR 10589, flyleaf, 2v

Plate III Longleat House, Marquess of Bath, NMR 10589, flyleaf, 3v

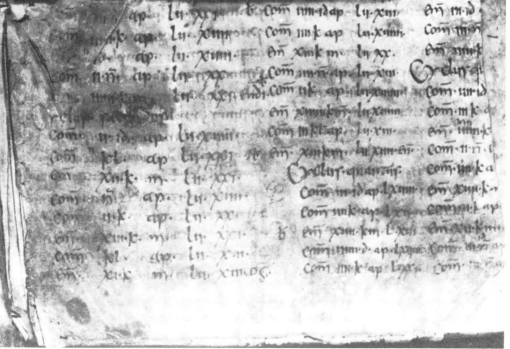

Plate IV Longleat House, Marquess of Bath, NMR 10589, flyleaf, 2r

Plate V Longleat House, Marquess of Bath, NMR 10589, flyleaf, 1v

scale capitalization marking major divisions, and a secondary system of enlarged initial letters which are not full capitals, and which mark the beginnings of periods. We have kept to this notation in our presentation of the text. Run-overs are normally carried to the line above and are marked by two oblique lines. Twice, run-overs carry to the line below and are marked off by a surrounding zig-zag line (lines 3 and 29). Corrections are noted with a single dot under the letter to be expunged. Accent marks are employed in a somewhat arbitrary fashion: for example, over *i* in final *-is* (*nobís, reliquís, electís, hereticís*; also in *síc*); over *u* in final *-ur* (*agnoscitúr*, etc.); over *a* (as in the preposition *á* and in *-ásci, dá, ác, -tántur*). In the Irish glosses length marks are used in *nésci* and *enáir*.[11]

Abbreviations include the following commonly found in Insular manuscripts: $\bar{a}$ = *-ari*; *k* = *autem*; *b:* = *bus*; *dr̄, dn̄r* = *dicitur, dicuntur*; ♯ = *enim*; + = *est*; *id* + = *id est* in main text by contrast with *·/·* in Irish gloss; *kl* = *kalendas*; $\bar{n}$ = *non*; *p* = *per*; *p̄* = *pre* (we have expanded to *prae* following the only instance written out [line 25]); *p* = *pro*; *q:* = *que*; *q̄si* = *quasi*; *q* = *quia*; *ꝗ* = *quod*; *qm̄d:* =

---

[11] It is possible that vowel length in the Irish gloss would have been marked by doubling rather than by the accent if the gloss were as early as the main text; see R. Thurneysen, *A Grammar of Old Irish* (Dublin, 1946), pp. 20–1. The marking of syllable length in *-is* endings and the marking of monosyllabic vowels is common in Irish Latin manuscripts. For comparative material on accent markings in early Irish manuscripts see *Adomnán's Life of Columba*, ed. A. O. Anderson and M. O. Anderson (Edinburgh, 1961), pp. 162–4.

quomodo; st̄ = sunt; l = uel. For *nomina sacra* the following abbreviations are used: *ds̄, dı̄, dm̄, dō, dn̄s, xpm̄ dm̄, scı̄, spū.*

The spelling variations are compatible with forms normally found in known Insular manuscripts.[12] Consonants show an occasional doubling: *dispossitum* (line 70),[13] *ussu* (line 162),[14] *repperitur* (line 181),[15] *addici* (line 159).[16] The common Late Latin epenthesis of *p* between *m* and *n* occurs: *condempn[ans]* (line 6), *praedampnauit* (line 25), *sollompnitas* (line 67).[17] So, apparently, does epenthesis of *c* before *x* in *sanc--nt* for *sanxerunt* (lines 32–3).

The vowels also show the kinds of variation derived from Vulgar Continental Latin and common to Hiberno-Latin texts: *a* for *e*, a rare confusion in Late Latin (and for the most part limited to -*er*- combinations, with opening to *a* under the influence of *r*) but much more common in Hiberno-Latin, as in *alaxundri-* (line 22), *alaxandrinus* (line 58), *alaxandriae* (line 63);[18] *o* for *u* in *commonique* (line 43) and *commoni* (line 45) is the common choice of Hiberno-Latin writers;[19] in Late Latin the groups -*ol*- and -*ul*- are interchangeable but the frequency of -*ul*- forms in Hiberno-Latin is reflected in *simbulum* (line 2) and *symbuli* (line 8); *i* for *e* as in *difiniuit* (lines 2–3), *[chal]cidonensis* (line 18), *hireticis* (line 24), and *decimnouenalis (line 80).*[20] *Sollompnitas* (line 67) is a

---

[12]   In what follows we are guided by the discussions and lists provided by Ludwig Bieler in *The Irish Penitentials*, Scriptores Latini Hiberniae 5 (Dublin, 1963), pp. 27–30; B. Löfstedt, *Der hibernolateinische Grammatiker Malsachanus* (Uppsala, 1965), pp. 86–107; and J. M. Picard, 'The Schaffhausen Adomnán – a Unique Witness to Hiberno-Latin', *Peritia* 1 (1982), 216–49. In particular, we have borne in mind Bieler's measured conclusion: 'It would be hazardous to declare as Hibernian this or that general type of spelling. There are, however, spellings of which Irish writers of Latin and Irish copyists of Latin texts seem to have been particularly fond' (p. 29). Picard's study is particularly useful as it is the only systematic analysis to date of the orthography of an early Hiberno-Latin manuscript. See also M. Herren, 'Sprachliche Eigentümlichkeiten in den hibernolateinischen Texten des 7. und 8. Jahrhunderts', in *Die Iren und Europa*, ed. Löwe, I, 425–33.

[13]   See Bieler, *The Irish Penitentials*, p. 29, and Picard, 'The Schaffhausen Adomnán', p. 242, n. 3, on *possitus* forms.

[14]   See Löfstedt, *Der hibernolateinische Grammatiker*, p. 102, on *ussu*.

[15]   See Picard, 'The Schaffhausen Adomnán', p. 243, for the morphological implications. He noted that the proportion of correct/incorrect forms for this spelling in Dorbéne's text was 21/7.

[16]   On possible Iona usage in the matter of prefixes see *ibid.* pp. 244–6.

[17]   Picard (*ibid.* p. 246) noted the comparative rarity of -*mpn*- forms in Dorbéne's usage; even in the very common *sollemnis* case, the *sollempn*- version occurs in only 40 per cent of the examples.

[18]   *Alaxander* is typically Hiberno-Latin; see examples cited in Löfstedt, *Der hibernolateinische Grammatiker*, p. 97.

[19]   See Bieler, *The Irish Penitentials*, pp. 5, 29–30; Löfstedt, *Der hibernolateinische Grammatiker*, pp. 100–1; Picard, 'The Schaffhausen Adomnán', p. 221.

[20]   In the case of *[chal]cidonensis* the medial *i* is a normal transliteration of η in the later Greek pronunciation. (We owe this observation to Michael Herren.) *Coietum* (line 39) may well be an example of a glide vowel representing scribal practice based on Old Irish. See Löfstedt, *Der hibernolateinische Grammatiker*, pp. 86–7 and notes; also Herren, 'Sprachliche Eigentümlichkeiten', p. 432, for the classification of *i/e* alternations. See also Picard's list, 'The Schaffhausen Adomnán', p. 226. In the main Picard's

rather eccentric rendering with apparent confusion of vowel quality before the nasal consonantal group -*mpn*-. We find two examples of *e* for *i*, as in *contenentur* (line 36) and *nonagenta* (line 64).[21] The common Late Latin practice of substituting *i* for *y* as in *sinodum* (line 37) and *ciclica* (line 77) occurs. There is, however, some evidence of the desire to retain *y*, as in *cyrillus* (line 63) and *cyclus* (line 69).[22] As is characteristic in Late Latin, *e* replaces *ae*: *[g]recorum* (line 9), *greco* (line 38), *presentem* (box, line 7). The reverse phenomenon is frequent in Hiberno-Latin texts where *ae* often replaces *e*, as in *aepiscopus* (line 64), *caelebrari* (line 67) and *saecundus* (line 97).[23] *Spaeculum* (line 180) is corrected from *saeculum* and hence does not count here. Other spellings of note are: *ag[ustus]* for *augustus* (line 12), a common Vulgar Latin feature, occurring frequently also in Hiberno-Latin texts;[24] *attamen* for *adtamen* (line 159) is the only example of assimilation, but is hardly in itself significant. The *u* of *alaxundri[num]* (line 22), involving a change of *a* > *u*, is unusual. It is possible that it reflects a misreading of an open *a* in the scribe's exemplar, but it could also represent a phonetic change influenced by phonological developments in Old Irish. In Old Irish, *a* > *o* > *u* was frequent when the following syllable had *u* and when *o* was followed by certain groups of consonants, of which -*nd*- was one. In certain conditions, moreover, an original *a* could appear as *u* when followed by a *u*-quality consonant as here.[25] The occurrence of *cognotionem* (line 178) – but note use of *cognitio* (line 173) – with confusion of *i* and *o* may reflect a levelling with related etymological forms, *cognoscere* etc.[26] There are a few examples of morphological confusion – common in Insular texts – in the matter of vowel contraction, as in -*atruum*

examples were drawn from the use of -*i*- forms with oblique cases of proper names such as *Brendini* etc.; for a morphologically similar form, however, with an -*i*- spelling, note *dulcidinem*; 'The Schaffhausen Adomnán', p. 226, n. 4. See Picard, *loc. cit.*, on the confusion of *de*- prefix forms, a confusion common for Irish scribes because of the *de*-/*di*- variation found in Old Irish, although this confusion occurs outside the Hiberno-Latin milieu as well – on which see M. Bonnet, *Le Latin de Grégoire de Tours* (Paris, 1890), pp. 108–9, 125, and C. H. Grandgent, *An Introduction to Vulgar Latin* (Boston, 1907), pp. 96–7.

21   The vowel confusion here may also be morphological rather than orthographical.
22   Picard, 'The Schaffhausen Adomnán', p. 229, noted that Dorbéne consistently gives *cyclus*.
23   There are no examples of *pre*- (with the exception of *presentem* in the box, line 7), and *prae*- is written out once in our text. This use of *prae*- contrasts with Iona practice as exemplified in Dorbéne's text. Nor does *ae* for *e*, common in Hiberno-Latin, appear in Dorbéne – see Picard, *ibid.* p. 232.
24   For the *agustus*/*augustus* variation see K. Jackson, *Language and History in Early Britain* (Edinburgh, 1953), pp. 93–4; Picard, 'The Schaffhausen Adomnán', p. 235; also H. Schuchardt, *Der Vokalismus des Vulgärlateins* (Leipzig, 1866), pp. 306 ff.
25   See Thurneysen, *A Grammar of Old Irish*, pp. 47–52. The relevant examples are listed on p. 51.
26   See Picard, 'The Schaffhausen Adomnán', p. 219, for the confusion between *cognitio* and *cognatio*. *a*/*o* confusion is extremely common in Insular texts: see Löfstedt, *Der hibernolateinische Grammatiker*, pp. 97–9.

for *patrum* (line 3) and -*sis* (line 10) for *ecclesiis*. Confusion is also seen between -*ensis*, -*iensis* formations, as in *caesarensis* (lines 57–8) for *caesariensis*.[27]

The script seems to be the work of a single scribe and is a clear and regular minuscule, compatible in its salient features with the work of Irish and Irish-influenced *scriptoria* from the late seventh to the mid-ninth centuries. The hand is neat, uniform and well spaced, a quality it shares with the Schaffhausen copy of Adomnán's *Vita S. Columbae* (Schaffhausen, Stadtbibliothek, Gen. 1 [*CLA* VII, 998]). In the hand of the scribe, Dorbéne, as displayed in the Schaffhausen text, the uniformity and spacing of the letters gives to the page a quality of dignity, maturity of conception, and general handsomeness which is not evident in our text. One might usefully compare the levelling-off of the tops of a series of minims and the close contiguity found in the writing of such words as *breuitate* (line 68) with similar treatment of such groupings in the Antiphonary of Bangor (Milan, Biblioteca Ambrosiana, C.5 inf. [*CLA* III, 311]); this remains a feature of some later Irish hands as in the St John's Gospel section of the Book of Dimma (Dublin, Trinity College 59 [A. IV. 23] [*CLA* II, 275b]).[28] The slightly wavy quality of the lines of writing resembles the treatment of the line in the Antiphonary of Bangor, as does the less set, rather free, quality of letter formation and forms in relation to each other. The Bangor hands are, however, much more varied and more predominantly cursive than our scribe's. The most striking resemblance to the Antiphonary of Bangor is the treatment of *a, e, r* and *t* at the end of the line where the final stroke of the letter is carried through and extended to create a finishing flourish. Our text – if one compares the general effect of the writing with Irish manuscripts at the later end of the period – has, on the whole, less pen-sharpness and angularity than representative later works like the Sankt Gallen Priscian (Sankt Gallen, Stiftsbibliothek, 904) or even the St John Dimma.

The treatment of the foot serifs is frequently awkward and inelegant. Majuscule and minuscule forms of *s* are used in upper-case letters with only one example of majuscule *s* in lower-case. The descenders of *s* and *r* are slightly longer and the *r* more compressed than in a comparable example like the Schaffhausen manuscript. The high shoulder and squared effect of *r* show more affinity with early rather than late examples. The frequent slight dip below the line of the last minim in *m* and *n* is not found in the hand of Dorbéne but is a feature shared with the Antiphonary of Bangor. The head of the tall *s* and the bow of the *p* have particularly low springing points, especially in *litterae notabiliores*. This is also a feature of the Antiphonary of Bangor. The sharply angled quality of the oblique stroke of capital *N* should be noted. Capital *A* is unusual in its finial flourishes, but there is no evidence

---

[27]   On -*uum* for -*um* see Löfstedt, *ibid.* p. 89; on -*is* for -*iis*, pp. 87–9; on -*iensis* for -*ensis*, pp. 89–92.

[28]   See T. O'Neill, *The Irish Hand: Scribes and their Manuscripts from the Earliest Times to the Seventeenth Century: With an Exemplar of Irish Scripts* (Dublin, 1984), plate IX and p. 67.

that the elaboration of finials amounts to a scheme of decorative capitals. There are no examples of *p* and *r* with clearly described open bow and retro point (*p*) as one would expect to find in Anglo-Saxon manuscripts of the eighth century such as the minuscule hands of the Leningrad Bede. There are, granted, some incipient examples (for example, at line 184, *speciem contemplentur*), but a tendency towards this habit also occurs in Dorbéne. In our text it is explained by the slight pooling of ink along the ruling line. The form of *g* with its closed, longish bow and capstroke which tilts downwards slightly on the right can also be compared with the Schaffhausen manuscript, the Antiphonary of Bangor and the St John section of the Book of Dimma: in the Antiphonary of Bangor the capstroke is invariably straight with a small closed bow at the end of a long downstroke which shows a marked turn to the right; in Schaffhausen the bow is occasionally closed and frequently the cap stroke tilts somewhat; in the St John Dimma, the flourish of the capstroke is quite level, the bow of the *g* is invariably closed but the down-curve of the capstroke is flatter than in our manuscript. The *a* is less squared than in Dimma and resembles the *a* of the Iona and Northumbrian traditions; there are no examples of open *a* although there are a few occurrences of triangular *a* with exaggerated extensions to the primary downstroke at the end of the line in the style of the Antiphonary of Bangor. On a few occasions the top extensions are also marked, thus yielding a resemblance to *ɑ*. On line 180 there occurs one example of *a* with a tall upward extension stroke.[29] The *ae* digraph is used frequently, but this is a general feature in Insular manuscripts from Dorbéne onwards. With one exception (line 179), there is only a single form for *d* (*ð*). It is uniformly uncial with a longer top-stroke than in Schaffhausen, and in size and direction the shaft resembles that of the *d* in the Antiphonary of Bangor but with less exuberant sinuousness. *I-longa* is heavily used at the beginnings of words. The occurrence of tall *c* and *e* with high bow may be considered as conservative features of Irish minuscule, which persist in Irish hands until the ninth century and cannot be used as dating criteria. The frequent flourish to the high-set tongue of *e* is also a feature of the very earliest Irish minuscule hands.[30] Ligatures of *ae*, *-li*, *-ti* (once with subscript *i*, line 160), *-si* (note *sicut*, line 163), *-ax* and *-et* occur, and there are few eccentricities in the matter of word division.

All the features taken together – especially the strong analogies with the Antiphonary of Bangor and the Schaffhausen Adomnán – indicate a date of *ca* 680x700 for the Longleat fragment.[31]

---

[29]   It should be noted that most Irish minuscule examples tend to use more than one form of *a*.

[30]   For these conservative features see W. O'Sullivan's review of T. O'Neill's *The Irish Hand* in 'Insular Calligraphy: Current State and Problems', *Peritia* 4 (1985), 346–59, at 350; also A. Breen, 'A New Irish Fragment of the *Continuatio* to Rufinus-Eusebius *Historia Ecclesiastica*', *Scriptorium* 41 (1987), 185–204, at 197.

[31]   Malcolm Parkes in a verbal communication and Bernhard Bischoff in written correspondence have, moreover, independently suggested that our fragment should be dated *ca* 700.

The text itself is taken from Isidore of Seville's *Etymologiae*, Book 6, chapter 16, and Book 7, chapter 1.[32] Apart from purely orthographical variations, there are readings which are not identical to those found in any other of the few reported copies (a study of the complex textual history of the *Etymologiae* remains to be undertaken):[33] at line 15 *haec* is added; *[nat]uras* for *naturis* (line 16); *[Constantin]opolinum* for *Constantinopolitanum* (line 20); *rursus* for *rursum* (line 23); *confiteatur* for *confiteamur* (line 28); *manente* for *manent* (line 34); *stabilito* (corrected from *stabilitate*) for *stabilita* (line 34); *cuiusque rationis* for *cuius quidem rationem* (line 62); *decinouies* for *decem nouies* (line 65); *die* added after *kalendas* (line 66);[34] *in ueritate. sine ueritate* (line 71) for *sine uarietate*; *cyclus . . . uocatus* for *cyclum . . . uocatum* (line 69); *sumptum sit* for *sumpsit* (line 162); *de deo* for *deo* (line 176); *domine* inserted into the Biblical quotation (lines 177, 178). Some of these variations may reflect the scribe's own rationalization or intervention in the text he was transcribing; for example, with *stabilito* for *stabilita* (line 34) he was obviously construing this as an adjective dependent on *uigore* and adjusting his text accordingly. With the insertion of *domine* in the quotation from Psalm 79 he was reverting to the common formula as found, for example, in Psalm 84, line 8, and subsequently in a variety of liturgical uses: *ostende nobis, Domine, misericordiam tuam.* Longleat shares a number of readings with Bern, Burgerbibliothek, 101 (Lindsay's B), Leiden, Bibliotheek der Rijksuniversiteit, Voss. lat. F. 74 (Lindsay's C), and Madrid, Biblioteca nacional, Tol. 15, 8 (Lindsay's T): *praedampnauit* for *condemnauit* (line 25); *uictorinus* for *uictorius* (line 60); *quia* for *qua* (line 174). The reading *deum* for *dominum* (line 26) occurs in B and T. At line 27 Longleat has a reading found otherwise only in C among reported copies: *in eum* for *in eo.*[35] All these variants may eventually lead to new conclusions about the version of Isidore's *Etymologiae* circulating in Ireland; what they immediately suggest, however, is that we have here a text which is somewhat carelessly copied by a scribe who was, perhaps, overly confident of his knowledge of Latin.

It is impossible to determine whether or not this fragment was originally part of a complete copy of the *Etymologiae*. It is worth noting that it consists

---

[32] See *Isidori Hispalensis Episcopi Etymologiarum sive Originum Libri XX*, ed. W. M. Lindsay, 2 vols (Oxford, 1911).

[33] See, however, M. Reydellet, 'La Diffusion des "Origines" d'Isidore de Séville au haut moyen-âge', *Mélanges d'archéologie et d'histoire publiés par l'Ecole Française de Rome* 78 (1966), 398–437.

[34] Dáibhí Ó Cróinín has informed us that the gloss *die* is also in the Augsburg, Stadtbibliothek, Lat. Frag. 42 text of Isidore's computus, incorporated into the text as here. In the quotations from Isidore in Cummian's paschal letter, moreover, there are over thirty variations from the textual readings cited by Lindsay. Thus considerable textual freedom appears to have been the norm in a seventh-century Irish centre of learning making use of the text of the *Etymologiae*.

[35] Interestingly, the Sankt Gallen fragments – assigned by Bischoff and others to Ireland – are more closely related textually to C than to any other manuscript; on which see J. N. Hillgarth, 'Visigothic Spain and Early Christian Ireland', *Proceedings of the Royal Irish Academy* 62 C (1961–3), 167–94, at 184–5.

primarily of a computistical section which was often excerpted.[36] At the bottom of 3rb, nevertheless, the number *luiii* appears under ultraviolet light; although this does not coincide with a new section heading in the standard version of the *Etymologiae*, scholars do not know when the text of Isidore was first laid out in chapters and sections. The number, therefore, does seem to indicate some sort of division and shows that we are dealing with more of the *Etymologiae* than the computistical section alone.[37]

Isidore took his Easter table from that of Dionysius Exiguus, which ran from A.D. 532 to 626; he believed mistakenly that this 95-year table would repeat itself in perpetuity. In the Longleat manuscript the table begins on 3v with 532 and carries down, although there are some problems with readings, to 541. Folio 2r begins at 545 (with three entries obscured by the binding) and carries through to 558. Moving back to 3v we get a boxed area containing independent numerical calculations – on which see below – which obstructs the next 11 entries (in column 3 rather than 2 because of the space occupied by the box), although the first component of each can just be made out. We then follow with 570 in column 2 and go down to 576. The second column in 2r begins with 580 and continues to 593. When we return to 3v – that is, the missing part – the box must have made it impossible to have a third column for much of the page, but there would presumably have been space lower down for 594 to 599 (matching 570 to 575). The third column of 2r, as would be expected, begins with 604 and carries on to 617. Allowing for trimmed sections this then represents substantially a copy of Isidore's table.

An odd feature of this manuscript is the pair of boxes enclosing dating calculations found within the paschal table. The boxed area disturbs the layout of the paschal table considerably, as indicated above, and this might suggest that it is an arrangement worked out by our scribe, even if the contents of the boxes do not originate with him. Possibly it stood in the exemplar as a long marginal gloss. There is, moreover, an arrow at the beginning of the second box, linking it with the final clause of the introduction to the paschal table (line 79).[38] Unfortunately, much of this boxed area is now illegible because of rubbing and our transcription is tentative at best; nevertheless it is clear that it concerns the translation of dating by *anno mundi* into dating by Spanish era. The inclusion of dating by Spanish era is a most

---

[36]   On Irish computistical writings in general see *Bedae Opera de Temporibus*, ed. C. W. Jones (Cambridge, Mass., 1943); W. Stevens, 'Scientific Instruction in Early Insular Schools', in *Insular Latin Studies*, ed. M. Herren (Toronto, 1981), pp. 83–111; D. Ó Cróinín, 'A Seventh-Century Irish Computus'; also D. Ó Cróinín, 'The Irish Provenance of Bede's Computus', *Peritia* 2 (1983), 229–47.

[37]   The fact that the fragment contains part of the following chapter of the *Etymologiae*, totally unrelated to computistical matters, also indicates that the original manuscript must have contained at least a portion of the *Etymologiae* rather than the computistical segment only.

[38]   At the end of the paschal table in the *Etymologiae* there is a statement on dating, 'A conditione mundi usque ad hunc nouissimum cyclum conputantur anni'; as Lindsay noted, there are actual date-insertions at this point in several manuscripts. This arrangement may have been the model from which our box derived.

unusual feature to find in any early medieval manuscript outside Spain and our example may possibly be unique in Insular manuscripts. We seem to have two dating statements, one in each box. Insofar as we can read box 1, the dating statement is confused; it may be simply a preliminary draft or it may be a rather botched attempt which is rendered more satisfactorily in box 2, as the similar figures in both boxes *dclxl + iii* seem to suggest.[39] Box 2 seems to present a fairly coherent statement. The *anno mundi* dating and Spanish era dating both yield the same year as follows. The Spanish era dating clause probably reads as 693 if we accept that there is run-over of the year number from line 4 to line 5. The *anno domini* date can be derived from this by subtracting 38, i.e., 655. *Anno mundi* 5854 (line 8), in turn, can be rendered *anno domini* by subtracting 5199, giving the required 655. The ancestor of our manuscript (whether immediate or at some remove), then, would appear to date from 655 and to be Spanish in origin.

As might be expected in an Irish computistical context, there are a number of marginal glosses. Most particularly, at line 65 we have *.i. numerans* glossing *calculans*, and at line 66 *.i. aes nésci for kalendas enáir* glosses *quota kalendas die uel luna debeat paschalis sollompnitas caelebrari*. It is, of course, the Irish gloss which is of primary interest here. The initial letters of the first grouping are difficult to read since they are written to accommodate the descenders of the *p* of *per* in the line above, but the most reasonable reading is as *.i. aes*. The *n* of *nésci* seems to be in a lighter ink than the rest of the gloss and to have shorter minim strokes than the usual *n* of the glossing hand. The marking of nasalization after neuter *o*-stem *aes* is grammatically correct, but is not at all consistently shown in Irish glosses of the eighth century. It is, however, standard by the ninth century, as the evidence of the Milan glossator attests.[40] The addition of *for kalendas enáir* – giving 'what the age of the moon is on the kalends of January' – renders the entire gloss somewhat inappropriate for its immediate context.[41]

The gloss *aes nésci* is of a common type, occurring in at least three computistical texts of Irish scribal origin:

[39] On the use of Greek counting in Irish computistical texts see D. Ó Cróinín, 'Mo-sinnu moccu Min and the Computus of Bangor', *Peritia* 1 (1982), 281–95, at 292–3.

[40] The frequency of the spelling *aesca* elsewhere in the gloss material for *esca* indicates a certain correctness on the part of the scribe, for whom *ae* would be simply a common confusion with *e* inherited from Late Latin. *Ae* is distinguished from the ligatured form in Old Irish and is reserved as an alternative spelling of the diphthong *ai*. (See Thurneysen, *A Grammar of Old Irish*, p. 18.) For the marking or non-marking of nasalization in Old Irish see Thurneysen, *A Grammar of Old Irish*, pp. 148–9, and p. 5 on the date of the Milan glosses.

[41] Though variants occur in the spelling of this loan word – *ienáir* in *Félire Oengusso*, January 1 (s. ix *in.*) and *enair* in *Saltair na Rann*, l. 7532 (s. x) – our spelling is normal. See *The Dictionary of the Irish Language*, s.n. *enáir* for these and other references.

i. The computistical fragments attached to Vatican City, Biblioteca Apostolica Vaticana, lat. 5755, 2r (*CLA* S, 1734).⁴² It occurs here as a series of glosses on finding the date of Easter: *do toscelad aiss aesci far caisc himart*; *do toscelad ais aesci farcaisc hinaapril; ais aesci farcaiscc.*

ii. Nancy, Bibliothèque Municipale, 317 (flyleaf), a single folio containing the Dionysiac Paschal Arguments xi and xiii with Latin and Irish notes and glosses.⁴³ It yields the same glossing formula in a slightly different context: *do toscelad cidaes nescai bíss for kl. Ian.*

iii. Karlsruhe, Badische Landesbibliothek, Aug. perg. 167. This Reichenau manuscript contains a selection of Bedan computistical work on fols 5–12 with copious Irish notes and glosses and has been tentatively dated by Charles W. Jones to the early ninth century.⁴⁴ The gloss occurs in the middle of a lengthy Latin and Irish gloss clarifying a difficult computistical point in chapter 20 of Bede's *De temporum ratione*: 'ní accomlatar epactae xi kl. ap. fri riaglóri in illo anno dothoscélad áis ésci bís for kl. cachmís in primo anno ithe riaglóri insin adchomlatar fri epacta xi kl. ap. hicach bliadin tresinnóedécde núile'. Later in this chapter the gloss occurs again: *aes nésci kl. ian. in primo anno.* The tone of confidence of the Karlsruhe Bedan glosses implies the presence of an assured tradition of computistical competence which may well pre-date the main text.

In all these examples a habit of mixing Latin and Irish glosses is standard and our fragment is entirely normal in this respect. The glossing hand is not the hand of the main text – which was itself, in fact, corrected by the original scribe. In general neatness the hand resembles the tiny Insular glossing hands of the late eighth and early ninth centuries, close to that found, for example, in the Irish Würzburg manuscript – i.e., Würzburg, Universitätsbibliothek, M.p.th.f.12 (*CLA* IX, 1403) – dated by Lowe to the end of the eighth century. The *s* and *r* have low-springing ascenders, and a high bowed *e* and high *c* appear. As for its content, it seems that there has been a slippage of the appropriate reference from a paschal calculation to a calculation

---

⁴² *Thesaurus Palaeohibernicus*, ed. W. Stokes and J. Strachan, 2 vols (Cambridge, 1901–3) II, 39–41. The editors believed the language of the Irish glosses to be that of the eighth century with no evidence that they had been copied; this was not contradicted by Lowe's dating of the fragments (i.e., s. viii–ix). The plate of this page in *CLA* is numbered as p. 3, counting another fragment – Milan, Biblioteca Ambrosiana, L. 22. sup., fols 146–7 – as p. 1.

⁴³ It may well be that these two fragments constitute a unified computistical text, and Lowe treated them as part of the same manuscript. Stokes and Strachan, on the other hand, did not think that this was the same manuscript as the Vatican fragment. They gave a ninth-century date for this page but provided no evidence concerning how they reached this conclusion.

⁴⁴ For a description see *Bedae Opera de Temporibus*, ed. Jones, pp. 145–6, 163–4; for the Irish glosses see *Thesaurus Palaeohibernicus*, ed. Stokes and Strachan, II, 10–30, at 17. Jones seemed to favour an earlier ninth-century date for the hand of the main text and did not discuss the Irish and Latin glosses. The glosses are in various hands and the editors of *Thesaurus Palaeohibernicus* accepted the evidence afforded by a datable note for 831 (p. x). There is one other datable note – *Aed rex hiberniae moritur* – which occurs in the Annals of Ulster, s.a. 819.

relative to the New Year in the context of a Dionysian table. In any case it is clear that the gloss itself is quite common. One might even speculate that these types of gloss first came into existence in a mid-seventh-century period of intense Irish computistical activity and that they then continued in use in Irish circles for quite some time thereafter.

A variety of evidence – in terms both of the hand and the gloss – indicates that this manuscript was written by an Irishman, and presumably (though not certainly) in Ireland. It must, however, have been at Glastonbury by 1189 to be dismembered and used as wrappers for Henry of Sully's book. At this time, moreover, it presumably was considered useless by the Glastonbury community. Why? Here, there seem to be a number of pertinent factors.

During his abbacy (1126–71) Henry of Blois had almost fifty books transcribed for the library: among these was *Ysidorus Ethimologiarum.*[45] When, moreover, the great catalogue of books *'de librario'* was put together in 1247/8 the compiler noted *Ysidorus Ethimologiarum. bon[us]*; this presumably is a reference to the copy made for Henry of Blois.[46] The catalogue also lists *Pars Ethimologiarum. Sinonima Ysidori. uetust[us] et inutil[is].*[47] It is clear, then, that there was more than one copy of the *Etymologiae* in the collection by the thirteenth century and that these copies had been there for some time. In 1189, therefore, the Longleat copy – if it were a complete or semi-complete text and not part of a computistical collection – may have been an old and useless duplicate, valuable only as scrap.

Another factor, however, may also be relevant. On St Urban's Day (25 May), 1184, there was a great conflagration at Glastonbury Abbey which destroyed almost the whole monastic complex. When the thirteenth-century chronicler Adam of Damerham described the fire, he specifically related that among other losses many books were destroyed.[48] After the fire the monks quickly turned to rebuilding and in 1186 the new Chapel of St Mary was dedicated.[49] Presumably, too, the book collection, of which the monks were so justly proud, was also being refurbished and reorganized. Although the Longleat Isidore shows no obvious sign of fire-damage, it is at least possible that it was one of the volumes weeded out as the new collection began to be assembled.[50]

[45] For these books see *AD*, ed. Hearne, II, 317–18; also T. W. Williams, *Somerset Mediaeval Libraries* (Bristol, 1897), pp. 49–51.
[46] The inventory was first printed in *JG*, ed. Hearne, II, 423–44, and was reprinted by Williams, *Somerset Mediaeval Libraries*, pp. 55–76.
[47] It is tempting to suppose that we have reference here to the manuscript from which our fragment was taken, especially since recent evidence suggests that the earliest copies of the *Etymologiae* to circulate in Ireland consisted of sections only. The catalogue also lists a contemporary copy of the works of Isidore: 'Item omnes libri Ysidori, de labore G. de Sowy, quos adhuc ipse habet.'
[48] See *AD*, ed. Hearne, II, 334.
[49] See Carley, *Glastonbury Abbey*, pp. 22–3.
[50] One might be tempted to speculate that perhaps the presence of Henry of Blois' new copy of the *Etymologiae* would have rendered the old manuscript in its 'difficult' Insular script redundant and more or less useless.

How – and where – the Irish gloss came to be placed in this manuscript is intriguing. If the manuscript was written in Ireland, as seems likely to have been the case, then it would seem logical to assume that the gloss was inserted before the book migrated to England. It is not impossible, however, that the manuscript came to England before the gloss was inserted by a visiting Irishman, although this seems an uneconomical hypothesis. It is even possible that both book and gloss were written by Irishmen living abroad.[51]

The question of the book's migration, too, is a fascinating one. There is a long tradition of connections between Ireland and the south-west of England. Recently Dáibhí Ó Cróinín has argued that much of the computistical material travelled from southern and south-midlands Irish schools in the mid-seventh century through a south-western English route.[52] As early as the mid-seventh century, too, Englishmen were going to Ireland for their studies.[53] In one of his letters, St Aldhelm (b. 630x640), abbot of Malmesbury and bishop of Sherborne, warned Wihtfrith of the moral hazards of Ireland: a dangerous fascination with classical pagan mythology and the temptations of bawdy houses.[54] In another letter to one Heahfrith (*ca* 675), Aldhelm set out arguments concerning the superiority of English education over Irish. 'Why', he asked, 'is Ireland, whither assemble the thronging students by the fleet-load, exalted with a sort of ineffable privilege, as if here in the fertile soil of Britain, teachers who are citizens of Greece and Rome cannot be found, who are able to unlock and unravel the murky mysteries of the heavenly library to the scholars who are eager to study them?'[55] A. S. Cook argued that the recipient of this letter must have been Ecgfrith, abbot of Glastonbury (*ca* 719), but Michael Herren has shown that his arguments were 'dubious' at best.[56] What the letter does indicate, however, is the continuing cultural relations between southern England and Ireland in the last quarter of the seventh century.

The Irish connections carried on throughout the Anglo-Saxon period, although there was active discouragement of pilgrimage by some members of

---

[51] On the inadvisability of drawing firm conclusions concerning date and/or provenance from the evidence of vernacular glosses see Vivien Law, 'Notes on the Dating and Attribution of Anonymous Latin Grammarians of the Early Middle Ages', *Peritia* 1 (1982), 250–67, at 251–4.

[52] Ó Cróinín, 'The Irish Provenance of Bede's Computus', pp. 232 ff.

[53] Ó Cróinín, *ibid*. p. 244, has observed that 'English connections with southern Ireland are well attested for the seventh century, as all readers of Bede's History will know. Indeed, there is some ground for saying that the English presence in Ireland has been unduly overshadowed by the more obvious role which the Iona paruchia played in the development of the Northumbrian schools. Travellers such as these could have been the means by which the Irish computus passed first to England and then to the continent.' See also *Aldhelm. The Prose Works*, trans. M. Lapidge and M. Herren (Ipswich, 1979), p. 139.

[54] See *Aldhelm. The Prose Works*, trans. Lapidge and Herren, p. 139.

[55] *Ibid*. p. 163.

[56] A. S. Cook, 'Who was the Ehfrid of Aldhelm's Letter?', *Speculum* 2 (1927), 363–73; *Aldhelm. The Prose Works*, trans. Lapidge and Herren, p. 145.

the Irish ecclesiastical hierarchy beginning in the late eighth century. Kathleen Hughes noted, however, that the ninth-century source material is very sparse and that by the tenth century – a period for which we have more evidence – there was an Irish presence at the court of King Æthelstan (924–39). She concluded, nevertheless, that 'the time of greatest mutual influence between the two churches was the seventh and eighth centuries'.[57]

Not surprisingly, books from Ireland arrived in England from the very earliest period of contact,[58] and this sort of exchange continued throughout the period, as in the case of the ninth- or tenth-century MacDurnan Gospels.[59] The Rushworth Gospels are particularly significant in the context of this paper since they were written by the Irishman Mac Regol and glossed in tenth-century Old English. As Hughes observed, the points of contact were so great that both the transmission of texts and the development of handwriting and manuscript layout were influenced.[60]

Even if one discounts the Heahfrith-Ecgfrith connection, there are early traditions concerning an Irish presence at Glastonbury itself.[61] Michael Lapidge, for example, has speculated that the Glastonbury association with

---

[57]   K. Hughes, 'Evidence for Contacts Between the Churches of the Irish and English from the Synod of Whitby to the Viking Age', *England Before the Conquest. Studies in Primary Sources Presented to Dorothy Whitelock*, ed. P. Clemoes and K. Hughes (Cambridge, 1971), pp. 49–67, at 67 (reprinted in her *Church and Society in Ireland A.D. 400–1200* [London, 1987], no. XVI).

[58]   For a seventh-century example see *CLA* A, 1864 (described by B. Bischoff and V. Brown, 'Addenda to *Codices Latini Antiquiores*', *Mediaeval Studies* 47 [1985], 317–66, at 348–9).

[59]   London, Lambeth Palace 1370. For a recent discussion of the manuscript see Simon Keynes, 'King Athelstan's Books', *Learning and Literature in Anglo-Saxon England*, ed. M. Lapidge and H. Gneuss (Cambridge, 1985), pp. 143–201, at 153–9.

[60]   See Hughes, 'Evidence for Contacts', pp. 59–61, 66–7; also *Aldhelm. The Prose Works*, trans. Lapidge and Herren, p. 32. For other recent studies of the relationships between Anglo-Saxon and Irish hands see Brown, 'The Irish Element', and P. McGurk, 'The Gospel Book in Celtic Lands before A. D. 850: Contents and Arrangement', *Irland und die Christenheit (Ireland and Christendom)*, ed. P. Ní Chatháin and M. Richter (Stuttgart, 1987), pp. 165–89. Two other early Irish-minuscule manuscripts which were in England by the tenth century are London, British Library, Add. 40618 (*CLA* II, 179) and the manuscript now found divided as Cambridge, Trinity College B. 10. 5 (216) and London, British Library, Cotton Vitellius C. viii. A radically dissenting view on the provenance of important Irish and Anglo-Saxon manuscripts of the late seventh and early eighth century was cogently presented by D. Ó Cróinín, 'Rath Melsigi, Willibrord and the Earliest Echternach manuscripts', *Peritia* 3 (1984), 17–49.

[61]   On Glastonbury and the Irish in general see J. F. Kenney, *Sources for the Early History of Ireland: Ecclesiastical* (New York, 1929), revised L. Bieler (New York, 1966), pp. 606–8. In 'Glastonbury Abbey', *The Quest for Arthur's Britain*, ed. G. Ashe (London, 1968), pp. 119–38, at 129, C. A. R. Radford argued that the Glastonbury cults of St Patrick and St Indract suggested an Irish influence at Glastonbury before the Anglo-Saxon conquest of Somerset in the mid-seventh century. Citing Hughes's more conservative approach, M. Lapidge, 'The Cult of St Indract at Glastonbury', *Ireland in Early Mediaeval Europe: Studies in Memory of Kathleen Hughes*, ed. D. Whitelock, R. McKitterick and D. Dumville (Cambridge, 1982), pp. 179–212, at 180, n. 9, has suggested that Radford has shown himself somewhat 'credulous' in this reasoning and that there is no real certainty in the matter.

St Indract may have a genuine basis to the extent that an Irishman called Indrechtach may indeed have been martyred near Glastonbury in 854.[62] If so, then, we do have an early tradition of at least one Irishman passing through Glastonbury on his Roman pilgrimage. The whole St Patrick/Glastonbury connection, moreover, must be considered.[63] Much of the evidence hinges on statements found in the *Vita S. Dunstani* composed by B. around 1000. In this *uita* the author seems to suggest that there was a well-established colony of Irish pilgrims at Glastonbury by the time of Dunstan's birth (probably in 909) and that they possessed books:[64]

> Porro Hibernensium peregrini locum, quem dixi, Glestoniae, sicut et caeterae fidelium turbae, magno colebant affectu, et maxime ob Beati Patricii iunioris[65] honorem, qui faustus ibidem in Domino quieuisse narratur. Horum etiam libros rectae fidei tramitem phylosophantes, diligenter excoluit, aliorumque prudentum, quos ab intimo cordis aspectu patrum sanctorum assertione solidatos esse persensit solubili semper scrutamine indagauit.[66]

H. P. R. Finberg traced this so-called Irish school at Glastonbury back to the reign of King Alfred, using the Anglo-Saxon Chronicle entry of 891 concerning the three Irishmen washed up in Cornwall as evidence, but (as Lapidge has observed) this reasoning is purely hypothetical; Lapidge himself concluded more tentatively that 'by the tenth century, then – and perhaps not earlier – Glastonbury was the centre of a cult of St Patrick and a destination of wandering Irish *peregrini*.'[67] Be that as it may, what does seem entirely possible is that Isidore's *Etymologiae* could have figured among the collection of books brought over by the Irish and that the Longleat fragment is a survivor from the Irish collection, one of the very books used by Dunstan himself as a student.[68]

---

62   Lapidge, 'The Cult of St Indract', p. 192.
63   On this topic see in particular C. H. Slover, 'William of Malmesbury and the Irish', *Speculum* 2 (1927), 268–83; H. P. R. Finberg, *West-Country Historical Studies* (Newton Abbot, 1969), pp. 70–88; and Lapidge, 'The Cult of St Indract', pp. 182–3.
64   On the increased stability of Irish pilgrims by the ninth century see K. Hughes, 'The Changing Theory and Practice of Irish Pilgrimage', *The Journal of Ecclesiastical History* 11 (1960), 143–51. In the later period, as she observed (p. 148), 'the perpetual pilgrim to the continent was now usually the ambitious scholar with a definite object in view . . . .' Also see, however, her somewhat changed views in *The Church in Early Irish Society* (London, 1966); T. M. Charles-Edwards, 'The Social Background of Irish Peregrinatio', *Celtica* 11 (1976), 43–59.
65   On the conflicting manuscript references to the older or younger St Patrick see Lapidge, 'The Cult of St Indract', p. 182, n. 20.
66   B., *Vita S. Dunstani*, ch. 5; *Memorials of St Dunstan*, ed. W. Stubbs, RS 63 (London, 1874), pp. 3–52, at 10–11. Michael Lapidge and Michael Winterbottom are preparing a new edition of this *uita* for the Oxford Medieval Texts series.
67   Lapidge, 'The Cult of St Indract', p. 183.
68   St Dunstan was a great collector of books – on which see J. P. Carley, 'Two Pre-Conquest Manuscripts from Glastonbury Abbey', *Anglo-Saxon England* 16 (1987), 197–212, at 197–8 – and it is at least possible, though not likely, that he himself acquired this manuscript. Nevertheless, all that can be definitively established in the

In the edition which follows we have observed scribal punctuation. At the bottom of the page we have included a parallel text taken from W. M. Lindsay's edition of Isidore's *Etymologiae*, maintaining the *'u'/'v'* distinction as Lindsay presented it.[69] Expansions have been marked in italics. Square brackets ([]) indicate conjectural readings where the original is badly blurred. The ellipsis sign (. . .) shows places where the original is entirely illegible or where there are sections of text missing through manuscript damage. Double oblique lines show page or column division. Single oblique lines slanting to the right (/) indicate runovers to the line above in the original manuscript; single oblique lines slanting to the left (\) indicate runovers to the line below. In the readings from Lindsay rounded brackets enclose sections missing from the Longleat text. Through the kindness of Peter Jones, Librarian of King's College, Cambridge, we were provided with an ultraviolet lamp and were able to expose sections of the text otherwise illegible. In the tables the abbreviations have not been expanded, in order to maintain the layout; macrons are used to indicate scribal practice.

---

final analysis – as David Dumville has pointed out to us (personal communication) – is that the fragments were at Glastonbury by the end of the twelfth century; they cannot be proved to have arrived as early as the times of St Dunstan.

[69]   Unfortunately Books VI and VII have not yet appeared in the new version of the *Etymologiae* being published in the Auteurs Latins du Moyen Age series headed by Jacques Fontaine and Yves Lefèvre.

TEXT

... tri d*eu*m filium   (3ra)
... simbulum difi
... atruu*m* \ niuit.
... Constantinopo
... e macedonium   5
... ntem condemp
... m patri et filio
... t. dans symbuli
... recorum et lati
... sis p*rae*dicat.   10
... na. prima^a .cc.
... e theodosio^b ag
... orium duas^c per
... em iusto anathe
... t. haec ostendens   15
... uras. unam d*omi*ni
... / xxx. sacerdotu*m*
... cidonensis .dc.

a   iiiia Fuit hunc missus *above in later hand*
b   ll lll *above in later hand*
c   due llll *above in later hand*

substantialem Deo patri Deum filium   (*Etymologiae* 6. 16.6)
idem sancta synodus per symbolum defi-
nivit. Secunda synodus centum quinquaginta Patrum
sub Theodosio seniore Constantinopo-
lim congregata est, quae Macedonium,   5
sanctum Spiritum Deum esse negantem, condem-
nans, consubstantialem Patri et Filio
sanctum Spiritum demonstravit, dans symboli
formam quam tota Graecorum et Lati-
norum confessio in ecclesiis praedicat.   10
Tertia synodus Ephesina prima ducentorum
episcoporum sub iuniore Theodosio Aug-
usto edita, quae Nestorium duas per-
sonas in Christo adserentem iusto anathe-
mate condemnavit, ostendens   15
manere in duabus naturis unam Domini
nostri Iesu Christi personam.
Quarta synodus Chalcedonensis sexcentorum triginta sacerdotum

... iano principe habita *est* in
       ... opolinum //   20
     ... eius defenso   (2va)
... orum quondam alaxundri
... scopum et ipsum rursus nes
... um reliquis hireticis una pa
... ntentia *prae*dampnauit. Prae   25
... adem synodus *christum deum* sic na
... irgine. ut in eum substantia*m*
... e et humanae confiteatur
... ii. synodi princi\naturae
... fidei doctrinam plenissime   30
... ntes. Sed et si qua s*unt* concilia
... *sa*ncti patres sp*iritu dei* pleni sanc
... nt. post istoru*m* .iiii. auctorita
... omni manente stabilito.^d ui
... e. quorum gĕsta in hoc opere   35
... ita^e contenentur. //
Sinodum a*utem* ex   (3rb)
greco interpr*ae*tari.

^d ate *expunged*, o *superscript*
^e *There is a space between these two words, but no erasure appears.*

sub Marciano principe habita est, in
qua Eutychem Constantinopolitanum   20
(abbatem Verbi Dei et carnis unam naturam)
pronuntiantem, et eius defenso
rem Dioscorum, quondam Alexandri-
num Episcopum, et ipsum rursum Nes-
torium cum reliquis haereticis una Pa-
trum sententia condemnavit; prae-   25
dicans eadem synodus Christum Dominum sic na-
tum de Virgine, ut in eo substantiam
et divinae et humanae confiteamur
naturae. Haec sunt quattuor synodi princi-
pales, fidei doctrinam plenissime   30
praedicantes; sed et si qua sunt concilia
quae sancti Patres spiritu Dei pleni sanx-
erunt, post istorum quattuor auctorita-
tatem omni manent stabilita vi-
gore, quorum gesta in hoc opere   35
condita continentur.
Synodum autem ex
Graeco interpretari

comitatum. uel coietum.[f]
Concilii uero nomen tractum   40
ex more romano. Tempore *enim* quo
causae agebantur conueniebant
omnes in unum. Commoniq*ue* inten
tione tractabant. Unde et conci
lium a commoni intentione dictum   45
q*uasi* consilium. Nam cilia oculorum
sunt. unde et considium consilum.[g]
.d. in .l. litter*am* transeunte. .
Coetus uero conuentus *est uel* congregatio
a coeundo. id *est* conueniendo in unum   50
unde et conuentum *est* nuncupatum
sicut conuentus coetus *uel* concilium
a societate multorum in unum.
de cyclo paschali[h]   luiii
Paschalem cyclum . . . olitus / /   55
atoris primus . . .   (2vb)
probatissimi auctores . . . cae
sarensis. thopilus alaxandrinus

---

[f]   i *superscript*
[g]   d *expunged after* i, l *superscript*
[h]   h *superscript*

---

comitatum vel coetum.
Concilii vero nomen tractum   40
ex more Romano. Tempore enim, quo
causae agebantur, conveniebant
omnes in unum communique intentione tractabant. Vnde et conci-
lium a communi intentione dictum,   45
quasi comcilium. Nam cilia oculorum
sunt. Vnde et considium consilium,
D in L litteram transeunte.
Coetus vero conventus est vel congregatio,
a coeundo, id est conveniendo in unum.   50
Vnde et conventum est nuncupatum,
sicut conventus coetus vel concilium,
a societate multorum in unum.
De cyclo paschali.
Paschalem cyclum Hippolytus   55
(episcopus temporibus Alexandri imper)
atoris primus conscripsit. Post quem
probatissimi auctores Eusebius Caesariensis, Theophilus Alexandrinus,

prosper quoq*ue* natione aquitanus
atq*ue* uictorinus amplificatis eiusdem   60
festiuitatis rationib*us* multiplices cir
culos ediderunt. Cuiusq*ue* rationis bea
tissimus cyrillus alaxandriae urbis
aepiscopus. in nonagenta quinq*ue* annos
per quinquies decinouies calculans.i   65
quota *kalendas* die*j* *uel* luna debeat pascha
lis sollompnitas caelebrari. summa
breuitate notauit. / sit et q*uasi* in cir
Cyclus *autem* uocatus eo q*uod* in orbem digestu[s]
culo dispossitum ordinem conplec   70
tat annorum. in ueritate. sine ueri
                                    tate //
et sine ulla   (3va)
arte. Unde fac
tum est ut cuiusque mate   75
riae carmina simplici for
mitate facta ciclica uoca[rentur]
hinc et laterculum dictum quod ordi

---

i   .i. nu[m]erans *superscript*
j   .i. aes nésci *for* *kalendas* enáir *superscript*

Prosper quoque natione Aquitanus
atque Victorius, amplificatis eiusdem   60
festivitatis rationibus, multiplices cir-
culos ediderunt. Cuius quidem rationem bea-
tissimus Cyrillus Alexandriae urbis
episcopus in nonaginta quinque annos
per quinquies decem novies calculans,   65
quoto Kal. vel luna debeat pascha-
lis sollemnitas celebrari, summa
brevitate notavit.
Cyclum autem vocatum eo quod in orbe digestum sit, et quasi in cir-
culo dispositum ordinem conplec-   70
tat annorum sine var-
ietatate
et sine ulla
arte. Vnde fac-
tum est ut cuiusque mate-   75
riae carmina simplici for-
mitate facta cyclica vocarentur.
Hinc et laterculum dictum, quod ordi-

nem habeat stratum annorum[k]

Cyclus primus decimnouen*alis* annor*um*			80	
ANnus com. iii id. ap. lu. xx		. . .		(532)
b	com. ui kl. ap.	lu. xui		(533)
	em. xui kl. mai	lu. xuii		(534)
	com. ui id. ap.	lu. xx		(535)
	com. uiii kl. ap.	lu. x . . .	85	(536)
	em. ii id. ap.	lu. xui		(537)
	com. ii n. ap.	lu. xuiiii		(538)
	. . .	lu. xx[l]		(539)
	. . .	lu. xui		(540)
	com. ii k. . . .	xuiii //	90	(541)
	. . .	lu. xuiii	(2ra)	(545)
	com. . . . id. ap.	lu. xxi		(546)
	com. uiii k. ap.	lu. xuii		(547)
	. . . id. ap.	lu. xuiii		(548)
	com. ii n. ap.	lu. xx	95	(549)
	em. uiiii k. m.	lu. xxi endi.		(550)
Cyclus saecundus				
	com. .u. id. ap.	lu. xuiii		(551)
	com. ii[m] kl. ap.	lu. xxi		(552)

k *An arrow points from the two boxed areas for their insertion/commentary at this point of the text. Because of bad rubbing the writing is almost illegible, even with the aid of ultraviolet light, and the readings given below are – with the exception of a few clear letters which show up on the photographs – very tentative:*

Era dc.lxl	1
iii . . . :xrec. . .s	2
pre . . . r in:	3

Era dc.lxx	4
a mundi [ix] ori	5
gin[e] usq*ue* In p*re*	6
sentem an*num*	7
u dcccxxx an*ni*	8
denumerant	9

a mundi ori	1
gine usque In	2
presen*tem* an*num*	3
que est dc.lxl	4
Ëra .iii. de	5
numer	6
antur an n[i]	7
u d ccc liiii	8

l *A later paper patch glued to the parchment partially obstructs readings for 539 and 540.*

m ii *superscript*

nem habeat stratum annorum.

	em.	xii k. m.	lu. xxi		100	(553)
	com.	n. ap.	lu. xuii			(554)
	com.	u k. ap.	lu. xx			(555)
	em.	xui k. m.	lu. xxi			(556)
	com.	kl. ap.	lu. xu			(557)
	em.	xi k. m.	lu. xui og. //		105	(558)
	com.	...		(3vb)		(559)
	com.	...				(560)
	em.	...				(561)
b.	com.	...				(562)
	com.	...			110	(563)
	em.	...				(564)
	com.	...				(565)
	com.	...				(566)
b.	em.	...				(567)
	com.	...			115	(568)
	com.	...				(569)
Cycl ...						
	com.	uiii id. ap.	lu. x[u]			(570)
	com.	iiii. k. ap.	lu. xui...			(571)
	em.	xiiii k. m.	lu. xx		120	(572)
b.	com.	u id. ap.	lu. xxi			(573)
	com.	uiii k. ap.	lu. xuii			(574)
	em.	xuiii k. m.	lu. xuiii			(575)
	com.	uiii ap.	lu. xx //			(576)
	em.	xii k. m.	lu. xxi	(2rb)	125	(580)
b	com.	uiii. id. ap.	lu. xui			(581)
	com.	iiii k. ap.	lu. xuiiii.			(582)
	em.	xiii k. m.	lu. xx			(583)
	com.	iiii. n. ap.	lu. xiii.			(584)
b	com.	ii k. ap.	lu. xuiiii.		130	(585)
	em.	xuiiii k. m.	lu. xuiiii			(586)
	com.	iii kl ap.	lu. xui.			(587)
b.	em.	xiii k. m.	lu. xiiii en.			(588)
Cyclus quartus						
	com.	iii. id. ap.	l. xuiii		135	(589)
	com.	uii k. ap.	l. xu			(590)
b	em.	xuii k m.	l. xui			(591)
	com.	uiii i.d. ap.	l. xuiii			(592)
	com.	iiii k. ap.	l. xxi //			(593)
	com.	xi...		(2rc)	140	(604)
	em.	iii. id. ...				(605)
	com.	iii. n. ...				(606)
	em.	uiii. k. ...				(607)
Cyclus qu ...						
	com.	uii. id. ...			145	(608)
	com.	iii k. ...				(609)

em. uiiiiⁿ k. . . .   (610)

com. ii. n. a. . . .   (611)

com. uii. k. a. . . .   (612)

em. xuii. k. m. . . .   150   (613)

com. ii. k. ap. . . .   (614)

em. xii k. m. . . .   (615)

com. iii n.º ap. . . .   (616)

com. iii n. a. . . . //   (617)

 . . .   gnificatur substantia   (1va)   155

 . . . uncta concludit. ipse a nullo

 . . . sed omnia intra eius omni

 . . . artantur. .   Perfectus d*icitur* q*uia*

 . . . addici.P attamen de consum

 . . . uius facti perfectio d*icitur* . . .   160

 . . . actus q*uomodo est* perfectus sed hoc

 . . . de ussu nostro sumptum sit.

 . . . opia sicut et reliqua uerba.

 . . . q*uod* ineffabile est. utcumq*ue* di

 . . . iam de deo nihil digne humanus   165

 . . . it sicut s*unt* et alia/ipso crea

 . . . dictus p*ro* totius mundi reb*us* ab

 . . . enim est q*uod* [non] originem a d*e*o trax

 . . . et unus q*uia* diuidi no*n* potest. .   //

ⁿ xiii *superscript*

^o id. *superscript*

P u *expunged after* d, i *added superscript*

spiritus, eius significatur substantia.   (*Etymologiae* 7. 1.30)

Inmensus, quia cuncta concludit, ipse a nullo   156

concluditur; sed omnia intra eius omni-

potentiam coartantur. Perfectus dicitur quia

nihil ei possit adici. Ad tamen de consum-

matione alicuius facti perfectio dicitur. Deus autem,   160

qui non est factus, quomodo est perfectus? Sed hoc

vocabulum de usu nostro sumpsit

humana inopia, sicut et reliqua verba,

quatenus id quod ineffabile est utcumque di-

ci possit, quoniam de Deo nihil digne humanus   165

sermo dicit, sicut sunt et alia.

Creator dictus pro totius mundi rebus ab ipso crea-

tis. Nihil enim est quod non originem a Deo trax-

erit. Ipse et unus, quia dividi non potest,

(vel quia nihil aliud esse potest quod tantundem capiat

potestatis. Haec igitur, quae de Deo dicta sunt, ad totam

pertinent Trinitatem propter unam et coaeternam substantiam,

sive in Patre, sive in Filio eius unigenito in forma Dei,

mam suam non q*uod* deus . . .   (1vb)   170
sed hoc nostro narrat . . .
Nam et facies d*ei* in scriptu . . .
caro sed diuina cognitio in . . .
eadem ratione q*uia* per faciem . . .
spectam quisq*ue* cognoscitur hoc   175
enim in oratione d*icitur* de d*e*o. ostende
nobis d*omi*ne faciem tuam. ac si dicatur
da nobis d*omi*ne cognotionem tuam..
Sic et uestigia d*ei* d*i*cuntur. q*uia* nunc d*e*us per
spaeculumq agnoscitur. ad perfecr   180
tum uero omnipotens repperitur
dum in futuros facie ad faciem
quibusq*ue* electis pr*ae*sentabitur. ut
ipsam speciem contemplentur.

q   p *superscript*
r   ro *deleted after* per
s   in *deleted*

sive in Spiritu sancto, qui unus Spiritus est Dei Patris et
Filii eius unigeniti. Sunt et quaedam vocabula ex usu
nostro ad Deum sumpta, de membris nostris, sive de
inferioribus; et quia in propria natura invisibilis et
incorporeus est, pro efficientiis tamen causarum in
ipso rerum species adscribuntur, ut more locutionis
nostrae facilius se ipsum insinuet: ut quia omnia videt,
dicatur oculus; et propter quod audit omnia, dicatur
auris; pro eo autem quod avertitur, ambulat; pro eo
quod spectat, stat. Sic et in ceteris horum similibus
ab humanis mentibus trahitur similitudo ad Deum, sicut est
obliviscens et memorans. Hinc est quod et Propheta
dicit: 'Iuravit Dominus exercituum per ani)
mam suam': non quod Deus animam habeat,   170
sed hoc nostro narrat affectu.
Nam et facies Dei in Scripturis sanctis non
caro, sed divina cognitio intellegitur,
eadem ratione qua per faciem con-
spectam quisque cognoscitur. Hoc   175
enim in oratione dicitur Deo: 'Ostende
nobis faciem tuam': ac si dicatur:
'Da nobis cognitionem tuam.'
Sic et vestigia Dei dicuntur, quia nunc Deus per
speculum agnoscitur, ad perfec-   180
tum vero omnipotens reperitur,
dum in futurum facie ad faciem
quibusque electis praesentabitur, ut
ipsam speciem contemplentur

Glastonbury's Early Abbots

SARAH FOOT

An attempt to identify the Anglo-Saxon abbots of Glastonbury and establish the order in which they ruled was made by William of Malmesbury in his *De antiquitate Glastonie ecclesie*, commissioned by the abbey in *ca* 1129.[1] William's intention in writing was to advance Glastonbury's reputation and prestige by demonstrating the monastery's antiquity and unbroken history, thus refuting the statement made at the end of the eleventh century by Osbern of Canterbury that St Dunstan had been the house's first abbot.[2] The *De antiquitate* therefore placed the origins of the house before the arrival of the Anglo-Saxons in Somerset (even hinting at the possibility of an apostolic foundation),[3] and traced a continuous sequence of abbots from A.D. 601 onwards.[4] It is, however, difficult to distinguish those portions of the *De antiquitate* written by William himself from the numerous interpolations made to its text by later generations of Glastonbury writers, among which was the addition of a list of the names of the abbots of the house from St Patrick to Abbot Michael of Amesbury (A.D. 1235–52), recording the date of each abbot's accession and the number of years for which he held the office.[5] Although this list is similar to the sequence of abbots reconstructable from the text of the *De antiquitate*, there are a number of discrepancies between the two, particularly in the order in which each placed the names of those who were reputed to have governed the minster in the period *ca* 750–940.[6]

---

[1]   *The Early History of Glastonbury: An Edition, Translation and Study of William of Malmesbury's 'De Antiquitate Glastonie Ecclesie'*, ed. John Scott (Woodbridge, 1981), pp. 1–5.

[2]   Osbern, *Vita S. Dunstani*, ch. 19 (*Memorials of St Dunstan*, ed. W. Stubbs, RS 63 [London, 1874], pp. 69–161, at 92); Stubbs discussed the date of this Life, *ibid.* pp. xxxi, 151. For William's rejection of Osbern's statement see *DA*, ch. 55 (ed. Scott, p. 114): 'Puto palam esse quantum a ueritate ille longe fuit, qui beatum Dunstanum primum abbatem Glastonia fuisse delirauit'. Compare also William of Malmesbury, *Vita S. Dunstani*, ch. 15 (*Memorials*, ed. Stubbs, pp. 250–324, at 271).

[3]   *DA*, ch. 2 (ed. Scott, pp. 46–50).

[4]   *Ibid.* ch. 35, p. 88. See below, n. 21.

[5]   *DA*, ch. 71 (ed. Scott, pp. 146–8). For discussion of the interpolations made to the *De antiquitate* see below, n. 22.

[6]   I am using the word 'minster' to describe all Anglo-Saxon religious houses, translating the Latin words *coenobium* and *monasterium* as well as the Old English *mynster*. My reasons for adopting this consistent vocabulary are given in my article, 'Anglo-Saxon Minsters: A Review of Terminology', *Pastoral Care Before the Parish*, ed. J. Blair and R. Sharpe (London, forthcoming).

The discovery in a manuscript from the second quarter of the eleventh century (London, British Library, Cotton Tiberius B. v, part 1, at 23va) of what has been presumed to be a list of the early abbots of Glastonbury compiled in the second half of the tenth century has led some historians to question the accuracy of the sequence of abbots established in the text of the *De antiquitate*. This list of Anglo-Saxon names from Tiberius B. v was first printed (side by side with the list of abbots from chapter 71 of the *De anti-quitate*) by William Stubbs, who assumed that its authority was to be preferred to that of the list in the *De antiquitate*, arguing that 'the order and dates of Malmesbury's list are quite at random; yet there is enough likeness between the two lists to show that he had older materials to work upon'.[7] J. Armitage Robinson made use of the Tiberius list in his essay on the Anglo-Saxon abbots of Glastonbury, but was inclined to place greater reliance on the actual sequence of abbots given in the text of the *De antiquitate*, which he also preferred to the abbatial list interpolated into chapter 71.[8] It is worth reconsidering the circumstances of the production of the Tiberius list, and exploring whether this collection of names can make any contribution to our knowledge of the early history of Glastonbury and the identity of the community's abbots, but before turning to this issue it is necessary to examine briefly the context of this list of Anglo-Saxon names within the Tiberius manuscript.

London, British Library, Cotton Tiberius B. v, part 1 (folios 2–73 and 77–88) is an illustrated miscellany copied in England probably in the second quarter of the eleventh century, perhaps at Christ Church, Canterbury.[9] Some of the material in the manuscript is, however, of south-western provenance, namely the genealogical tract on the kings of Wessex (23r) and Hampson's metrical calendar (3r–8v), both of which may be associated with Glastonbury: the West Saxon genealogy contains an allusion to Glastonbury in attributing the minster's foundation to King Ine,[10] and the grading of feasts for January in

---

[7]   *Memorials*, ed. Stubbs, pp. lxxxi–lxxxii, n. 1. The Tiberius list has also been printed by several other people, including J. B. Davidson, 'On the Charters of King Ine', *PSANHS* 30 (1884), 1–31, at 24; T. Scott Holmes, 'The Abbey of Glastonbury', in the *Victoria History of Somerset*, ed. W. Page (London, 1911) II, 82–99, at 98; J. Armitage Robinson, *Somerset Historical Essays* (London, 1921), pp. 41–2; and H. Edwards, *The Charters of the Early West Saxon Kingdom*, BAR Brit. ser. 198 (Oxford, 1988), p. 8.

[8]   Robinson, *Somerset Historical Essays*, pp. 26–53; Robinson made one mistake in his transcription of the list, reading *Ændhun* for the manuscript's *Andhun*, as pointed out by David Dumville, 'The Anglian Collection of Royal Genealogies and Regnal Lists', *Anglo-Saxon England* 5 (1976), 23–50, at 43, n. 5.

[9]   A facsimile of the manuscript has been edited by P. McGurk *et al.*, *An Eleventh-Century Anglo-Saxon Illustrated Miscellany: British Library Cotton Tiberius B. V Part 1 Together with Leaves from British Library Cotton Nero D. II*, Early English Manuscripts in Facsimile 21 (Copenhagen, 1983). See P. McGurk, 'Contents of the Manuscript', *ibid.* pp. 15–24, and 'The History of the Manuscript', *ibid.* pp. 25–7.

[10]   Tiberius B. v, part 1, 23r: 'Ingeld wæs Ines broðor West seaxna cyninges. 7 he heold rice .vii. 7 .xxx. wintra, 7 he getimbrade þæt beorhte mynster æt Glæstinga-byrig, 7 æfter þam fyrde to Sancte Petres . . .'. For discussion of the genealogical material in this manuscript and the manuscript itself see Dumville, 'The Anglian

the metrical calendar concurs with Glastonbury practice.[11] In Tiberius B. v, part 1, following a miscellany of chronological matter (2r–19r), there is (19v–24r) a collection of lists and catalogues among which is found (23va) a list of nineteen names without a heading.[12] The absence of a heading for the list in Tiberius B. v may be a failure of rubrication, a feature common to the manuscript, and need not therefore signify anything about the provenance of this material,[13] but such a collection of names would not readily be identifiable outside Glastonbury and it is hard to imagine where else it might have been compiled.[14] The last name in this list, Ælfweard, may refer to the abbot of Glastonbury *ca* 975x985 to ?1009,[15] but David Dumville has shown that the list's context in the manuscript renders it more likely that it was originally compiled before Ælfweard's time. The Tiberius manuscript also contains (16r) two decennovenal Easter cycles for A.D. 969–1006 which fit chronologically with the West Saxon genealogy (23r), datable to 966x970/1.[16] Dumville has argued that the genealogy (with its reference to Glastonbury) and the Easter tables were both produced at that house in the year 969, and that the production of the abbatial list (which follows immediately after the West Saxon genealogy in the manuscript) should probably be dated to the same year.[17] According to this argument, the last name, Ælfweard, was thus an addition made to the list in or before 990 when the south-western material found in Tiberius B. v was taken to Christ Church, Canterbury, by Sigeric, bishop of Ramsbury, or by one of his followers, on Sigeric's translation to the see of Canterbury in that year.[18]

The Tiberius list contains the following nineteen names:

Hemgils
Wealhstod
Coengils

Collection', pp. 26–8 and 43–5. Ine's association with the minster at Glastonbury is discussed further below, pp. 168–9.

[11] See P. McGurk, 'The Metrical Calendar', in *An Eleventh-Century Anglo-Saxon Illustrated Miscellany*, ed. McGurk *et al.*, pp. 44–50. See also Jennifer Morrish's review of the facsimile of Tiberius B. v in *Modern Philology* 83 (1985/6), 298–303, at 302, where she suggested that the whole manuscript might have been copied in the south-west.

[12] This list occurs in the Tiberius manuscript immediately after a genealogy of the West Saxon kings. The context of this material in Tiberius B. v was discussed by Dumville, 'The Anglian Collection', pp. 26, 43.

[13] D. Dumville, 'The Catalogue Texts', in *An Eleventh-Century Anglo-Saxon Illustrated Miscellany*, ed. McGurk *et al.*, pp. 55–8, at 57, n. 22.

[14] *Ibid.* p. 57.

[15] D. Knowles *et al.*, *The Heads of Religious Houses: England and Wales, 940–1216* (Cambridge 1972), p. 51. See below, no. 19 (Ælfweard).

[16] Dumville, 'The Anglian Collection', p. 43.

[17] *Ibid.* pp. 43–4.

[18] *Ibid.* p. 44. These arguments were accepted by Edwards (*The Charters*, pp. 8–9), who suggested that a list of abbots of which the collection of names in Tiberius B. v represents an expanded version could first have been compiled before the other Glastonbury material in the manuscript, but she doubted that the original compilation could date from earlier than the abbacy of Dunstan.

Beorhtwald
Cealdhun
Luca
Wiccea
Bosa
Stiðheard
Herefyrð
Hunbeorht
Andhun
Guðlac
Cuðred
Ecgwulf
Dunstan
Ælfric
Sigegar
Ælfweard

Although the initial letters of some of the names appear to have been corrupted in copying (a characteristic of the rubrication of this manuscript, and perhaps also of its exemplar), ten of these nineteen men can be identified as abbots of Glastonbury from other surviving Anglo-Saxon texts.[19] If this does indeed purport to represent a chronological list of the minster's abbots, however, the order in which some of the earlier names are listed should probably be revised. Previous analysis of the Tiberius list has always compared it with the history of the abbey presented in the *De antiquitate*, a post-Conquest compilation which itself needs a much closer and more critical evaluation. No one has yet attempted to assess the reliability of the Tiberius list by comparing its testimony solely with the evidence for the identity of Glastonbury's early abbots which is provided by the surviving pre-Conquest materials relating to that minster.[20] It has already been noted that there are marked differences between this list and the sequence of abbots presented by the *De antiquitate*, and, before the names given in Tiberius B. v are examined in detail, it is necessary to consider briefly the reliability of that account.

With the intention of demonstrating not only the antiquity of the foundation at Glastonbury but also the unbroken history of the minster, William used the charters which he found in the abbey's archives together with the evidence of tombstones and other physical remains to trace the succession of

[19]   See the appendix below, pp. 188–9. Edwards (*The Charters*, p. 9) argued that all but four of those named – Wealhstod, Bosa, Cuthred and Ecgwulf – represented abbots of Glastonbury, but her identification of several of the others is dependent on the unsupported testimony of the *De antiquitate*.
[20]   Robinson (*Somerset Historical Essays*, pp. 26–53) considered the names in the Tiberius list in the context of the evidence for Glastonbury's early abbots found in the history of the abbey and in early Anglo-Saxon charters in the house's favour, but he placed undue reliance on the reliability of the *De antiquitate*, and on a number of charters to which that text is now the sole witness.

Glastonbury's abbots from at least the early seventh century onwards.[21] Although the text of the *De antiquitate* was tampered with by later generations of Glastonbury writers who made a number of interpolations and additions, much of William's original account can be disentangled from the later accretions; however, even those portions for which William himself seems to have been responsible can be shown to have been based on documents and legends which would not satisfy modern critical standards.[22]

When he was writing the *De antiquitate*, William of Malmesbury would seem to have had access to a number of documents in Glastonbury's archives which no longer survive; record of some of these texts is, however, preserved in a list of the contents of a lost Glastonbury cartulary known as the *Liber terrarum*, found in a manuscript now in Trinity College, Cambridge, under the heading 'Cartae contentae in libro terrarum Glastonie'.[23] Some of these lost documents may indeed have recorded genuine transactions, but even should they appear to have been included in the *Liber terrarum*, the testimony of the *De antiquitate* alone is not sufficient to establish their authenticity.[24] In the absence of any other evidence to corroborate these readings, considerable

---

[21]   Although the *De antiquitate* attributed the first foundation of a church at Glastonbury to the missionaries sent by Pope Eleutherius to Lucius, king of the Britons (*DA*, ch. 2; ed. Scott, pp. 46–8), and repeated the legend which identified St Patrick as the first abbot of Glastonbury (*ibid*. ch. 8, p. 54), the earliest abbot purportedly identifiable from a documentary source in the abbey's archive was one *Worgret*, who supposedly received a grant of land at *Inesuuitrin* from a British king in A.D. 601 (*ibid*. ch. 35, p. 88). There, are however, no grounds for placing any reliance on this 'document'; it seems most likely that the house was created at some time in the second half of the seventh century.

[22]   The interpolations made to William's text of the *De antiquitate Glastonie ecclesie* were explored by Robinson, *Somerset Historical Essays*, pp. 1–25, and by E. Faral, *La Légende arthurienne: études et documents*, 3 vols (Paris, 1929) II, 403–9, 421–32. In his edition of the *De antiquitate* Scott made a generous assessment of which passages might have originally been written by William; see *The Early History*, ed. Scott, pp. 27–33, and 168–72. However, only those extracts which are included in William's own revision of the text of his *Gesta regum Anglorum* can certainly be ascribed to William himself: *Willelmi Malmesbiriensis Monachi de Gestis Regum Anglorum*, ed. W. Stubbs, 2 vols, RS 90 (London, 1887–9) I, lviii–lxii.

[23]   Cambridge, Trinity College R. 5. 33, 77r/v; for an account of this manuscript see Julia Crick, 'The Marshalling of Antiquity: Glastonbury's Historical Dossier', in this volume. Although the *Liber terrarum* (hereafter *LT*) was still in the abbey's possession in 1247, when it was included in a catalogue of Glastonbury's library (R. 5. 33, 103ra), the entry was deleted the following year when the list was revised. The lost *Liber terrarum* was discussed by Simon Keynes, *Studies on Anglo-Saxon Diplomas*, 2 vols (unpublished fellowship dissertation, Trinity College, Cambridge, 1976) I, 164–86.

[24]   In his edition of the *De antiquitate*, Scott attempted as far as possible to equate those charters quoted or cited in the *De antiquitate* (of which texts seem no longer to survive) with the charters from the *Liber terrarum* as listed in the contents-list of that cartulary preserved in R. 5. 33. However, just as there are a good many spurious and interpolated texts among the charters copied into the abbey's fourteenth-century cartulary (Longleat House, Marquess of Bath 39, printed as *The Great Chartulary of Glastonbury*, ed. A. Watkin, 3 vols, SRS 59, 63–4 [1947–56]) and its contemporary copy, the *Secretum Domini* (Oxford, Bodleian Library, Wood empt. 1 [*S. C.* 8589]), so only

caution must thus be exercised in attempting to use the information about the identity and relative chronology of the abbey's Anglo-Saxon abbots which the *De antiquitate* provided from charters which are no longer extant.[25]

It is, however, possible that additional information about Glastonbury's early abbots might be derived from the list of Anglo-Saxon names in Tiberius B. v, even though, if it does constitute a list of the minster's abbots, it may well be incomplete.[26] It also seems, if some of the names in the Tiberius list are correctly to be identified with abbots named in extant pre-Conquest charters, that little reliance can be placed on the order of the earlier names in that list, particularly of those apparently relating to abbots of the eighth century. I shall consider each of the men listed in Tiberius B. v in turn, attempting to identify them and to establish the nature of their association with Glastonbury from the evidence of the surviving pre-Conquest sources.

1. HEMGILS

There seems no reason to doubt that the first person named in the list in Tiberius B. v, Hemgils (for Hæmgils), should be identified as the first abbot of Glastonbury, although there is no acceptable evidence to indicate just when the minster at Glastonbury was founded.[27] The abbey's cartulary preserves neither an authentic nor a fabricated foundation-charter. In a marginal addition to the A-text of the Anglo-Saxon Chronicle beside the entry for A.D. 688, Ine, king of Wessex (688–726), was credited with building the minster at Glastonbury;[28] the same legend is preserved in the genealogy of the West

some of those copied into the *Liber terrarum* are likely to have been entirely genuine texts. The reliability of the documents to which William supposedly referred cannot be determined from the summaries given of their contents in the *De antiquitate*.

[25]   In adopting this circumspect approach I depart markedly from the opinions expressed by Robinson and Edwards; the latter argued (*The Charters*, p. 9) that, even though some of the names listed in Tiberius B. v might be identified as abbots only from William of Malmesbury's account, 'as William was working from charters in the Glastonbury archives, it seems reasonable to accept his information on this point'.

[26]   Other surviving pre-Conquest sources permit the identification of additional men as abbots of Glastonbury whose names are not included in the Tiberius list.

[27]   The legends preserved at Glastonbury and reported in the *De antiquitate*, which maintain that there was a religious house at Glastonbury in the pre-English period, may be dismissed as being quite without documentary foundation.

[28]   ASC 688 A: *The Anglo-Saxon Chronicle MS A*, ed. J. Bately, The AS Chronicle: A Collaborative Edition, gen. ed. D. Dumville and S. Keynes 3 (Cambridge, 1986), p. 32: '7 he [Ine] getimbrade þæt menster æt Glæstingabyrig'. This marginal note was present in A when G was copied (1001x1013). Compare the entry in the Annals of St Neots, s.a. 726: *The Annals of St Neots with Vita Prima Sancti Neoti*, ed. D. Dumville and M. Lapidge, The AS Chronicle: A Collaborative Edition, gen. ed. D. Dumville and S. Keynes 17 (Cambridge, 1985), p. 29: 'hoc anno Ine rex Occidentalium Saxonum .xxxviii. anno regni sui, monasterium constructum atque dedicatum apud Glastoniam, regnum reliquit'. See also the discussion of this entry *ibid.* pp. xviii, xxxvi–xxxvii, lxix.

Saxon kings in Tiberius B. v,[29] and in the *Textus Roffensis*.[30] However, Ine cannot have been Glastonbury's founder, for it seems that there was already a religious community on the site before the beginning of his reign. Three charters survive in favour of an Abbot Hæmgils which are assignable to the years 680–2; all three show signs of interpolation and corruption in transmission, but they appear to be based on seventh-century originals.[31] Moreover, among the *Index chartarum* in R. 5. 33,[32] the list of royal charters in Glastonbury's favour concerning land still held by the abbey in the mid-thirteenth century begins with four grants linked together as having been given *Hemgillo abbati*, including one which is no longer extant.[33] Hæmgils would also seem to have been remembered in later years at Glastonbury, since a spurious charter of King Cuthred – confirming all the grants made to Glastonbury by earlier kings – referred to the sarcophagus of Abbot Hæmgils,[34] which suggests that at the time this document was forged Hæmgils may have been held in some veneration by the community, possibly because he was known to have been the minster's first abbot. Ine's posthumous reputation as the founder of the house may have originated because he had endowed a new church or been a particularly generous benefactor to the minster,[35] but, if reliance may be placed on the information contained in the three earlier grants (680x682) to Hæmgils, it seems reasonable to presume that the minster was in fact founded before Ine's reign, and that all the grants made by King Ine were to a pre-existing house.[36]

[29]   See above, p. 164, n. 10.
[30]   Rochester, Cathedral Library, A. 3. 5, 104r.
[31]   S.1249 (A.D. 680), preserved in the Great Cartulary, a grant from Hædde, bishop of Winchester (Edwards, *The Charters*, pp. 18–19); S.236 (A.D. 681), a grant made by a West Saxon sub-king, Baldred, which survives in the Great Cartulary and as a ?tenth-century single sheet (*ibid.* pp. 11–15); and S.237 (A.D. 682), granted by Centwine, king of the West Saxons, which survives in a late register, Longleat House, Marquess of Bath, NMR 10586 (*ibid.* pp. 15–17).
[32]   The *Index chartarum* (hereafter *IC*), R. 5. 33, 77r–78v, contains lists of charters preserved in the Glastonbury archive in 1247; see Crick, 'The Marshalling of Antiquity', elsewhere in this volume.
[33]   *IC* A1–4 (S.236, S.1665, S.1249, S.238).
[34]   S.257 (A.D. 745); Edwards (*The Charters*, pp. 45–8) argued that this charter may have some basis in an authentic charter of Cuthred, but was substantially rewritten at a later date.
[35]   Elsewhere, William of Malmesbury reported that King Ine built a new church at Glastonbury in addition to the ancient one already on the site, and that Ine's church was dedicated to the apostles Peter and Paul: *Gesta regum Anglorum*, ch. 35 (ed. Stubbs, I, 34). The archaeological evidence for the succession of buildings at Glastonbury was summarized by H. M. Taylor and Joan Taylor, *Anglo-Saxon Architecture*, 3 vols (Cambridge, 1965–78) I, 252–7. See also C. A. R. Radford, 'Glastonbury Abbey before 1184: Interim Report on the Excavations, 1908–64', *Medieval Art and Architecture at Wells and Glastonbury*, British Archaeological Association Conference Transactions 4 (1981 for 1978), pp. 110–34.
[36]   Several charters in Glastonbury's Great Cartulary are attributed to King Ine: S.238 (A.D. 663 for ?693), S. 246 (A.D. 704), S.247 (A.D. 705), and S.250–1 (A.D. 725). One further grant from Ine is preserved in a single-sheet copy, S.248 (A.D. 705); see below p. 172, n. 53, and also Lesley Abrams, 'A Single-Sheet Facsimile of a Diploma of King

2. WEALHSTOD

No pre-Conquest evidence survives to confirm that there was an abbot named Wealhstod at Glastonbury at any time in the Anglo-Saxon period, nor did William of Malmesbury identify an abbot of this name on the basis of any of the materials to which he had access. There was, however, apparently a priest of this name in the community in 744, who was listed among the witnesses to a transaction made between the community and a religious woman, Lulla, in that year.[37] This may be a case of the preservation of the name of a former member of the Glastonbury community who was still remembered and commemorated by the house in the second half of the tenth century.[38]

3. COENGILS

An Abbot Coengils does seem to have governed the minster at Glastonbury in the first half of the eighth century, although he should probably be placed chronologically after, not before, the fourth name on the Tiberius list, Beorhtwald.[39] Only one surviving charter from Glastonbury's archives purports to be in favour of an Abbot *Coengisl*, a suspicious text attributed to Æthelheard, king of Wessex, and dated A.D. 729.[40] However, the name *Cynegysl abbas* appears also in an apparently genuine witness-list datable to A.D. 726x737 appended to a forged charter from Winchester attributed to King Æthelheard.[41] The *De antiquitate*, moreover, identified Coengils as the recipient of a grant of five hides at Brompton from Æthelheard's wife, Frithugyth;[42] the text of this charter is now lost, but it was apparently recorded in the *Liber terrarum*, since a grant described simply as *Fridogida de Brunamtone* was listed among that cartulary's contents in R. 5. 33.[43]

Further evidence relating to Coengils is found in a letter (datable to 729x *ca* 744) of which the Glastonbury abbot was the joint recipient. This letter (which is preserved with the Boniface correspondence) was from an Abbot Aldhun and the abbesses Cneuburga and Coenburga to Abbot Coengils, Abbot Ingeld, and the priest Wiehtberht, and concerned an agreement of mutual intercession between their houses.[44] Neither Aldhun nor the two

---

Ine for Glastonbury', in this volume. A number of other grants were apparently made by Ine to Glastonbury, but their texts no longer survive; Glastonbury's lost charters have been discussed by Edwards, *The Charters*, pp. 62–78.

[37] S.1410 (A.D. 744); see below, no. 11 (Hunbeorht).
[38] See below, p. 185.
[39] See below, no. 4 (Beorhtwald).
[40] S.253. The form of this charter is suspicious, but Robinson (*Somerset Historical Essays*, p. 36) suggested that there may have been a genuine charter underlying this text; Edwards (*The Charters*, pp. 40–1) accepted it as a genuine early document. See also Abrams, 'A Single-Sheet Facsimile', elsewhere in this volume.
[41] S.254 (A.D. 737); Edwards, *The Charters*, pp. 137–40.
[42] *DA*, ch. 44 (ed. Scott, p. 102).
[43] *LT* 16; S.1677.
[44] *Die Briefe des heiligen Bonifatius und Lullus*, ed. M. Tangl, MGH Epistolae selectae I

women can be identified with certainty, but Ingeld and Wiehtberht were apparently members of another community in the neighbourhood of Glastonbury: Wiehtberht later joined Boniface's mission, and on his arrival in Germany wrote to 'the fathers and brothers living in the minster at Glastonbury' asking them to send his greetings to 'the brothers round about, particularly Abbot Ingeld and my own community'.[45]

4. BEORHTWALD

The fourth name given in the Tiberius list, Beorhtwald, would seem to be an error for the different name, Beorwald or Berwald; there is no acceptable evidence for the existence of an Abbot Beorhtwald at Glastonbury at any time in the Anglo-Saxon period. This issue has, however, been greatly confused both by the identification as abbots of Glastonbury in the *De antiquitate* of two separate individuals called Beorhwald or Beorwald (to the first of whom was also attributed the different name 'Beorhtwald', variously spelt *Berthwald*, or *Bertuuald*),[46] and by the inclusion of both these persons in the interpolated abbatial list inserted in chapter 71.[47] According to the *De antiquitate*, the last British abbot of Glastonbury – a certain Bregored, identified as an abbot on the basis of a painting found near the high altar of the church – was succeeded by one *Berthwald*.[48] This *Berthwald* supposedly received a grant of land at *Ferramere* from King Cenwalh of Wessex in A.D. 670, but the charter recording this donation (which was preserved in the Great Cartulary and summarized in the *De antiquitate*), is completely fabricated.[49] The first of the two abbots *Berthwald* was equated in the *De antiquitate* with Beorhtwald, the archbishop of Canterbury (A.D. 692–731), who was said, after a rule of ten years, to have 'renounced the rule of Glastonbury against the will of the king and of his diocesan bishop'.[50] There is, however, no evidence to support this identification; according to Bede, Archbishop Beorhtwald had pre-

---

(Berlin, 1916), pp. 97–8 (no. 55): 'Fratribus in Christo carissimis Coengilso et Ingeldo abbatibus et singulariter cognato nostro Uuietberto presbytero omnis congregatio trium monasteriorum, id est Aldhuni patris reuerentissimi et Cneuburge Christi famulae necnon et Coenburge abbatissarum, perennem atque insolubilem in domino salutem'.

[45] *Die Briefe*, ed. Tangl, pp. 224–5 (no. 101); this letter is datable to 732x754.

[46] Julia Crick has very kindly verified the various spellings of these names in the manuscript of the *De antiquitate*.

[47] *DA*, ch. 71 (ed. Scott, p. 146).

[48] *Ibid.* ch. 35, p. 88. In his *Gesta regum Anglorum* (ch. 21; ed. Stubbs, I, 26), however, William of Malmesbury said that Beorward [sic] as well as Bregored was abbot *tempore Britonum*.

[49] S.227. *DA*, ch. 36 (ed. Scott, p. 90); William of Malmesbury, *Gesta regum Anglorum*, ch. 29 (ed. Stubbs, I, 29). Edwards (*The Charters*, pp. 20–3) suggested that S.227 may have been compiled at Glastonbury in the tenth century.

[50] *DA*, ch. 36 (ed. Scott, p. 90). The same identification was made later in the *De antiquitate*, where '*Berhtuualdus*, archbishop of Canterbury, one time abbot of Glastonbury' was included in a list of members of the Glastonbury community who went on to become bishops and archbishops: *ibid.* ch. 67, p. 136.

viously been abbot of Reculver.[51] Although the supposition in the *De anti-quitate* (based largely on the text of the spurious *Ferramere* charter) that there was an abbot at Glastonbury in the 670s called Beorhtwald must therefore be rejected, there does appear to have been an abbot by the name of Beorwald at the minster early in the eighth century; it is presumably this individual who was named in the Tiberius list.

Two charters, one in the Great Cartulary,[52] the other surviving as a single sheet,[53] record grants of land in Somerset made by King Ine to an Abbot Beorwald in A.D. 705. Moreover, two additional grants supposedly made to 'Beorwaldo abbati' are mentioned in the *Index chartarum*, although these do not now survive.[54] There is further evidence, independent of the abbey's archives, for the presence of an abbot of this name at Glastonbury early in the eighth century. Willibald's Life of St Boniface (written 754x769) described how a synod of West Saxon ecclesiastics held in Ine's reign appointed Boniface, then a priest at Nursling, as an envoy to the archbishop of Canterbury. He was nominated by the abbots of Nursling and Tisbury, and by 'Beorwald who governed by divine ordinance the minster which is called by the name given of old, Glastonbury'.[55] A further reference to an abbot of the same name is found in a letter (datable to 709x731) from Beorhtwald, archbishop of Canterbury, to Forthhere, bishop of Sherborne, about the ransoming of a Kentish girl apparently held captive by Abbot Beorwald.[56] From these vari-

---

[51]   *Historia ecclesiastica*, V.8 (*Bede's Ecclesiastical History of the English People*, ed. B. Colgrave and R. A. B. Mynors [Oxford, 1969], p. 474). The identification of Beorht-wald as both abbot of Glastonbury and archbishop of Canterbury was, however, accepted by Robinson (*Somerset Historical Essays*, pp. 27–9) and by Scott (*The Early History*, p. 197, n. 80). Compare William of Malmesbury, *Gesta regum Anglorum*, ch. 29 (ed. Stubbs, I, 29), where William stated that *Bertuualdus* had left Glastonbury to go to Reculver, whence he was made archbishop of Canterbury.

[52]   S.247 (A.D. 705). This document was copied twice into both the Great Cartulary and the *Secretum Domini* and is not genuine in its present form, being a revised version of the single sheet, S.248. See Edwards, *The Charters*, pp. 33–4, and Abrams, 'A Single-Sheet Facsimile'.

[53]   S.248 (A.D. 705) is preserved in a single-sheet copy (Taunton, Somerset Record Office, DD/SAS PR 501 c/795). Scott (*DA*, ch. 40, p. 95) erroneously called the recipient of this charter, and of S.247, Beorhtwald, rather than the *Beruuald* of the original document (*Berwaldus* in the manuscript of the *De antiquitate*: R. 5. 33, 8v); Edwards (*The Charters*, pp. 27–33) gave the same name as Berhtwald. See further Abrams, 'A Single-Sheet Facsimile'.

[54]   IC A6 and C2 (S.1670 and S.1674). In the first of the lists which comprise the *Index chartarum* (that recording royal grants to Glastonbury of lands still held by the abbey in 1247) four grants (A5–8; S.247, S.1670, S.251, S.1705) are bracketed together as having been received by Beorwald. The abbot who received S.251 from King Ine is not named in the surviving text; the recipient of S.1705 was reported in the *De antiquitate* (ch. 54; ed. Scott, p. 114) to be an Abbot *Aldhunus*.

[55]   Willibald, *Vita S. Bonifatii*, ch. 4 (*Vitae Sancti Bonifatii Archiepiscopi Moguntini*, ed. W. Levison, MGH Scriptores rerum germanicarum in usum scholarum [Hanover, 1905], pp. 1–57, at 4): '. . . et Beorwald, qui diuina coenobium gubernatione quod antiquorum nuncupatur uocabulo Glestingaburg regebat'.

[56]   *Die Briefe*, ed. Tangl, p. 2 (no. 7). Beorhtwald was archbishop of Canterbury A.D. 692–731, and Forthhere bishop of Sherborne A.D. 709–37.

ous pieces of evidence it may be inferred that there was an Abbot Beorwald at Glastonbury from at least A.D. 705 until 709x731.

The dates of the abbacies of Beorwald and Coengils could be defined with greater accuracy if the evidence of a charter of Forthhere, bishop of Sherborne, dated A.D. 712, granting land at Bleadney in Somerset to an Abbot Ealdberht, were accepted.[57] This brief text is found only in the Great Cartulary and the *Secretum Domini*,[58] and there are no other surviving grants made by Forthhere with which it can be compared; but it displays no suspicious features.[59] If this may be taken as a record, albeit an imperfect and possibly abbreviated one, of a genuine grant, it might suggest that there was an abbot called Ealdberht at Glastonbury, perhaps in 712.[60] Alternatively, it might relate to an abbot of a different (unidentifiable) house, whose charter passed into Glastonbury's hands at a later date when the abbey obtained the land to which the document related. It is not known who possessed Bleadney in 1066, since the ownership of the estate was not recorded in Domesday Book.[61] Ealdberht was not named in the list in Tiberius B. v, yet he was assumed to have been abbot of Glastonbury in both the *De antiquitate* and the thirteenth-century *Index chartarum*.[62] There is thus insufficient evidence to confirm or deny whether Ealdberht was an abbot of Glastonbury.[63]

[57] S.1253.

[58] The charter was also included in the *Liber terrarum* (*LT* 11), where it was designated as a grant in the abbey's favour, but Ealdberht was not mentioned.

[59] It was accepted as authentic by Robinson (*Somerset Historical Essays*, p. 34, n. 1) and by Edwards (*The Charters*, pp. 34–6).

[60] The indictional and incarnational dates borne by this charter are not compatible; see Robinson, *Somerset Historical Essays*, p. 34, and Edwards, *The Charters*, p. 35.

[61] Bleadney was included among the lands belonging to Glastonbury which were supposedly confirmed by King Ine in A.D. 725, but the evidence is a forged charter, S.250. Interestingly, it was also claimed by Wells in a fabricated grant of privileges from Edward the Confessor, S.1042 (A.D. 1065).

[62] *DA*, chs 40, 71 (ed. Scott, pp. 92, 146). The list of royal diplomas relating to lands still held by Glastonbury in 1247 ends with five charters said to have been granted to *Albertus abbas* (A16–20). In Sawyer's handlist these are S.1775, 1668, 1253, 1410 and 1675; apart from S.1253, the only other to be equated with a surviving text is that identified with S.1410. This grant made by Lulla to Glastonbury of land at Baltonsborough and elsewhere, dated A.D. 744, has been equated with A19 in the list of royal charters: 'Lulla femina de Baltenesbeorge'. According to the cartulary-text of S.1410, however, the recipient of the Baltonsborough estate was Abbot Tunbeorht, not Ealdberht (see below, no. 11 [Hunbeorht]). While it is conceivable that Ealdberht could have received S.1675 (which, if it is really a garbled reference to a donation from Bishop Wilfrid, can be dated 705x709), it is most improbable that he was the recipient of S.1668 (A.D. 676x685), or of S.1775 (dated by the *De antiquitate* to A.D. 1000: *DA*, ch. 63; ed. Scott, p. 130).

[63] Between Ealdberht and Coengils, the main text of the *De antiquitate* placed yet another abbot, *Echfrid* (viz. Ecgfrith). According to that text (*DA*, ch. 40; ed. Scott, p. 94) an Abbot *Echfrid* received one hide on the River Axe from King Ine in A.D. 719, and a grant at *Ora* from an Abbess Bugu. No other record of the grant from Ine survives; a charter of Ine relating to land at *Ora* was preserved as *LT* 12 (S.1693), but there is no evidence there that it was associated with either Bugu or Ecgfrith. The Abbot Ecgfrith mentioned in the *De antiquitate* has tentatively been identified with the Heahfrith who received a letter from Aldhelm datable to some time before A.D. 690

5. CEALDHUN

It is possible that the fifth name found in the Tiberius B. v list, that of Cealdhun, may be that of an abbot of Glastonbury from the second half of the eighth century; he can, however, be identified only from evidence provided by the *De antiquitate* and, even then, only if it be assumed that the initial letter of his name in the Tiberius list is corrupt. In that text the recipient of a charter of Cynewulf, king of Wessex, granting land at *Cumtun* to Glastonbury in A.D. 762 was named as Abbot Wealdhun.[64] This charter is now lost, although it may have been preserved in the *Liber terrarum*.[65]

6. LUCA

Presuming that the initial letter of the name has been corrupted, Luca, the sixth person listed in Tiberius B. v, might be equated with an abbot called Muca at Glastonbury at the beginning of the ninth century. A certain Muca *abbas* witnessed a charter to a layman, Eadgils, preserved in the Great Cartulary,[66] and is also found among the subscriptions to the canons of the Council of *Clofesho* of A.D. 803.[67] According to the *De antiquitate*, the same abbot obtained five manors near the River Torridge from King Ecgberht in A.D. 802,[68] but the charter recording this transaction is no longer extant, although it was seemingly copied into the *Liber terrarum*.[69] In the same chapter of the *De antiquitate*, William of Malmesbury (or an interpolator to the text) stated

---

(*Aldhelmi Opera*, ed. R. Ehwald, MGH Auctores antiquissimi 15 [Berlin 1913–19], 488–94 [no. 5]); A. S. Cook, 'Who was the Ehfrid of Aldhelm's Letter?', *Speculum* 2 (1927), 363–73. This identification has, however, been questioned by M. Lapidge, 'The Cult of St Indract at Glastonbury', *Ireland in Early Mediaeval Europe: Studies in Memory of Kathleen Hughes*, ed. D. Whitelock *et al.* (Cambridge, 1982), pp. 179–212, at 180, n. 11.

[64]   *DA*, ch. 48 (ed. Scott, p. 106); S.1685.

[65]   *LT* 39. The *De antiquitate* also identified two further eighth-century abbots at Glastonbury, Guba and *Beadeuulfus*, whose existence is not attested elsewhere: *DA*, ch. 48 (ed. Scott, p. 106). Guba was reputed to have received a grant from King Cynewulf of land at Wootton and Houndsborough in A.D. 760, which might be identifiable with *LT* 27 (S.1684), although the *Liber terrarum* reference makes no mention of Abbot Guba. The *De antiquitate* (*DA*, ch. 48; ed. Scott, p. 106) made Beaduwulf the recipient of S.1692, a grant from King Offa dated A.D. 794, which is again otherwise known only from a reference in the contents-list in R. 5. 33 (*LT* 28), where the name of the recipient was not given. Beaduwulf was also, according to the *De antiquitate* (*DA*, ch. 51; ed. Scott, p. 111), a witness to King Cynewulf's confirmation (S.152, A.D. 797) of the privilege granted by Pope Leo III, which gave King Cynehelm and his successors perpetual ownership of the minster at Glastonbury. Both of these texts are attested only in the *De antiquitate*: see Robinson, *Somerset Historical Essays*, p. 38, n. 3; W. Levison, *England and the Continent in the Eighth Century* (Oxford, 1946), pp. 32 and 249–52; and Edwards, *The Charters*, pp. 52–5.

[66]   S.270a (A.D. 801).

[67]   *Councils and Ecclesiastical Documents Relating to Great Britain and Ireland*, ed. A. W. Haddan and W. Stubbs, 3 vols (Oxford, 1869–78) III, 545–7.

[68]   *DA*, ch. 52 (ed. Scott, p. 110).

[69]   *LT* 30; S.1693. Robinson, *Somerset Historical Essays*, p. 39; Lapidge, 'The Cult of St Indract', p. 181, n. 13.

that in A.D. 800 a certain 'Cuman' had succeeded as abbot and ruled the minster for twenty-two (or two) years;[70] although no charters are attributed to the abbacy of 'Cuman', that name is also found in the list of Glastonbury's abbots given in chapter 71 of the *De antiquitate*, where the year of his ordination as abbot is given as A.D. 746, and the length of his rule as two years.[71] Robinson suggested that 'Cuman' could be a 'ghost-word', a scribal error for Muca;[72] if so, the mistake must have been made before the abbatial list found in chapter 71 was interpolated into the *De antiquitate*, since the error is perpetuated there.

7. WICCEA

The seventh on the list of names in Tiberius B. v is Wiccea; Robinson suggested that if this name had also been corrupted in transmission, it could be identified with the abbot *Tica* (for Tyccea) mentioned in the *De antiquitate*.[73] That text reported an Abbot Tyccea's purchase of two estates in the Polden Hills from King Sigeberht for fifty gold *solidi* each in 754;[74] no texts recording these transactions survive, but there is corroboration in an entry in the contents-list of the *Liber terrarum*.[75] Before he came to Glastonbury, Tyccea was said to have been abbot of a northern minster which he had fled, bearing the relics of various northern saints, in the face of Danish raids;[76] Tyccea's tomb was described as lying in the right-hand corner of the great church at Glastonbury,[77] inscribed with an epitaph bearing his name.[78]

No surviving Anglo-Saxon charters mention an abbot called Tyccea at Glastonbury. A *Tyccæa abbas* is found among the witnesses to S.96, a charter of King Æthelbald of Mercia, datable to 757, which survives as a tenth-century single sheet; however, the house which this abbot governed was not named in that charter.[79]

---

[70] *DA*, ch. 52 (ed. Scott, p. 110). In the earliest manuscript of the *De antiquitate* (Cambridge, Trinity College R. 5. 33, at 11r), 'Cuman' was originally said to have ruled the minster for 'xxii' years, but this was later corrected to 'ii'.

[71] *DA*, ch. 71 (ed. Scott, p. 146).

[72] Robinson, *Somerset Historical Essays*, p. 39. See also *The Early History*, ed. Scott, pp. 200–1, n. 103; Lapidge, 'The Cult of St Indract', p. 181 and nn. 14 and 17.

[73] Robinson, *Somerset Historical Essays*, p. 44.

[74] *DA*, ch. 47 (ed. Scott, pp. 104–6).

[75] *LT* 63; S.1680.

[76] *DA*, ch. 21 (ed. Scott, p. 68). It is unlikely that there were Danish raids on Northumbria as early as 754, but this legend (which conflicts with the evidence given elsewhere in the *De antiquitate* as to the means by which Glastonbury acquired its collection of relics) may have been developed at the abbey in order to account for its possession of the relics of a number of notable Northumbrian saints.

[77] *DA*, ch. 21 (ed. Scott, p. 68).

[78] *Ibid.* ch. 47, p. 106.

[79] See also Robinson, *Somerset Historical Essays*, p. 37.

8. BOSA

From the surviving Anglo-Saxon materials no pre-Conquest abbot of Glastonbury may be identified with the eighth name given in the Tiberius list, Bosa, nor did the *De antiquitate* attribute this name to any ruler of the minster. A priest of this name did, however, witness the grant made to the minster by Lulla in A.D. 744.[80] It is possible that Bosa and Wealhstod (the second name on the Tiberius list) both became abbots of Glastonbury later in the eighth century (in which case they have both been dislocated chronologically in this list) but there is no other evidence that either of them held this office.[81]

9–10. STIÐHEARD AND HEREFYRÐ

The ninth and tenth individuals named in the Tiberius list cannot be identified as abbots of Glastonbury from any surviving pre-Conquest materials, but in the *De antiquitate* these men are both identified as ninth-century abbots. Although no charters concerning Abbot Stithheard are recorded, reference is made to a picture of this abbot, whose accession is dated to 981;[82] this is obviously wrong, and might perhaps be corrected to 881.[83]

The *De antiquitate* associated a certain Abbot Hereferth with a grant by King Æthelwulf (A.D. 839–58) to Glastonbury of ten hides at *Branucminster*, to which the impossible date of A.D. 867 is attributed.[84] The evidence of this text cannot be corroborated since the charter is now lost; although it was included in the list of the contents of the *Liber terrarum* in R. 5. 33, no reference was made there to Abbot Hereferth.[85] According to the *De antiquitate*, Abbot Hereferth ruled the minster at Glastonbury for fourteen years, during which time King Alfred was said to have given the house a piece of the Lord's cross which he had received from Pope Martin.[86]

Since the chronology in the *De antiquitate* for the period A.D. 800–940 is hopelessly confused and dependent on evidence for which it is now the sole witness, little reliance may be placed on the details provided by that text, and no further conclusion can be drawn other than that there were perhaps two persons called Stithheard and Hereferth at Glastonbury at some time before the mid-tenth century, who were still remembered by the community at the time the Tiberius list was compiled. Either or both of them could have been

---

80   S.1410; see below, no. 11 (Hunbeorht).
81   Neither Bosa nor Wealhstod were named in the list of abbots interpolated into *DA*, ch. 71 (ed. Scott, p. 146).
82   *DA*, ch. 54 (ed. Scott, p. 114).
83   Reading DCCCLXXXI for the manuscript's DCCCCLXXXI. Scott (*The Early History*, pp. 201–2, n. 109) corrected this date to 891.
84   *DA*, ch. 53 (ed. Scott, p. 112).
85   *LT* 19; S.1695.
86   *DA*, ch. 53 (ed. Scott, p. 112). This story receives no support from the contemporary references to the Pope's gift to Alfred: ASC 883, 885; Asser, Life of King Alfred, ch. 71 (ed. W. Stevenson [Oxford, 1904; rev. imp. 1959], pp. 53–4).

abbots of Glastonbury at some time during the period for which no other sources survive, but this cannot now be proved.

11. HUNBEORHT

The eleventh name listed in Tiberius B. v might with greater certainty be equated with an eighth-century abbot of Glastonbury, if it were presumed that the first letter of his name had been altered in copying. A charter dated A.D. 744, by which Lulla, *militancium Christo humilis ancilla*, sold some land in Somerset to Glastonbury Abbey with the consent of Æthelbald, king of Mercia, was witnessed by a *Tunbert abbas*,[87] who may be identified with the Hunbeorht of the Tiberius list.[88] Other members of the Glastonbury *familia* witnessed Lulla's grant: Bosa, Urta, *Walcstod* and Tidbert, *sacerdotes*, and Tida, *prepositus*. Two of these, Bosa and Wealhstod, might be identifiable with the individuals of the same names included in the Tiberius list.[89] Abbot Tunbeorht did not receive or witness any other surviving charters, but the *De antiquitate* identified one *Tumbertus* as the recipient of two further grants dated A.D. 745 and 746.[50] Although the texts of these documents are now lost, they have been identified as two of the charters from the *Liber terrarum* on the basis of the summaries of their contents given in the *De antiquitate*.[91] However, since the contents-list of this cartulary does not indicate the name of the abbot who received this gift on the minster's behalf, the assertion that the grants were made to Tunbeorht cannot be verified.

In the ninth century there was apparently a monk at Glastonbury called Tunbeorht (*Tumbert*) who might, rather than the eighth-century abbot of the same name, be the individual commemorated in the Tiberius list as Hunbeorht.[92] In the *De antiquitate*, among a list of members of the Glastonbury community who were chosen to be bishops and archbishops elsewhere, there is a reference to a Bishop Tunbeorht, a monk of Glastonbury, who died in 876.[93] There was a bishop of this name at Winchester A.D. 871x877–878x879 to whom this entry presumably refers.[94] A Bishop Tunbeorht re-

---

[87] S.1410 (A.D. 744). Birch, taking his text from the *Secretum Domini* (Wood empt. 1, 169v), gave the name of this abbot as *Cunbert* on the first occasion on which it occurred, but as *Tunbert* subsequently: *Cartularium Saxonicum*, ed. W. de G. Birch, 3 vols (Oxford, 1885–93), pp. 241–3 (no. 168). In the Great Cartulary, however, the name is consistently spelt *Tunbert*.

[88] The text of this charter has been much manipulated: see Robinson, *Somerset Historical Essays*, p. 36; Edwards, *The Charters*, pp. 41–5. Although Hunbeorht is a perfectly good Anglo-Saxon name (W. G. Searle, *Onomasticon Anglo-Saxonicum: A List of Anglo-Saxon Proper Names from the Time of Beda to that of King John* [Cambridge, 1897], p. 305), the initial letters of several of the names in the Tiberius list are corrupted, and it seems reasonable to equate Hunbeorht with Tunbeorht.

[89] See above, no. 2 (Wealhstod); no. 8 (Bosa).

[90] *DA*, ch. 46 (ed. Scott, p. 104).

[91] *LT* 18 and 22; S.1678 and 1679.

[92] See further below, p. 188.

[93] *DA*, ch. 67 (ed. Scott, p. 136).

[94] S. Keynes, 'Episcopal Succession in Anglo-Saxon England', *Handbook of British Chronology*, ed. E. B. Fryde *et al.*, 3rd ed. (London, 1986), pp. 209–24, at 223.

putedly granted an estate at *Logderesdone* to Glastonbury, although the charter recording that transaction does not survive.[95]

12–15. Andhun, Guðlac, Cuðred and Ecgwulf

Very little is known about events at Glastonbury during the ninth century and no abbots may be identified with any confidence in this period.[96] The four persons named next in the Tiberius list, Andhun, Guthlac, Cuthred and Ecgwulf, may all have been abbots of Glastonbury at various times during this period for which no other sources survive, but equally they may have been other members of the community who were still commemorated in the tenth century, as apparently were Bosa and Wealhstod, and those former monks whose names are recorded in chapter 67 of the *De antiquitate*.[97]

The names Andhun and Ecgwulf occur in no other pre-Conquest text relating to Glastonbury, nor does any source refer to an Abbot Cuthred at this minster. Stubbs did equate the Cuthred of the Tiberius list with the name *Cudret* entered with a number of other English names into the confraternity book of Sankt Gallen on the occasion of the visit of Cenwald, bishop of Worcester, to Germany in 929,[98] but *Cudret* is not actually identified in the Sankt Gallen manuscript as an abbot (although the two names preceding his, *Kenod* and *Albrich*, are both designated *abba*).[99] It seems more likely that this *Cudret* should be grouped with the laymen listed after him in the confraternity book than that he be taken as an abbot, let alone an abbot of Glastonbury. Robinson reasonably equated the *Cudret* of the confraternity book with the *Cuðerð minister* whose name is found among the witnesses to a charter of

---

[95]   *LT* 33; S.1703.

[96]   There is one charter in favour of Glastonbury dating from the mid-ninth century which was copied into the Great Cartulary, a general grant of lands and privileges made to the minster by King Æthelwulf and dated A.D. 854 (S.303; *DA*, ch. 53, ed. Scott, p. 112), but it is unlikely to represent a genuine donation. Some discussion of the minster at Glastonbury in this period is found in Lapidge, 'The Cult of St Indract', pp. 180–3.

[97]   *DA*, ch. 67 (ed. Scott, pp. 136–8).

[98]   *Memorials*, ed. Stubbs, pp. lxxv–lxxvi, n. 8, and pp. lxxxi–lxxxii, n. 1. Sankt Gallen, Stiftsarchiv, Cod. C 3 B 55, p. 77, in *Libri Confraternitatum Sancti Galli Augiensis Fabariensis*, MGH Libri Confraternitatum, ed. P. Piper (Berlin, 1884), p. 100, col. 332. The English names recorded in this manuscript were also printed and discussed by S. Keynes, 'King Athelstan's Books', *Learning and Literature in Anglo-Saxon England: Studies Presented to Peter Clemoes*, ed. M. Lapidge and H. Gneuss (Cambridge, 1985), pp. 143–201, at 200. See also J. Armitage Robinson, *The Saxon Bishops of Wells: A Historical Study in the Tenth Century*, British Academy Supplemental Papers 4 (London, 1918), p. 61.

[99]   Stubbs (*Memorials*, p. lxxvi, n. 8) suggested that *Kenod* might be identifiable as abbot of either Evesham or Abingdon, but J. Armitage Robinson (*The Times of Saint Dunstan* [Oxford, 1923], pp. 35–40) identified him with *Cynath* of Evesham. Abbot *Albrich* cannot be identified with certainty, but an Abbot Ælfric attested a number of King Æthelstan's charters; Keynes, 'King Athelstan's Books', p. 200. There may have been an abbot of this name at Glastonbury in the tenth century: below, no. 17 (Ælfric).

King Æthelstan dated A.D. 932, preserved in the *Codex Wintoniensis*.[100] It is, however, more difficult to accept Robinson's conjecture that *Cuðerð/Cudret* might have been a 'lay abbot' of Glastonbury, by which he apparently meant a 'king's thegn' who held the 'royal island' of Glastonbury from the king as a layman, but accorded himself the title of abbot.[101]

The *De antiquitate* made no reference to an Abbot Cuthred at Glastonbury at any period, but did assign two further abbots to the ninth century in addition to Stithheard and Hereferth: Guthlac and *Elmund* (presumably Æthelmund). Again, in identifying these individuals as abbots, the *De antiquitate* relied on information which no longer survives. Abbot Guthlac was apparently responsible for selling part of one hide at *Brunham* to a certain Eanulf.[102] There is no record of an abbot whose name could be represented as *Elmund*, nor of the transaction which he supposedly made in A.D. 851, beyond the account given in the *De antiquitate*;[103] this name is not found in the Tiberius list.

16. DUNSTAN

King Edmund's appointment of St Dunstan to the abbacy of Glastonbury in A.D. 940 or 943 is traditionally regarded as the beginning of the movement for the reform of English religious life according to the Benedictine rule,[104] which reached its height during the reign of Edgar as king of all England (A.D. 959–75). It is, however, impossible to provide precise dates for the abbacy of St Dunstan, the sixteenth name on the list in Tiberius B. v; he was appointed in either A.D. 940 or 943, and had perhaps resigned his authority by the time he became archbishop of Canterbury in 959 or 960.

The earliest charter purporting to represent a grant to Dunstan *abbas* from King Edmund survives only in the Great Cartulary but there seem to be no obvious diplomatic grounds for rejecting it; it is dated A.D. 940.[105] However, an addition in a late eleventh-century hand to the A-manuscript of the Anglo-Saxon Chronicle relating to A.D. 943 states 'in this year King Edmund entrusted Glastonbury to St Dunstan, where he afterwards first became abbot'.[106] Charters witnessed by Dunstan as abbot are of equally little assist-

---

[100] S.417.

[101] Robinson, *Somerset Historical Essays*, p. 43.

[102] *DA*, ch. 52 (ed. Scott, p. 110).

[103] *Ibid.* ch. 53, p. 112.

[104] For example, it was with the date A.D. 940 that D. Knowles and R. Hadcock chose to begin their catalogue, *Medieval Religious Houses: England and Wales*, 2nd ed. (London, 1971).

[105] S.466. The witness-list of this charter (like those of so many others in the Great Cartulary) has been abbreviated and now has only three names, those of the king, his brother Eadred, and Wulfhelm, archbishop of Canterbury. If the attestation of Wulfhelm is accepted, the charter must be dated before 12 February 941; it bears the A.D. date 940, and the thirteenth indiction, which is correct for that incarnational year.

[106] ASC 943 A: 'Her Eadmund cing Sancte Dunstane Glæstingeberig betæhte ðær he syððan ærest abbud wearð' (*ASC MS A*, ed. Bately, p. 73; see also p. xl, n. 121). Com-

ance in determining the precise dates of his abbacy, since they can be dated only to the period from 946 to 956x957.[107] On his return from exile, Dunstan was appointed bishop of Worcester and then of London before being elevated to Canterbury in 959 or 960;[108] it is nevertheless possible that he resumed and retained the abbacy of Glastonbury for some or all of his time as bishop. Of the three Glastonbury charters in Dunstan's favour, King Edmund's grant of privileges dated A.D. 944 must be rejected as spurious,[109] but King Eadred's grant of land at Badbury, made in 955, may be genuine.[110]

Dunstan was included in the *De antiquitate* among the list of former members of the Glastonbury community who became archbishops and bishops; at the time that chapter was compiled Dunstan was remembered for having effected an improvement in the minster's fortunes and for having organs, bells, and a new holy water vat made.[111]

17. ÆLFRIC

There is some confusion about the identity of Dunstan's successor as abbot. According to the *De antiquitate*, when Dunstan was exiled by King Eadwig in 956, a certain *Elsius, pseudo-abbas*, was given possession of the minster by the king, together with an estate at Panborough.[112] Although the charter recording the latter donation survives in the Great Cartulary, its text makes no mention of the abbot at the time;[113] it is possible that the name *Elsius* was obtained from another charter of King Eadwig (S.625, A.D. 956) granting an estate at Nettleton to a certain *Elswyus*, described as *uidelicet abbati Glastingens'*. Watkin suggested plausibly that the words identifying the recipient as abbot of Glastonbury were an interpolation into what was originally a grant to a layman.[114]

pare ASC 943 F (*The Anglo-Saxon Chronicle According to the Several Original Authorities*, ed. B. Thorpe, 2 vols, RS 23 [London, 1861] I, 211).
[107] S.509, 520 (A.D. 946); S.544, 546, 552 (A.D. 949); S.553 (A.D. 950, *recte* 953x955); S.555 (A.D. 951); S.559 (A.D. 952); S. 571, 597, 605 (A.D. 956); S.663 (A.D. 955x957).
[108] Dunstan's appointments to the bishoprics of Worcester and London cannot be dated more closely than 957x959: S. Keynes, 'Episcopal Succession', pp. 220, 224. For Dunstan's elevation to Canterbury see N. Brooks, *The Early History of the Church of Canterbury* (Leicester, 1984), pp. 243–4.
[109] S.499. King Edmund was apparently buried at Glastonbury: John of Worcester, *Chronicon ex chronicis*, s.a. 946 (*Monumenta Historica Britannica*, ed. H. Petrie and J. Sharpe [London, 1848], pp. 522–644, at 574).
[110] S.568. The formulae of this charter are very similar to those of S.563, a grant by Eadred also dated 955, which survives as a single-sheet apparent original from the Glastonbury archive. S.553, however, Eadred's grant of land at Pucklechurch to Glastonbury in A.D. 950, which also survives as a single-sheet copy, is probably an eleventh- or twelfth-century forgery: L. Abrams, ' "Lucid Intervals": A Rediscovered Anglo-Saxon Royal Diploma from Glastonbury Abbey', *Journal of the Society of Archivists* 10 (1989), 43–56.
[111] *DA*, ch. 67 (ed. Scott, p. 136).
[112] *DA*, ch. 58 (ed. Scott, p. 120).
[113] S.626 (A.D. 956).
[114] *The Great Chartulary*, ed. Watkin, III, ccxvi and 646.

In the list of names in Tiberius B. v, Dunstan's name is followed by that of Ælfric, and an Abbot Ælfric is found among the witness-lists of a number of charters dating from ?959 to 975, but it is difficult to assign him to any one house with any confidence.[115] A putative abbot of this name at Glastonbury cannot be distinguished from the abbots called Ælfric who were found at St Augustine's, Canterbury, from ?959 to 971,[116] and at Malmesbury between ?*ca* 965 and 977.[117] Nor, if Ælfric were an abbot of Glastonbury, could he have retained this position until A.D. 975; there is greater certainty about the identity of the next abbot, Sigegar, who is found witnessing charters in 974 and 975.[118]

No surviving pre-Conquest source apart from the Tiberius list attests to the presence at Glastonbury of an Abbot Ælfric, although some lost Anglo-Saxon text may lie behind the statement, 'In the year 988 died Bishop Ælfric, an abbot of Glastonbury', which is found in the *De antiquitate* among the list of obits of former members of the abbey's community.[119] It is uncertain of which see this Ælfric was bishop; he may have been bishop of Crediton from 977x979 to 986x987.[120] Scott erroneously equated the Ælfric referred to in the *De antiquitate* with the Ælfstan who was bishop of Ramsbury from 970 to 981.[121] His confusion of these two names may have been caused by the suggestion that the reference to Ælfric in the Tiberius B. v list might in fact be an error for Ælfstan.[122] According to John of Worcester, there was an Abbot Ælfstan of Glastonbury in A.D. 970, in which year he attended the translation of the relics of St Swithhun at Winchester before he was appointed bishop of Ramsbury.[123] Possible corroboration of this account may be found in Wulfstan's *Vita S. Æthelwoldi*, where we read of a miracle concerning a monk of Abingdon called Ælfstan, who became an abbot (clearly of some house other than Abingdon) and later bishop of Ramsbury.[124] Ælfstan is also named as abbot of Glastonbury in two spurious charters in favour of Crowland Abbey, S.741 and S.1294, both dated A.D. 966,[125] and an Abbot Ælfstan is found witnessing charters from A.D. 965 to 970.[126] No Abbot Ælfstan is

---

[115] For example S.586 (A.D. 956 for 959) and S.802 (A.D. 975).

[116] S. Kelly, 'The Pre-Conquest History and Archive of St Augustine's, Canterbury' (unpublished PhD dissertation, University of Cambridge, 1986), p. 232.

[117] Knowles *et al.*, *The Heads of Religious Houses*, p. 54.

[118] See below, no. 18 (Sigegar).

[119] *DA*, ch. 67 (ed. Scott, p. 138).

[120] Keynes, 'Episcopal Succession', p. 215.

[121] *The Early History*, ed. Scott, p. 206, n. 134.

[122] Knowles *et al.*, *The Heads of Religious Houses*, p. 50.

[123] John of Worcester, *Chronicon ex chronicis*, s.a. 970 (ed. Petrie and Sharpe, p. 577).

[124] Wulfstan, *Vita S. Æthelwoldi*, ch. 14 (*Three Lives of English Saints*, ed. M. Winterbottom [Toronto, 1972], p. 41).

[125] Further confusion is caused by the fact that the *liber uitae* of Hyde Abbey identified the future bishop of Ramsbury as a monk of the Old Minster, Winchester; his name (identified as bishop of Wiltshire) is included in a list entitled: 'Nomina fratrum ueteris cenobii Uuentone ecclesiae' (*Liber Vitae: Register and Martyrology of New Minster and Hyde Abbey, Winchester*, ed. W. de G. Birch, Hampshire Record Society 5 [London, 1892], p. 23).

[126] For example, S.734 (A.D. 965); S.779–81 (A.D. 970). Ælfstan's name is also found

included among those described in the *De antiquitate*, nor is an abbot of that name included in chapter 71 of that work; however, among the *alumni* of Glastonbury whose obits are recorded in chapter 67 is a Bishop Ælfstan, *monachus Glastonie*, who was said to have died on 13 February.[127] It is presumably he who should be identified with the bishop of Ramsbury, 970–81.

There is one alternative possibility: that the Ælfric placed after Dunstan in the Tiberius list should be identified with the Abbot Ælfric mentioned before Dunstan's time in the *De antiquitate*.[128] According to that text, this abbot ruled for fourteen years during the reign of Æthelstan (A.D. 924–39);[129] the list of abbots found later in the same work placed Ælfric's accession in 927.[130] An Abbot Ælfric did attest a number of King Æthelstan's charters, and it might have been on the basis of some of these charters that Ælfric was identified in the *De antiquitate* as an abbot of Glastonbury.[131] In his Life of St Dunstan, William of Malmesbury stated that Dunstan was appointed abbot of Glastonbury on the elevation of the previous abbot, Ælfric, to the episcopate,[132] a supposition which, as Robinson showed, could be supported by the fact that an Ælfric became bishop of Hereford in either 934 or 937x940, and the existence of a bishop of the same name at Ramsbury from 941x949 to 949x951.[133] It is, however, difficult to prefer the testimony of William of Malmesbury or of the *De antiquitate* to that of the Tiberius list, particularly so close to the time at which the latter was apparently compiled; it seems more probable that an Abbot Ælfric ruled Glastonbury after Dunstan, was elevated from that minster to a bishopric, possibly Crediton, and that it is his obit (given as A.D. 988) which is recorded in chapter 67 of the *De antiquitate*.

The *De antiquitate* identified a further abbot in the 960s, called *Egeluuardus* (Æthelweard); the list of abbots in chapter 71 placed Æthelweard between Dunstan and Sigegar and accorded him a rule of ten years from A.D. 962,[134] but no man of this name was included in the Tiberius list.[135] This abbot

among the witnesses to two dubious charters dated 964: S.725, 731; see Knowles *et al.*, *The Heads of Religious Houses*, p. 50. A complete list of the charters witnessed by Ælfstan may be found in W. de G. Birch, *Index Saxonicus: An Index to all the Names of Persons in 'Cartularium Saxonicum'* (London, 1899), p. 12.

127 *DA*, ch. 67 (ed. Scott, p. 138). See also Scott's note 135, p. 206, where he has tentatively assigned this bishop to London.

128 Robinson, *Somerset Historical Essays*, pp. 42–3.

129 *DA*, ch. 54 (ed. Scott, pp. 112–14).

130 *Ibid*. ch. 71, p. 146.

131 Robinson, *Somerset Historical Essays*, pp. 42–3. A complete list of charters whose witness-lists include the name of an Ælfric *abbas* is given by Birch, *Index Saxonicus*, p. 10. The relevant Æthelstan charters witnessed by Ælfric are preserved in the cartularies of Abingdon (S.410, 413), Sherborne (S.423), and the Old Minster, Winchester (S.379, 393, 412, 416); two of them also survive as apparent originals (S.416 and 425).

132 *Vita S. Dunstani*, ch. 15 (ed. Stubbs, p. 270).

133 Robinson, *Somerset Historical Essays*, p. 43; Keynes, 'Episcopal Succession', pp. 217, 220.

134 *DA*, ch. 71 (ed. Scott, p. 146).

135 The name *Egeluuardus* cannot represent the Old English name Ælfweard, so the Abbot *Egeluuardus* placed by the *De antiquitate* in the 960s cannot be equated with the

supposedly received a grant of privileges from Pope John XII in 965, which was recorded in the *De antiquitate* and in the Great Cartulary, and is also found in some recensions of William of Malmesbury's *Gesta regum Anglorum*.[136] The *De antiquitate* also attributed to *Egeluuardus* receipt in A.D. 963 of a charter from King Edgar which granted four separate estates (at Sturminster Newton, Podimore Milton, Luccombe and Blackford) and returned a piece of land at Marksbury;[137] as no such charter now survives, a composite document incorporating several individual grants seems to have been copied as if it were a single donation.[138] Among the extant charters of King Edgar there are texts of his separate donations of Sturminster and Podimore to Glastonbury,[139] while the grants of Luccombe and Blackford were apparently copied in the *Liber terrarum*.[140]

18. SIGEGAR

The penultimate name on the Tiberius list is that of Sigegar. No abbot of this name is mentioned in any of Glastonbury's surviving charters, but a Sigegar *abbas* witnessed charters of King Edgar in favour of other recipients in A.D. 974 and 975,[141] and could have governed the minster at Glastonbury. In the list of obits of Glastonbury *alumni* in the *De antiquitate* it was stated that Bishop Sigegar of Wells (975x979–996) had formerly been abbot of Glastonbury,[142] but it is impossible to accept that he had ruled that house for twenty-eight years before he was made bishop.[143] Abbot Sigegar was said to have received a number of grants from King Edgar and King Æthelred from 965 to 989;[144] although these donations are no longer recorded in extant documents, some of them may be identified with charters copied into the *Liber terrarum*.[145]

Ælfweard named last in the Tiberius list; I am grateful to David Dumville for bringing this point to my attention.

[136] *DA*, ch. 61 (ed. Scott, p. 128); *The Great Chartulary*, ed. Watkin, I, 146; William of Malmesbury, *Gesta regum Anglorum*, ch. 149 (ed. Stubbs, I, 168–9), in which text the name of the abbot who received the privilege was given as *Aelfuuardus*.

[137] *DA*, ch. 62 (ed. Scott, p. 128).

[138] Robinson, *Somerset Historical Essays*, p. 41.

[139] S.764 (A.D. 968); S.743 (A.D. 966). Neither of these documents mentions the name of the abbot of Glastonbury at the time these grants were made.

[140] *LT* 72 (S.1769) for Luccombe; *LT* 81 (S.1768) for Blackford. There is no other record of Edgar's return of an estate at Marksbury.

[141] S.795 (A.D. 974), S.801–2 (A.D. 975). Knowles *et al.* (*The Heads of Religious Houses*, p. 50) also stated that John of Worcester mentioned an Abbot Sigegar without identifying his house and presumed that this must be a reference to this abbot of Glastonbury.

[142] *DA*, ch. 67 (ed. Scott, p. 138). The identification of the bishop of Wells with an abbot of the same name at Glastonbury has been accepted, for example, by Knowles *et al.*, *The Heads of Religious Houses*, p. 50. See also Robinson, *The Saxon Bishops of Wells*, p. 48.

[143] *DA*, ch. 62 (ed. Scott, p. 128).

[144] *DA*, chs 62–3 (ed. Scott, pp. 128–30).

[145] *LT* 83 and 86 (S.1773 and 1770), both ascribed to Edgar; *LT* 133 (S.1774) ascribed to

19. ÆLFWEARD

No extant grants in Glastonbury's archive were made directly to an Abbot Ælfweard, the last individual named in the Tiberius list, but an abbot of this name is found witnessing charters between A.D. 985 and 1009,[146] who, in the witness-lists of two charters, is identified as abbot of Glastonbury.[147] If the previous abbot, Sigegar, did relinquish the abbacy of Glastonbury in order to become bishop of Wells in 975, Ælfweard may have succeeded him soon thereafter, even though his name does not appear in charter witness-lists until 985.[148]

The Glastonbury obit-list found in the thirteenth-century custumary of Abbot Michael of Amesbury (London, British Library, Add. 17450, at 5v) is headed by the name *Alwardus abbas*, which would seem to relate to the tenth-century Abbot Ælfweard.[149] Although the *De antiquitate* identified no abbot between Sigegar and *Brihtred* (and hence attributed a twenty-eight-year rule to Sigegar),[150] there seems to be no reason to doubt that there was another head of the minster, whose name was Ælfweard, between those two men.

CONCLUSION

The list of names in Tiberius B. v has previously been presumed to represent a catalogue of the early abbots of Glastonbury, even though it has been recognized that the compiler of the list dislocated several from the proper chronological sequence, and that others of those whom he named are not elsewhere identified as abbots of this minster. The Tiberius list has most recently been printed and discussed by Heather Edwards, who restated that it was intended as a list of the abbots of Glastonbury (even though it included the names of some men who never apparently held that office), and suggested that it might have been compiled on two or more occasions in the tenth century, the later names being additions to an earlier list.[151] The four persons named in the Tiberius list whom she was unable to equate with abbots of that house Edwards argued might have been mistakenly included

---

Æthelred. The other three charters which according to the *De antiquitate* Sigegar had received from Æthelred (S.1780, 1778, 1777) were not listed among the contents of the *Liber terrarum*, but may be equated with references in the *Index chartarum* to charters once given to Glastonbury which the abbey had since lost: C13, C12 and C11.

[146] For example, S.860 (A.D. 985, preserved in the Winchester archive), and S.921 (A.D. 1009, from the archive of Athelney). The next identifiable abbot of Glastonbury, Beorhtred, is first found attesting charters in A.D. 1013 (S.931).

[147] S.876 (A.D. 993, from Abingdon's archive); and S.891 (A.D. 998, preserved in the *Codex Wintoniensis*).

[148] This was presumably the assumption made by Knowles *et al.* (*The Heads of Religious Houses*, p. 51), who dated Ælfweard's accession to the abbacy to *ca* 975.

[149] See M. Blows, 'A Glastonbury Obit-List', elsewhere in this volume.

[150] *DA*, chs 63 and 71 (ed. Scott, pp. 130 and 146). The *Egeluuardus abbas* referred to in the *De antiquitate* in the 960s cannot be this Abbot Ælfweard, but rather an otherwise unknown Æthelweard; see above, pp. 182–3.

[151] Edwards, *The Charters*, pp. 8–9.

if the list had been constructed from 'some form of commemorative record, probably either a *Liber Vitae* or a necrology' in existence at the abbey.[152]

It is, however, equally possible that what survives in Tiberius B. v is not in fact an abbatial list compiled from such earlier materials, but is rather a copy of such a memorial record, a list of members of the community of Glastonbury who were deemed worthy of veneration by later generations of monks in the same house. As one of the leading houses in the tenth-century monastic reform movement, Glastonbury is likely to have had a number of monks whom later generations revered, and it is clear that records of past members were indeed preserved at the abbey, for example the list of archbishops and bishops chosen from the minster community and the record of the obits of Glastonbury *alumni* included in chapter 67 of the *De antiquitate*,[153] and the obit-list preserved in Abbot Michael of Amesbury's custumary.[154] Similar records were kept at Malmesbury and at Abingdon. A list of *alumni* survives for the abbey of Malmesbury from the seventh to the thirteenth century; the early portion of that list (which includes the names of a number of individuals who do not appear ever to have been abbots of Malmesbury) seems also to have been compiled in the tenth century on the basis of commemorative records and possibly of oral traditions current in the minster.[155] At Abingdon during the eleventh century a collection of almost ninety obits was copied (mostly by one scribe) from a calendar into the margins of a martyrology in the abbey's possession.[156]

If the list in Tiberius B. v were taken to be no more than a collection of the names of certain men commemorated at Glastonbury *ca* A.D. 1000, then it could not be used to establish the identity or sequence of Glastonbury's early abbots. The fact that this list appears to present a rather different picture of the early history of Glastonbury from that obtainable from the earliest surviving narrative source (the interpolated version of William of Malmesbury's *De antiquitate*), would thus be irrelevant, and the problem of determining the succession of the heads of the minster could only be approached through the evidence of the surviving Anglo-Saxon charters. There is not, however, a *prima facie* case for rejecting the conclusion that this represents a list of the abbots of Glastonbury covering the period *ca* 670 to *ca* 1009, albeit an imperfect and not wholly accurate one. Its apparent inaccuracies may stem from the fact that it was compiled from that sort of commemorative record which by its nature tends to obscure those details which might help to date or identify a given person more closely. Nevertheless, there is no reason to accept the Tiberius list as the best witness to the identity of Glastonbury's

---

[152] *Ibid.* p. 9.

[153] *DA*, ch. 67 (ed. Scott, pp. 136–8).

[154] BL Add. 17450, 5v; see M. Blows, 'A Glastonbury Obit-List'.

[155] This list is in London, British Library, Cotton Vitellius A. x, 160r; it has been printed and discussed by Edwards, *The Charters*, pp. 82–3.

[156] Cambridge, Corpus Christi College 57. The obits have been printed by M. R. James, *A Descriptive Catalogue of the Manuscripts in the Library of Corpus Christi College Cambridge*, 2 vols (Cambridge, 1912) I, 115–18. See also S. Keynes, *The Diplomas of King Æthelred 'the Unready' 978–1016* (Cambridge, 1980), p. 239, n. 22.

early abbots simply because it is the earliest available source. Instead, the list should more properly be used as just one of the fallible records which comprise the sum of the extant materials relating to the pre-Conquest minster at Glastonbury.

Since the surviving evidence is so partial, it may now be virtually impossible to determine with any confidence the identity of all the pre-Conquest abbots of Glastonbury, nor is it necessarily possible to place in proper chronological sequence more than a few of those abbots to whom reference is made in extant contemporary materials. Some of the individuals named in the Tiberius list were indubitably abbots of the Anglo-Saxon minster, but so many of the abbey's pre-Conquest charters have been lost that it is impossible to state categorically that the nine persons named in the Tiberius list who cannot now be identified with any known Anglo-Saxon abbots did not in fact hold this office.[157] Four of those nine not mentioned as abbots in surviving contemporary sources are reported by the *De antiquitate* to have ruled the minster;[158] however, it should be remembered that if memorial records were used by the compiler of the Tiberius list, such materials could also have been available to William of Malmesbury and to those who revised the *De antiquitate*. Any (or all) of these writers could have been mistaken about whether a person included in an obit-list or some other such source had indeed once been abbot; apparent corroboration in the *De antiquitate* of the existence of an abbot bearing a name witnessed otherwise only in the Tiberius list may thus demonstrate nothing but that the compilers of each text had access to the same records. Equally the absence from the Tiberius list of the name of a man attested in other sources as an abbot of Glastonbury is not conclusive. Should it represent a list of the abbey's early abbots the list in Tiberius B. v may well be incomplete.

This question is of particular relevance when it comes to consideration of the identity of the abbots who governed Glastonbury in the ninth and early tenth centuries. In the First Viking Age the continuing existence of many religious houses was threatened, but the absence of information about this minster's abbots at this time may more confidently be attributed to the shortage of surviving charters for Wessex in this period than to the possibility that the house temporarily ceased to function.[159] Indeed, Glastonbury

---

[157] These nine are Wealhstod, Wealdhun, Bosa, Stithheard, Hereferth, Andhun, Guthlac, Cuthred and Ecgwulf. See appendix below.

[158] Wealdhun, Stithheard, Hereferth and Guthlac.

[159] M. Deanesly (*The Pre-Conquest Church in England*, 2nd ed. [London, 1963], p. 297) asserted that the house at Glastonbury had been wrecked by the Danes in the later ninth century, but no contemporary accounts confirm this view. The only evidence for viking activity is the (unsupported) statement of William of Malmesbury that the minster flourished until the arrival of the Danes in Alfred's reign, after which time it was deserted until restored by Dunstan: *Gesta pontificum Anglorum*, ch. 91 (*Willelmi Malmesbiriensis Monachi de Gestis Pontificum Anglorum*, ed. N. E. S. A. Hamilton, RS 52 [London, 1870], p. 196). This statement conflicts with the information given in the *De antiquitate* about an Abbot Hereferth who was said to have been contemporaneous with King Alfred: *DA*, ch. 53 (ed. Scott, p. 112). Passing reference was made to the assaults of the Danes (and of the Normans) in the *De antiquitate* in an attempt to

is one of the few religious houses for which there is any near-contemporary evidence relating to the first half of the tenth century. The earliest Life of St Dunstan (written 995x1005 by a priest known only by his initial, B.)[160] described how the young Dunstan, having taken 'the proper tonsure of the clerical office', spent his adolescence at Glastonbury, studying widely.[161] Since the date of Dunstan's birth is unknown, this part of his life cannot be dated more precisely than to the early part of the tenth century, but this text does provide clear evidence that the minster at Glastonbury was not only still functioning at that time, but was able to provide some sort of education.[162] The possibility that the house was ruled at some time between *ca* 800 and 940 by one or more of those persons named in the Tiberius list but not identifiable as abbots from other reliable sources cannot be ruled out, nor can the existence of abbots such as *Elmund* who are attested only in the *De antiquitate* (or indeed of others whose names have been forgotten) be totally discounted.[163]

In view of the nature of the surviving materials relating to the history of Glastonbury, it would be difficult to produce an accurate list of the Anglo-Saxon abbots of the minster unless one of the lost sources such as the *Liber terrarum* were rediscovered. But whether the list of names in Tiberius B. v was designed to represent either an abbatial list or a catalogue of worthy *alumni* of the abbey remembered in the later tenth century, it can usefully clarify some aspects of the minster's early history if used in conjunction with the other pre-Conquest materials. I have therefore appended a revised version of the list, emending the spelling of some of the names and indicating beside each what (if anything) can be determined on the basis of surviving pre-Conquest evidence of that individual's connection with the abbey. Mention has been made of the evidence provided by the *De antiquitate* only where that text is the sole witness other than the Tiberius list to the existence of a particular abbot.

account for the reputedly impoverished state of Glastonbury Abbey in the eleventh century: *DA*, chs 68, 74 (ed. Scott, pp. 138–40, 152).

[160] The evidence for the identity of B. has been examined by Michael Lapidge, 'B. and the *Vita S. Dunstani*' (forthcoming); I am grateful to him for allowing me to see a copy of this article in advance of its publication.

[161] B., *Vita S. Dunstani*, ch. 5 (*Memorials*, ed. Stubbs, pp. 3–52, at 10).

[162] According to B. (*ibid.* ch. 3, p. 6), Dunstan was born in the reign of King Æthelstan (A.D. 924–39); yet B. admitted that he did not know the names of any English kings before Æthelstan and it seems much more likely that Dunstan's birth should be placed earlier in the century. It is most improbable that Dunstan could have been appointed abbot of Glastonbury in 940 (or 943) if he had not been born before 924; it has often been suggested, for example by Robinson (*The Times of St Dunstan*, pp. 92–4), that Dunstan might have been born *ca* 909.

[163] The following men are identified as abbots of Glastonbury in the *De antiquitate* only: St Patrick, St Benignus (also called *Beonna*), Worgret, Lademund, *Echfrid*, Guba, *Beadeuulfus*, *Cuma* and *Elmund*. There are others, whose names are not found on the Tiberius list, who are mentioned as abbots of Glastonbury in the *De antiquitate* and in other texts (William of Malmesbury's *Gesta regum Anglorum* and documents surviving in the abbey's archive): Bregored, Beorhtwald, Ealdberht and *Egeluuardus*.

APPENDIX

1. H<æ>mgils   The first abbot of Glastonbury; he received S.1249 (A.D. 680), S.236 (A.D. 681), S.237 (A.D. 672). His sarcophagus is mentioned in S.257 (A.D. 745). Four charters listed in the *Index chartarum* are said to have been granted to Abbot Hæmgils (A1–4).

2. Wealhstod   A *Walcstod, sacerdos*, attested S.1410 (A.D. 744). He was not identified as abbot of Glastonbury in any other pre-Conquest text or in the *De antiquitate*.

3. Coengils   Received S.253 (A.D. 729), witnessed S.254 (A.D. 737). One recipient of a letter from Abbot Aldhun *et al.*, A.D. 729x744 (Tangl, no. 55).

4. <Beor>wald   Received S.247 and S.248 (A.D. 705) and supposedly S.1670 and S.1674 (*IC* A6 and A7). He was mentioned as abbot of Glastonbury by Willibald in *Vita S. Bonifatii*, ch. 4, and in a letter from Beorhtwald, archbishop of Canterbury, to Forthhere, bishop of Sherborne, A.D. 709x731 (Tangl, no. 7). Four charters listed in the *Index chartarum* are said to have been granted to Abbot Beorwald (A5-8).

5. <W>ealdhun   Not identified as abbot of Glastonbury in any other pre-Conquest text, but mentioned in the *De antiquitate* as the recipient of the lost charter S.1685 (A.D. 762).

6. <M>uca   Witnessed S.270a (A.D. 801) and the canons of the 803 council of *Clofesho* as *abbas*.

7. <T>iccea   Witnessed S.96 (A.D. 757) as *abbas*.

8. Bosa   A Bosa *sacerdos* attested S.1410 (A.D. 744). There is no evidence that there was an abbot of this name at Glastonbury.

9. Stithheard   Not identified as abbot of Glastonbury in any other pre-Conquest text, but mentioned in the *De antiquitate* as an abbot in the late ninth century.

10. Herefyrth   Not identified as abbot of Glastonbury in any other pre-Conquest text, but mentioned in the *De antiquitate* as the abbot who received the lost charter S.1695 (A.D. 839x855).

11. <T>unbeorht   Received S.1410 (A.D. 744) as abbot. The obit in 876 of a Bishop Tunbeorht, a former monk (not abbot) of Glastonbury, was recorded in chapter 67 of the *De antiquitate*.

12. Andhun   Not identified as abbot of Glastonbury in any other pre-Conquest text or in the *De antiquitate*.

13. Guthlac   Not identified as abbot of Glastonbury in any other pre-Conquest text; mentioned in the *De antiquitate* as an abbot in relation to a transaction concerning the sale of a piece of land which is otherwise unknown.

14. Cuthred   Not identified as abbot of Glastonbury in any other pre-Conquest text or in the *De antiquitate*.

15. Ecgwulf   Not identified as abbot of Glastonbury in any other pre-Conquest text or in the *De antiquitate*.

16	Dunstan	Received S.466 (A.D. 940), S.499 (A.D. 944), S.568 (A.D. 955) as *abbas*; witnessed many other charters as *abbas*. Five charters in the *Index chartarum* are said to have been granted to Dunstan (A9-13). His name was included in the list of archbishops and bishops chosen from the Glastonbury community found in chapter 67 of the *De antiquitate*. Dunstan's abbacy of Glastonbury was described by 'B.' in his *Vita S. Dunstani*, chs 14–22.
17.	Ælfric	Not identified as abbot of Glastonbury in any other pre-Conquest text, but an abbot of this name did witness a number of charters between ?959 and 975. The obit in 988 of a Bishop Ælfric, an abbot of Glastonbury, was recorded in chapter 67 of the *De antiquitate*.
18.	Sigegar	Witnessed S.795 (A.D. 974) and S.801–2 (A.D. 975) as *abbas*. The obit on 28 June of Sigegar, bishop of Wells and abbot of Glastonbury, was recorded in chapter 67 of the *De antiquitate*.
19.	Ælfweard	Attested a number of charters between 985 and 1009, in two of which (S.876, A.D. 993, and S.891, A.D. 998) he is identified as abbot of Glastonbury. His name was included in the obit-list found in Abbot Michael of Amesbury's custumary: BL Add. 17450, at 5v.

Glastonbury and the Glastening

DAVID EWAN THORNTON

In the tenth-century collection of Old Welsh royal genealogies contained in London, British Library, Harley 3859, at 192v–195r (hereafter HG), there is a retrograde pedigree of a patriline which both later medieval and modern historians have sought to associate with Glastonbury. The extant pedigree (HG §25) reads:

> <I>udnerth map Morgen map Catgur map Catmor map Merguid map Moriutned map Morhen map Morcant map Botan map Morgen map Mormayl map Glast, unum sunt Glastenic qui uenerunt que uocatur Loytcoyt.[1]

Another redaction of this pedigree, entitled *Y Glastyniaid* by its modern editor, occurs as part of the later tract *Achau Brenhinoedd a Thywysogion Cymru* (hereafter ABT), a possible reconstruction of which has been offered by Peter Bartrum. This redaction of the pedigree (ABT §19) offers a number of variant readings when collated against the Harleian version:

> Ednyfed ap Morien ap Kadgwr ap Kadvor ap Merwydd ap Morvynydd ap Morith ap Morgwn ap Botan ap Morien glas.[2]

ABT §19 lacks one generation (*Mormayl* of HG) and presents the personal name Glast as a cognomen *glas* (blue). As it stands, the pedigree does not fit automatically into any known historical context, and the only readily identifiable name is that of the place *Loytcoyt* (Modern Welsh Llwyd-goed, Romano-British *Letocetum*), which has been identified with Lichfield.[3] However, a version of the pedigree can also be found in chapter 4 of the history of Glastonbury, the *De antiquitate Glastonie ecclesie*, where it takes the form of a list of brothers:

> Legitur in antiquis Britonum gestis, quod a boreali Britannie parte uenerunt in occidentem xii fratres et tenuerunt plurimas regiones Uenedociam, Demeciam, Guther, Kedweli, quas proauus eorum Cuneda tenuerat. Nomina eorum fratrum interius annotantur: Ludnerth,

---

[1] E. Phillimore, 'The *Annales Cambriæ* and Old-Welsh Genealogies in *Harleian MS. 3859*', *Y Cymmrodor* 9 (1888), 141–83, at 180; P. C. Bartrum, *Early Welsh Genealogical Tracts* (Cardiff, 1966), p. 12. This (non-Welsh) manuscript dates from *ca* 1100.

[2] *Ibid.* pp. 106–7.

[3] H. Bradley, 'Ectocetum or Letocetum?', *The Academy* 30 (1886), 294; and 'The Etymology of "Lichfield" ', *The Academy* 36 (1889), 305–6.

Morgen, Catgur, Cathmor, Merguid, Moruined, Morehel, Morcant, Boten, Morgent, Mortineil, Glasteing.[4]

The chapter continues to relate how the last-named 'brother', Glasteing, discovered the deserted Glastonbury, having followed his sow 'per mediterraneos Anglos secus uillam que dicitur Escebtiorne . . . usque ad Wellis'. The sow is said to have been found under an apple tree (*sub malo*), and these events are then employed as etymological explanations for what appear to be local traditions concerning the 'Sow's Way' (*sugewege*), the 'Old Church apples' (*ealdecyrcenas epple*), and the 'Old Church sow' (*ealdecyrce suge*). Although the *De antiquitate* was originally the work of William of Malmesbury, in its extant form the text has been heavily interpolated by later monks of Glastonbury, and this fact bears somewhat on the elucidation of the material quoted above.[5]

No member of the pedigree seems to be attested convincingly in any independent source, and consequently scholars have depended upon their own ingenuity in order to explain this otherwise enigmatic piece of genealogical information. It has been suggested that the form of the personal name Glasteing, as used in the *De antiquitate*, is the result of a confusion over a version of the Old Welsh name *Glastenic* (= Glastening) of HG §25, with a possibly unexpanded contraction-mark over the *e* resolving to the variant form Glastening.[6] This name would sit neatly among a series of attested early medieval Welsh regional and kindred-group names comprising a personal name plus the suffix -*ing*, so that Glastening would be translated as 'descendants of Glasten'.[7] Technically, therefore, the figure Glasteing in the *De antiquitate* is a misnomer, arising presumably from the identification of an equivalent of Glast (HG) or Glas (ABT) of the pedigree with the contracted form of the name of the kindred-group.[8] On the basis of the similarity of Glast(en) and Glastonbury, those scholars who have paid attention to the pedigree have generally accepted its association with the site, despite its apparently altered form in the *De antiquitate*.[9] However, a close analysis of the available material would seem to suggest that the historicity of this association is more apparent than real.

[4]   *DA*, ch. 4 (ed. Scott, p. 52).
[5]   *The Early History*, ed. Scott, pp. 27–33.
[6]   A. W. Wade-Evans, 'The Origin of Glastonbury', *Notes and Queries* 193 (1948), 134–5.
[7]   M. Richards, 'Early Welsh Territorial Suffixes', *Journal of the Royal Society of Antiquaries of Ireland* 95 (1965), 205–12, at 206 and 208–9. Wade-Evans regarded 'Glastan' as a diminutive form of Glast ('The Origin of Glastonbury', p. 134).
[8]   In the ensuing discussion I shall use 'Glastening' when referring to the kindred-group, and 'Glasteing' to denote the character who features in the *De antiquitate*. 'Glast' will be used to denote the member of HG §25, and 'Glast(eing)' will be employed in cases of ambiguity.
[9]   Bartrum, *Early Welsh Genealogical Tracts*, p. 128; Wade-Evans, 'The Origin of Glastonbury'; E. W. B. Nicholson, 'The Dynasty of Cunedag and the "Harleian Genealogies"', *Y Cymmrodor* 21 (1908), 63–104, at 100–3; L. H. Gray, 'The Origin of the Name Glastonbury', *Speculum* 10 (1935), 46–53. But see the more cautious approach of Bradley, 'The Etymology of "Lichfield" ', p. 306.

According to the *De antiquitate*, Glasteing was one of twelve brothers who migrated from the north and assumed control of various parts of Wales. The great-grandfather (*proauus*) of these brothers was said to have been one Cunedda. Cunedda wledig is an important figure in early Welsh pseudo-history. According to the anonymous ninth-century text, the *Historia Britto-num*, and various medieval Welsh genealogical tracts, Cunedda and his numerous sons, having migrated to Wales from Manaw of Gododdin in north-eastern Britain, expelled Irish settlers from various parts of Wales and established a series of Welsh kingdoms.[10] This claim is allegedly vindicated by the fact that the names of his sons as recorded in the sources would appear to be preserved in names of certain medieval *cantrefi* and some attested early medieval kingdoms.[11] It has been noted that among the Cuneddan genealogies copied on 33r–41r of the fourteenth-century codex, Oxford, Bodleian Library, Jesus College 20, the following pedigree occurs (§50):

> <M>euruc m. Elaed m. Elud m. Glas m. Elno m. Docvael m. Cuneda wledic.[12]

The relationship of Glas ab Elno to Cunedda described in this pedigree has been taken as confirmation of that of Glasteing to his *proauus* Cunedda as stated in the *De antiquitate*.[13] A second version of this genealogy of Dogfeiling in North Wales exists in *Achau Brenhinoedd a Thywysogion Cymru*, where – as in the case of that text's recension of the Glastening pedigree – Glas has been reduced to a cognomen;[14] and he has been omitted altogether from the copy made in 1640 by John Jones of Gelli Lyfdy in Cardiff, Public Library, 25, p. 81.

There are two sections of the *Historia Brittonum* which relate to Cunedda (chapters 14 and 62):

> . . . filii autem Liethan obtinuerunt in regione Demetorum et in aliis regionibus, id est Guir <et> Cetgueli, donec expulsi sunt a Cuneda et a filiis eius ab omnibus Brittanicis regionibus.

> Mailcunus magnus rex apud Brittones regnabat, id est in regione Guenedotae, quia atauus illius, id est Cunedag, cum filiis suis quorum numerus octo erat, uenerat prius de parte sinistrali, id est de regione quae uocatur Manau Guotodin, centum quadraginta sex annis ante-

---

[10] The text of the material from the *Historia Brittonum* (HG §§32, 33) is given below; *Bonedd yr Arwyr* §29 (Bartrum, *Early Welsh Genealogical Tracts*, pp. 13, 91–3); see also *Vita II S. Carantoci*, chs 2–3 (*Vitae Sanctorum Britanniae et Genealogiae*, ed. and trans. A. W. Wade-Evans [Cardiff, 1944], p. 148).

[11] M. Miller, 'The Foundation-Legend of Gwynedd in the Latin Texts', *Bulletin of the Board of Celtic Studies* 27 (1976–8), 515–32. J. E. Lloyd, *A History of Wales from the Earliest Times to the Edwardian Conquest*, 2 vols, 3rd ed. (London, 1939) I, 116–19.

[12] E. Phillimore, 'Pedigrees from Jesus College MS. 20', *Y Cymmrodor* 8 (1887), 83–92, at 90; Bartrum, *Early Welsh Genealogical Tracts*, p. 49.

[13] Nicholson, 'The Dynasty of Cunedag', p. 100.

[14] 'Gwehelyth Dogveiling yNyffryn Klwyd: Kenwrik ap Elaeth ap Elgud glas ap Ilon ap Dogvael Dogveiling ap Kunedda wledic' (ABT §27; Bartrum, *Early Welsh Genealogical Tracts*, pp. 108–9).

quam Mailcun regnaret, et Scottos cum ingentissima clade expulerunt ab istis regionibus et nusquam reuersi sunt iterum ad habitandum.[15]

Drawing on all the available material – often with scant regard for its reliability – scholars have attempted to weave the Glastening pedigree into a neat historical context. For example, calculating roughly twenty-five years per generation and placing Cunedda's obit *ca* 410 – that is 146 years before the death of Maelgwn of Gwynedd according to the *Annales Cambriae*[16] – E. W. B. Nicholson dated that of Glas ab Elno *ca* 510.[17] In Nicholson's estimation, such a date would have enabled Glas to have been present at Arthur's battle of *Kaerluideoit* mentioned by Geoffrey of Monmouth in chapter 145 of his *Historia regum Britannie*, which may, Nicholson then argued, provide a context for Glasteing's migration to Glastonbury, and explain the reference to *Loytcoyt* in HG §25! However, a *Kaer Loytcoyt* is not included in the earlier list of battles of Arthur given in chapter 56 of the *Historia Brittonum* – although it does appear among the *ciuitates* of Britain listed in that text (chapter 66a) – and indeed Geoffrey identified *Kaerluideoit* with Lincoln, not Lichfield.[18] Geoffrey's contemporary, Henry of Huntingdon, also made this identification with Lincoln when giving a version of the list of *ciuitates* from the *Historia Brittonum* in his *Historia Anglorum* (chapter 3).[19] Wade-Evans, in turn, drew attention to the alliteration of the names Elaed, Elud and Elno of the pedigree of Dogfeiling (Jesus College 20 §50) and postulated some 'family connection' with the line of Cerdic (son of *Elesa* son of *Esla*), the founder of

15   *Nennii Historia Britonum*, ed. J. Stevenson (London, 1838), pp. 12, 52–3; *Chronica Minora saec. IV.V.VI.VII*, ed. T. Mommsen, 3 vols (Berlin, 1891–8) III, 156, 205–6.

16   s.a. [547] (Phillimore, 'The *Annales Cambriæ* and Old-Welsh Genealogies', p. 155).

17   Nicholson, 'The Dynasty of Cunedag', pp. 100–1.

18   *The Historia Regum Britannie of Geoffrey of Monmouth*, ed. N. Wright (Cambridge, 1984) I, 102.

19   *Henrici Archidiaconi Huntendunensis Historia Anglorum*, ed. T. Arnold, RS 74 (London, 1879), p. 7. The inclusion of *Kair Glou*, *Kair Ceri*, *Kair Merdin*, and perhaps also *Kair Cei* in Henry's list indicates that the source was a copy of the expanded list characteristic of the 'Vatican' recension of the *Historia Brittonum*; and it shares some variant readings with the text of that recension in the later twelfth-century manuscript Paris, Bibliothèque Nationale, lat. 11108 (J), for which see *The Historia Brittonum: 3. The 'Vatican' Recension*, ed. D. N. Dumville (Cambridge, 1985), pp. 29–31, 49, 62–3. The list given in the *Historia Anglorum* has some omissions and has been re-ordered into two parts: the first part comprising names which – with the exception of *Kair Bristou* – are identified in the text, and the second of names for which – with the exception of *Kair Peris* – no identification is offered. Ifor Williams noted the similarity of this arrangement of the names and the list entitled *Enweu Ynys Prydein* given in the Red Book of Hergest of *ca* 1400: I. Williams, 'Enwau ac Anryfeddodau Ynys Prydain', *Bulletin of the Board of Celtic Studies* 5 (1929–31), 19–24, at 19–21. Furthermore, the vernacular list shares some readings with those of J and Henry of Huntingdon, against the other 'Vatican' and 'Harleian' texts of the *Historia Brittonum*: *Kaer Dawri* being closer to *Cair Dauri* (J, also Henry) than to *Cair Daun* (Harleian and Vatican recensions); or, *Kaer Cusrad* being closer to *Cair Cuscerat* (J) or *Kair Cucerat* (Henry) than to *Cair Custeint* (Vatican recension). Similarly, if Henry's *Kair Cei* is equivalent to *Cair Ceim* of J – *Cair Teim* (Vatican recension) – then so is *Kaer Gei* of the vernacular list.

the West Saxon dynasty.[20] However, it has been argued that the 'Anglian' descent of Cerdic to Woden as recorded in most sources represents an altered version of an earlier, more overtly 'Saxon', ancestry, and that the name Esla is a later addition, intended to enhance the alliterative character of the genealogy.[21]

John Morris identified *Mormayl* (that is, Morfael), the son of Glast according to HG §25,[22] with the Morfael who is described in the poem *Marwnad Cynddylan* as having fought alongside Cynddylan ap Cyndrwyn at Llywdgoed, and – presumably drawing on the account of Glasteing's migration in the *De antiquitate* – he suggested that this 'last British lord of Lichfield' fled to Glastonbury in response to the English incursions which seem to form the background to the Cynddylan cycle of Welsh poetry.[23] However, without supporting evidence, the mere correspondence of names is insufficient to justify the association of these sources. Indeed, Ifor Williams's edition of the poem on which these arguments are based has modernized the orthography, and the form of the name in the manuscripts is *Moriael*.[24] In fact, Williams had earlier suggested that this form might reflect a confusion of the names Morial and Morfael (or a miscopying of the form *Moruael*) and subsequently arguments in favour of both names have been ventured.[25] Although the ambiguity of the poem prevents *Moriael* from being definitely identified as one of the *meibion Cyndrwynyn* mentioned there,[26] a *Morvael* is enumerated among the children of Cyndrwyn in the genealogical tract *Bonedd yr Arwyr* (§1).[27] Thus, if Morfael is regarded as the brother – not just military ally – of Cynddylan,[28] then his identification with Morfael *son of Glast* of the pedigree must surely collapse. A similar conclusion would be reached if the correct explanation of *Moriael* were not Morfael, but Morial.[29]

The account given in the *De antiquitate* is clearly very close at a number of points to these two extracts from the *Historia Brittonum* – the enormity of the offspring, its northern origin, and the order of the names Dyfed, Gower and

20   Wade-Evans, 'The Origin of Glastonbury', p. 134.
21   K. Sisam, 'Anglo-Saxon Royal Genealogies', *Proceedings of the British Academy* 39 (1953), 287–348, at 300–7; D. N. Dumville, 'Kingship, Genealogies and Regnal Lists', *Early Medieval Kingship*, ed. P. H. Sawyer and I. N. Wood (Leeds, 1977), pp. 72–104, at 78. The latter has been reprinted; see D. N. Dumville, *Histories and Pseudo-histories of the Insular Middle Ages* (Aldershot, 1990), ch. 15.
22   This name is lacking in ABT §19, and is given as *Mortineil* in the *De antiquitate*.
23   J. Morris, *The Age of Arthur. A History of the British Isles from 530 to 650* (London, 1973), pp. 243, 308; *Canu Llywarch Hen*, ed. I. Williams (Cardiff, 1935), p. 52.
24   *Ibid.*; J. Rowland, *Early Welsh Saga Poetry. A Study and Edition of the Englynion* (Cambridge, 1990), p. 176; R. G. Gruffydd, 'Marwnad Cynddylan', *Bardos. Penodau ar y Traddodiad Barddol Cymreig a Cheltaidd*, ed. R. G. Gruffydd (Cardiff, 1982), pp. 10–28, at 20; I. Williams, 'Marwnad Cynddylan', *Bulletin of the Board of Celtic Studies* 6 (1931–3), 134–41, at 136.
25   *Ibid.* p. 140; Rowland, *Early Welsh Saga Poetry*, pp. 177, 187; Gruffydd, 'Marwnad Cynddylan', pp. 15, 24.
26   Rowland, *Early Welsh Saga Poetry*, pp. 187, 611.
27   Bartrum, *Early Welsh Genealogical Tracts*, p. 85.
28   W. Davies, *Wales in the Early Middle Ages* (Leicester, 1982), p. 100.
29   Gruffydd, 'Marwnad Cynddylan', p. 15.

Kidwelly – and it would not be unreasonable to suggest that a version of the *Historia* may be among the *antiqui Britonum gesta* cited in the *De antiquitate*.[30] A more detailed comparison of the Glastonbury account of Cunedda with its alleged sources in the *Historia Brittonum* will be given below; for present purposes, it is worth drawing attention to some differences which would imply that the author of this section of the *De antiquitate* either misunderstood or consciously altered the account in the *Historia*. For instance, according to the latter text it was the Irish, not the descendants of Cunedda, who had held Dyfed, Gower and Kidwelly, and indeed these three southern Welsh regions lie outside the area encompassed by the kingdoms which were associated in the genealogies with Cunedda's sons. Similarly, the migration from the north was undertaken by Cunedda and his sons, not some more distant descendants. The problem is compounded by the fact that according to the Harleian genealogies and *Achau Brenhinoedd a Thywysogion Cymru* we are dealing with a pedigree, not a list of brothers. Cunedda is credited with eight immigrant sons in chapter 62 of the *Historia Brittonum*[31] or with nine sons and one grandson in HG §32, and since a larger figure is achieved only in later genealogical tracts (*Bonedd yr Arwyr* §29) – which can be regarded as an extension of the earlier pattern – the number twelve given in the *De antiquitate* was probably derived from the pedigree/list, rather than from the Cuneddan material used in the compilation of chapter 4. These characteristics of the account in the *De antiquitate*, when contrasted with the testimony of the *Historia*, would facilitate the inclusion of the 'list' into the Glastonbury text and seem to be the product of a conscious alteration of the information derived from the *Historia* for this purpose. The pedigree/list need have had no textual association with Cunedda prior to the writing of the *De antiquitate*.

Although Jesus College 20 §50 does appear to provide convenient genealogical confirmation of the relevant material in the *De antiquitate*, the evidence for manipulation of the material derived from the *Historia Brittonum* might arouse suspicion concerning the Cuneddan aspect of the Glastonbury account, and indeed neither HG §25 nor the variant ABT §19 traces the ancestry of the Glastening beyond the eponymous ancestor Glast. It is possible to envisage a medieval scholar – probably the author of chapter 4 of the *De antiquitate* – who, having access to one or more collections of Welsh genealogies, made the identification of Glast(eing) of the Glastening with Glas ab Elno of Dogfeiling and was thus able to credit Glast(eing) and his descendants/brothers with a Cuneddan ancestry.[32] Indeed, according to HG §§32–3, Dogfael ap Cunedda (the grandfather of Glas ab Elno in the Jesus

---

30   R. Thurneysen, 'Zu Wilhelm von Malmesbury', *Zeitschrift für romanische Philologie* 20 (1896), 316–20, at 319.

31   See text above.

32   Thurneysen seems to have been unaware of the Jesus College pedigree, and postulated ('Zu Wilhelm von Malmesbury', p. 319) that Glast(eing) might have been credited with a Cuneddan ancestry because Cunedda appeared as the founder of the line of Ceredigion as represented by the pedigree which immediately succeeds that of the Glastening in the Harleian collection (HG §26).

College pedigree) took part in the migration from Manaw of Gododdin to Wales with Cunedda. Consequently, unless one would wish to argue (rather convolutedly) that either he or one of his immediate descendants subsequently returned north, thereby providing a context for the migration of Glasteing and his brothers recounted in the *De antiquitate*, the main outline of the Glastonbury account is not compatible with that represented by the *Historia Brittonum* and the Harleian genealogies. Furthermore, if the account in the *De antiquitate* is dismissed, then the grounds for arguing that HG §25 and Jesus College 20 §50 represent two branches of the same lineage become even less acceptable. Once Glast(eing) had been identified with Glas ab Elno the incorporation of the material about Cunedda from the *Historia Brittonum* would be a relatively simple process, facilitated by a small number of textual alterations as outlined above.

The corrupt material following the pedigree in HG §25 offers little help in suggesting a context for the Glastening, whether Glastonbury or not. Phillimore emended 'unu*m* sunt' to 'un*de* est',[33] and Bartrum offered 'Glastenic qui uenerunt <per uillam> que uocatur Loytcoyt'. As noted above, *Loytcoyt* has been identified with Lichfield. However, the choice of emendation, particularly of the missing preposition, is theoretically very wide.[34] The transitory character of Bartrum's 'per' is probably dependent upon an acceptance of the account of Glasteing's route described in the *De antiquitate*: Wade-Evans tentatively associated *Escebtiorne* – arguably containing the Welsh word *esgob* ('bishop') – with Lichfield, a bishop's see in the Anglo-Saxon period, which could be regarded as a point of contact between the two texts.[35] It is always possible, of course, that the description of Glasteing's route in the *De antiquitate* was inspired by, or even based upon, some version of the mangled non-genealogical material which concludes HG §25. According to Bartrum's critical apparatus, the copy of ABT §19 in the mid-sixteenth-century collection, Aberystwyth, National Library of Wales, Peniarth 177 (p. 217), would appear to be introduced by a passage which clearly bears some relation to this concluding material.[36] I have italicized those phrases which seem to be common to both pedigrees:

> *Oddyna y Glastyniaid a dyvodd* o Gaer *Llwydkoed* i Gaer *a elwir* yr awr honn Aldüd.[37]

This might be understood as describing the journey of the Glastening from Lichfield to *Aldüd*. The latter place-name is arguably a corruption of *Alclud*,

---

[33] Phillimore, 'The *Annales Cambriæ* and Old-Welsh Genealogies', p. 180, n. 4.
[34] Wade-Evans ('The Origin of Glastonbury', p. 134) would have *secus uillam*; Thurneysen ('Zu Wilhelm von Malmesbury', p. 319) inserted *a regione*; and Bradley ('The Etymology of "Lichfield" ', p. 306) gave *a ciuitate*.
[35] Wade-Evans, 'The Origin of Glastonbury', p. 134. Furthermore, Bradley ('The Etymology of "Lichfield" ', p. 306) suggested that the second element of *Escebtiorne* might contain *ty* ('house').
[36] Peniarth 177 contains three hands – one of which has been identified as that of Griffith Hiraethog – and was written between 1544 and 1565: J. G. Evans, *Report on Manuscripts in the Welsh Language*, 2 vols (London, 1898–1910) I, 982.
[37] Bartrum, *Early Welsh Genealogical Tracts*, pp. 106–7.

an attested form of Old Welsh *Alt Clut*, the Brittonic name for Dumbarton,[38] but this is hardly in the vicinity of Glastonbury. An alternative interpretation of this material might be ventured. The collection of genealogical and miscellaneous material by Hugh Thomas (d. 1720) in London, British Library, Harley 2289 contains a second vernacular version of this passage:

> Odhyna Glastyneyt a dynaud o Gaer o Gaer Lugthoet.[39]

Henry Bradley emended *Lugtheot* to *Luytkoet* and stated that the scribe 'has added a gloss identifying *Luytkoet* with Alclud – an arbitrary guess scarcely worth notice'. The exact date of Harley 2289 is uncertain,[40] but since it postdates Peniarth 177, the mention of Alclud ought not to be attributed to Thomas. However, the possibility of its being a gloss should not be discounted automatically. Peniarth 177 introduces its reference to *Aldüd* with *i*, which – according to the interpretation offered above – could represent the preposition 'to', but could equally be derived from the abbreviation for *id est*. Furthermore, the *caer* is said to be called *Aldud* 'at *this* time' – 'yr awr *honn*', rather than *honno* ('that'). The implication might be that the author of the statement believed that the *caer* had been known earlier by a different name – the only apparent candidate being *Llwyd-goed*. As indicated above, the true identification of Llwyd-goed as Lichfield does not seem to have been known to Geoffrey of Monmouth and Henry of Huntingdon in the twelfth century.[41] Consequently, it is possible that the reference to *Alclud* in Peniarth 177 and Harley 2289 is a brave attempt by a Welsh scholar to make sense of an irretrievably corrupt source and has no bearing on the reading of HG §25.[42]

The account in the *De antiquitate* of Glasteing's journey to Glastonbury

---

[38]   The form *Alclud* is attested in a number of sources. The A-text of the *Annales Cambriæ* (s.a. [870]) contains the form *Alt Clut*, whereas the B-text (in London, Public Record Office, E. 164/1) gives *Alclut*, and the vernacular *brutiau* have *Alclut* and *Alklud* (Phillimore, 'The *Annales Cambriæ* and Old-Welsh Genealogies', p. 166; *Brut y Tywysogyon. Peniarth MS. 20*, ed. T. Jones [Cardiff, 1941], p. 5; *Brut y Tywysogyon, or The Chronicles of the Princes. Red Book of Hergest Version*, ed. and trans. T. Jones, 2nd ed. [Cardiff, 1973], p. 8; *Brenhinedd y Saesson, or The Kings of the Saxons*, ed. and trans. T. Jones [Cardiff, 1971], p. 22). Geoffrey of Monmouth seems to have used *Alclud*, among other forms (*The Historia Regum Britannie*, ed. Wright, I, 17, 33, 96, 104; J. S. P. Tatlock, *The Legendary History of Britain. Geoffrey of Monmouth's Historia Regum Britanniae and its Vernacular Versions* [Berkeley, 1950], pp. 14–16).
[39]   The piece is quoted by Bradley ('The Etymology of "Lichfield" ', p. 306); I have capitalized the initials of names. For the genealogical work of Hugh Thomas, see F. Jones, 'An Approach to Welsh Genealogy', *Transactions of the Honourable Society of Cymmrodorion* (1948), 303–466, at 421–8. Another manuscript by Thomas – London, British Library, Harley 4181 – contains a copy of the Glastening pedigree (107v, 113v), said there to have been extracted from a codex by William Salesbury: *A Catalogue of Manuscripts Relating to Wales in the British Museum*, ed. E. Owen (London, 1903), p. 421.
[40]   Owen (*A Catalogue of Manuscripts*, p. 384) dated it to the end of the seventeenth or the beginning of the eighteenth century.
[41]   Bradley, 'The Etymology of "Lichfield" ', p. 306.
[42]   It can be seen from the italics in the passage from Peniarth 177 that *a elwir* refers to *Aldud*, whereas *que uocatur* of HG §25 refers to *Loytcoyt*. Both the vernacular versions

serves only to complicate matters. The theme of the discovery of a future monastic site or hermitage either by following or encountering an animal – often a boar or a sow with young – is not an uncommon convention in the hagiography of the Celtic-speaking areas,[43] but more directly relevant for Glasteing's association with his sow is the description in various Lives of St Patrick of the resurrection and baptism by that saint of a swineherd called Glas mac Cais.[44] That Glasteing of the *De antiquitate* and Glas mac Cais are both associated with pigs may be more than fortuitous, and it has been suggested that the Irish Glas provided the direct inspiration for the porcine interests of Glasteing.[45] Indeed, *Sanas Chormaic*, the Glossary of Cormac mac Cuilennáin (d. 908), contains at §883, as part of a discussion of Irish settle-

contain the preposition *o* ('from'), which – if they are to be trusted – might provide the key to emending the Harleian reading. Thus, as noted above, Bradley offered *a ciuitate*. However, the version of the passage in Harley 2289 as given by Bradley is clearly corrupt at a number of points. For example, Bradley understood *a dynaud* to comprise the conjunction *a* ('and') plus the personal name Dunod, rather than the relative pronoun *a* plus the verb *dyfod* (*dy<u>aud*) as witnessed in Peniarth 177 and as might be surmised from the *qui uenerunt* of HG §25.

[43] It has been suggested that the description of the discovery of the site of *Alba Longa* in Virgil's *Aeneid* (VIII. 42–8) was the ultimate source for the Glastonbury account: W. W. Newell, 'William of Malmesbury on the Antiquity of Glastonbury', *Publications of the Modern Language Association of America* 18 (1903), 459–512, at 476. For purposes of comparison with the *De antiquitate*, the following examples extracted from Celtic saints' lives have been limited to references to pigs: *Vita S. Ciarani de Saigir*, ch. 5 (*Vitae Sanctorum Hiberniae partim hactenus ineditae*, ed. C. Plummer, 2 vols [Oxford, 1910] I, 219), and *Betha Ciaráin Saighre*, ch. 2 (*Bethada Náem nÉrenn*, ed. C. Plummer, 2 vols [Oxford, 1922] I, 113); *Vita S. Pyrani*, ch. 4 (P. Grosjean, 'Vita Sancti Ciarani Episcopi de Saigir ex Codice Hagiographico Gothano', *Analecta Bollandiana* 59 [1941], 217–71, at 229–30); *Vita S. Ruadani*, chs 2–3 (*Vitae Sanctorum*, ed. Plummer, II, 240–1); *Betha Ruadháin*, ch. 2 [4]–[5] (*Bethada Náem*, ed. Plummer, I, 317); *Vita S. Mochoemog*, ch. 19 (*Vitae Sanctorum*, ed. Plummer, II, 170); *Vita S. Finani abbatis de Cenn Etigh*, ch. 8 (*ibid.* 88); 'Tripartite Life of Patrick', ch. [191] (*Bethu Phátraic. The Tripartite Life of Patrick*, ed. K. Mulchrone [Dublin, 1939] I, 116); *Vita S. Finniani*, ch. 18 (*Vitae Sanctorum Hiberniae ex Codice Salmanticensi*, ed. W. W. Heist [Brussels, 1965], p. 101); *Vita S. Mochtei*, ch. 9 (*ibid.* 170); *Vita S. Kentigerni* by Jocelyn of Furness, ch. 24 (*Lives of S. Ninian and S. Kentigern Compiled in the Twelfth Century*, ed. A. P. Forbes [Edinburgh, 1874], pp. 74, 202); *Vita S. Bernachii*, ch. 7 (*Vitae Sanctorum Britanniae et Genealogiae*, ed. Wade-Evans, pp. 8–9); *Vita S. Cadoci*, chs 8, 20 (*ibid.* 44–5, 64–5); *Vita S. Iltuti*, ch.7 (*ibid.* 202–3); *De Sancto Cungaro Heremita et Confessore*, ch. [7] (J. A. Robinson, 'A Fragment of the Life of St Cungar', *Journal of Theological Studies* 20 [1918–19], 97–108, at 101); *Lectiones de Vita S. Dubricii* (*The Text of the Book of Llan Dâv*, ed. J. G. Evans and J. Rhys [Oxford, 1893], pp. 80–1); *Vita S. Pauli Aureliani*, ch. 15 (F. B. Plaine, 'Vita Sancti Pauli Episcopi Leonensis in Britannia Minori Auctore Wormonoco', *Analecta Bollandiana* 1 [1882], 208–58, at 241). A similar theme might be reflected in *Betha Phátraic* from the Book of Lismore (*Lives of Saints from the Book of Lismore*, ed. and trans. W. Stokes [Oxford, 1890], p. 6). For an extra-Celtic attestation, see M. Lapidge, 'Byrhtferth and the *Vita S. Ecgwini*', *Mediaeval Studies* 41 (1979), 331–53, at 346–7, 349–50.

[44] *Four Latin Lives of St. Patrick: Colgan's Vita Secunda, Quarta, Tertia, and Quinta*, ed. L. Bieler (Dublin, 1971), p. 165. The *Vita Auctore Probo* gives the swineherd's name as *mac Maic Cais maic Glais* (*ibid.* p. 213). The form in the 'Tripartite Life' is *Cáss macc Glaiss qui fuit subulcus Lugair ríg Iruatáe* (*Bethu Phátraic*, ed. Mulchrone, p. 77).

[45] Newell, 'William of Malmesbury on the Antiquity of Glastonbury', pp. 474–6; see also Thurneysen, 'Zu Wilhelm von Malmesbury', p. 320.

ment in Britain, a reference to the swineherd Glas mac Cais at *Glastimbir na nGaoidel* ('Glastonbury of the Irish'?), mentioning his resurrection by Patrick, and locating him and his pigs 'beside a fruit tree' (*for mess*).[46] As stated above, Glasteing's sow is found *sub malo* in the Glastonbury account. In the preface to the *De antiquitate*, William claimed to have written the Lives of a number of Irish saints, including Patrick, and a summary of this *Vita S. Patricii* has been preserved by John Leland in his *Collectanea*.[47] From this summary it has been demonstrated that William drew mostly on the so-called 'English recension' of the *Vita Tertia* and (for chapters 1–11) on a text of the *Vita Secunda/ Quarta* type.[48] Although Leland's extant summary does not indicate that William used the material in the *Vita Tertia* relating to Glas mac Cais (namely, chapter 67),[49] it has been argued on the basis of his knowledge of Patriciana that William himself was the author of chapter 4 of the *De antiquitate*.[50] In general, however, chapters 4–5 have been regarded as later interpolations,[51] and it is not impossible that either the sources used by William at Glastonbury when he was composing his *Vita S. Patricii* or indeed the Life itself – if Leland's summary is incomplete – provided the inspiration for a later monk to connect the swineherd Glas mac Cais with Glast(eing) of the genealogies and thereby introduce the pig-theme into the *De antiquitate*. Alternatively, a local version of the account in *Sanas Chormaic* may have acted as an intermediate stage.[52]

Some light might be thrown on this problem if the relationship between the *De antiquitate* and the Cuneddan material in the *Historia Brittonum*, upon which it would seem to be dependent, is studied more closely. Of the two passages concerning Cunedda in the *Historia Brittonum*, it may be noted that, according to Mommsen's critical apparatus, while the first (chapter 14) is present in all the texts except the fragmentary copy in the now destroyed Chartres, Bibliothèque Municipale, 98 (Mommsen's MS. Z), the second (chapter 62) is to be found only in the texts of Mommsen's H (London, British Library, Harley 3859) and K (London, British Library, Cotton Vespa-

---

46   'Et inde est Glastimbir na nGaoidel .i. cell for brú Marae hIcht. Iss ed árus indsin i rraba Glass mac Caiss muccid rígh Hirúaite oc a muccaib for mess, is é indsin rodersaig Patraic íartoin sé fichit blíadain íarna guin do fíanaib Maic Con. . . .' (*Sanas Cormaic. An Old-Irish Glossary Compiled by Cormac Úa Cuilennáin*, ed. K. Meyer in *Anecdota from Irish Manuscripts*, ed. O. J. Bergin, R. I. Best, K. Meyer and J. G. O'Keeffe, 5 vols [Dublin, 1907–13] IV, 75).

47   *DA*, prologue (ed. Scott, p. 40); C. H. Slover, 'William of Malmesbury's *Life of St. Patrick*', *Modern Philology* 24 (1926–7), 5–20, at 10–19; *Joannis Lelandi Antiquarii De Rebus Britannicis Collectanea*, ed. T. Hearne, 6 vols, 2nd ed. (London, 1774) III, 273–5.

48   *Four Latin Lives*, ed. Bieler, pp. 21–4. Scott (*The Early History*, pp. 7, 175) would also include Patrick's own *Confessio* among these sources.

49   The sections of the *Vita Tertia* used by William are chapters 1–26 (with omissions), 36, 72–3, 78, 87, for which see Slover, 'William of Malmesbury's *Life of St. Patrick*', pp. 10–19.

50   C. H. Slover, 'William of Malmesbury and the Irish', *Speculum* 2 (1927), 268–83, at 275–80.

51   J. Armitage Robinson, *Somerset Historical Essays* (London, 1921), pp. 11–12; *The Early History*, ed. Scott, p. 188, n. 24.

52   Newell, 'William of Malmesbury on the Antiquity of Glastonbury', p. 476.

sian D. xxi). If it could be determined that the *De antiquitate* was dependent on both chapters from the *Historia Brittonum*, then the source-recension used by the compiler of the Glastonbury text might be more easily identified. The statement in the *De antiquitate* that Glasteing and his brothers 'tenuerunt plurimas regiones Uenedociam, Demeciam, Guther, Kedweli' would seem to derive from chapter 14 of the *Historia Brittonum*,[53] although there is no mention of Gwynedd (the *Venedocia* of the *De antiquitate*) in that chapter. However, the Cuneddan ancestry of the Venedotian ruler Maelgwn is mentioned explicitly in chapter 62 of the *Historia*, and that might explain why that first Welsh region – along with Dyfed, Gower and Kidwelly – is said in the Glastonbury account to have been held by the brothers. Similarly, according to the *De antiquitate* the brothers 'a boreali Britannie parte uenerunt in occidentem', but chapter 14 of the *Historia Brittonum* – being primarily concerned with the phenomenon of Irish migration to parts of Britain – simply describes how Cunedda and his sons dealt with the Irish settlement in Wales, without giving the Cuneddan place of origin. Chapter 62 of the *Historia Brittonum*, on the other hand, is more specific: 'Cunedag . . .uenerat prius de parte sinistrali, id est de regione quae uocatur Manau Guotodin.' The absence of Manaw of Gododdin from the Glastonbury account may seem a little surprising if chapter 62 of the *Historia Brittonum* was being drawn upon at this point. However, the brothers' journey 'from the North' and 'into the West' would presumably place their origin to the north-east of their destination, and that is how one might very roughly describe the accepted location of Gododdin with respect to Wales.[54]

Arguably, therefore, in order to allow us to account for all his information about the Cuneddan migration, we must suppose that the author of chapter 4 of the *De antiquitate* had access to chapters 14 and 62 of the *Historia Brittonum*, and would therefore have been drawing on a text of the 'Harleian' recension. The line of argument here is tentative, and against such a conclusion it might be suggested that if the author of chapter 4 of the *De antiquitate* had extracted his 'list' of brothers from a collection of Old Welsh genealogies related to that found in Harley 3859 (HG §25), then in that source he could also have found evidence of Maelgwn's Cuneddan descent (HG §1) and Cunedda's association with Manaw of Gododdin prior to the alleged migration to Wales (HG §32).

William of Malmesbury seems to have drawn on the *Historia Brittonum* when compiling the description, given in his *Gesta regum Anglorum*, of the dealings of Vortigern with the English settlers,[55] and he introduced this section on Vortigern 'ut in gestis Britonum legitur'.[56] Much of the information given here by William is common to most of the recensions of the *Historia*

---

[53] 'Filii Liethan obtinuerunt in regione Demetorum et in aliis regionibus, id est Guir <et> Cetgueli.'

[54] *The Gododdin. The Oldest Scottish Poem*, trans. K. H. Jackson (Edinburgh, 1969), pp. 69–75.

[55] *Gesta regum Anglorum*, chs 4–8; *Willelmi Malmesbiriensis Monachi de Gestis Regum Anglorum*, ed. W. Stubbs, 2 vols, RS 90 (London, 1887–9) I, 7–8, 10, 12.

[56] *Ibid*. ch. 4, ed. Stubbs, I, 7.

Brittonum, and the degree of rewording and of interpolation of material from other sources, such as Bede's *Historia ecclesiastica gentis Anglorum* and the Anglo-Saxon Chronicle, makes comparatively difficult the task of identifying the recension of the *Historia Brittonum* on which he drew. However, he incorporated verbatim into his *Polyhistor* the section on *mirabilia* from the *Historia Brittonum*, and an analysis of William's text shows that his source at this point was of the 'Gildasian' recension created in Anglo-Norman England *ca* 1100.[57] The 'Gildasian' recension omits chapter 62 of the *Historia Brittonum*, and therefore, if the reasoning above holds, a text of that recension could not have furnished all the Cuneddan material apparent in chapter 4 of the *De antiquitate*. Although the results of this analysis of William's use in his various works of the *Historia Brittonum* are far from satisfactory – for instance, it is not impossible that William had access to texts of more than one recension at different points in his career – it might be argued – in support of others who would regard chapters 3–5 of the *De antiquitate* as later interpolations – that, since William can only be shown to have used the 'Gildasian' recension, he is possibly not the author of chapter 4, which seems to be dependent on the 'Harleian' recension.

In conclusion, it may be stated that there is no strong evidence whatsoever for the association of the pedigree of the Glastening (HG §25 and ABT §19) with Glastonbury. As it stands, the pedigree offers nothing towards this hypothetical association beyond the mere correspondence of the personal name Glast and *Glast*onbury – hardly the basis for a compelling argument. It is the *De antiquitate* which provides the primary material which scholars have employed when attempting to cast light on the genealogy. However, the relevant section of that tract appears to depend ultimately on reworked information drawn from the *Historia Brittonum*, and that reworking, in turn, may have been executed after the original composition of the *De antiquitate*

---

[57]   *William of Malmesbury, Polyhistor*, ed. H. T. Ouellette (Binghamton, N.Y., 1982), pp. 153–5. I am grateful to David Dumville for supplying me with the relevant information concerning the textual history of the *Historia Brittonum* and for discussing the evidence for William's use of that text in the *Gesta regum* and *Polyhistor*. There are three defining characteristics of the 'Gildasian' recension at this point: the *saut du même au même* '. . . *se* [in modum arietum et procedit unusquique ad alterum et collidunt *se*] ad inuicem . . .' (*Polyhistor*, ed. Ouellette, p. 153, line 26; *Chronica Minora*, ed. Mommsen, III, 214, lines 5–7); the *saut du même au même* '. . . *sissam* [et mare inundatur similiter in ostio supra dicti fluminis et in stagno ostii recipitur in modum uoraginis et mare non uadit sursum et est litus iuxta flumen et quamdiu Sabrina inundatur ad *sissam*] istud. . .' (*Polyhistor*, ed. Ouellette, p. 153, line 30; *Chronica Minora*, ed. Mommsen, III, 214, lines 15–20); and, the inversion of the order of the last sections of the *mirabilia*, chs 74–6 (*Polyhistor*, ed. Ouellette, p. 155, lines 5–19 [=chs 75, 76], & lines 20–30 [=ch. 74]). Furthermore, Ouellette has suggested (*Polyhistor*, p. 34) that William's material 'shows most agreement and the least disagreement' with the Gildasian text of Durham, Cathedral Library, B. 2. 35, pp. 235–49, which was written in the first half of the twelfth century: D. N. Dumville, 'The Corpus Christi "Nennius" ', *Bulletin of the Board of Celtic Studies* 25 (1972–4), 360–80, at 372; reprinted as *Histories and Pseudo-histories of the Insular Middle Ages*, ch. 9. William is known to have visited Durham *ca* 1125: R. M. Thomson, *William of Malmesbury* (Woodbridge, 1987), pp. 73–4.

by William of Malmesbury – thereby calling its reliability further into question. The Glastening must remain in obscurity: they are first witnessed in a
genealogical tract of the mid-tenth century and would appear – from the
corrupt passage which follows their pedigree – to have had some sort of
association with Lichfield. The nature of that association is uncertain due to
the degree of textual corruption. Their sojourn in Glastonbury, however, is
the product of medieval pseudo-historical thought supported by the zealous
ingenuity of subsequent scholars.

Eadmer's Letter to the Monks of Glastonbury Concerning St Dunstan's Disputed Remains

RICHARD SHARPE

During the ninth, tenth, and eleventh centuries the notion was widely accepted that the remains of a saint might be removed illicitly from their place of rest and appropriated by another church. Such *furta sacra* could take place only with the consent of the saint in question: without this the tomb could not be opened. Saints stolen in this way were in most cases little-known figures removed from little-known churches. Almost invariably our knowledge of the theft derives from an account written by the successful church, describing how it acquired its new patron and setting out the saint's *uirtutes*. Such accounts tend to have many features in common. In word and deed these *furta sacra* conform to a widely distributed tradition.[1]

The story of how Glastonbury came to possess the relics of St Dunstan differs in many respects from this tradition. The theft supposedly took place in 1012 but the earliest account of it from Glastonbury was not written until after 1184. This account is one of the interpolations added to William of Malmesbury's *De antiquitate Glastonie ecclesie*. It specifically says that Dunstan's remains were removed from Canterbury in 1012; they were hidden at Glastonbury for 172 years and were rediscovered only in the aftermath of the fire which destroyed much of the abbey in 1184.[2] The discovery of St Dunstan's relics at this stage may have been motivated by the need to increase the number of attractions drawing pilgrims to the abbey in order to raise funds necessary for rebuilding. Although Dunstan had been abbot of Glastonbury before his appointment as bishop of Worcester and later archbishop of Canterbury, the story in the *De antiquitate* was not founded on any actual association between Dunstan and Glastonbury; it was framed within the tradition of pious thefts. In 1012, the story goes, Canterbury lay desolate after its destruction by the Danes in the previous year. King Edmund – anachronistically titled, since Æthelred was still king – came to Glastonbury, described the sorry state of Canterbury, the *uirtutes precelsas* of St Dunstan, and encouraged the abbot of Glastonbury to rescue the archbishop's body from this neglect. Four monks carried out the removal: according to this story they were monks of Glastonbury who had accompanied Dunstan to

---

[1] Discussed on the basis of evidence mostly from France by P. J. Geary, *Furta Sacra* (Princeton, 1984).
[2] For the account of the translation, concealment and recovery of the relics, see *DA*, chs 23–5 (ed. Scott, pp. 72–9).

Canterbury and remained with him presumably from 960 until his death in 988; they had laid him in his grave in the cathedral of Christ Church and had continued there a further twenty-three years until the abduction of Archbishop Ælfheah in 1011. They knew exactly where to find St Dunstan's body but, when they had brought it to Glastonbury, it was felt prudent to keep its presence a secret lest Canterbury should soon reclaim its saint.

The principal departure from the usual tradition depends on the fame of St Dunstan and of his burial at Canterbury. Not only did everyone know that he was buried in his cathedral there but they also knew that Glastonbury had never publicly vindicated its claim to have the archbishop's remains. Hence nearly two centuries of silence. Canterbury was not known to be bereft. Canterbury's desolation was a brief episode but it was at least historically attested. In the thirteenth-century manuscript of the interpolated *De antiquitate* a contemporary hand noted in the margin both the anachronistic reference to King Edmund and the account of how the Danes had slaughtered the monks of Canterbury from Osbern's *Vita S. Elphegi*.[3] Such evidence lent weight to the story which was otherwise exceedingly and irredeemably improbable.

William of Malmesbury made no reference to this story in his own *Vita S. Dunstani*, though this was written to please the monks of Glastonbury, by correcting the Canterbury bias of Osbern's *Vita*. It may therefore be assumed that the interpolated account in the *De antiquitate* did not merely rewrite a version of the story in William's work: William did not admit any claim on the part of Glastonbury to possess, openly or privily, the relics of St Dunstan.

Yet William must have known such a claim. The tale inserted into the *De antiquitate* after 1184 is a modification of a story which we know was in circulation around the year 1120 when William was at the height of his powers. This earlier story does not survive as a Glastonbury claim but, unusually for the tradition of *furta sacra*, as a refutation by Eadmer, monk of Christ Church, Canterbury. Eadmer wrote to the monks soon after 1120, relating all the elements in their story of the theft of St Dunstan's body, ridiculing the claim in every possible way, and condemning the act (if it had been true) as sacrilege. Eadmer cannot have been unaware that saints' relics had often been translated without the consent of their custodians – Christ Church had acquired relics of St Wilfrid from Ripon in this way – but he never conceded even the possibility that the saint might have consented to such a translation regardless of the views held by the deprived party. The fact of the matter was that St Dunstan's body had never left Canterbury. Any supposed removal of his relics could not have been pious but would have been nothing less than sacrilege, if the claim were not itself a fraud. Condemnation of what was claimed went hand in hand with ridicule of the claims. There is a certain irony here, for Eadmer had himself described how Arch-

---

[3]   *The Early History*, ed. Scott, p. 72, note h, appears not to have recognized that the marginal note quotes five lines ('ita quod ex omni numero . . . secum abduxerunt') from Osbern's *Vita S. Elphegi*, as printed in *Anglia Sacra*, ed. H. Wharton, 2 vols (London, 1691) II, 122–47, at 136.

bishop Oda found Ripon deserted and took the opportunity to translate St Wilfrid's bones to Canterbury.[4] Eadmer made no mention of sacrilege there, but in that case what Eadmer described had actually happened, and Ripon was powerless to stop the archbishop. Here Eadmer's indignation at Glastonbury's false claims is understandable, but his contention that the acts – if the claims were true – were themselves shameful carries a shade of hypocrisy. Right, none the less, was on his side here: the arguments he deployed rested on his acquaintance with the facts as he accepted them and as he could support them from written and oral testimony. His presentation of the case is not without its amusing side.

The particulars of this earlier claim by the community of Glastonbury must be reconstructed from Eadmer's arguments against them. The premise, as in the later version, is that Canterbury was left desolate after the Danish attack in 1011. In this story monks from Glastonbury acted as guards during Canterbury's troubles: their actions, therefore, if they stole what they had come to guard, were treacherous as well as sacrilegious. St Dunstan's grave was opened, his body was removed and taken to Glastonbury, but its removal was apparently concealed because a substitute corpse, a deceased abbot of Glastonbury, was placed in the grave. As a result of Lanfranc's opening of the grave in 1070 it was public knowledge that the body it contained was dressed as an archbishop, a fact which Glastonbury's fiction had to accommodate. The carrying of corpses across southern England, the leaving open of the grave while this was done, and the dressing of the substitute in archiepiscopal insignia offer ample room for Eadmer's mocking rhetoric. In addition Eadmer was able to add arguments showing that Glastonbury had continued to acknowledge that Canterbury was the resting-place of the former abbot.

The letter in which all this is set out has been printed twice.[5] It has been cited chiefly as a witness to the location of St Dunstan's tomb in the cathedral at Christ Church. The evidence on this subject given by Eadmer here and elsewhere has been interpreted in several ways.[6] It is however quite clear that Dunstan's grave was in a prominent location between the choir altar in the chancel and the steps leading to the main altar in the eastern apse. After the cathedral was destroyed by fire in 1067, all the tombs had to be moved during the rebuilding. This was done about 1070 by Archbishop Lanfranc

---

[4] Eadmer, *Vita Wilfridi episcopi*, in *The Historians of the Church of York*, ed. J. Raine, 3 vols, RS 71 (London, 1879–94) I, 161–226, at 223–5.

[5] The text was printed in *Anglia Sacra*, ed. H. Wharton, II, 222–6, from a collection of Canterbury transcripts made at the beginning of the sixteenth century, now Lambeth Palace Library, 159; *Memorials of St Dunstan*, ed. W. Stubbs, RS 63 (London, 1874), pp. 412–22, gives a better text from Eadmer's personal collection of his writings in Cambridge, Corpus Christi College 371.

[6] The primary investigation is that by Robert Willis, *The Architectural History of Canterbury Cathedral* (London, 1845), in which he collected the relevant evidence from the works of Osbern and Eadmer, then largely unprinted, and offered a plan of the Anglo-Saxon cathedral. Willis's and later reconstructions are discussed by H. M. Taylor, 'The Anglo-Saxon Cathedral Church at Canterbury', *Archæological Journal* 126 (1969), 101–30; Taylor there set out (pp. 125–9) the extracts relevant to the problem.

and the new cathedral was finished in 1077. St Dunstan was reinstated and his cult continued to be one of the two most favoured of the several saints whose relics were enshrined at Christ Church: these were Dunstan and Ælfheah, Oda and Bregwine, Wilfrid and Audoen. They were celebrated in hagiography by Osbern, precentor of Christ Church in the time of Lanfranc, and their Lives were rewritten a generation or so later by Eadmer. This interesting series of *uitae* has received less attention than it deserves. The letter translated here provides a sidelight on Christ Church's devotion to its saints and a hostile commentary on the whole tradition of *furta sacra*.

The force of Eadmer's arguments may account for William of Malmesbury's silence on the subject. Its revival after 1184 did not become the object of such reproof or, if it did, no trace survives. By then Christ Church had in St Thomas a new saint whose fame and reputation greatly exceeded Dunstan's. The Glastonbury claim, however, did not die away completely. It was repeated – one suspects with little conviction – in later histories of the abbey, and was revived again in 1508.[7] At that date the abbot of Glastonbury once again set up a shrine to St Dunstan and was roundly condemned by the archbishop of Canterbury for promoting a false cult. History can be made to repeat itself.

TRANSLATION

How it is that the monks of Glastonbury claim to have the body of St Dunstan[8]

Brother Eadmer, one of the least in goodness and learning among the sons and brethren of Christ Church, Canterbury, greets the glorious community of monks at Glastonbury Abbey with loyal friendship and loving service in our Lord Jesus Christ.

I remember how I came to visit you once, some time ago. You received me with great rejoicing and honour, and for as long as I wished to remain with you you kept me with great celebration and jubilation. Even now I feel grateful to you for this and I shall continue grateful to you as long as I live. While this, therefore, ought to be and is my attitude towards you, I fancy it will surprise no one if I love your honour, if I applaud those things which benefit you, and if I loathe and detest whatever causes you shame. If I did otherwise, how could I be your loyal friend? How could I be said truly to observe the duty of brotherly love? The importance this should have for a Christian who would attain the kingdom of God is seen by the man who puts his faith in the words of the Apostle, saying that everyone who does not

---

[7]   *AD*, ed. Hearne, II, 336; *Cronica*, chs 76, 97 (ed. Carley, pp. 142–7, 178–81). The revived claim of 1508 was described and refuted in a statement by the prior of Christ Church; this together with letters by the archbishop of Canterbury and the abbot of Glastonbury concerning this dispute was printed in *Anglia Sacra*, ed. Wharton, II, 227–33, and reprinted in *Memorials*, ed. Stubbs, pp. 426–39.
[8]   I am grateful to Michael Winterbottom for his many improvements to this translation.

love his brother is a homicide and that such a man should have no share in the kingdom of God and Christ [cf. 1 John 3:15]. You will see my reasons for saying this at the beginning.

There are some among you – recent members of your community, as I think – who claim that your fathers of old were thieves and robbers and, worse, that they committed sacrilege. They make it a point of praise that they did so,[a] perhaps drunk on the same desire, ignoring the words of sacred scripture, 'nor thieves nor robbers shall inherit the kingdom of God' [1 Cor. 6:10]. Moreover they reinforce their point, affirming that those men were like Judas the traitor who, though he kept the Lord's purse, wickedly stole what he should have kept. Oh, men, who honour your brethren! who hear attentively the Lord's words! A hundred and more years have passed since they left this present life, those men whom these now claim to have been thieves and robbers. And now, only at this late stage is such a grave reproach brought against them, and[b] most unhappily they are now newly consigned to eternal punishment, to which according to the judgement of these accusers they are condemned for torment. Truly a great irreverence. For if those of old were not such as these now claim they were, the irreverence of their accusers is not lessened; no, without a doubt, it is worse, because they defame the innocent and reveal themselves to all and sundry as shameless liars. God's truth is my witness, all-knowing and all-ruling. For, when I was still a boy at school, Archbishop Lanfranc of blessed memory, primate of all Britain, had all this performed: the whole people of Canterbury were ordered to fast; the body of the blessed father Dunstan was lifted from its first burial-place, in the presence of Scotland, abbot of St Augustine's, and of Gundulf (who was later to become bishop of Rochester) and of the whole company of monks of both churches, that is of our own Christ Church and of the neighbouring church of St Peter and St Paul, now usually called St Augustine's. An untold crowd of men and women assembled, who all followed that heavenly treasure, rejoicing with voice and heart, to the place where it was to be reburied. The whole day was spent full of joy and solemnity and made bright with divine miracles.[9] It is fifty years since that happened and now some of your community – if they really are of your community – have stood up and put it about wherever they like that, a hundred years ago, there were monks from your church assigned as keepers

---

[a] In the phrase *idque illorum praedicandi laudi ascribunt* the word *praedicandi* seems redundant.
[b] Reading *et aeterna poena . . . innouatur* with the Lambeth MS rather than *ut . . .* with the Corpus MS.

---

[9] Eadmer's account here is in some respects more detailed than the longer description by Osbern in his *Miracula S. Dunstani*, chs 17, 19 (*Memorials*, ed. Stubbs, pp. 129–61, at 142–3 and 148–50). Eadmer revised Osbern's account in his own *Miracula S. Dunstani*, chs 14, 16 (*Memorials*, ed. Stubbs, pp. 223–49, at 232–3 and 236–7), but he did not there add any of the particulars he gave here.

for ours, which was at that time left desolate, so they say, on account of the martyrdom of our glorious father Elphege, and that these keepers with deceitful cunning stole what was held most precious. Alas, men more wicked than all others! The mother church of all Britain was afflicted by the death of its father and its sons, and she took refuge as with a uniquely beloved daughter and – supposing for the sake of argument that this happened – they thereby trusted that your church should safeguard her relics and her very self. Your church, as you yourselves claim, sent the best of her sons to do what was requested, but these men, having become keepers of the relics, invaded the womb of the mother they had come to protect, tore it open, looted her heart and bowels, snatched and carried away. The Jews, when they took custody of our Lord's body for fear that it might be carried off by the apostles, did not fail to guard it as long as they were able, nor did they attempt to steal it or otherwise to make off with what was entrusted to them. Rather they accused others of having stolen it while they themselves slept. If those keepers from Glastonbury had done this, that is, if they had said that the sacrilege for which they are praised had been committed by others while they themselves were asleep,[c] perhaps they would have had some regard for their own reputation and would not have besmirched it in this detestable way. As it is, what are we to say? As we set it out at the beginning, we show that they were like Judas in their theft. But it is not we who say so; rather, it is their own modern brethren at Glastonbury. Assuredly we know for certain that those men are not guilty of this sin. What does this matter to the fellows who accuse their own brethren, nay, their own fathers, with such silly concocted lies? Surely neither brethren nor fathers. For if these fellows were brethren or sons of those men, surely natural affection or even common decency would teach them to curb their tongues and to mind their own reputations. But granted that the holy brethren of Glastonbury used their cunning to make possible the concealment of their theft from everyone, they are said to have brought with them the corpse of one of their own abbots, whose name is unknown to those who put about the story, and to have set this in the holy father Dunstan's coffin so that it should not stand empty. What forethought! Were there not bones of dead men between Canterbury and Glastonbury that it should have been necessary for them, in order to conceal their theft, to have carried the corpse of someone they knew not over a distance of perhaps 200 miles?[d] Your reverence must understand how, writing this, I am confounded by such patent stupidity, worthy of everyone's scorn, especially because it is said that these tales were made up by Englishmen. Alas, why did you not look overseas, where they have more experience, more learning, and know better how to make up such stories? You could even have paid someone[e] to make up a plausible lie for you on a matter of such importance. Oh, poor pitiable you, and men of my nation, to

---

[c] Wharton and Stubbs both printed *commissum fuisse, ab aliis se somno depressis*, but the comma ought to follow *aliis*.

[d] It is M. Winterbottom's suggestion that this sentence be read as a question.

[e] Reading *ut uel pretio ageretis* in place of *et uel pretio ageretis*.

be blackened with such stupidity that you are forever judged worthy of universal derision.

So I ask these men who lay claim to this remarkable sacrilege that they tell me, their compatriot, Did they really carry the body of their supposed abbot, recently deceased and still intact, from Glastonbury to Canterbury? And did he wear the chasuble and the pallium with its pin, as an archbishop should, was he shod with bishop's sandals, or not? And if he had all these, how did it come about? Forgetting the rest for the moment, how did he come to have the pallium? Surely the abbots of Glastonbury did not wear the pallium in days gone by? This is only granted by Rome and the Holy See to patriarchs and primates and archbishops. No one has ever heard of a patriarch of Glastonbury, or even of a bishop. So if your predecessors carried to Canterbury a body dressed as an archbishop in order to deceive posterity, they were committing an affront to the Roman pontiff and to all Christian men who keep the faith under the direction of St Peter, a notorious affront which deserves all manner of disgrace. It is known that they had no authority from the Apostolic See. They made it up at the devil's prompting or they got it made up by persons like themselves. For I can assure you that the body we found was in this condition, intact and fittingly adorned with chasuble, ring, pallium, pin, and sandals. With it was found an inscription on a lead tablet which clearly stated that there lay the body of St Dunstan, archbishop of Canterbury. Have you, pray, any writings to prove matters stood thus? namely to say that the body of that abbot was decked out as I have described? Again, I ask, Did your fathers and brethren of old, who were brought – so you say – to guard the relics of our deserted church, did they bring with them that body to replace St Dunstan's as being without worries as to the success of the coming theft? Or did they come here first and take away to Glastonbury the exhumed body of our father, and did they there despoil it of its pontifical garments, and then bring back here your own abbot, dressed in St Dunstan's robes, to be placed in the grave from which our father was taken? Whichever of these you may say happened, it is easy even for a blind man to see that it would be madness to believe you. Oh unhappy men! who are so entangled in their own stupidity that they cannot understand how wiser men could not fail to detect this blundering. Christ who is the Truth says, 'The truth shall make you free' [John 8:32]. Yet your soothsayers today say, 'Our fathers' theft and sacrilege and our own lies will bring honour to our church and to ourselves'. What a lie! 'Our fathers', they say, 'stole the body of St Dunstan, archbishop of Canterbury and primate of all Britain, from his church, and they took our own abbot, removed for such sacrilege,[f] since he was no use to us, to Canterbury and set him in St Dunstan's grave'. Oh, joy! Oh, sorrow! Oh, that your church should be enhanced by so great a gain. But what will you do, I beg you, enemies of pure truth, when Truth Himself will come to destroy all who spread lies? For

---

[f] I cannot make sense of *nostrum abbatem tali sacrilegio emptum, quia nobis inutilis erat*; M. Winterbottom suggests *aptum*, 'well-fitted for such sacrilege, since . . .'.

it is clearer than the light of day to all that what you claim about your fathers is lies. When they were invited to Canterbury, they did not bring with them their abbot's corpse. Nor, when they dwelt here, did they remove Dunstan's body and bring in the other. The former would be an act of extreme and incredible stupidity – no, extreme and incredible madness; but the latter would be an act of audacity impossible to bring about. For when the saint himself had his grave dug, the account of his life truly bears witness to the fact that the depth of his grave was sunk as much as a man's height into the ground.[10] What possibility could there have been for such a scandalous theft? Moreover the church was at no point destitute of its own sons, nor was the city of Canterbury ever emptied of its people. In addition one should consider that when the blessed martyr suffered death the church itself was not burnt nor were its roof or walls damaged. For we know it was profaned and looted of many ornaments, and that an attempt was made to burn it, by a fire started from outside, so that the savage troops could force out the bishop, protecting himself within when the invader had ordered him to leave. When he came out and they seized him, they abandoned their fire and their other traps set to catch him. They killed a few monks in his sight and took him away, bringing him to the place intended for his death, where they afflicted him with tortures and injuries and destroyed him.[11] Since these are the facts, how much effrontery does it take to claim that, in the sight of everyone, the floor of the church was dug up to the depth of the grave – seven feet on all sides, for otherwise they could not reach the body? Then, the story goes, having removed the body of the holy father Dunstan, they left the grave open for a fortnight while the monks returned to Glastonbury with what they had stolen. There they found that their abbot was dead on their arrival (I shall not say he was done to death), so they removed St Dunstan's pontifical adornments and dressed the abbot's body in them. Then they hastily carried this body – was it on an ass's back? – to Canterbury and placed it in the grave. How much effrontery? Again I ask. Was all the land between Glastonbury and Canterbury a deserted waste in those days, that they should be free to go and return without hindrance, carrying such a treasure wherever they would? Or was it not? Surely at the date when you claim this was happening, the terror of the Danes swarmed all over. Nowhere was peaceful, nowhere safe, wars and troubles raged all around. On top of all this, as is surely known, the body of St Dunstan had been buried in the

---

10   The depth of Dunstan's grave was also remarked on by Eadmer in his *De reliquiis S. Audoeni* (see below, n. 12).

11   Eadmer here appears to telescope the months which elapsed between the attack on Canterbury and Ælfheah's martyrdom in 1012. Other accounts of the attack on the town can be found in the Anglo-Saxon Chronicle, s.a. 1011, and in Osbern's *Vita S. Elphegi* (*Anglia Sacra*, ed. Wharton, II, 134–6). Later in this paragraph Eadmer cited Osbern by name as his source for the survival of only four monks. In specifying the limits to the destruction he was perhaps extrapolating from what Osbern said, viz. that the fire had *begun* to melt the lead of the roof (implying perhaps that the roof was not destroyed) and that, whereas the city was burnt, the church was violated.

middle of the choir at the foot of the steps leading to the high altar, in a lead coffin, and at a great depth, as the English once used to bury their dead.[12] How can it have happened, therefore, that the monks of Canterbury tolerated such a gaping hole for so many days until the nameless abbot was brought and deposited in Dunstan's empty grave? We know from what Osbern relates that at least four monks survived the slaughter, not to mention the clerks who assisted them in maintaining the service of the church. Their patience was wonderful, and more wonderful was their awaiting the arrival of the abbot, whose name was perhaps Wlsinus.[13]

For God's sake, is there anyone who can help but laugh at such nonsense? We could go on to pile up more arguments, no less suited to show the foolishness of this pretence, but we should spare the embarrassment of your sacred abbey. It is a shame and a disgrace that Glastonbury fosters, feeds, embraces such men as so defame it. No monks of Glastonbury came to Canterbury in those days as they make out, nor did they dwell here. There were none to snatch St Dunstan's body, and it was never taken from us nor ever brought to you. But your claim is not that it was brought by others nor on any other occasion. Confess therefore that your soothsayers have spoken falsehoods, and that it is in every way untrue to claim that you have anything of St Dunstan's body. Look to your reputation, therefore, and curb your tongues from such vanities. Let truth be brought to mind, even if you have forgotten it.

Know – there is no room for doubt – that once Æthelnoth, abbot, or rather former abbot, of Glastonbury, and one or two of his monks lived for a long time at Canterbury. I call him former abbot because at a general synod of the English Church he was deposed from his abbacy by Lanfranc, archbishop of Canterbury, and he was placed under such confinement at Canterbury as

---

[12] The location of St Dunstan's grave in front of the steps leading to the altar of Christ is given in Eadmer's *Vita S. Dunstani*, ch. 42 (*Memorials*, ed. Stubbs, p. 221). Here Eadmer added that Dunstan's grave reached as far west as the matutinal altar in the chancel. The grave was at a great depth with a monument (*pyramis*) raised over it. All this is set out quite precisely in Eadmer's *De reliquiis S. Audoeni*, ed. A. Wilmart, 'Edmeri Cantuariensis cantoris nova opuscula', *Revue des sciences religieuses* 15 (1935), 184–219 and 354–79, at 365. The description is complicated by a reference to the strong wall (*maceria fortis*) between the grave and the (? later) eastern crypt. The problem of the relationship of Dunstan's grave and this crypt was discussed by R. D. H. Gem, 'The Anglo-Saxon Cathedral Church at Canterbury: A Further Contribution', *Archaeological Journal* 127 (1970), 196–201. The position of the tomb between the rows of monks' stalls is confirmed by the Old English story edited by A. S. Napier, 'An Old English Vision of Leofric, Earl of Mercia', in *Transactions of the Philological Society* (1907–10), 180–88, at 184–5.

[13] I assume that this is Abbot Wulfsine of Malmesbury (occ. *ca* 1023, d. *ca* 1033), though it is not apparent what part he played in the restoration of ecclesiastical life. His tenure of office did not demonstrably begin earlier than 1020 when Æthelnoth, prior of Christ Church, was consecrated archbishop, and one must assume that conventual life had resumed before then. Nor was Wulfsine mentioned in the account of the translation of St Elphege in 1023 written by Osbern (*Anglia Sacra*, ed. Wharton, II, 143–7).

fitted his position.[14] At that time the number of monks serving Christ and St Dunstan here exceeded sixty. If then there were ever monks of Glastonbury who stole St Dunstan's body, I think it was those. Yet during the period when they were at Canterbury, the body had already been translated, as I have described above, from its first burial-place into a place where they could have had no access. It was not taken by them; therefore it was not taken by any of your monks. If you will listen to my advice, you will remove those bones which you have loaded on to the image of our Redeemer, before He is Himself angry with you.[15] It is sufficient that He be honoured for Himself, and there is no need to heap up holiness on Him through dead men's bones or otherwise. My brethren, think and think again, what is it honourable for you to think, what is it proper for you to say, what is it right for you to do? One hundred years and more have passed since the martyrdom of St Elphege. No one who was present is still alive today, or at least no one who remembers being present. To this day I have never heard that anyone who was there at the time has ever said or written anything concerning these matters which you have put about – not a single word, spoken or written, that any sane man could accept. Drop these playground stories, therefore, and behave like mature and intelligent men. Love St Dunstan as your father and patron and speak the truth about him. Then truly you will deserve his love. He is a member and a friend of the highest Truth and he cannot admit to the bosom of his love any who depart from the truth. God knows, and he knows too who is our father and our most sweet advocate that what I say I say for your honour and help, nor do I have any purpose other than that God who is the Truth should be magnified, praised, and proclaimed in St Dunstan, as is right, by you as well as by us and, if I could achieve it, by the whole world. I know that I have gone a little beyond the usual length of a letter addressing you so, but my subject was so important that, although I intended to use few words, my speech spread to the length it has. Do not wonder. The way of man is not His way.

So, my lords and my brethren, to whom God has opened the means of understanding matters of reason, bridle the wanton violence of your foolish young men who open their mouths only in order to seem to know how to speak, on whatever the flightiness of their hearts leads them to, thinking that they are something because others are innocent enough to listen to what they say. I once knew such youths, and perhaps I was one, so I do not doubt that young men are the same these days. I am now old and white-haired, and

---

[14]   The deposition of Æthelnoth, abbot of Glastonbury since 1053, took place at a council held in London in 1078; *Councils & Synods with Other Documents relating to the English Church*, ed. D. Whitelock, M. Brett and C. N. L. Brooke (Oxford, 1981), pp. 624–5. It is the only act of that council to have been recorded, and that only in the *Acta Lanfranci* added to the Anglo-Saxon Chronicle at Canterbury. Our letter is the sole evidence for his 'dignified confinement' at Christ Church.

[15]   This passage seems to imply that the bones purported to be St Dunstan's were in some manner disposed about a crucifix at Glastonbury, but it is hard to imagine how this could be achieved: perhaps Eadmer was merely using strong figurative language.

many things which I valued greatly as a youth I now rate as nothing. This will come to today's young men too by God's gift.

The length of this letter, however, demands an end, so this is my last word. Although your fathers of old are now dead who lived at Glastonbury a century ago, I think there will be some still living who were fostered in the monastic life before our Norman age. If there are, ask them whether they remember an abbot there who every year on St Dunstan's Day used to come to Canterbury with four monks or more.[16] They would stay among our brethren for six days and longer, giving themselves to rejoicing and celebration for reverence of the holy father. If any of these men remains alive today, I fancy he will confirm that what I say was the case. Anything else would be far from the truth. If then these men knew that they had St Dunstan's body at Glastonbury, why did they come to Canterbury to do reverence to it on his feast day? I say this to confound the errors of the foolish and to strengthen the sacred love of the wise towards us, which we much hope to receive. Farewell, therefore, in Christ Jesus. Pray for us.

[16]   This must be either Æthelweard, abbot of Glastonbury from *ca* 1024 to 1053, or Æthelnoth – already named in the letter – who was abbot from 1053 to his deposition in 1078. Glastonbury's participation in the celebration of St Dunstan's day (19 May) at Christ Church is not otherwise recorded. One might have supposed that there would have been special commemorations at Glastonbury since he was a former abbot.

The Marshalling of Antiquity: Glastonbury's Historical Dossier

JULIA CRICK

The use to which history was put by the monks of Glastonbury forcefully demonstrates the importance of the past to a medieval religious community. Although Glastonbury Abbey was an exceptionally powerful house – it was frequently richer than Christ Church, Canterbury, from the time of the Domesday survey onwards[1] – succeeding generations of its inhabitants were involved in generating, or at least nurturing, a cult of venerability which was spurious in the extreme. Why they felt impelled to do this, what they thought they were doing, and how they tackled their task are questions which underlie the following paper,[2] but its subject is the mechanics of the process and in particular its earliest extant product, a mid-thirteenth-century manuscript in the library of Trinity College, Cambridge: R. 5. 33 (724).

R. 5. 33 postdates by more than a century the first tangible signs of Glastonbury's pretensions to remote antiquity.[3] These come from the writings of the noted twelfth-century authors William of Malmesbury, Caradog of Llancarfan and Giraldus Cambrensis.[4] The actual age of the institution with which they were dealing is unknown but some confidence can be placed in certain charters attesting its existence in the later seventh century;[5] whatever the exact date, Anglo-Saxon origins were clearly insufficiently venerable for twelfth-century purposes.[6]

---

[1] For 1086 see *The Early History*, ed. Scott, p. 2; for the thirteenth century, D. Knowles, *The Religious Orders in England*, 3 vols (Cambridge, 1948–59) I, 44; at the Dissolution, D. Knowles and R. N. Hadcock, *Medieval Religious Houses. England and Wales* (London, 1971), pp. 53–4.

[2] On their motives, see A. Gransden, 'The Growth of Glastonbury Traditions and Legends in the Twelfth Century', *Journal of Ecclesiastical History* 27 (1976), 337–58, at 337–9; V. M. Lagorio, 'The Evolving Legend of St Joseph of Glastonbury', *Speculum* 46 (1971), 209–31, at 211; J. Armitage Robinson, *Somerset Historical Essays* (London, 1921), pp. 1–2.

[3] For earlier indications see H. P. R. Finberg, 'St Patrick at Glastonbury', *The Irish Ecclesiastical Record*, 5th ser. 108 (1967), 345–61, at 347–54, reprinted in his *West-Country Historical Studies* (Newton Abbot, 1969), pp. 70–88.

[4] Gransden, 'The Growth of Glastonbury Traditions', pp. 342–7 and 353–4.

[5] S.1249, 236, 237: discussed by Sarah Foot, 'Glastonbury's Early Abbots', p. 169, n. 31, in this volume. See also Finberg, 'St Patrick', p. 346.

[6] For rival antique monastic origin-legends see *The Early History*, ed. Scott, pp. 27–30.

In his *De antiquitate Glastonie ecclesie*, written shortly after 1129, William of Malmesbury traced the foundation of the house to certain missionaries sent by the second-century pope, Eleutherius, during the conversion of Britain under the mythical king, Lucius; William also described how St Patrick himself was an early abbot of the house.[7] Fabulous though it was, this account must have commanded credence: apart from William's reputation as an unusually discriminating historian, Lucius appears as a historical figure in Bede's *Historia ecclesiastica gentis Anglorum*, and Patrick's association with Glastonbury seems to have been well established.[8]

Caradog contributed to Glastonbury's claims by elaborating a statement of William's: that Gildas, the sixth-century author of the famous polemic *De excidio Britannie*, had lived at Glastonbury.[9] Caradog's *Vita Sancti Gilde* describes how Gildas, one of the twenty-four sons of a king of Scotia, came to the monastery of Glastonbury and there wrote his famous History. After his arrival the area was attacked by a large army from Cornwall and Devon led by Arthur, who was attempting to reclaim his wife, Guennouar, from Meluas, king of the region, who had abducted her. Gildas and the monks and abbot of Glastonbury succeeded in making peace between the two kings and received as a result substantial grants of land.[10]

The traditions recorded, or created, by the *Vita* found more graphic expression in the event reported by Giraldus: the exhumation of the bodies of Arthur and Guinevere at Glastonbury by the monks in 1191. The account in his *De principis instructione* (1193–9?) offers the earliest version of the story, but it was later retold both by him and others.[11] This episode provides the first example of active royal involvement in the pseudo-history of the abbey: Giraldus makes clear that the initiative for the excavation came from Henry II,[12] and a visit of Richard I to the abbey has been taken as the occasion for

---

[7]   *DA*, chs 2 and 8 (ed. Scott, pp. 46–50, 54). See also Scott's reconstruction of the original text: *ibid.* pp. 168, 170. The same information is found in the C-recension of William's *Gesta regum* (chs 19 and 22): *Willelmi Malmesbiriensis Monachi de Gestis Regum Anglorum*, ed. W. Stubbs, 2 vols, RS 90 (London, 1887–9) I, 23–4, 26 (hereafter *GR*). More extreme elements of the Glastonbury story were later interpolated into the *De antiquitate: The Early History*, ed. Scott, pp. 2 and 5–25, especially 23–4; J. Armitage Robinson, *Two Glastonbury Legends: King Arthur and St Joseph of Arimathea* (Cambridge, 1926), p. 2; A. Gransden, *Historical Writing in England c. 550 to c. 1307* (London, 1974), pp. 184–5. William cannot escape charges of either credulousness or invention, however: A. Gransden, 'Propaganda in English Medieval Historiography', *Journal of Medieval History* 1 (1975), 363–82, at 365, and Robinson, *Two Glastonbury Legends*, pp. 3–4.

[8]   Bede, *Historia ecclesiastica*, I.4 (*Bede's Ecclesiastical History of the English People*, ed. B. Colgrave and R. A. B. Mynors [Oxford 1969], p. 24). Finberg, 'St Patrick'.

[9]   For example, *GR*, ch. 20 (ed. Stubbs, I, 24).

[10]   *Chronica minora saec. iv. v. vi. vii.*, ed. T. Mommsen, 3 vols (Berlin, 1892–8) III, 107–10.

[11]   Distinctio I, ch. 20 (*Giraldi Cambrensis Opera*, ed. J. S. Brewer *et al.*, 8 vols, RS 21 [London, 1861–91] VIII, 126–9). This and other accounts were printed by E. K. Chambers, *Arthur of Britain* (Cambridge, 1927; rev. imp., 1964), pp. 268–74.

[12]   *Giraldi Cambrensis Opera*, ed. Brewer *et al.*, VIII, 127–8.

the exhumation.[13] This combination of public display and royal ceremonial was reinvoked nearly a century later when, in 1278, Edward I and Queen Eleanor visited Glastonbury and witnessed the opening of the tombs of their mythical predecessors.[14]

Finally, the seal was set on Glastonbury's claims by documentation. By the thirteenth century, Glastonbury had acquired, retrospectively, an impressive array of patrons, including St Patrick and Cnut, whose 'gifts', recorded in charter form, lent formidable support to the abbey's pretensions.[15]

Narrative, public display, and documentation were of course means widely used by medieval monks to build the prestige of their houses, generally by association with a saint. The deeds of patron saints were celebrated in *uitae*, sometimes performed publicly.[16] In the Celtic world, the practical value of such hagiography might lie not only in establishing prestige but also in laying claim to territory: rights to property and privilege might be traced back to the actions of the patron saint in his or her lifetime.[17] However, although the target of a cult might often be far from religious – the commemoration of a king,[18] the material aggrandizement of a house – its subject generally retained the pious cloak of conventional saintly attributes.[19] The case of Glastonbury is unusual in that two important focuses of attention – Arthur and Guinevere – remained unambiguously secular.[20] It is intriguing to speculate why this might have been. Perhaps the figures of Arthur and Guinevere were already too well known to be moulded by the hagiographers in the conventional way. Perhaps the monks recognized that they could secure royal support by championing Arthur and Guinevere as king and queen of Britain: only a few years before Edward I's visit, the monks had secured freedom from episcopal interference by appealing to royal protec-

---

[13] W. A. Nitze, 'The Exhumation of King Arthur at Glastonbury', *Speculum* 9 (1934), 355–61, at 356.

[14] Nitze, 'The Exhumation of King Arthur', pp. 356–60; R. S. Loomis, 'Edward I, Arthurian Enthusiast', *Speculum* 28 (1953), 114–27, at 115–16; Gransden, 'The Growth of Glastonbury Traditions', pp. 349–52 and 356.

[15] See the charter of St Patrick, *AD*, ed. Hearne, I, 19–22, also *DA*, ch. 9 (ed. Scott, pp. 54–8).

[16] M. D. Legge, *Anglo-Norman in the Cloister: The Influence of the Orders upon Anglo-Norman Literature* (Edinburgh, 1950), pp. 10–12.

[17] See W. Davies, 'Property Rights and Property Claims in Welsh "Vitae" of the Eleventh Century', *Hagiographie, cultures et sociétés ive–xiie siècles*, ed. E. Patlagean and P. Riché (Paris, 1981), pp. 515–33, at 522–4 and 527.

[18] For example, Oswald (culted at Bamburgh, Bardney and Lindisfarne) or Edward the Confessor (at Westminster).

[19] Compare the *Liber Landauensis*: C. N. L. Brooke, *The Church and the Welsh Border in the Central Middle Ages* (Woodbridge, 1986), pp. 18–21; W. Davies, *An Early Welsh Microcosm: Studies in the Llandaff Charters* (London, 1978), pp. 3–6.

[20] On hagiography and romance see V. M. Lagorio, 'Pan-Brittonic Hagiography and the Arthurian Grail Cycle', *Traditio* 26 (1970), 29–61, at 31–3, and Gransden, 'The Growth of Glastonbury Traditions', p. 341. On the secular nature of the story of even a Biblical figure, see V. M. Lagorio, 'The *Joseph of Arimathie*: English Hagiography in Transition', *Medievalia et Humanistica* ns 6 (1975), 91–161, at 93.

tion.[21] Certainly the monks' cause can only have been advanced by the evidence that their house had enjoyed a special relationship with the Crown from time immemorial.[22]

In the same way as saints' cults often derived impetus from material factors – relics being paraded to raise funds for monastic buildings, for example[23] – it is clear that practicalities lay behind Glastonbury's researches into antiquity, at least initially. The ultimate explanation for the historical and hagiographical creations of William of Malmesbury and Caradog of Llancarfan probably lies in the reduced circumstances in which Henry of Blois found the monastery in the 1120s when he came to be its abbot: Henry sought to repair the reputation of the house together with its more tangible assets.[24] The unearthing of Arthur's grave came soon after a fire in 1184 which destroyed many of the abbey's documents, its ancient church and new buildings,[25] and even sooner after the death of an important patron, Henry II.[26] It has also been noted that the entry into Glastonbury's written origin-story of such romantic figures as Arthur and Joseph of Arimathea is not unconnected with the efforts of the monks to maintain their independence from the bishop of Bath and Wells in the mid-thirteenth century.[27]

The evidence for accretions to the story comes from R. 5. 33, a collection of historical and documentary material, both fantastic and real, central to the history of the abbey and its estates. This includes the only entire copy of William's *De antiquitate*, extensively annotated.[28] The marginalia include notes on Joseph of Arimathea, Lancelot, and Arthur.[29] It is followed by a chronicle of the history of Glastonbury from 1126 to 1291 entitled *Libellus de rebus gestis Glastoniensibus* and attributed to the Glastonbury monk Adam of Damerham. The bulk of the *Libellus* consists of transcriptions of documents relating to the abbey's estates and privileges, interspersed with accounts of the activities of the abbots and of various internal and external disputes.

Documents also form much of the rest of the volume. There is a list of the contents of the so-called *Liber terrarum*, a cartulary, now lost, of Anglo-Saxon charters held by the abbey; this contents-list provides the only record of many of the documents, although some were also transcribed in the Great

---

21   *AD*, ed. Hearne, II, 539. See also below, note 62, on Henry III's acquisition of the abbey's advowson *ca* 1250.

22   Giraldus described Morgan, Arthur's *propinqua*, as *dominatrix atque patrona* of the region: *De principis instructione*, Distinctio I, ch. 20 (*Giraldi Cambrensis Opera*, ed. Brewer *et al.*, VIII, 128).

23   Cf. P. J. Geary, *Furta Sacra: The Theft of Relics in the Central Middle Ages* (Princeton, 1978), pp. 24–5.

24   *The Early History*, ed. Scott, p. 1. William's history was dedicated to Henry.

25   See C. M. Church, *Chapters in the Early History of the Church of Wells A.D. 1136–1333* (London, 1894), p. 56.

26   Cf. R. F. Treharne, *The Glastonbury Legends: Joseph of Arimathea, The Holy Grail and King Arthur* (London, 1967), pp. 99–101.

27   *The Early History*, ed. Scott, p. 27. On Joseph, see also Lagorio, 'The Evolving Legend', pp. 209–31.

28   Described in *The Early History*, ed. Scott, pp. 27–33 and 186–210.

29   *DA*, chs 1 and 31 (ed. Scott, pp. 46 and 82–4, notes a and 74).

Cartulary in the mid-fourteenth century.[30] The list in R. 5. 33 heads a series of inventories of royal grants, papal privileges, charters, letters, and other documents. Most of these relate to the twelfth and thirteenth centuries but sections entitled *antiqua indulgencia* and *antiqua priuilegia* include such exotic items as a second-century papal indulgence from Eleutherius, another to St Patrick, and Patrick's own charter in favour of the house. There is also a copy of the Domesday entry for Glastonbury and records of the thirteenth-century holdings of the abbey, added when the original core of the manuscript was revised and expanded, as it was several times during the first century of its existence.

Given the importance of the manuscript and its complexity, little consideration has been accorded to the manner of its compilation: this has tended to be overshadowed by the interest of its individual items. In particular, almost no attention has been paid to how and when the additions to the original manuscript were made.[31] Attempting to identify and describe the separate parts of the compilation is a detailed and lengthy business; the following formal description of the manuscript is intended primarily for reference. The conclusions which can be drawn from it are discussed in the accompanying commentary.

CAMBRIDGE, TRINITY COLLEGE R. 5. 33 (724)

CONTENTS[32]

i r
Blank flyleaf. Wormholes run from it into the first quire (to fol. 8).

i v   (s. xiv [Anglicana] and later hands)
Two notes (described by James, *The Western Manuscripts*, II, 199), an ex-libris (in late medieval Gothic Textura) and an early modern contents-list.

1r–18v   (s. xiii *med.*)
'Prologus W. Malmesbur. de antiquitate Glastoniensis ecclesie'. Prologue and text.
   Ed. Hearne, *AD*, I, 1–122. Ed. Scott, *The Early History*, pp. 40–210.

---

[30]   S. D. Keynes, *Anglo-Saxon Manuscripts and Other Items of Related Interest in the Library of Trinity College, Cambridge* (typescript catalogue, Cambridge, 1985; to be reprinted in *Old English Newsletter*, Subsidia), no. 29. See also Keynes, *The Glastonbury Liber Terrarum* (Cambridge, forthcoming). The cartulary survives in the manuscript Longleat House, Marquess of Bath 39: P. H. Sawyer, *Anglo-Saxon Charters: An Annotated List and Bibliography* (London, 1968), p. 44.
[31]   Although see the description by M. R. James, *The Western Manuscripts in the Library of Trinity College, Cambridge*, 4 vols (Cambridge, 1900–4) II, 198–202.
[32]   *Incipits* and *explicits* are given only for works of which no printed version exists or for documents which would otherwise be difficult to identify.

19r/v (in similar hand)
'Consuetudo luminarii seu cereorum in ecclesia Glaston. per sacristam loci ad diuinum officium exhibendorum'.
Ed. Hearne, *JG*, II, 358–65.

19vb (same hand)
Note under text 'Memor. quod in primo sabbato . . . .
Ed. Hearne, *JG*, II, 365.

20ra/b (largish hand, s. xiii/xiv)
'Iste sunt uillate que claudere debent in parco'.
Dultyng to *Pultona*. (In three hands of similar date – s. xiv *in./med.*)

20va/b (imitation of late medieval formal cursive, s. xvi)
'Constructiones quorundam monasteriorum'.
'Constructio monasterii Glastoniensis anno Domini 166 . . . . Remocio ueteris et constructio noue abbatie de Leystone. Anno Domini 1363.'

21r–73vb (s. xiii *med.* and later)
'Libellus de rebus gestis Glaston. et primo de .H. episcopo' (History of Glastonbury Abbey attributed to Adam of Damerham).
Ed. Hearne, *AD*, II, 303–596.
Fol. 27 is an inserted two-thirds-leaf containing documents relating to the *Libellus*, printed by Hearne, *AD*, II, 345–9.

73vb–74ra (s. xiii/xiv)
'Hec sunt mete et termini foreste domni regis de Blakemor. . . . usque Puttestaple'.
Ed. Hearne, *AD*, II, 653.

74ra[33]
'[O]mnes dominici bosci domni regis pertinentes ad manerium de Porstoke . . .'.
Ed. Hearne, *AD*, II, 654.

74ra/b
'[H]ec sunt mete et termini foreste domni regis de Gilling. . . . Heggecliffe'.
Ed. *ibid.*

74va–75rb
Documents relating to a dispute between John Louel and John, abbot of Glastonbury (?John of Kent, 1291–1303).
'Edwardus Dei gratia rex Anglie . . . nec honeste domino suo nudi seruire propter' (incomplete).

75v–76r (s. xiv ?*in.*, different hand, single column)
'[H]ec sunt nomina eorum quibus tenebatur [ ] abbatis pro predecessoribus suis'.

76r/v
Two charters, printed by Hearne, *JG*, II, 366–9.

---

[33] No indication of date is given when the previous description still applies.

76v (beneath, in tiny script)

'Hec sunt que dimisit frater Adam de Domerham de bonis sancti Dunstani in thesauraria Glast. Anno Domini .m.cc.lxxxix'.

Ed. Hearne, *JG*, II, 369.

77ra–87v (s. xiii *med.*)

Lists of charters and other documents pertaining to Glastonbury.

1. 'Carte contente in libro terrarum Glaston.'
2. 'Carte ueteres regum de terris datis Glaston. quas adhuc habent et sunt sine sigillis'
3. 'Carte ueteres regum de terris datis suis seruientibus quas adhuc Glaston. sine sigillis'
4. 'Carte ueteres de terris datis Glaston. inmediate quas non habent.'
5. 'Carte ueteres regum de terris datis suis seruientibus quas creditur habuisse Glaston. ecclesia. Sed modo non habent.'
6. 'Antiqua indulgencia Glaston. in carta sine sigillo'
7. 'Dies indulgenciarum Glaston. unde cartas non habemus licet habuerimus'
8. 'Antiqua priuilegia'
9. 'Carte regum signate licet uetuste et pene consumpte'
10. 'Priuilegia summorum pontificum'
11. 'Carte pontificum de indulgenciis concessis Glastoniensi ecclesie siue fabrice ecclesie'
12. 'Carte de indulgenciis datis ad ecclesiam de la Torre'
13. 'Carte de pensionibus debitis Glaston. ecclesie'
14. 'Carte de archidiaconatu Glaston.'
15. 'Carte de annexis ecclesie'
16. 'Carte de diuersis redditibus uel rebus datis ecclesie Glaston.'
17. 'Recogniciones'
18. 'Finales concordie'
19. 'Carte de conuencionibus'
20. 'Carte de quietis clamanciis'
21. 'Diuerse carte transitorie'
22. 'Transitorie littere'
23. 'Carte de rebus datis specialiter conuentui'
24. 'Carte pertinentes ad celerarium'
25. 'Carte pertinentes ad hostelerium'
26. 'Carte pertinentes ad prioratum scilicet de Winfrod [*sic*]'
27. 'Carte pertinentes ad elemosinariam'
28. 'Carte pertinentes ad sacristariam et primo de ecclesia sancti Iohannis in Glaston.'
29. 'Carte de redditu ad lumen sancti Dunstani'
30. 'Carte infirmaria'

Ed. Hearne, *JG*, II, 370–418. On 77ra/vb, see S. Keynes, 'Studies on Anglo-Saxon Royal Diplomas', 2 vols (unpubl. fellowship dissertation, Trinity College, Cambridge, 1976) I, 165–82. See now *idem, The Glastonbury Liber Terrarum* (Cambridge, forthcoming).

85v is blank except for four erased lines at the top. Several leaves, written in hands of the second half of the thirteenth century, are additions; 79 is an added two-thirds-leaf, 82–83 a full bifolium, 87A an added half-leaf.

88r/v (s. xiii/xiv)
Confirmation of King Henry to Glastonbury.
Ed. Hearne, *JG*, II, 419–22.

89r–95va (s. xiii, new quire)
Papal privileges

1. 89r
'Priuilegium Calixti pape'. Calixtus II, A.D. 1123.
  'Religiosis desideriis . . . .' P. Jaffé, *Regesta pontificum Romanorum ab condita ecclesia ad annum post Christum natum mcxcviii*, 2 vols (Leipzig, 1885–8) I, 813, no. 7071 (cf. 18va/vb). Ed. Hearne, *AD*, I, 120–1.

2. 89r/v
'Priuilegium Innocencii pape secundi'. Innocent II, A.D. 1137.
  'Uenerabilium locorum . . . .' Jaffé, *Regesta*, I, 875, no. 7834 (cf. 23va/vb). Ed. A. Watkin, *The Great Chartulary of Glastonbury*, 3 vols, SRS 59, 63–4 (1947–56) I, 125–6 (hereafter *GC*).

3. 89v–90r
'Priuilegium domni Lucii pape'. Lucius II, A.D. 1144.
  'Pie postulacio uoluntatis . . . .' Jaffé, *Regesta*, II, 12, no. 8601 (cf. 23vb–24ra). Ed. Watkin, *GC*, I, 130.

4. 90r
'Forma priuilegii Alexandri pape'. Alexander III, A.D. 1168.
  'Pie postulacio . . . .' Jaffé, *Regesta*, II, 223, no. 11615 (cf. 24ra/b). Ed. Watkin, *GC*, I, 128–9.

5. 90r
Short note of documents of popes Alexander, Celestine, and Honorius.

6. 90r/v
'Priuilegium Celestini pape de usu ornamentorum pontificalium et de benedicendo uestimenta sacerdotal.'. Celestine III, A.D. 1192.
  'Decor apostolici . . . .' Jaffé, *Regesta*, II, 587, no. 16823 (cf. 26vb). Ed. Watkin, *GC*, I, 137.

7. 90v
Alexander III, A.D. 1160x1178.
  'Cum deceat nos . . . .' Jaffé, *Regesta*, II, 317, no. 12985.

8. 90v–91v
'Confirmacio composicionis facte apud Scephtebur. auctoritate domni Honorii pape'. Honorius III, A.D. 1219.
  'Cum desideremus materiam . . . .' Cf. A. Potthast, *Regesta pontificum Romanorum inde ab a. post Christum natum mcxcviii ad a. mccciv*, 2 vols (Berlin, 1874–5) I, 531, no. 6067 (cf. 45va–46va). Ed. Watkin, *GC*, I, 93–4.

9. 91v
'Priuilegium Honorii pape de protectione'. Honorius III, A.D. 1218.
  'Sacrosancta romana ecclesia deuotos . . . .' Potthast, *Regesta*, I, 512, no. 5832. Ed. Watkin, *GC*, I, 140.

10. 91v–92r
'Renouacio priuilegii de usu insignium pontificalium et de benedicendo uestimenta sacerdotal. [*sic*]'. Honorius III, A.D. 1219.
  'Ut pulcra et decora filia Ierusalem . . . .' Potthast, *Regesta*, I, 532, no. 6076 (cf. 46va/b). Ed. Hearne, *AD*, II, 474–5.

11. 92r
'Confirmacio Honorii pape de ecclesiis sancti Iohannis in Glastonia et de Estpennard'. Honorius III, A.D. 1218.
   'Cum a nobis petitur . . . .' Potthast, *Regesta*, I, 508, no. 5789. Ed. Watkin, *GC*, I, 22.

12. 92r/v
'Confirmacio Honorii pape de ecclesia sancti Iohannis in Glastonia'. Honorius III, A.D. 1223.
   'Cum monasterium uestrum multipliciter . . . .' Ed. Watkin, *GC*, I, 20.

13. 92v
'Priuilegium ut clerici collatis uel oblatis ecclesiasticis resignent pensionibus'. Honorius III, A.D. 1225.
   'Ex parte uestra fuit propositum . . . .' Potthast, *Regesta*, I, 644, no. 7479. Ed. Watkin, *GC*, I, 131–2.

14. 92v
'Personalis exempcio a cognicione causarum'.
   'Tua nobis deuocio supplicauit . . . .'

15. 92v
'Generalis indulgencia super beneficiis possessis ab Italicis'. Gregory IX, A.D. 1230.
   'Ecclesiarum indempnitatibus quarum cura nobis imminet . . . .' Potthast, *Regesta*, I, 732–3, no. 8531.

16. 92v–93r
'Aliud priuilegium indultum Anglis super collacionibus ecclesiarum'. Gregory IX, A.D. 1232.
   'Graue gerimus et indignum . . . .' Potthast, *Regesta*, II, 2104, no. 8984a–26222.

17. 93r
'Priuilegium super usu mitre et anuli'. Gregory IX, A.D. 1241.
   'Sedes apostolica non numquam illos . . . .' Potthast, *Regesta*, I, 931, no. 11004. Ed. Watkin, *GC*, I, 138.

18. 93r
'Indulgencia .xx. dierum ad capellam beati Dunstani'. Pope Innocent (unidentified).
   'Licet is de cuius munere uenit . . . misericorditer relaxamus.'

19. 93r
'Confirmacio libertatum et immunitatem Gl. in [ ]i forma'. Pope Innocent (unidentified).
   'Solet annuere sedes apostolica piis uatis. . . . Nulli ergo etc.'

20. 93r/va
'Confirmacio archidiaconatus'. Innocent IV, A.D. 1246.
   'Iustis petencium desideriis dignum est . . . .' Ed. Watkin, *GC*, I, 7–8.

21. 93va
'Priuilegium ne teneatur ecclesia Glast. ad prouisionem clericorum et cet.'. Innocent IV, A.D. 1246.
   'Paci et tranquillitati uestre paterna . . . .' Ed. Watkin, *GC*, I, 133–4.

22. 93va/vb
'De eodem in forma'. Innocent IV, A.D. 1245.
   'Etsi clericorum prouisio . . . .' Ed. Watkin, *GC*, I, 134.

23. 93vb
'Indulgencia de utendis pilleis'. Innocent IV, A.D. 1247.
'Ex parte dilectorum filiorum . . . auctoritate nostra dispenses.'

24. 93vb–94rb
'Confirmacio super possessionibus et libertatibus [ ] Glaston.'. Innocent IV, A.D. 1245.
'Religiosam uitam eligentibus . . . .' Potthast, *Regesta*, I, 1002, no. 11798. Ed. Watkin, *GC*, I, 132–3.

90r–94r (Additions in lower margins in various hands of perhaps slightly later date than above)

1. 90r
Innocent IV, A.D. 1245.
'Dilecti filii abbas et conuentus mon. Glast. . . . .' Ed. Watkin, *GC*, I, 134–5.

2. 90v
Alexander IV, A.D. 1259.
'Meritis tue deuocionis inducimur . . . .' Potthast, *Regesta* II, 1438, no. 17658. Ed. Watkin, *GC*, I, 139.

3. 91r
Innocent IV, A.D. 1253.
'Deuocionis uestre precibus inclinati . . . .' Ed. Watkin, *GC*, I, 135.

4. 91v
John XX, A.D. 1277.
'Ex parte uestra fuit propositum . . . .' Ed. Watkin, *GC*, I, 136–7.

5. 92r
'Confirmacio libertatis Glastonie'. Nicholas III, ?A.D. 1278.
'Cum a nobis petitur quod iustum est . . . communimus.'

6. 92v
'Confirmacio libertatis Glastonie'. Gregory X, A.D. 1272.
'Cum a nobis petitur quod iustum est . . . .' Ed. Watkin, *GC*, I, 136.

7. 93r
'Confirmacio libertatis Glastonie'. Innocent V, A.D. 1276.
'Cum a nobis petitur quod iustum est . . . .' Potthast, *Regesta*, II, 1706, no. 21121. Ed. Watkin, *GC*, I, 135–6.

8. 93v
Boniface of Savoy, archbishop of Canterbury, A.D. 1247.
'Noueritis nos domni pape . . . duximus disspensandum [*sic*].'

9. 94r
Innocent IV, A.D. 1248.
'Ex parte dilectorum filiorum abbatis . . . .' Ed. Watkin, *GC*, I, 139.

94v–95va (Papal privileges written in rather later hands than nos 1–24)

25. 94v
'Appropriacio ecclesie de Domerham'. Alexander IV, A.D. 1255.
'Sincere deuocionis . . . .' Potthast, *Regesta*, II, 1297, no. 15738. Ed. Watkin, *GC*, I, 56–7.

26. 94va/b
'Executoria eiusdem'. Alexander IV, A.D. 1255.
'Sincere deuocionis . . . .' Ed. Watkin, *GC*, I, 57.

27. 94vb
'Ratificacio episcopi Sar.'. Walter, bishop of Salisbury, A.D. 1267.
 'Ut possessionem ecclesie de Dom. . . . .' Ed. Watkin, *GC*, I, 57–8.

28. 94vb
'Ratificacio decani et capituli'. A.D. 1268.
 'Noueritis nos litteras uenerabilis patris nostri domini W . . . .' Ed. Watkin, *GC*,
I, 58.

29. 94vb
'Priuilegium ne ten. ad soluc. debit. nisi fuerit in utilitat. monasterii'. ?John XXII,
A.D. 1267–77. This and the next item written over erasure.
 'Indempnitati tui monasterii . . . .'

30. 95ra
Alexander IV, A.D. 1255. Over erasure.
 'Ut erga sedem apostolicam eo amplius crescat . . . .' Ed. Watkin, *GC*, I, 138–9.

31. 95rb
'Appropriacio ecclesie de Sowy'. Alexander IV, A.D. 1259.
 'Prouisionis nostre prouenire debet auxilio . . . .' Potthast, *Regesta*, II, 1438, no.
17656. Ed. Watkin, *GC*, I, 22–3.

32. 95rb/va
'Executoria eiusdem'. Alexander IV, A.D. 1259.
 'Prouisionis nostre etc. . . . .' Ed. Watkin, *GC*, I, 23.

33. 95va
'Priuilegium de parciendum fructibus primi anni'. Alexander IV, A.D. 1255.
 'Cum sicut nobis significare . . . .' Ed. Watkin, *GC*, I, 104–5.

34. 95va
Beneath, in different hand. Cardinal Octobon, A.D. 1267.
 'Noueritis nos uidisse litteras . . . .' Ed. Watkin, *GC*, I, 105.

95vb
William I, bishop of Bath and Wells, A.D. 1267.
 'Uniuersis presentis litteras inscripturis Willelmus miseracione diuina . . .
apponi.'

95vb
'De priuilegiis utendis'. Pope Nicholas (unidentified).
 'Cum sicut ex parte uestra . . . facultatem. Si quis autem hoc etc.'

96ra–98vb (s. xiii *med.*)
Charters of Henry III. 'Transcripta cartarum regiarum' (Magna Carta, A.D. 1224–
5; liberties of the forest).
 Ed. Hearne, *AD*, II, 597–9.

99r (s. xiv 1)
'De phisica' (later medieval title).
 'Quoniam per opiliones antiquas infirmitates periculose corpori humane
superueniunt . . . .'

99r/v (s. xiv 1)
'Consuetudo luminarii seu cereorum in ecclesia Glaston. per sacristam ad diuinum officium exhibendorum'. As on 19r/v. Runs on to the foot of 100r.

100ra–vb (s. xiii *med.*)
Four texts found also in London, British Library, Cotton Cleopatra D. viii and
Oxford, Bodleian Library, Bodley 622 (*S.C.* 2156)

1. 100ra/va
'Compendium de Britannia siue Anglia'.
   'Quoniam simplicioribus foret difficile prolixiores historias tam regum Brito-
num quam Anglorum legendo percurrere . . . uel pro ignauia amiserunt.'

2. 100va
'Sequitur de episcopatibus. De archiepiscopatu Eboracensi.'
   'Archiepiscopatus Eboracensis . . . quibus tota Northamhimbria subiacet.'

3. 100va/b
'De archiepiscopatu Cantuarie'.
   'Archiepatus [*sic*] Cantuarie . . . et Danis sepius infestarentur.'

4. 100vb
'De Normannis'.
   'Anno ab incarnacione Domini .mlxvi. a conuersione uero Anglorum .cccc.lxxx.
. . . commutans.' Notes on roads in Britain added in different hand: 'Sciendum
quod .iiii. in Britannia . . . per Lincolniam.'

100va (foot) (Added in different, rather later, hand.)
Version of the *Epitaphium* of King Ceadwalla (Bede, *Historia ecclesiastica*, V.7; ed.
Colgrave and Mynors, pp. 470–2). Ten lines of verse.

100vb–101ra
'Reges Britonum'. Left-hand column added to table on 101r.

101r (in similar hand to 100ra/vb)
King-lists of heptarchic kingdoms arranged in six columns (*Reges Cancie, Reges
Merciorum, Reges Westsaxonum* [with a drawing of Ecgberht; list continues in
original hand to Henry III, with continuations to Edward I, Edward II, Henry VI,
and Edward VI], *Reges Northammibrorum, Reges Orientalium Anglorum, Reges
Orientalium Saxonum*).

101v (s. xiv; cf. hand of 75v)
'Redditus maneriorum baronie Glastonie anno Iohannis abbatis de Cancia nono'
(A.D. 1300). Followed by *redditus* for fourth year of Abbot Fromund (Geoffrey
Fromond, 1303–22).

102r–103v (s. xiii *med.*)
Library list. 'Numerus librorum Glaston. ecclesie qui fuerunt de librario. Anno
gratie .m.cc.xl.vii' (additional minim – correcting to 1248 – entered in different
hand).
   Ed. Hearne, *JG*, II, 423–42. Reprinted by T. W. Williams, *Somerset Mediaeval
Libraries and Miscellaneous Notices of Books in Somerset Prior to the Dissolution of the
Monasteries* (Bristol, 1897), pp. 55–76.

102r–103v (s. xiii 2 – xiv *in.*)
Marginalia, alterations, additions (for example, on 103vb, books of Richard de
Culmton).

104r (s. xiv; cf. hand of 99r/v)
'Libri recepti a fratre Galfrido de Bathon. . . . .'
   Ed. Hearne, *JG*, II, 443–4; Williams, *Somerset Mediaeval Libraries*, p. 77.

104r–105v   (s. xiv)

Account of relics headed 'De sanctis Beda et Gilda'.

'Hec continentur in duobus feretris de nouo ornat. . . . .' Ed. Hearne, *JG*, II, 445–54. On Glastonbury's relic-lists see *The Chronicle of Glastonbury Abbey*, ed. Carley, p. xlvi.

105v–107r   (in similar script, several hands)

Charters relating to Glastonbury estates.

Ed. Hearne, *AD*, II, 599–612.

107v   (in similar hand)

French documents. 'De terris in Hibernia' (late medieval title).

'Sire asez se uent tute gent ke Phylype de Wyrcestre . . . .'

108ra   (s. xiii *med.*)

'Confirmacio cartarum libertatum Anglie et de foresta', A.D. 1253.

'H. Dei gratia etc. thesaur. et baronibus de scaccar. iusticiar. suis de bancho . . . dux apponend. Datum apud Westmonast. xvi die Maii anno regni nostri xxxviii.'

108ra/b

'Forma sententie[?] late in uiolatores ipsarum lib.'.

'Anno Domini .m.cc.liii. .ii. idus maii. in maiori aula regia Westmon. . . . . duximus apponenda.' (Found also in the Glastonbury manuscript London, British Library, Add. 22934, 42ra/b.)

108rb/va   (s. xiv *in.*)

More documents, one dated 1282.

108vb

Blank.

109ra–110rb   (*ca* 1300)

'Appropriacio parochialis ecclesie de Moorlinch.', 'appropriacio ecclesiarum de Dultyng et Estbrente', 'appropriacio ecclesie de Nyweton'.

Ed. Hearne, *AD*, II, 612–8.

110v–115r   (s. xiv 1)

'Inquisicio magistri Reginaldi de Fontibus clerici domini Huberti Cantuar. archiepiscopi per maneria abbatie Glaston. de ualencia eorum', A.D. 1201.

Ed. N. E. Stacy, 'The Estates of Glastonbury Abbey c. 1050–1200' (unpubl. D.Phil. dissertation, Univ. of Oxford, 1971), pp. 247–66. Discussed by M. M. Postan, *Essays on Medieval Agriculture and General Problems of the Medieval Economy* (Cambridge, 1973), pp. 249–77.

115r–116v, 116Ar

'Inquisicio Hilberti Cantoris de ualencia abbatie Glaston. post mortem Henrici Winton. episcopi quantum ualuit tempore regis Henrici filii Willelmi'.

Ed. Stacy, 'The Estates of Glastonbury Abbey', pp. 238–44. Discussed by Postan, *Essays on Medieval Agriculture*, pp. 249–77.

116Ar/v

Survey by Bishop Savaric, A.D. 1198.

Ed. Stacy, 'The Estates of Glastonbury', pp. 245–6. Discussed by Postan, *Essays on Medieval Agriculture*, pp. 249–77.

116Av–117r
Diuisio of meadow at *Kynwardesmore*, A.D. 1189.

117r/v, 119r (s. xiv)
Thomas atte Nye's list of military tenants of the abbey (*ca* 1197). Dated and identified by Stacy, 'The Estates of Glastonbury', pp. 6–7. Cf. *Rentalia et Custumaria Michaelis de Ambresbury, 1235–1252, et Rogeri de Ford, 1252–1261, Abbatum Monasterii Beatae Mariae Glastoniae*, ed. C. J. Elton and E. Hobhouse, SRS 5 (1891), p. 4.
    Ed. Stacy, 'The Estates of Glastonbury', pp. 267–9.

118ra/vb (s. xiii)
'Carte de rebus assignatis specialiter conuentui et primo carta .H. abbatis . . .', A.D. 1193.
    Ed. Watkin, *GC*, III, 702.

118rb–vb
Other documents in the same hand.
1. 'Rob. senior de decimis ecclesie de Niweton'
2. 'De remissione cere et mellis ad opus conuentus'
3. 'R. iunior de remissione .c. sol. quos percipere consueuit de camera'
4. 'Confirmacio eiusdem super redecimacione frumenti tocius abbacie'
5. 'De remissione oblacionis duorum festorum'
6. 'Carta .M. abbatis de ecclesia de Lim et quibusdam aliis assignatis conuentui'.
    Ed. Watkin, *GC*, III, 710–11.
7. 'De redditu in Bristollis'
8. 'Eiusdem de datis ad feretrum'

119r/v
Note of fire at abbey in 1184 (continued from 117v); *inquisiciones* into the rights of churches of Wrington, *Buddeclegh*, and Walton, A.D. 1261.

120ra/b (s. xiii *med.*)
'Ad coquinam'. Documents relating to the kitchen.
1. 'H. de Northilod. de .xl. solidis debitis conuentui.'
2. 'Sauar. de .i. mar. in Assebir.' Ed. Watkin, *GC*, III, 698.
3. 'W. de Moun. de quadam terra in Uplim remissa Glast.' Ed. Watkin, *GC*, III, 584.

120rb/va (s. xiii *med.*, as above)
'De capitalibus'.
    'Abbatis de Niwenham de remissione secte hundred. et torno uic. de Uplim.'
Ed. Watkin, *GC*, III, 579.

120va (s. xiv, cursive; cf. 105v)
'De iuribus ecclesie de Strete'.
    'Iuris Regin. de Legh. Iocelin de Legh . . . per ipsum cuius fuerunt aueria.'

120va/b (s. xiv, different hand)
'Inquisicio capta per quatuor uillat. dicit quod abbas Glaston. reddit decano Well. per annum . . . nec optenta fuit'.
(Beneath, on 120vb, in same hand) 'Ces sunt les cours k. dussent e soleynt estre ouers en yuer . . .'.

121ra–122rb (s. xiii, as 120rb/va)
'De prioratu'. Charters relating to the church of Winford.
  Ed. Hearne, *AD*, II, 618–27.

122rb–123v (s. xiv; larger, more informal hand)
'Feouda [*sic*] Glaston. Sumerset'. Account of abbey's tenants in Somerset, Dorset, Wiltshire, and Berkshire.

124ra/b (s. xiii)
Documents relating to the appropriated church of Shapwick.
1. 'De ecclesia de Sapewick assignata elemosinarie.' Ed. Watkin, *GC*, I, 35–6.
2. 'Assensus capituli Bathon. super eodem.' Ed. Watkin, *GC*, I, 36.
3. 'Cirographum quod capitula de Escote ecclesie de Sapewik tamquam matrici debet respondere.'
4. 'Sampson. decani de capella de Escote'. Ed. Watkin, *GC*, I, 39–40.

124v–125v (s. xiv, informal hand)
'Hide que pertinent ad abbathiam Glaston.'. List of holdings of the abbey in the hundreds of *Wytheleghe* and *Wystan*.

125ra/b (s. xiii)
Charters relating to the appropriated church of St John's, Glastonbury.
1. 'H. episcopi de ecclesia sancti Iohannis assignata ad usus sacristarie Glaston. ecclesie'. Ed. Watkin, *GC*, I, 16–17.
2. 'Sauarici episcopi de eodem'. Ed. Watkin, *GC*, I, 19.
3. 'Confirmacio capituli Bathon. super eodem'.
4. 'Willelmi Blundi de quadam terra in Glaston. data sacristarie'.

126ra/b (s. xiii)
Charters relating to the appropriated church of East Pennard.
1. 'Sauarici Bath. episcopi de ecclesia de Estpennard data in usus sacristarie Glaston. ecclesie'. Ed. Watkin, *GC*, I, 21.
2. 'Confirmacio Iocel. super eodem'. Ed. *ibid.*
3. 'Confirmacio capituli Bath. super eodem'. Ed. *ibid.*
4. 'Capituli Wellensis super eodem'. Ed. *ibid.*
Most of 126rb and all verso blank.

127r–129v (?s. xiv bookhand, later than any seen so far)
List of holdings in each shire (*Sumersete, Dorsete, Wyltesire, Barokesyre, Glocestresyr*).
  Cf. *Rentalia et Custumaria*, ed. Elton and Hobhouse, pp. 228–33.

129r (foot) (s. xiv, informal hand)
Note of holding in *Schapwyk*.

129v–130r (in hand of 127r until middle of 130r)
Series of memoranda of homage done in 1255 and 1264.
  Ed. Elton and Hobhouse, *Rentalia et Custumaria*, pp. 233–4.

130v (s. xiv, cursive hand)
1. 'Wyltechyr'. 'Inquisicio facta de expedicione canum abbatis Glaston. et hominum suorum de precepto domini regis'. Cf. Watkin, *GC*, I, 175–6.
2. *Inquisiciones* at *Bryweton*, Dorset and Wilton.

131r–137ra (later hand, s. xiv)

Entries for Glastonbury Abbey from Domesday Book. *Sumersete, Wiltesir, Dorsete, Deuon, Berksyre.*

Ed. Hearne, *AD*, II, 627–53. See also *Domesday Book: A Survey of the Counties of England*, gen. ed. J. Morris, 35 vols in 40 (Chichester, 1975–86) VIII, fols 90a–91a; VI, fols 66c–d; VII, fol. 77c; IX, fol. 103c; V, fol. 59c.

137ra/vb (s. xiv)

'Estimacio ualoris omnium maneruorum [*sic*] abbatie Glastonie in omnibus exitibus tam in redditibus . . .'.

138–139 (written on an inserted bifolium in a fourteenth-century hand different from that of the preceding folio)

Accounts

1. 138r
'Taxacio Norwicensis'

2. 138v
'Ecclesie appropriate'

3. 138v
'Pensiones'

4. 139r/v
'Ualorum bonorum temporalium et spiritualium abbatie Glaston. abstractus de rotulis compoti primorum trium annorum abbatis Iohannis' (? John of Taunton, A.D. 1274–91, John of Kent, A.D. 1291–1303, or John of Breynton, A.D. 1334–42).

139v (s. xiv, different hand)

'Ceo le entendement coment le tenement Roberd Moryz de Mynterne en la manere de Boclande de Veynt Frank . . .'.

140r/v (in different hand, s. xiv)

Latin tale of a soldier from Devon who fell in love with the daughter of a king of Mercia.

141r (in different hand, s. xiv)

'Memorandum quod cum die mercur. proxima post purificationem . . .', A.D. 1255. (Copy of first memorandum on 129v, with fuller witness-list.)

141r/v

'Nomina militum qui tenent de domo Glaston. per seruic. militar. fac. scuagium [*sic*]'.

142r (Early Modern, apparently imitating s. xiii)

Copy of a note of contents (sixteenth-century) on i v. In late medieval hand, lists of early (British and Anglo-Saxon) kings, bishops, saints and archbishops. Note of ownership, 1565.

142v

Blank flyleaf. Wormholes extending back from it into fol. 141.

DESCRIPTION

Size. 27.5 x 16.5/17 cm.

Quiring. No signatures.
a ?2 (2 cancelled: fol. i), I^{10} (1–10), II^{10} (11–20), III^{10} (+ two-thirds-leaf [fol. 27] after 6: 21–31), IV^{10} (32–41), V^{10} (42–51); VI^{12} (52–61, 61A, 62), VII^8 (63–70), VIII^6 (71–76); IX^{10} (lacks 4, + two-thirds-leaf [79] after 2, + bifolium [82–83] after 5, + half-leaf [87A] before 9: 77–86, 87A, 87–88); X^{10} (89–98), XI $?^{10}$ (lacks 1, 7; + bifolium inserted before 2 and after 9 [99:107]: 99–108), XII^{10} (109–116, 116A, 117); XIII^{10} (one leaf [?7] lacking: 118–126; originally only rectos written), XIV^4 (127–130), XV^{12} (5 and 7 cancelled, bifolium [138:139] after 9: 131–142).

Ruling. QQ. I–V, IX, 100r/v, 118, 120, 121r–122r, 124r, 125r, 126r – two columns, ruling above top written line, 45 lines.
QQ. VI, VII, VIII to 75r – similar layout but 43–31 lines.
Q. X – single column of 41/42 lines but after 93v in two columns of 44 lines.
75v–76v – single column, 39–44 lines.
Folio 99 – single column, 42 lines.
102r–104v – double column, 49–51 lines.
104r–107v, 110v–117v, 119r/v, 122v–123v – single column, 47–58 lines.
108r – two columns of 44 lines.
109r–110r – single column of 43/44 lines.
127–130r – single column of 34 lines.
130v – single column of 41 lines.
131–146 – 32/34 lines, two columns, etc.

Script. The *De antiquitate* (1r–18v) in small mid-thirteenth-century bookhand with cursive features. Brown ink. Fairly compact; not angular. Simple round *d* occasionally but sometimes loops back with hairline top. Slight splitting at tops of ascenders, sometimes split and looped; *t* is pierced, *a* single-compartment. Juncture of *e* and *o* after *d* etc.; *g* rarely crank-tailed. N.B. 16ra – list of abbots after Michael of Amesbury (1235–52) continued in later hands.
Libellus, 21v to 51v – ?Slightly later-looking but with less juncture. Ascender of *d* slanting and heavy; thick horizontal of crank-tailed *g* and *-us* abbreviation but *g*, *a*, and *et*-nota comparable with those in hand of the *De antiquitate* (changes to less ornate type on 23rb). By 46r, the hand seems to be that of the *De antiquitate* (both grades evident on 42va).
Q. IX (77–86, 87A, 87–8) – Small mid-thirteenth-century bookhand with some hairline flourishes. Additions in hand similar to this in aspect but more upright, with fewer hairlines and generally simpler forms, more like bookhand. Written in conjunction with an Anglicana hand with split ascenders and crank-tailed *g* but lacking fully developed fourteenth-century characteristics.
Q. X (89r–94r, 96–8) – Mid-thirteenth-century bookhand (latest document 1247). Laterally compressed with frequent high *a*. Generally formal in appearance. Script of additions to this quire has more hairline flourishes, split and looped ascenders. Sometimes two-compartment *a*. Pierced *t*.
100r–101r – Cf. list of documents (quire IX) and the *De antiquitate*. Names of kings written in this hand as far as Henry III (viz. before 1272). Library catalogue on thinner membrane, in paler ink but hand comparable to those seen elsewhere in earlier part of the volume. Single compartment *a* (often high), some split and looped ascenders. The pigment of the rubrication is also different from that found elsewhere in the volume.

Libellus, 52r–75rb – Script initially remains small (brown ink), but closer to Anglicana with split and looped ascenders, curled round *d*, small, usually monoline minim letters with longer and heavier ascenders and descenders. Two-compartment *a* usually, long cursive *r*. Several changes of hand (?56ra, 56vb, 60ra, 60va); the script becomes increasingly large and displays in exaggerated form the characteristics of Anglicana.

Fourteenth-century additions are in several hands, predominantly a large, crude post-Anglicana English cursive. Two-compartment *a*, looped ascenders, looped *d*, long descenders on *r* and initial and medial *s*. Brown ink.

Decoration. In mid-thirteenth-century section, large initials, red/blue parti-coloured with filigree, red rubrication. Small initials are red or cobalt blue with filigree.

52r–74r – Initials of the Lombardic type, unfiligreed red or blue. Rubrics in red Anglicana.

94v–95v, 109r–110r and 131r–137r – Red Lombardic initials and red rubrication.

Later history. Notes of ownership in same hand at top 1r 'Su*m* Guiliel. Bɷwyer. 1565' and on 142r (line 4) 'Sum Guiliel. Bɷwyer primo Septemb. 1565'; William Bowier was Keeper of the Records at the Tower of London and owner of a number of manuscripts.[34]

THE COMPILATION

Although Thomas Hearne edited many items from R. 5. 33, he gave little account of the volume as a whole; his attention was chiefly focussed on the two histories which stand at the beginning of the manuscript. Indirectly, however, he suggested a date for this *cod[ex] peruetust[us]*. He ventured the opinion that the manuscript might have been in the possession of the author of the second of the two histories and was perhaps even his autograph.[35] The author in question was Adam of Damerham; the work attributed to him, the *Libellus de rebus gestis Glastoniensibus*, concludes in 1291.

Little work has been done on the text of the *Libellus* since Hearne, and the *De antiquitate* was only re-edited in 1981,[36] but study of other parts of the manuscript has caused Hearne's view of its dating to be revised. Folios 102–3 contain a list of the books in the library at Glastonbury which bears the date 1247, altered by the addition of a minim to 1248. The list seems to have been revised at the same time as the date: various titles were deleted from it and others added. Hearne seems not to have attached any significance to the list for dating of the manuscript,[37] but scholars commenting on the list alone

---

[34]   C. E. Wright, 'The Dispersal of the Monastic Libraries and the Beginnings of Anglo-Saxon Studies. Matthew Parker and his Circle: A Preliminary Study', *Transactions of the Cambridge Bibliographical Society* 1 (1949–53), 208–37, at 231–2.

[35]   *AD*, ed. Hearne, I, xvi.

[36]   *The Early History*, ed. Scott.

[37]   He had printed the list without comment together with other material from R.5.33 ('Ex cod. MS. veteri membraneo') as an appendix to his edition of the *Cronica* of John

have taken the dates attached to it at face value and regarded it as an original of 1247/1248.[38] In his catalogue of the Trinity manuscripts, M. R. James made nothing of the date of the library list, but described the manuscript as 'cent. xiii early and xiii–xiv'.[39]

The implications of the library list for the dating of the manuscript seem to have been noticed only recently. Simon Keynes, in an unpublished work, noted that the scribe responsible for the library list had also copied 'the greater part of this manuscript', including William's History and the first part of that attributed to Adam.[40] John Scott, who edited the *De antiquitate*, endorsed and elaborated this observation. As a result he assigned the production of the first part of R. 5. 33 to *ca* 1247.[41]

Keynes's and Scott's dating of the earliest (mid-thirteenth-century) part of R. 5. 33 depends on the distribution of scribal stints within the manuscript. The relevant sections apart from those already mentioned – the *De antiquitate*, the *Libellus* to *ca* 1230 (quires I–V),[42] and the library list (fols 102–3) – comprise quire IX (the lists of documents), quire X (papal privileges), and folios 100r–101r (the *Compendium*, notes on bishops and Normans, and king-lists). The papal privileges may be separated from the remainder: they are written in various hands clearly different from the almost homogeneous script of the other items listed above.

This homogeneity is not at first apparent, however. The opening script of the *De antiquitate* is a bookhand of greater formality than the tiny, hairlined script in which the *Libellus* begins. Nevertheless scribal portions are almost impossible to identify. There are numerous changes of aspect but one cannot attribute these to anything more than a change in the quality of the writing surface (as on the reverse of a leaf) or to the trimming of a pen. The script hovers between a fairly classic bookhand with pierced *t*, eight-shaped *g*, simple round *d* (although sometimes looped back by a hairline), single-compartment *a* and something approaching charter script with forked ascenders, high *a* and crank-tailed *g*. The two styles are evident together on 42va (lines 24–6 and the surrounding text). Certain habits are evident: final *m* is sometimes finished with an oblique stroke rising upwards from the baseline at the right of the final limb of the letter, the vertical abbreviation stroke of the -*orum* abbreviation tends to come at the extreme right of the *r*, the -*us* abbreviation is continued leftwards under the preceding letters in a thick horizontal flourish similar to that of crank-tailed *g*, and round *d* sometimes

---

of Glastonbury, which appeared a year before his edition of the other Glastonbury histories. *JG*, ed. Hearne, II, 423–42.

[38]   For example, A. Anscombe, 'Numerus librorum Glastoniensis, A. 1248', *The Athenaeum* 3589, 8 August 1896, p. 194; Williams, *Somerset Mediaeval Libraries*, pp. 55–76.

[39]   James, *The Western Manuscripts in the Library of Trinity College*, II, 198. His first date is clearly unacceptably early.

[40]   Keynes, 'Anglo-Saxon Royal Diplomas', I, 165.

[41]   *The Early History*, ed. Scott, pp. 36 and 6. The volume was not included by P. R. Robinson in *Catalogue of Dated and Datable Manuscripts c. 737 – 1600 in Cambridge Libraries*, 2 vols (Cambridge, 1988).

[42]   As far as *AD*, ed. Hearne, II, 502.

has a hairline loop. These features appear and disappear unpredictably.[43] If not the work of a single scribe, these sections were produced by a group of well-trained collaborating scribes writing a particularly successful house style.

The early parts of R. 5. 33 are evidently interrelated. The hand of 100–101r is remarkably similar to the main hand of the *De antiquitate* and also the lists of documents (quire IX). Moreover, most of the sections detailed above (all dating from the mid-thirteenth century) are identically arranged (in tens), laid out (in two columns of 45 written lines, beginning below the top ruled line) and have similar decoration (blue or red filigreed capitals with parti-coloured initials at major divisions).

The only sections of appropriate date arranged differently are quire X, which contains the papal privileges (a single column of 41/42 lines, then a double column of 44 lines), and the library list on folios 102–3 (49 lines). The papal privileges have already been distinguished from the remainder on grounds of script; the status of the library list within the compilation is ambiguous. It is written on thinner parchment and in paler ink than the surrounding material in similar script.

The physical composition of the quire in which it is found is unclear. James regarded it as a gathering of ten with the sixth cancelled and the first added. This leaves two folios unaccounted for. I too consider that quire XI originally had ten leaves, but that the first and seventh were cancelled or lost and that a fourteenth-century bifolium (99:107) was inserted into the quire within the original outer bifolium (whose first leaf may already have been lacking), before the original second leaf of the quire and after the ninth. As the library list constitutes the central two bifolia of the quire (their last leaf is apparently now lacking) it is conceivably separable. However, to envisage the bifolia as an addition would require either that the quire had originally had only eight leaves and so disrupted the established pattern of quiring in tens, or that a bifolium has disappeared without trace. Either argument introduces complications which are not justified by internal evidence; this provides no grounds for supposing that the central bifolia are additions. The library list suggests a date of 1247/8 which accords with indications from the remainder of the would-be associated material. The abbatial list found in the *De antiquitate* (16ra) is written in the original hand as far as Michael of Amesbury (1235–52); the regnal list on 101r ends with Henry III (1216–72) (and is continued in later hands). It seems most likely, despite slight physical differences, that the library list belongs to the original phases of compilation.

So far, little has emerged which brings into question conclusions pre-viously reached about this manuscript and the texts which it contains: 1247 seems a reasonable date to assign to much of the manuscript. However, the

---

[43] For example the decorated final *m* appears on 4va (line 36, *Glastoniensem*), 34vb (line 10, *impetratam*), 42v (line 29, *ambicionem*), 50va (line 20, *perpetuum*), and on 51va, 85r, 125ra, and elsewhere. It also occurs in a plainly different hand in the papal privileges (94va, line 6, *quantum*; 95 va, line 37, *eodem*), as does the form of *-orum* abbreviation (94va, line 11, *quorum*).

hiatus in the middle of the *Libellus* (between 51v and 52r) is less easily reconciled to received opinion about that text. Thomas Hearne, following John of Glastonbury himself (writing *ca* 1342), attributed the whole work (anonymous in the manuscript) to a single author, Adam of Damerham, who appears in the *Libellus* as a monk of Glastonbury.[44] The composition of the Trinity manuscript puts this attribution under some strain. We have just seen that the first three quires of the *Libellus* belong to the earliest part of the manuscript, approximately datable to 1247. This part of the *Libellus* covers the years 1126 to about 1230 (the first date in the following section is 1234). However, the *Libellus* ends at the death of Abbot John of Taunton, attributed to 1290 (actually 1291). Thus there is a forty-year time-lapse between the copying of the earliest part of the *Libellus* and the completion of the work. Given the life expectancy of a man in the thirteenth century, we must suppose that if only one author was responsible, he started writing at a tender age and completed his composition near the end of his life.

While the range of time is not impossible, the evidence of R. 5. 33 allows a different interpretation. Keynes, despite the traditional attribution of the *Libellus*, concluded from looking at the manuscript that 'the earlier part of the work (21r–51v), which brings the account down to about 1230, was written in the late 1240s, while the rest (52r–73v), which takes it on to 1290, is plainly of different (and complex) origin'.[45]

John of Glastonbury's attribution should not be rejected without careful consideration. He was writing only half a century (about two generations), at the most, after the completion of the *Libellus*. Adam is not an unlikely candidate as author: he is known to have entered the abbey under Michael of Amesbury (1235–52) and to have been active in the politics of the house in 1255 and 1274.[46] Given that he held a position of some seniority in 1255, it is quite conceivable that he could have been at work on a history of his monastery some ten years before. But it seems improbable that he would have undertaken to update his work fifty years later. Moreover, the *Libellus* was not the property of a single author. It received anonymous continuations elsewhere: London, British Library, Add. 22934 is a copy of the work extended to 1313.[47] The second part of the *Libellus* in the Trinity manuscript could consist of one or more similar continuations, extending to 1291.

It may be that John was correct about one author of the *Libellus* but that

---

[44]   John of Glastonbury, in his prologue, described Adam's History as covering the years between 1126 and 1290, exactly the period of the *Libellus* in R. 5. 33: *The Chronicle of Glastonbury Abbey*, ed. Carley, p. 6, and *JG*, ed. Hearne, I, 6.

[45]   Keynes, *Anglo-Saxon Manuscripts*, no. 29.

[46]   See *The Chronicle of Glastonbury Abbey*, ed. Carley, p. xxxvi.

[47]   *The Early History*, ed. Scott, pp. 37–8. The bulk of BL Add. 22934 consists of the *De antiquitate* and *Libellus* (heavily interpolated with documents) copied end to end and followed by a continuation. The manuscript was apparently compiled in a single process. The *De antiquitate* and *Libellus*, both anonymous here, were copied almost as a single text with no spacing or major rubrication marking off one from the other. There is no sign of intermittent updating. However, a change of hand is apparent at the point in the *Libellus* where in R.5.33 the first continuation begins (52r in R.5.33, 50r in BL Add. 22934; both begin at the top of a new folio).

his information was inaccurate as to the extent of the work in its original state. Adam may have been responsible for the initial section at the time when the codex was first compiled, or possibly the first continuation, but it seems probable that some parts of the work were carried out by other Glastonbury monks. The chronicle which bears Adam's name ought to be viewed not as the work of a single author but as a house production.

A tentative estimate can be made of the duration of the hiatus between the copying of the initial section of the *Libellus* and that of its first continuation. The scribe who began the new section on quire VI (52r–56ra) evidently wrote in or after 1252, the year of the death of Abbot Michael, the latest event in the portion copied by him to which a date can be assigned. This scribe also copied a privilege of Alexander IV, dated 1259 (on 95rb). Although this document in itself offers no more than a *terminus post quem*, further precision about the date of its copying can be reached by examining its position in the quire of papal privileges, the only part of the mid-thirteenth-century section of the manuscript not yet discussed here.

The first seven folios of this quire (fols 89–95) contain papal privileges; the last three (fols 96–8) bear royal documents. The papal material is arranged in roughly chronological order (1123, 1137, 1144, 1168, 1192, 1219, 1218, 1223, 1225, 1230, 1232, 1246, 1245, 1247, 1245; 1255, 1267, 1268, 1255, 1259, 1255, 1267). The eleven documents at the end of the sequence dated in and after 1255 (from 1255, 1259, 1267, and 1268) are written on 94v and folio 95 in hands not found in the earlier, or indeed the final, part of the quire (89r–94r; 96r–98v). Folios 94v–95v are also distinct from the remainder in their decoration: plain red Lombardic capitals, not the filigreed sort found in the remainder of the quire and the early part of the manuscript. The end of the quire, the charters of Henry III on 96r–98v, is written in hands matching those before 94v and contains nothing dated later than the twenty-seventh year of Henry's reign, viz. 1243. It is possible then that the original part of the quire dates from about 1247: it certainly cannot be earlier. At that initial stage, all the papal privileges to date were copied and a few leaves left blank before the next item (the Henrician charters) so that the dossier could be kept up to date. The entries on 94v and folio 95 demonstrate that this happened in perhaps the later 1260s: the ratifications of 1267 and 1268 found on 94v are written in the same hand as the two documents of 1255 (Alexander IV) which precede them.[48]

This examination shows that the internal dating of the quire of papal privileges places them in or after 1247 (allowing time for the documents to reach Glastonbury);[49] there are accordingly good grounds for associating them with the initial compilation. Their inclusion is apt. The early part of the

---

[48] While this consistency of hand provides no absolute guarantee that the four documents on 94v were written at the same time, this possibility is more likely than not. There is also no perceptible change of ink between the documents of 1255 and 1267/8.

[49] The latest document from the original part of the quire is dated Lyon, 4 ides March, 1247.

Libellus constitutes our main narrative of the long dispute between Glastonbury and the see of Bath in which the pope was arbiter. Bishop Savaric (1192–1205), with papal sanction, secured direction of the abbey, which he was able to bequeath to his successor, Jocelin (1206–42). Glastonbury only regained independence in 1219, with the backing of Pope Honorius III.[50] The document issued on this occasion appears in the collection in R. 5. 33 (90v–91r), as do several statements about the abbey's liberty secured from later popes. The privileges supporting the bishops of Wells are of course absent (they were not addressed to Glastonbury).

It seems that after the initial compilation the quire of privileges developed in tandem with the *Libellus*. Both were continued in what constitutes the first extension of the oldest part of the manuscript. The hiatus between the initial copying of the *Libellus* and its first continuation may have been of the order of twenty years.

This interpretation may have to be revised in one respect. Two charters of Henry III datable to 1253 are found on 108r, at the end of the original part of quire XI, in a mid-thirteenth-century hand. While this is not the hand of the *De antiquitate* and the early part of the *Libellus*, it resembles closely that of the Henrician material on folios 96–8. It may be that the *terminus post quem* argued for the copying of most of that quire – 1247 – is too early, and the whole should be ascribed to the 1250s. This seems unlikely, given that the hand of folio 108 looks later than that of the *De antiquitate* and the rest. Alternatively the charters on folios 96–8 could have been copied after 89r–94r, but still with space left for further papal privileges. Or it is conceivable that quire X was indeed originally written *ca* 1247 and that 108r was copied by the same scribe some years later.

The completion of quire X – the papal privileges – in the 1260s or later (the script does not suggest a date much later) was not an isolated act of addition to the manuscript. Quire IX, which contains the lists of documents, seems to have received attention at about the same time. The quire contains two added leaves (79, 87A: not full size) and an added bifolium (fols 82–3) which bear material very similar to the original contents. The additions were written not by the mid-thirteenth-century scribe who completed most of the quire, but mainly in a bookhand of similar appearance to the main hand and also (on 82r, 83r, 87A) in a more cursive, erratic script of about the same period; this is difficult to compare with the bookhand on account of the difference in grade.

The additions are not easy to date. Many of the documents listed on the added leaves may be found in the Great Cartulary,[51] but few are dated. An exception is the charter of John Thusard relating to Wrington and datable to 1257 (found on 82v).[52] This dating accords with a second indication. There is

[50] For one account of the dispute see Church, *Chapters in the Early History of the Church of Wells*, pp. 89–107, 115–16 and 134.

[51] For example, charters of William de Monketone, Robert Sutor and Henry de Alweton are equivalent to those of *GC*, ed. Watkin, II, 260, 259, and III, 617.

[52] *GC*, ed. Watkin, II, 547.

an entry in the cursive hand described above (which does not appear on folio 79), at the foot of 78vb and therefore in the original part of the quire. This is a note of the privileges of Pope Alexander about the appropriations of Damerham and *Sowy*, documents dated 1255 which, transcribed in full, constitute the first of the additions to the quire of privileges (94v). It would seem therefore that quire IX, in particular the list of contents of the *Liber terrarum* which stands at its beginning, received additions in the later 1250s. Leaves subsequently added to the quire contain documents which bear dates as late as 1276 and 1278 (confirmations by Innocent V and Nicholas III, both on 79r).

It may be possible to go a stage further. The cursive hand seen in the additions in quire IX (on 82r, 83r, 87A, and elsewhere) bears a strong similarity to that found on the main part of 94v; exact identification is difficult but the resemblance is to be noted. Additions were made to the lists of documents, therefore, at about the same time as, if not in one of the hands of, the continuation of the papal privileges. This process, as the work of the other continuator-scribe shows (above), may be associated with the first continuation of the *Libellus*.

The *Libellus* received several further continuations. Distinct changes of hand are evident at 56rb, line 7, and 60ra, line 20. Each stint takes the narrative into a new abbacy: that beginning at 56rb continues to the succession of Robert of Petherton (1261–74), that at 60ra stops with the abbacy of John of Taunton (1274–91). Similarly, the first continuator-scribe ended his stint after recording the death of Michael of Amesbury (1252). The impression of occasional but regular updating is reinforced by the script. The hands show increasingly the features of Anglicana script – the flourished, heavily shaded documentary hand written in the later thirteenth century.[53] The final hand perhaps postdates 1295/6.[54]

While these hands cannot be identified in any other part of the manuscript, the second (from 56rb) is similar to that which appears on 140r/v, the tale of the West Saxon *miles*. This story occurs towards the end of the final quire, apparently filling in space after documents about the holdings of Glastonbury (written in various hands datable to about the end of the thirteenth century). The preceding quire (XIV) of four leaves contains similar material and may date from approximately the same time.

Any blank space originally left in these final quires disappeared in the last major phase in the completion of the present manuscript. This, to judge from the script, took place in the first half of the fourteenth century. Many docu-

---

53   Described by M. B. Parkes, *English Cursive Book Hands 1250–1500* (Oxford, 1969; rev. ed. London, 1979), pp. xiv–xvi.

54   The copyist who completed the *Libellus* also transcribed (below it) an account of a dispute between John, abbot of Glastonbury, and one John Lovel which took place in the fourteenth year of the king (unnamed). The abbot in question could be either John of Taunton, 1274–91, or John of Kent, 1291–1303. As the document refers to a record kept 'per cartam Iohannis quondam abbatis Glaston. predecessoris predicti abbatis', John of Kent seems the likely candidate. The regnal year is problematic, however: the 14th of Edward I was 1285/6. To achieve a date within John of Kent's abbacy, one would need to envisage a missing .x. and redate to 1295/6.

ments – (mostly in Latin, but a few in French) about Glastonbury, the abbey's estates, and their dues – were entered in semi-cursive hands on any empty space in the manuscript. Only a couple of extra leaves were added (in quires XIV and XV, see below). Thus the existing collection was extended by charters, lists of tenants, lists of books and relics, *inquisiciones* into its estates, accounts of holdings and tax assessments. These were accommodated on blank leaves at the end of quires II (20r), VI (75r–76v), X (88), XI (104–107), XIV (129r–130v) and XV (141r/v). In addition the blank versos of a slip in quire IX (79v) and those in quire XIII were used (122v–125v). Despite adding a substantial amount of new material, the revisers made minimal physical changes to the manuscript. Quire XI gained a new outer bifolium; a bifolium was inserted into quire XV.

These additions were carried out in several hands. One seems to recur particularly. It is largish, informal, lacks the more extreme flourishes and shading of Anglicana, and is written in brown ink.[55]

It is difficult to assign a precise date to this last phase. Few of the documents offer a date close enough to that indicated by the script to be helpful. Some material is apparently of the fourteenth century. A return written (on 101v) in the ubiquitous hand just described is dated in the fourth year of Abbot Geoffrey Fromond (1303–22). There is besides a document (in French, on 120vb) mentioning Simon de Montacute, who witnessed a Glastonbury document in 1319.[56]

Given that the fourteenth-century continuators seem to have included historical rather than contemporary material, one would not want to assume that these two documents offer a precise date, but it may be significant that they both fall within Fromond's abbacy. He was an energetic defender of the abbey's prestige and followed the example set by certain thirteenth-century predecessors who took care to maximize profits from the house's estates and to extend the abbey's buildings.[57] The continuation of the *Libellus* to 1313 may suggest that the history of the abbey was also attended to under his abbacy.[58] However, it may be that the final phase of R. 5. 33 should be placed rather later. Abbots John de Breynton (1334–42) and Walter de Monyngton (1342–75) ruled at a period of intense interest in the abbey's history and rights. The Great Cartulary was compiled *ca* 1338–40, the *Secretum Domini* (a copy of the cartulary for the abbot's own use) in 1340–2,[59] and the Glaston-

---

[55] Seen, for example, on 75v. It has looped ascenders, two-compartment *a*, looped *d*, long *r* and crossed *et*-nota.

[56] *GC*, ed. Watkin, II, 517.

[57] I. Keil, 'The Abbots of Glastonbury in the Early Fifteenth Century', *The Downside Review* 82 (1964), 327–48, at 347.

[58] But note that Scott's assertion that BL Add. 22934 was copied *ca* 1313 (*The Early History*, ed. Scott, p. 37) is brought into question by a charter which appears on 119ra of that manuscript – apparently part of the original compilation – and is dated 1322, the year of Fromond's death. Fromond was asked by Edward II to supply historical information in another connection: E. L. G. Stones and I. J. E. Keil, 'Edward II and the Abbot of Glastonbury: A New Case of Historical Evidence Solicited from Monasteries', *Archives* 12 (1975/6), 176–82.

[59] See Watkin, *GC*, I, x–xi.

bury Feodary in 1342–3; at about the same time John of Glastonbury completed his chronicle of the abbey.[60]

From this examination, it seems that R. 5. 33 was compiled in four phases. The first – the copying of the historical texts, papal privileges (notably those guaranteeing the abbey's liberty), and the lists of charters and library books – dates from 1247 or shortly afterwards. A little later, minor additions were made to the papal privileges and *Libellus* in order to bring them up to date. The third stage was more protracted and entailed more substantial additions: the updating of the house history and the dossier of documents in the second half of the century. The final additions to the manuscript were the documents and accounts relating to the abbey's estates entered in the early fourteenth century.

All these stages represent written expression of claims to rights, lands, and prestige which the monks of Glastonbury were pursuing actively in other ways. In the 1240s, under the direction of Abbot Michael of Amesbury, a strenuous upholder of the abbey's privileges,[61] the monks were attempting to recover rights and property from the bishop of Bath and Wells. This campaign was boosted *ca* 1250 by the king's issue of a writ against the bishop, claiming the advowson of the abbey for himself.[62] It is interesting that the abbey's ancient royal connection – with Arthur – should have been recorded in writing at about the same time. John of Taunton (1274–91), with whose career the final instalment of the *Libellus* in R. 5. 33 ends, was another active defender of the abbey's position.[63] The final phase of the manuscript's production falls into another period of consolidation, in the fourteenth century, as we have seen. However romantic some of its subject matter, the interest of the monks of Glastonbury in history, especially Arthurian history, was plainly far from fanciful.

APPENDIX

The stages of the manuscript's growth suggested by this description may be summarized as follows.

s. xiii med. ?ca 1247

William of Malmesbury's *De antiquitate*; *Consuetudo luminarii*; *Libellus de rebus gestis Glaston.* (to A.D. 1223) (quires I–V); the list of documents in quire IX; the *Compendium de Britannia* and list of the kings of England (fols 100–101: quire XI); and the grants to Glastonbury in quire XIII (118r–122r). These form the earliest unit identifiable in the manuscript. The whole is connected by script, decoration,

---

[60]　*A Feodary of Glastonbury Abbey*, ed. F. W. Weaver, SRS 26 (1910); *The Chronicle of Glastonbury Abbey*, ed. Carley, p. xlvii and n. 11 and p. xxvi.

[61]　On whom see Knowles, *The Religious Orders*, I, 45 and 315.

[62]　S. Wood, *English Monasteries and their Patrons in the Thirteenth Century* (Oxford, 1955), p. 30.

[63]　Knowles, *The Religious Orders*, I, 45 and 315.

layout (in two columns of 45 lines, beginning below the top ruled line)[64] and quiring (in tens).

Parts of quire X (the papal privileges and Magna Carta) were copied in a slightly different script (with a layout different from the above) at approximately the same time. The library list in quire XI may be contemporary with this activity.

s. xiii med. ?1260s

Additions were made to the papal privileges in quire IX (in blank spaces and on added leaves) and the *Libellus* was continued.

s. xiii 2/xiv in.

Further continuations were made to the *Libellus* (quires VI–VIII)[65] and to the existing collections of documents. New quires containing records of the abbey's estates and entitlements were added at the end in various hands (quires XIV and XV).

s. xiv 1

Additional charters and documents were entered, mostly on blank leaves in the mid-thirteenth-century quires II, VIII, IX, and XI (often at the ends of texts) and in the later quires XIV and XV. Bifolia were added to quires XI and XV.[66]

---

[64] This practice began to be followed by professional scribes in the early thirteenth century and by non-professionals after the middle of the century: N. R. Ker, 'From "Above Top Line" to "Below Top Line": A Change in Scribal Practice', *Celtica* 5 (1950), 13–15.

[65] An indication of the dating of the continuations is provided by the record of the division of goods on 76v dated 1289 (found at the end of quire VIII).

[66] I am grateful to Lesley Abrams, David Dumville and Simon Keynes for reading this paper in draft and for suggesting numerous improvements.

Glastonbury's Cornish Connections

O. J. PADEL

Glastonbury Abbey had two unrelated links with the county of Cornwall in the Middle Ages. One consisted in a chapel in Cornwall dedicated to a saint, Indract, who was distinctively honoured at Glastonbury; as will be seen, the dedication can probably be ascribed to the pre-Conquest period. The other link was with the parish of Talland, some twelve miles away from that chapel, and belonged to the post-Conquest period. The earlier connection has received little discussion, partly because of its obscurity and uncertain nature; it has been treated by Doble and Finberg, but the latter account is misleading, as will be seen.[1] The later connection has received excellent recent discussion by Picken and Olson;[2] the chief addition to be made here is to give some improvements in the text of a charter concerning Glastonbury's interest. The charter was formerly known only from a later copy, but the original text has recently come to light.

In the parish of St Dominick in Cornwall, at a farm now called Chapel on the bank of the River Tamar, there was formerly a chapel apparently dedicated in honour of St Indract,[3] the saint whose body lay at the north side of the high altar in St Mary's church at Glastonbury. This is the only such dedication known in Britain, for the saint's cult was otherwise restricted to Glastonbury.[4] The earliest mention of the name of the saint at the Cornish site is as *St Ildrayth* in 1351, and other fourteenth-century forms are similar: *St Ildreyth* (1352) and *St Ildreith* (1362); but also '*St Ildract*, confessor' (1419).[5]

---

[1]   G. H. Doble, 'St Indract and St Dominic', in *Collectanea III: A Collection of Documents from Various Sources*, ed. T. F. Palmer, SRS 57 (1942), 1–24, and separately, Cornish Saints Series, no. 48 (no place, no date); H. P. R. Finberg, 'Sherborne, Glastonbury and the Expansion of Wessex', in his *Lucerna. Studies of Some Problems in the Early History of England* (London, 1964), pp. 95–115, at 101–2.

[2]   W. M. M. Picken, 'Light on Lammana', *Devon and Cornwall Notes and Queries* 35 (1982–6), 281–6; Lynette Olson, *Early Monasteries in Cornwall* (Woodbridge, 1989), pp. 97–104.

[3]   The chapel is at grid reference SX 417658.

[4]   M. Lapidge, 'The Cult of St Indract at Glastonbury', in *Ireland in Early Mediaeval Europe: Studies in Memory of Kathleen Hughes*, ed. D. Whitelock, R. McKitterick and D. Dumville (Cambridge, 1982), pp. 179–212, at 198; Doble, 'St Indract', p. 21; and G. H. Doble, 'St Indract at Glastonbury', *SDNQ* 24 (1943–6), 126.

[5]   In 1351 and 1352: *The Hylle Cartulary*, ed. R. W. Dunning, SRS 68 (1968), p. 76 (the cartulary was compiled in *ca* 1416). In 1362: *The Register of Edward the Black Prince*, ed. M. C. B. Dawes, 4 vols (London, 1930–3) II, 188. In 1419: *The Register of Edmund Stafford (A.D. 1395–1419)*, ed. F. C. Hingeston-Randolph (London, 1886), p. 313. The

Apart from this last instance, the names referred not to the saint himself as patron saint of the chapel, but to a secular property which evidently took its name from the chapel situated in its territory.

There are several points of significance in the dedication and in the forms of the saint's name. The dedication provided a focus for an episode in one of the surviving medieval accounts of the martyrdom of St Indract, that of John of Tynemouth composed in the first half of the fourteenth century.[6] John related that, on their way to Rome, St Indract and his companions had paused for a while at a place called *Tamerunta*; numerous miracles occurred there, and John recounted them in such a manner as to give the impression that St Indract was still honoured at the spot.[7] As Doble saw, it was evidently the chapel in St Dominick parish that John of Tynemouth had in mind as the site of the events. In the first place, St Indract was credited in the episode with a sister called St Dominica – a reference to the dedication of the parish church to an unknown female saint, Dominica.[8] Secondly, *Tamerunta* must be a copyist's error for *Tamertuna*, a normal medieval form for any of the three places called Tamerton, named from their location near to the River Tamar: North Tamerton in Cornwall, and King's Tamerton and Tamerton Foliot in Devon.[9] However, none of these places is actually at the site of St Indract's chapel, and the discrepancy is curious. The best candidate, since it is closest to St Dominick, is Tamerton Foliot; but even that village is not immediately across the River Tamar from St Dominick, being a few miles down-river. Perhaps 'Tamerton' was used by John of Tynemouth as a generic term for what is now known as the port of Plymouth, at the entrance to the River Tamar. This large estuary embraces access to both King's Tamerton and Tamerton Foliot, on its east side, and the parish of St Dominick higher up on its west side. 'Tamerton', used loosely to mean the ports at the mouth of the River Tamar, would thus include the Cornish parish where St Indract's chapel lay. At all events, John must have known of the dedication of the Cornish chapel to the Glastonbury saint; it seems likely that the legends

manuscript of the latter reads *Sancti Ildracti*: S. Baring-Gould and John Fisher, *The Lives of the British Saints*, 4 vols (London, 1907–13) III, 320.

6   For details of the various accounts see Lapidge, 'Cult of St Indract'. John of Tynemouth is known to have travelled to Cornwall, among other places. His *Sanctilogium Anglie*, written in the first half of the fourteenth century, was arranged according to the liturgical calendar. It was rearranged into alphabetical order by an anonymous compiler, and published by Wynkyn de Worde as *Nova Legenda Anglie* (London, 1516). The account of St Indract appears on 188va–189va; *Nova Legenda Anglie*, ed. C. Horstman, 2 vols (Oxford, 1901) II, 56–8.

7   *Nova Legenda*, 188vb (ed. Horstman, II, 56). John's account is mainly based on a Latin *passio* of St Indract, written before the early twelfth century, but that work does not contain an equivalent of John's Cornish episode (Lapidge, 'Cult of St Indract', p. 197).

8   O. J. Padel, *A Popular Dictionary of Cornish Place-Names* (Penzance, 1988), p. 79; cf. Doble, 'St Indract', appendix, pp. 23–4.

9   J. E. B. Gover *et al.*, *The Place-Names of Devon*, 2 vols, English Place-Name Society 8–9 (Cambridge, 1931–2) I, 237 and 242; Padel, *Popular Dictionary*, p. 161. Tamerton Foliot is at grid reference SX 4760, King's Tamerton at SX 4558, and North Tamerton at SX 3197.

which he recounted were locally current in Cornwall in the fourteenth century, and that he decided to incorporate them into his re-telling of the Glastonbury account of St Indract's martyrdom.[10]

There is a further point of interest in the references to the Cornish chapel, and that lies in the forms of the name. It will be noted that the forms in use in Cornwall were different from those at Glastonbury. This has caused some doubt whether the two saints were actually the same;[11] however, the doubt is unnecessary, as will be seen, and the discrepancy is instructive. At Glastonbury itself, the form *Indract(us)* was normally used. This is rightly considered to be a Latinization of the Irish name *Indrechtach*, borrowed through the medium of Old English, which would have had a hypothetical intermediate form **Indrac(h)te* or the like.[12] In addition to the standard form *Indractus*, one or two Glastonbury references show that in spoken Old English the Irish *ch* in the second syllable was in fact represented by the expected spirant, instead of the Latinized plosive: the form *S. Indrahte* occurs in a litany written in the second quarter of the eleventh century, and, about a century later, William of Malmesbury once used the form *Indrahtus*.[13] These show what must have been the spoken form of the name as borrowed from Irish into Old English, as opposed to the learned form with *c*, *Indractus*, which is the form more often used in the manuscripts of William of Malmesbury's texts.[14] The other feature to be noted in the form of the name is that for some unknown reason English usage substituted *a* for Irish *e* in the second syllable.

The expected Old Cornish or Welsh form of the name would have been **Indraith* (or *Indraeth* in later Welsh), where the final *-cht* has regularly become *-ith*: compare, for example, Irish *tracht*, Modern Welsh *traeth*, 'shore, strand'. The hypothetical form *Indraith* is attractively similar to the one actually found attached to the Cornish site in the fourteenth century, *Ildreyth*. No regular parallel is forthcoming for the interchange of *l* and *n*, but it occurs sporadically elsewhere, and can be plausibly taken to be a spoken corruption which occurred locally in Cornwall. It might have occurred, in Cornish speech, by analogy with other Cornish personal names starting *Il-*.[15] Apart

---

[10] Doble's suggestion ('St Indract', p. 16) that the information was first written up at St Germans was speculation, based solely on incorrect hypotheses regarding certain place-names in the area. Tavistock, St Germans and Launceston were the religious houses nearest to the parish of St Dominick, and any of them might have preserved the local legends and made them available to John of Tynemouth.

[11] Doble, 'St Indract', p. 17.

[12] Lapidge, 'Cult of St Indract', p. 187, n. 38.

[13] Lapidge, 'Cult of St Indract', p. 184; Bernard J. Muir, *A Pre-Conquest English Prayer-Book*, Henry Bradshaw Society 103 (Woodbridge, 1988), p. 127; William of Malmesbury, *Gesta pontificum Anglorum*, ch. 91; *Willelmi Malmesbiriensis Monachi de Gestis Pontificum Anglorum*, ed. N. E. S. A. Hamilton, RS 52 (London, 1870), p. 197.

[14] For example, *DA*, ch. 12 (ed. Scott, p. 61).

[15] Compare Old Cornish personal names such as *Illcum*, *Iliuth* and *Ylcerthon*: M. Förster, 'Die Freilassungsurkunden des Bodmin-Evangeliars', in *A Grammatical Miscellany Offered to Otto Jespersen*, ed. N. Bøgholm et al. (London and Copenhagen, 1930), pp. 86, 87 and 94 (nos. 16, 18 and 36). Compare also Old Welsh personal names in *Il-*:

from that one discrepancy, the two names are etymologically identical, and there seems therefore no need for Doble's doubt as to whether it was actually the Glastonbury saint who was honoured at the Cornish chapel. No alternative St Ildreyth is known elsewhere.

The question arises: when did the Cornish dedication come into being? It is not recorded before the mid-fourteenth century, when it appeared both in local records and, as already seen, by implication in John of Tynemouth's narrative. That does not mean that the dedication had only recently arisen, however. It was already sufficiently well established to have become an alternative name of the manor in which the chapel lay (on which see further below); and, if it is right to deduce that John was drawing upon indigenous local legends, the dedication would need already to have been in existence for a substantial while.

The form of the name can perhaps give some clue to the origins of the dedication. The existence of the Cornish form for the dedication of the chapel indicates that the personal name had, at some time, been current upon Cornish-speaking lips in the area. That explains, incidentally, why the change did not occur at Glastonbury itself, where neither Welsh nor Cornish was a spoken language during the period when there was an interest in the saint. The change of -ac(h)t to -aith took place probably in the late sixth century.[16] This might have made one suppose that the name was already current locally before that date, so that it could take part in the sound-change when that occurred. However, that is very unlikely in this instance, not least because St Indract himself is probably to be dated considerably later than the sound-change. Lapidge has tentatively suggested that the Glastonbury St Indract probably lived and was martyred in the mid-ninth century.[17] We must suppose that *Indrac(h)t* was changed to *Indraith* in Cornish speech at a time later than the date of the regular sound-change; it must have occurred simply by analogy with similar words which had undergone the change.

The earliest likely date for the dedication to have arisen is thus provided by the tentative date of the saint himself, in the mid-ninth century. A latest likely date for the dedication can also be suggested. In this part of Cornwall, right on the bank of the River Tamar, the place-names indicate considerable English settlement, probably from the eighth century onwards, and it is most unlikely that Cornish was a spoken language after *ca* 1100; so a dedication which arose after that date would not have been affected by Cornish sound-changes. The creation of the dedication can thus be dated to some time between the mid-ninth century and *ca* 1100; however, that dating could be overridden in either direction if cogent evidence were forthcoming, for example to indicate that the saint himself should be dated earlier than the

J. Gwenogvryn Evans and J. Rhys, *The Text of the Book of Llan Dâv* (Oxford, 1893), p. 405. Note also instances of *l/n* interchange in, for example, the following Cornish place-names: Lamorna (formerly *Nansmornou*), Lelant (formerly *Lananta*) and Newlyn (formerly *Lulyn*); Padel, *Popular Dictionary*, pp. 105, 108 and 128.

[16]   K. H. Jackson, *Language and History in Early Britain* (Edinburgh, 1953), p. 411.

[17]   Lapidge, 'Cult of St Indract', pp. 187–93.

mid-ninth century, or to demonstrate a later link of some kind between Glastonbury Abbey and the parish of St Dominick. In the later Middle Ages, the manor of Halton (including the chapel of St Indract) belonged to a family with close Somerset connections, the Fichets of Spaxton and elsewhere. However, they did not acquire their Cornish lands until the later fourteenth century, by the marriage (in about 1370) of Sir Thomas Fichet II to Ricarda, heiress of Nicholas Inkpen;[18] that connection therefore cannot account for the dedication to St Indract, recorded at a slightly earlier date.

There is one indication that the hypothetical Cornish or Welsh pronunciation of the saint's name, *Indraith*, was known at Glastonbury. In the twelfth-century Irish Martyrology of Tallaght the saint occurs in the form *sancti Indrathi* (Latin genitive);[19] he is recorded there as being honoured specifically at Glastonbury, and his day is given, as also is the Irish form *Indrechtaig* (genitive), as a translation. The information about the saint was presumably obtained from Glastonbury itself, and the form *Indrathi* constitutes the sole item of evidence suggesting that the vernacular Cornish or Welsh form of the saint's name was known there.[20]

If *Indrathi* indicates knowledge of the Cornish or Welsh pronunciation at Glastonbury, then in theory one might suppose that the Cornish dedication could have arisen later than *ca* 1100, for the vernacular pronunciation might have been introduced from Glastonbury along with the dedication, instead of being due to local Cornish speech. However, it would be difficult to sustain that suggestion, for one would then need to explain how the vernacular Cornish or Welsh pronunciation had arisen at all, since St Indract was not honoured elsewhere in the Brittonic world, as far as is known. The Cornish form, with *l* instead of *n*, would also be harder to explain under that theory (since the Glastonbury form to be introduced would have had the expected *Indr-*, not the irregular Cornish *Ildr-*), and it would lack even the tentative explanation suggested above (a change which Cornish-speakers might have effected, by analogy, before 1100); and, finally, there is no tenurial link between Glastonbury Abbey and the Cornish parish, either before or after *ca* 1100, such as might have given rise to the dedication. One might say, rather, that the form *Indrathi* in the Glastonbury material in the Martyrology of Tallaght suggests that the Cornish dedication, and thus its name-form, might have been known in Glastonbury. (If so, then the saint's name travelled in its true form, before the corruption of *n* to *l*.) Doble has pointed out that there was information available at Glastonbury about several other more or less obscure Cornish saints.[21]

Since a tenurial link would have been the best explanation for the dedica-

---

[18] *Hylle Cartulary*, ed. Dunning, pp. xvii and xxi.
[19] *The Martyrology of Tallaght*, ed. R. I. Best and H. J. Lawlor, Henry Bradshaw Society 68 (London, 1931), p. 110.
[20] However, an alternative explanation of *Indrathi* could be that it was a copyist's error for *Indrahti* (compare *Indrahte*, etc., above); in that case, the following suggestions would be invalid.
[21] Doble, 'St Indract', p. 18; G. H. Doble, 'The Celtic Saints in the Glastonbury Relic Lists', *SDNQ* 24 (1943–6), 86–9 and 128.

tion of the Cornish chapel, it is worth examining two possible hints of such a connection, although it will be seen that neither stands up to close inspection.

As mentioned above, the name of the Cornish chapel, St Ildreyth, was also used as an alternative name for the manor in which it lay; and that had already happened by the date of the earliest mentions of the Cornish saint.[22] Such a transfer is an unusual occurrence, even in Cornwall with its great frequency of saints' names occurring as place-names, and it implies some considerable significance for the chapel within the territory of the manor. Previous to that, the manor was known by the name of Halton, which has continued to the present day as the standard name.[23]

It would have been tempting, but unfortunately it is not legitimate, to suggest that this Cornish manor of Halton, containing within its lands the chapel dedicated to St Indract, might be equated with a property given to Glastonbury in King Edgar's reign: 'Edgarus de Healtone dat. Byrnsige .S.',[24] and 'Brinsige dedit Healtone v hidas'.[25] This estate is normally, and rightly, identified instead with Holton in Somerset, where the abbey had an interest after the Norman Conquest, so that these references unfortunately cannot constitute possible evidence for a tenurial link between the abbey and the area in Cornwall where the chapel of St Indract lay.[26]

Among the lands mentioned in William of Malmesbury's *De antiquitate Glastonie ecclesie* as having been given by the West Saxon king Ine to Glastonbury Abbey is an estate specified as 'iuxta Tamer, scilicet Linig, xx hidas'.[27] Elsewhere in the text, the same grant is mentioned as 'xx hidas iuxta Tamer', and an annotator of the mid-thirteenth century has added 'scilicet Linis'.[28] In the course of a discussion of the Saxon conquest of Devon and Cornwall, Finberg suggested that this estate could be identified as the whole area lying, in Cornwall, between the rivers Tamar and Lynher, an area including the parish of St Dominick.[29] As mentioned earlier, this area is known to have been subjected to English settlement at an early date (say, the eighth century) because it has a high proportion of English, instead of Cornish, place-names, as compared with most other areas of east Cornwall. In making this sugges-

---

[22]   *Hylle Cartulary*, ed. Dunning, p. 76: the manor of *Seint Ildreyth*, 1352.
[23]   For instance, the manor is referred to as *Haltone* in 1086, *Halton'* in 1337, and *Haltone* in 1375.
[24]   From the surviving contents-list of the lost Glastonbury cartulary known as the *Liber terrarum*, cited in *JG*, ed. Hearne, II, 370–5, at 373.
[25]   *DA*, chs 62 and 69 (ed. Scott, pp. 130 and 144).
[26]   S. C. Morland, 'The Glastonbury Manors and their Saxon Charters', *PSANHS* 130 (1986), 61–105, at 74 (no. 32), 'Holton with Lattiford'; compare p. 69 (no. 10), 'Blackford near Wincanton', and p. 70 (no. 14), 'Butleigh'. My thanks to Mr Morland for kindly discussing in correspondence some aspects of these holdings.
[27]   *DA*, ch. 69 (ed. Scott, p. 140; misprinted as *Lining*, but correctly cited as *Linig* at pp. 141 and 198, n. 87; the manuscript reads *Linig*).
[28]   *DA*, ch. 40 (ed. Scott, p. 94 and note z). My thanks to Julia Crick for her comments on the manuscript.
[29]   Finberg, 'Sherborne', pp. 101–2; H. P. R. Finberg, *The Early Charters of Devon and Cornwall*, 2nd ed. (Leicester, 1963), p. 17 (no. 73).

tion, Finberg was following a comment made earlier by Doble, who had hoped that the dedication to St Indract might be explained by the existence of an outpost of Glastonbury Abbey in this part of Cornwall.[30]

Finberg's suggestion has received little attention in print, though some commentators have accepted it.[31] There are several reasons why it cannot stand, and it may be appropriate here to refute it outright. His argument was primarily a linguistic one. *Linig* is not a known place-name anywhere 'iuxta Tamer', but Finberg suggested that the name could be broken down as *Lin-ig*, where *Lin-* would supposedly be a reference to the River Lynher, bounding the western edge of Finberg's chosen area, and the ending *-ig* would be a form (found also in other early spellings of place-names) of Old English *eg*, 'island', which is indeed often found as a termination in English place-names. The whole name would then mean 'Lynher-island', that is, the 'island' of land between the rivers Lynher and Tamar.

There are at least two reasons why this suggestion is inappropriate. In the first place, the name of the river, throughout its early history, is *Linar* (a spelling of the late eleventh century) or *Liner*, not *Lin*;[32] so a name meaning 'Lynher-island' ought to be *Linar-eg* (or *Linar-ig*), not *Lin-eg*. There would be no reason for the English to have dropped a part of the Celtic river-name in forming their compound, when they did not do so in borrowing the river-name on its own. Secondly, the English word *eg* does not bear the meaning required by Finberg. It can have a variety of meanings in addition to that of 'island'; one such is 'low-lying land near a river', and another may be 'land almost surrounded by water'.[33] But such meanings are necessarily very localized; they can apply only when the nature of the land so described could be felt to have some affinity with that of a small island. This cannot apply in the case of the large and hilly tract of land lying between the rivers Lynher and Tamar, for it has no such affinity.

There is also a third reason why Finberg's identification must be wrong. The context of the grant, as listed twice by William of Malmesbury, shows that it is to be identified with a grant whereby King Ine gave land in several parts of Somerset to Glastonbury Abbey. That grant survives in a facsimile copy (of uncertain date) of what appears to be a genuine lost charter dated A.D. 705.[34] In the text of that charter, of which the various parcels of land correspond to those also mentioned in the context of the grant 'iuxta Tamer' in the *De antiquitate*, the latter phrase appears instead as 'iuxta flumen quod

---

[30] Doble, 'St Indract', p. 18.

[31] For example, W. G. Hoskins, *The Westward Expansion of Wessex* (Leicester, 1960), p. 19; Susan Pearce, *The Kingdom of Dumnonia* (Padstow, 1978), p. 113.

[32] Padel, *Popular Dictionary*, p. 112.

[33] A. H. Smith, *English Place-Name Elements*, 2 vols, English Place-Name Society 25–6 (Cambridge, 1956) I, 147; compare Gover *et al.*, *Place-Names of Devon*, II, 677: '*eg* is practically unknown in Devon and is not found in Cornwall.'

[34] S.248; W. de G. Birch, *Cartularium Saxonicum*, 3 vols and index (London, 1885–99) I, no. 113. See the discussion of this charter by Lesley Abrams elsewhere in this volume. My thanks to Lesley Abrams for kindly discussing this charter and other aspects of the Glastonbury properties.

appellatur *Tan'*. This refers to the River Tone, in Somerset, not the River Tamar, and that makes much better sense of the whole group of lands in the grant, placing them all within the single county of Somerset. It seems highly probable, then, that the river *Tamer* in the *De antiquitate* is simply an error for the river *Tan* in the charter itself. It is unclear how, or when, the error arose, but an error is anyway what it must be.[35]

This means that it is misguided to seek for *Linig* or *Linis* anywhere near the River Tamar, and it is near the Tone that it should be sought. One possible candidate is the unidentified territory called *Lini* in which Glastonbury had an interest in the Middle Ages: it was in the manor and parish of *Sowy* (Zoy), situated near where the River Tone joins the River Parrett (though not actually on the River Tone). *Lini* is mentioned in documents dated 1122 (for 1192?) and 1330.[36] This would not necessarily mean that *Lini* in Zoy was actually the territory granted by Ine in 705, but merely that the thirteenth-century glossator thought that it might be.

However, the question arises why such an error, *Tamer* for *Tan*, should have been made – whether by William, by some lost source which William was following, or, most likely, by the thirteenth-century copyist of William's text. It is not a natural mistake, in the context of the grant. Scribally it might be explicable, for a reader could have mistakenly supposed that a meaningless final flourish in the spelling of the river-name stood for an abbreviated -*er*; but geographically speaking the River Tone, being near Glastonbury, is far more natural in the context of the other lands, all in Somerset, mentioned in the same grant; so that *Tamer* is an improbable error for anyone working on Glastonbury materials to have made.

It is tempting to suggest that the error of writing *Tamer* for *Tan* in the account of the grant of King Ine might have been due to a knowledge, at Glastonbury, of the chapel situated on the banks of the River Tamar and dedicated to the Glastonbury saint. However, in the Glastonbury accounts of St Indract, including those of William, there is no hint that there was any knowledge there of the existence of the Cornish chapel, so that explanation too fails on present knowledge. As mentioned above, the form *Indrathi* in the Martyrology of Tallaght constitutes the only possible evidence that there may have been some knowledge at Glastonbury of the saint's Cornish dimension; and the reason for the dedication of the Cornish chapel remains a mystery. At the moment the most likely explanation seems to be an actual visit by the saint on his way to or from Rome, as indicated by John of Tynemouth in his account of the saint.

---

[35] Scott, *The Early History*, pp. 95 and 141, translated William's *Tamer* as the River Tone, though without entering into any detail; compare p. 198, n. 87.

[36] *The Great Chartulary of Glastonbury*, ed. A. Watkin, 3 vols, SRS 59 and 63–4 (1947–56): II, 375, 'totam terram de Lini in manerio de Sowy', and II, 517, '[in parochia de Sowy] in Lini et iuxta Lini'. Compare also Richard de *Lini*, having rights in the parish of *Sowy*, in 1302: *ibid.* II, 516. The place called Lyng, situated on the River Tone a few miles to the south, is not a suitable identification, since its other early spellings are *to Lengen* (ca 910), *Lenga* (ca 1180), and *Leng* (1225): E. Ekwall, *The Concise Oxford Dictionary of English Place-Names*, 4th ed. (Oxford, 1960), p. 310.

Glastonbury Abbey, then, had no territorial interest in the county of Cornwall before the Norman Conquest, as far as our information goes. In the twelfth century, however, it did acquire land there, in a different part of the county from that where the chapel of St Indract was situated. This was the property called Looe Island, together with a piece of land on the mainland facing the island in the parish of Talland, near Looe on the south coast of Cornwall. The name Lammana seems to have referred to both the mainland and the island properties. As mentioned above, this interest of the abbey has been recently discussed by Picken and Olson.[37] The property had already been given to the abbey by 1144, when it appeared in a list of the abbey's possessions, found in a confirmation of Pope Lucius II; it appears again in another papal confirmation of 1168.[38] In the late thirteenth century the abbey had a dispute with Launceston Priory over the ownership of the tithes. This dispute has been discussed by Picken.[39] It is unknown what the history of the property may have been before it was given to Glastonbury, but the most recent authority is of the opinion that there may well have been a small Celtic monastic community there in the Dark Ages.[40]

The papal confirmations are the sole items of evidence from the twelfth century concerning Lammana, and they survive only in later copies. So the earliest local charter dealing with the property, datable to 1199x1220, is of considerable interest. It constitutes a further confirmation to the abbey of the possession of the island. The grantor of the confirmation is Hasculf de Soligny, whose family held lands both in Somerset, at Kilmersdon, and in Cornwall. As the charter states, it was a predecessor of Hasculf's who had given the Cornish property to Glastonbury in the first place. No doubt it was the Somerset connection of this family that influenced their choice of recipient for the grant. Hasculf succeeded his father John de Soligny in about 1199, and he held the estates until 1220, when he resigned them in favour of his son and took the Cross.[41] The charter can thus be dated with some assurance to 1199x1220. Its text was previously known only from the copy printed by Hearne.[42] This was taken from the manuscript in Trinity College, Cambridge, which also contains the historical works of Adam of Damerham and William of Malmesbury concerning Glastonbury, and which is described by Julia

---

[37] Picken, 'Light on Lammana'; Olson, *Early Monasteries*, pp. 97–104.

[38] W. Dugdale, *Monasticon Anglicanum*, 6 vols in 8 (London, 1817–30) I, 37–8 (*Lamane* 1144); *ibid.* 36–7 (*Lamane* 1168).

[39] Picken, 'Light on Lammana'. Two documents relating to the dispute are now readily available in calendared form: *The Cartulary of Launceston Priory (Lambeth Palace MS. 719): A Calendar*, ed. P. L. Hull, Devon and Cornwall Record Society ns 30 (Exeter, 1987), pp. 167–9.

[40] Olson, *Early Monasteries*, p. 103.

[41] In the Pipe Rolls his first appearance is in 1199: *The Great Roll of the Pipe for the First Year of the Reign of King John, Michaelmas 1199*, ed. D. M. Stenton, Pipe Roll Society 48, ns 10 (London, 1933), p. 241. His taking of the Cross appears in *Rotuli Litterarum Clausarum*, ed. T. D. Hardy, 2 vols (London, 1833–44) I, 410b (A.D. 1220).

[42] *AD*, ed. Hearne, II, 599–600. From Hearne's text, the charter was also printed by George Oliver, *Monasticon Dioecesis Exoniensis* (Exeter, 1846), p. 70 (no. 1).

Crick elsewhere in these essays.[43] However, among the papers of the Somerset family of Trevelyan, recently deposited at the Somerset Record Office in Taunton, is the original of the deed.[44] Since the printed texts are both slightly inaccurate, as well as being taken from the thirteenth-century copy of the deed instead of the original, it is worth printing the text of the charter once more.

The text is printed as it appears in the document except that expanded abbreviations are shown with italics; some abbreviated names, where the expansion would be open to doubt, have been left as they are. Punctuation is modern, but is restricted to points indicated in the manuscript. Capital letters are used according to modern conventions.

HASCULF'S CHARTER

Vniuersis Christi fidelibus ad quos presens scriptum peruenerit, Hascutus filius Iohannis de Solenneio salutem in domino. Vniuersitati uestre notificetur quod ego Hascutus filius Iohannis de Solenn' concessi et presenti carta mea confirmaui deo et ecclesie beate uirginis Marie Glast'onie et eiusdem loci conuentui totam insulam Sancti Michaelis de Lammana cum omnibus pertinentiis suis, et terris et decimis, quam ab antiquo dono predecessorum meorum tenent, ut in omnibus tam libere et quiete et honorifice ab omni seruicio seculari et exactione seruili ipsam possideant, integre plenarie et pacifice in planis et pascuis et in omnibus consuetudinibus liberis, sicut ego melius et liberius terram meam in dominiis meis possideo, et ut omnia peccora sua cum meis ubique pascantur. Concedo etiam eis plenarie decimas dominii mei omnes de Porlo et ut iura libertates et consuetudines sicut ego in mea curia ita ipsi in sua curia habeant. Prohibeo siquidem ne aliquis ex balliuis uel seruientibus meis illis quacumque occasione aliquam molestiam inferant uel seculare seruicium ab eisdem exigere presumant, unde fratres mei monachi Glast' in prefato loco de Lammana deo seruientes ab eiusdem famulatu ullatenus prepediantur. Siquis autem huic concessioni mee fidem et effectum adhibuerit, a pio iudice mercedem condignam inueniat. Qui uero eam in irritum ducere presumpserit, deleat eum deus de libro uite et cum Iuda proditore sine fine penas exoluat. Ne igitur facti mei tenor uacillet in dubio, presentis scripti paginam sigilli mei appositione roboraui. His testibus, Helia tunc eiusdem loci priore et eius socio monacho Iohanne, Henrico filio Milonis, Willelmo milite, Grimbaldo, Roberto clerico, Iordano decano, Angero de Luitcote, Iocelino milite fratre eius, Geruasio capellano de Sancto Marco, Rogero rufo, Rogero de Cilimenaut, Willelmo filio Roberti, et multis aliis.

[43]   Cambridge, Trinity College R. 5. 33, 105v.
[44]   Somerset Record Office, DD/WO 23/1. I am grateful to Steven Hobbs, then of the Somerset Record Office, for drawing the charter to my attention and for assistance regarding its provenance; and to the Somerset Record Office for permission to print the text.

The text is very close to those printed by Hearne and Oliver. In those versions, which follow the manuscript in Trinity College, there are some insignificant variations of spelling, and the omission of a few short words. The sole textual point of note, apart from variations in the forms of the names, is that the original text, like the copy in the Trinity manuscript, has the verbs *inferant* and *presumant* incorrectly in the plural (their subject is *aliquis*, singular). Hearne realized the difficulty, and suggested the singular forms *inferat* and *presumat*. He was silently followed by Oliver, but the error is now seen to be original.

The variations in the forms of the names are of greater interest. Among these, the following points deserve comment. *Hascutus*: so, too, the Trinity manuscript, but Hearne, followed by Oliver, printed *Hastutus*. The normal form of his name was *Hasculfus*, and the replacement of *lf* with *t* is curious. *Glast'onie*: it is unclear how this ought to be expanded. *Porlo*: the Trinity manuscript, followed by Hearne and Oliver, reads *Portlo*. Curiously enough, *Portlo* is actually the more ancient form. The name refers to the manor of Portlooe, in the parish of Talland near to Looe Island.[45] The form *Porlo* can readily be explained, since there are other equally early instances of the loss of *th* in Cornish *porth*;[46] but it is strange to find the *t* inserted in the later, non-Cornish, copy. The scribe of the Trinity manuscript must have known the more ancient form from other documents concerning this property of the abbey, and he must have inserted it into this document.[47] Anger de *Luitcote*: the Trinity manuscript, followed by Hearne, has *Luit cote* as two words; Oliver has *Luitecote*. The form of the original deed is again preferable. The man is known from other records around the date 1200; he probably took his name from Lydcott, near to Lammana and in the parish of Morval.[48] Roger de *Cilimenaut*: the Trinity manuscript, followed by Hearne and Oliver, has the corrupt form *Cileintenat*; that of the original deed is a great improvement. It refers to the place now called Kilminorth, which lies in the same parish, Talland, as Lammana itself.[49] The presence of Anger and Roger as witnesses, taking their surnames from small places near to Lammana, suggests that the deed was a local Cornish one.

The deed has been preserved among the papers of the Trevelyan family, who have been established at Nettlecombe in Somerset since the fifteenth century. However, as their name implies, the Trevelyans have Cornish, as well as Somerset, interests, for they originated at Trevelyan in the parish of St Veep in Cornwall. St Veep is not far from Looe, where the Glastonbury

---

[45] Portlooe is at grid reference SX 2452.

[46] Padel, *Popular Dictionary*, p. 33.

[47] There is at least one other such form in the manuscript, Odo de *Portlo* occurring on 106r (*AD*, ed. Hearne, II, 602).

[48] The latest reference to Anger de Ludcuit known to me is in 1214: *The Great Roll of the Pipe for the Sixteenth Year of the Reign of King John, Michaelmas 1214*, ed. Patricia M. Barnes, Pipe Roll Society 73, ns 35 (London, 1959), p. 61. Lydcott (Morval) is at grid reference SX 293578. My thanks to Keith Hamylton Jones for some references to Anger de Ludcuit.

[49] Kilminorth is at grid reference SX 233539.

property lay; moreover, John Trevelyan in the fifteenth century held various administrative posts which might have brought documents his way. So the transmission of the deed could have taken place either through Cornish channels, or through the Somerset connections of the Soligny and the Trevelyan families.

To sum up, Glastonbury's two medieval connections with the county of Cornwall were as follows. A chapel on the banks of the River Tamar was dedicated to St Indract, whose only other known place of veneration in Britain was Glastonbury. The form of his name, as attested locally in the fourteenth century, suggests that the dedication had already existed when the Cornish language was still current in the area, that is, before about 1100. There is no satisfactory explanation for the existence of the dedication. Various attempts have been made to create a tenurial link between Glastonbury and the Cornish place in order to account for it, but none of them is persuasive; so at the moment, an actual visit by the saint, as recounted in the story of his martyrdom, seems to be the most likely explanation.

After the Norman Conquest, the abbey was given land in another part of the county, where there may possibly have been a small Celtic monastic settlement at an earlier date. *Lammana* was the Cornish name of Looe Island and of the mainland property adjacent to it. It contains the Cornish word **lann*, 'church-site', which may imply the former existence of a Dark-Age religious community there. If that is so, then its remains should be sought on the island, rather than on the mainland side of the property, for Picken has recently shown that the name belonged on the island originally.[50] It may be that the donation of the property to Glastonbury Abbey in the twelfth century, as confirmed by Hasculf de Soligny in *ca* 1210, perpetuated a memory of such an earlier community.

---

50   Picken, 'Light on Lammana', p. 284.

A Glastonbury Obit-List

MATTHEW BLOWS

A thirteenth-century custumary from Glastonbury Abbey, now London, British Library, Add. 17450, contains on 5v a unique list of twenty-seven obits.[1] Although the custumary was edited for the Somerset Record Society in 1891,[2] the primary interest of the editor was not the list but rather the customs of the abbey's knights and tenants. The list was printed with some errors and omissions. I propose, therefore, to provide a new edition of the list with a discussion of its contents. The list is particularly important since it contains several unusual obits and has hitherto not been noticed in discussions of the abbots or patrons of Glastonbury.

The obit-list has survived in the rent-book of Abbot Michael of Amesbury (1235–52).[3] The obits appear on 5v under the heading 'Notatio anniuersariorum in quibus requiritur mandatum' and follow lists of the abbey's knights, tenants, and allowances of wax and candles. The provisions to be supplied by the *medarius* (the officer in charge of the mead) to the refectorer for the use of the monastic community on each anniversary are noted after the list: 'five measures, two gallons and two parts of one gallon of good mead, neither more nor less'. The importance of these festivals is suggested by the fact that the provisions were made *pro magno mandato*.[4] In his *De antiquitate Glastonie ecclesie*, William of Malmesbury noted that 'on the anniversaries of kings, bishops, abbots and ealdormen who helped build the church, the brethren were obliged to celebrate mass for their souls at each altar, and, in particular, in the presence of the whole convent, to do so respectfully using the orna-

[1]   I would like to acknowledge the generous help of Janet Nelson in writing this article and also that of David Carpenter, David Crouch, Stephen Church, John Gillingham, Patrick McGurk, Ann Williams and the editors of this volume.
[2]   *Rentalia et Custumaria Michaelis de Ambresbury, 1235–1252, et Rogeri de Ford, 1252–1261, Abbatum Monasterii Beatae Mariae Glastoniae*, ed. C. J. Elton and E. Hobhouse, SRS 5 (1891); the list appears on p. 6.
[3]   The custumary of Abbot Michael records rents and services owed in the first, third and fourth years of his abbacy and hence the survey may have been completed by *ca* 1239. See *Rentalia*, ed. Elton and Hobhouse, pp. 12, 26, 72, 81 and 114. For Michael's abbacy see *Cronica*, chs 113–18 (ed. Carley, pp. 210–21).
[4]   *Mandatum* was a term which could be used in the general sense of 'requirement' or 'order' as well as in the specialized sense of 'maundy'. See *Custumaries of St Augustine's Canterbury and St Peter's Westminster*, ed. E. M. Thompson, 2 vols, Henry Bradshaw Society 23, 27 (London, 1902–4), index s.n. *mandatum*, p. 337.

ments that they had given the church'.[5] The list in Michael's rent-book would appear to include just such a group of benefactors, almost all of whom had made gifts to the abbey and may be said to have helped to build the church.

A thirteenth-century Glastonbury manuscript (Cambridge, Trinity College R. 5. 33 [724]) also records the abbey's customs concerning the lights on the anniversaries of the dead.[6] Eleven of the twenty names of those to be remembered are the same as those in the BL list, the most notable omissions being the names of the Anglo-Saxon abbots and the *benefactrices*.[7] The latest name to be preserved is that of Michael of Amesbury, in whose time the customs (like those of the BL manuscript) were probably copied.[8] It may be that both the BL and the Trinity manuscripts used a common source, perhaps a (lost) custumary of the abbey. Such a book must have provided William of Malmesbury with the details of the customs of the time of abbots Thurstan and Herluin.[9]

The BL list, however, differs from that of the Trinity manuscript in that it provides the dates of the individual anniversaries. Hence it is conceivable that the BL list itself may have been copied from a (lost) *liber uitae*. These 'books of life' preserved the names of lay benefactors and members of the community in order that the most important of their anniversaries could be observed.[10] The endowment of an anniversary rewarded the monks for their

---

5   *DA*, ch. 80 (ed. Scott, p. 162); William also described the custom at Glastonbury concerning dress on Maundy Thursday.

6   Cambridge, Trinity College R. 5. 33 (724), 19rv. For a full account of this manuscript, see the discussion by Julia Crick elsewhere in this volume.

7   The names are graded into major and minor feasts, those of King Edgar, King Henry II and Bishop Henry of Winchester being the most important. They are followed by King Ine, bishops Brihtwold and Brihtwig, and abbots Robert, William and Michael. The final group includes the names of Edmund *senior*, Edmund Ironside, priors Thomas and Eustachius, Bishop Lyfing, Ælfhere, Æthelwine, Eadwine, Ælfheah *dux*, Radulfus son of Stephen and Radulfus the priest.

8   The manuscript is written in a hand of the mid-thirteenth century. A catalogue of the contents of the library, in the same hand, is dated to 1247. This was revised by another hand to 1248, suggesting that the material was completed by that date. See *The Early History*, ed. Scott, p. 36, and M. R. James, *The Western Manuscripts in the Library of Trinity College, Cambridge*, 4 vols (Cambridge, 1900–4) II, 198–202.

9   *DA*, ch. 80 (ed. Scott, pp. 162–3).

10   The most famous surviving English examples of lists of those to be commemorated are those for Durham and Hyde abbeys, which record material from widely differing periods; see *Liber Vitae Ecclesiae Dunelmensis*, ed. A. H. Thompson, Surtees Society 136 (Durham, 1923), and *Liber Vitae: Register and Martyrology of New Minster and Hyde Abbey, Winchester*, ed. W. de G. Birch, Hampshire Record Society 5 (London, 1892). For early *libri uitae*, and for the possible commemoration of Glastonbury monks, see H. Hahn, 'Die Namen der Bonifazischen Briefe im *Liber Vitae Ecclesiae Dunelmensis*', *Neues Archiv für ältere Deutsche Geschichtskunde* 12 (1887, for 1886), 111–27. A wider study of Anglo-Saxon necrologies can be found in J. Gerchow, *Die Gedenküberlieferung der Angelsachsen mit einem Katalog der* libri uitae *und Necrologien* (Berlin, 1988), although there is no discussion of the evidence from Glastonbury. On later confraternities involving the Glastonbury community, see *Liber Vitae*, ed. Birch, pp. 47–50, and below, no. 26. Much has been written on continental *libri uitae*; good introductions to the earlier historiography can be found in K. Leyser, 'The German Aristocracy from the Ninth to the Early Twelfth Century, A Historical and Cultural

labour of annual and sometimes weekly commemoration of the dead, as well as providing alms for the poor. This was eventually to become an important source of revenue for monasteries.[11] It is likely that at Glastonbury the earliest anniversaries for the abbots Ælfweard, Brihtred, Brihtwig, Æthelweard and Æthelnoth would have been endowed by these men themselves, but only Brihtwig and Æthelnoth are recorded as having made gifts to the abbey. Possibly Thurstan and certainly Henry and Robert also endowed their own anniversaries.[12] Of those others in the list almost all made gifts to the abbey but it is not known upon what terms. One type of agreement was that of confraternity; in return for a gift the name of the *confrater* would be inscribed in a book and recited during the mass. Connected with confraternity was the custom of taking the monastic habit *ad succurendum*, usually shortly before death, which entitled the deceased to burial in the habit within the monastic enclosure.[13]

Whilst names may have been recorded in a *liber uitae*, the anniversaries might also have been noted in a calendar or martyrology. Again, such a source for the Glastonbury list must remain hypothetical, since no calendar of this type has survived for Glastonbury. The only calendar certainly from Glastonbury is the Up Holland calendar surviving in a fifteenth-century psalter (now London, British Library, Add. 64952).[14] Other calendars thought to have been based on a lost Glastonbury exemplar survive in the Leofric Missal and in the Bosworth Psalter, but neither calendar includes obits for Glastonbury.[15] A further calendar attributed to Glastonbury (Cambridge,

Sketch', *Past & Present* 41 (1968), 25–53, at 32–4, and G. Constable, 'The Liber Memorialis of Remiremont', *Speculum* 47 (1972), 261–77. For more recent literature, see *Memoria: der geschichtliche Zeugniswert des liturgischen Gedenkens im Mittelalter*, ed. K. Schmid and J. Wollasch (Munich, 1984).

[11] See B. Harvey, *Westminster Abbey and its Estates in the Middle Ages* (Oxford, 1977), pp. 29–36 and 365–401; D. Knowles, *The Monastic Order in England*, 2nd ed. (Cambridge, 1963), pp. 475–9; and D. Whitelock, *Anglo-Saxon Wills* (Cambridge, 1930), nos 1, 8, 23 and 33 (pp. 2–5, 20–3, 66–7, 86–9).

[12] See below, p. 260.

[13] On the phrase '*ad succurendum*' see C. Du Cange, *Glossarium Mediae et Infimae Latinitatis*, 6 vols (Paris, 1840–50) IV, 475–6, s.v. *monachi ad succurendum*. For an early example see the case of the seventh-century king, Sebbi, in *Venerabilis Baedae Opera Historica*, ed. C. Plummer, 2 vols (Oxford, 1896) I, 225–7. More generally the evidence is discussed by Knowles, *The Monastic Order*, pp. 475–9. See also the infamous case of Walter and Glastonbury in H. P. R. Finberg, *Lucerna. Studies of Some Problems in the Early History of England* (London, 1964), pp. 204–21.

[14] F. Wormald, 'The Liturgical Calendar of Glastonbury Abbey', in *Festschrift Bernard Bischoff*, ed. J. Autenrieth and F. Brunhölzl (Stuttgart, 1971), pp. 325–45. Wormald suggested that the calendar might date from the twelfth century.

[15] The calendar in the Leofric Missal is said to have been based upon a Glastonbury exemplar primarily because the relics of a number of 'Celtic' and northern saints whose names are preserved in the calendar were claimed by Glastonbury. Two of these saints, Ceolfrith and Aidan, are noted as resting *in glaston*. The calendar in the Bosworth Psalter, whilst adapted for use at Christ Church, Canterbury, records that Ceolfrith and Patrick *senior* were *in glaston*. See *The Leofric Missal*, ed. F. E. Warren (Oxford, 1883), pp. liii and 30–1, and *The Bosworth Psalter*, ed. F. Gasquet and E. Bishop (London, 1908), pp. 18 and 21. See also C. Hohler, 'Some Service Books of the

University Library, Kk. 5. 32, 50–5v; hereafter cited as G) does contain several obits, but they differ from those in the BL list.[16] G, however, shares the rare obit of Ine, 22 July, with our list and with a Muchelney calendar, as well as the obit of Edmund I, on 26 May.[17]

The list must have been compiled from earlier records in several stages.[18] The first eighteen names are in monthly order from January to December but thereafter the entries show no such ordering. It is possible that the first series might represent all or part of a lost obit-list, which – since Thurstan is the last mentioned of the abbots – could date from his death in 1096. But after Æthelwine (no. 18) three tenth-century obits are given, which might suggest that some names were overlooked when the first series was written or possibly that another source was used. No attempt was made to correct the sequence of obits when the list was copied in the thirteenth century.

The list of obits seems to have reached its present form well before the date of the manuscript itself, for the last two entries in the list, and the most recent of the obits, are those for Abbot Robert of Winchester (1173–80), whose obit is given as 28 April, and King Henry II (1154–89).[19] Entry no. 25, for Robert's parents, gives the date 29 April. It is not clear whether this refers to a separate date for the parents' anniversary, or whether it refers to 28 April as a joint anniversary for Robert and his parents; the discrepancy could be explained as the result either of a scribal error or of the custom of starting the liturgical day on the previous evening.[20]

Since no obit of an abbot later than Robert of Winchester is recorded, the list was presumably compiled after the death of Henry II and before the death of Robert's successor as abbot, Henry of Sully (1189–93).[21] Adam of

---

Later Saxon Church', in *Tenth-Century Studies*, ed. D. Parsons (Chichester, 1975), pp. 68–83, at 69; P. Korhammer, 'The Origin of the Bosworth Psalter', *Anglo-Saxon England* 2 (1973), 173–87; and N. Brooks, *The Early History of the Church of Canterbury. Christ Church from 597 to 1066* (Leicester, 1984), pp. 252–3.

[16]   The manuscript as a whole was attributed to Glastonbury by N. Ker, *Medieval Libraries of Great Britain*, 2nd ed. (London, 1964), p. 90. H. Gneuss, 'A Preliminary List of Manuscripts Written or Owned in England up to 1100', *Anglo-Saxon England* 9 (1981), 1–60, at 7, suggested a Glastonbury provenance for fols 49–73. J. Armitage Robinson suggested, however, that the calendar itself was probably not written at Glastonbury; see 'The Mediaeval Calendars of Somerset', in *Muchelney Memoranda*, ed. B. Schofield, SRS 42 (1927), pp. 143–83, at 144, 174 and 178. G was printed by F. Wormald in *English Kalendars Before 1100*, Henry Bradshaw Society 72 (London, 1934), 71–83. The obits are printed by Gerchow, *Die Gedenküberlieferung*, pp. 330–1.

[17]   Robinson, 'The Mediaeval Calendars', pp. 172–8.

[18]   The maximum number of stages is as follows: [1]–[18]; [19]–[20]; [21]; [22], [23]–[24] or [22]–[24]; [25]–[27]. These divisions are based upon the sequence of months in the list. Where an entry records a date earlier in the year than the preceding one, it has been taken to represent an addition to the original sequence.

[19]   On Robert, see *Cronica*, ch. 93 (ed. Carley, pp. 170–3).

[20]   Such is the explanation suggested by Marjorie Chibnall for the discrepant dates given for Henry I's death. See *The Ecclesiastical History of Orderic Vitalis*, ed. and trans. M. Chibnall, 6 vols (Oxford, 1969) VI, 43, n. 6. For a comparable record of a family being commemorated on the same day see Knowles, *The Monastic Order*, p. 476.

[21]   Henry of Sully was clearly interested in the abbacy of his predecessor, since the survey of abbey lands he compiled makes frequent mention of the customs of

Damerham described Robert as endowing his own anniversary with the tithes (*decimas*) of *Newitone* (Sturminster Newton) and *Kenteleswrthe* (Marnhull), part of which was to go to the poor and part to the community, that they might revere his memory with more devotion (*quo eius memoriam deuocius recolerent*). Robert also gave the monks the same wax and honey from the *medarius* that they were accustomed to receive in the time of his predecessors, and he further established that the community might have wine on the festivals of the apostles Peter and Paul, the conception of the Virgin Mary, St John the Apostle, St John the Evangelist, St Thomas the Martyr and on the anniversary of Bishop Henry, his predecessor.[22] The last two feasts were instituted at Glastonbury by Robert; Henry died in 1171 and Thomas was canonized on 21 February 1173.[23]

Although no necrology or *liber uitae* has survived from Glastonbury, William of Malmesbury in the *De antiquitate* did give some obits of ecclesiastics from what appear to be two separate lists. One includes a series of obits of the eighth and ninth centuries and might conceivably have been copied in that period. The second list preserves obits from the mid-tenth century: these were all (or all thought to have been) members of the community who went on to become bishops elsewhere.[24] It is possible that the obits in the *De antiquitate* and those in BL Add. 17450 are derived from the same, now lost, source. But this does not seem likely since the lists in the *De antiquitate* have only two names in common with those of the BL manuscript: Sigefrith and Brihtwig.[25]

A thirteenth-century marginal addition to the Trinity College text of the *De antiquitate* has noted the obit for Bishop Lyfing, monk of Glastonbury,

---

Robert's time: *Liber Henrici de Soliaco, Abbatis Glaston. An Inquisition of the Manors of Glastonbury Abbey*, ed. J. E. Jackson (London, 1882).

[22] *AD*, ed. Hearne, II, 331–2.

[23] For the date of Bishop Henry's death see *The Early History*, ed. Scott, p. 185. On the date of Thomas Becket's canonization see *English Historical Documents 1042–1189*, ed. D. C. Douglas *et al.*, English Historical Documents II, 2nd ed. (London, 1981), no. 157 (p. 827).

[24] *DA*, ch. 67 (ed. Scott, pp. 136–9 and 206–7). The two lists are distinct in their content and format: the first records the year of death of two bishops in the eighth century, four in the ninth century and two in the tenth century; the second list records the day, but not the year, of the deaths of ten bishops *tempore Edgari regis*. For a discussion of the lists see F. Birkeli, 'The Earliest Missionary Activities from England to Norway', *Nottingham Mediaeval Studies* 15 (1971), 27–37, at 28–9, and S. Keynes, *The Diplomas of King Æthelred 'the Unready' 978–1016. A Study in their Use as Historical Evidence* (Cambridge, 1980), p. 239, n. 23. William also knew of two laymen buried at Glastonbury: he noted that Æthelstan *comes* and one Brihtric commended their bodies to Glastonbury, although he gave no dates for their deaths; see *DA*, chs 53 and 58 (ed. Scott, pp. 113 and 121). It is worth observing the similarity of the wording with which William recorded these entries; this could suggest a common source. If William's source was a written one, it may have supplied the chronicler Æthelweard with the obit of another layman, Eanwulf (d. 867); see *The Chronicle of Æthelweard*, ed. A. Campbell (London, 1962), p. 36.

[25] Although the Æthelstan *comes* recorded in the *De antiquitate* could be the same as Æthelstan *dux* in our list.

which is similarly preserved in the BL list.[26] The information supplied by the marginal note may have come either from the BL manuscript itself or from the hypothetical lost exemplar.[27]

The list in BL Add. 17450 does show some resemblance to an early chapter (chapter 31) interpolated into the *De antiquitate*. The chapter recalls those kings and nobles who were buried at Glastonbury: Arthur, his wife, Centwine, Edmund *senior*, Edmund *minor*,[28] Edgar, bishops Brihtwig, Brihtwold, Lyfing and *Seifrid*[29] and the ealdormen Ælfhere,[30] Æthelstan, Æthelwine and Æthelnoth. All but Centwine, Arthur, his wife and Æthelnoth have obits recorded in the BL list. It is possible that the author of this passage used the list in BL Add. 17450 or its exemplar, among other sources, whilst adding the illustrious names of Arthur and Centwine.[31]

The BL list as a whole records the otherwise unknown obits of lay benefactors as well as those of several abbots of Glastonbury. If the *Cilnothus abbas* (no. 7) is an error for Æthelnoth, then the ten abbots named might represent a complete abbatial list from Ælfweard (d. *ca* 975)[32] to Robert (d. 1180) though, of course, not in chronological order. The list would, therefore, provide independent support for the abbatial sequence reconstructed by Knowles as opposed to that preserved in the surviving text of the *De anti-*

---

26   Cambridge, Trinity College R. 5. 33, 15r; *DA*, ch. 67 (ed. Scott, p. 138).

27   Lyfing's obit is recorded in ASC 1046 CD under 20 and 23 March, respectively. See S. Keynes, 'Episcopal Succession in Anglo-Saxon England', *Handbook of British Chronology*, ed. E. Fryde *et al.*, 3rd ed. (London, 1986), pp. 209–24, at 215; and see below, no. 4.

28   The use of *senior* and *minor* to distinguish the two Edmunds is like the *senior* and *iunior* of our list.

29   *Seifrid* could be either Sigefrith, bishop of Norway, or Seffrid, bishop of Chichester. But since Sigefrith went to Norway and Seffrid may have retired to Glastonbury (see below, no. 24), it is perhaps more likely that the bishop of Chichester was intended.

30   See *DA*, ch. 31 (ed. Scott, pp. 82–5). 'Alfari' should be Ælfhere not Ælfheah, as Scott translated.

31   Since William of Malmesbury probably did not connect Arthur with Glastonbury and since he believed Lyfing to have been buried at Tavistock (*Willelmi Malmesbiriensis Monachi de Gestis Pontificum Anglorum*, ch. 94; ed. N. E. S. A. Hamilton, RS 52 [London, 1870], p. 201), the chapter is unlikely to have been his work as it stands. Also, since Seffrid did not die until 1150 this chapter cannot have been interpolated until after that date; see *The Early History*, ed. Scott, pp. 195–6.

32   Compare the tenth-century list which ends with Ælfweard, discussed elsewhere in this volume by Sarah Foot. The list is preserved in London, British Library, Cotton Tiberius B. v, pt i, 23v. A facsimile was published in *An Eleventh-Century Anglo-Saxon Illustrated Miscellany: British Library Cotton Tiberius B v Part 1, Together With Leaves from British Library Cotton Nero D. II*, ed. P. McGurk *et al.*, Early English Manuscripts in Facsimile 21 (Copenhagen, 1983), p. 74. On the manuscript see D. Dumville, 'The Anglian Collection of Royal Genealogies and Regnal Lists', *Anglo-Saxon England* 5 (1976), 23–50. The abbatial list was discussed by J. Armitage Robinson in his *Somerset Historical Essays* (London, 1921), pp. 26–53; see also D. Knowles *et al.*, *The Heads of Religious Houses in England and Wales 940–1216* (Cambridge, 1972), pp. 50–2. The list was transcribed by H. Edwards, *The Charters of the Early West Saxon Kingdom*, BAR Brit. ser. 198 (Oxford, 1988), pp. 7–9; Edwards suggested (p. 9) that the source for the list was either a *liber uitae* or a necrology.

quitate.[33] This would further suggest that the list in BL Add. 17450 was not constructed simply from the obits and information given in the *De antiquitate.*

The commemoration of three members of the same family, that of Ealdorman Ælfhere of Mercia, one of the most powerful families of the tenth century, is especially important. If the identifications suggested are correct, then lay people – and this family in particular – played an exceptional role in the life of Glastonbury.

In the edition which follows I have numbered each entry for reference and standardized punctuation and capitalization. I have expanded only those unambiguous abbreviations.

For the dates of the abbots I have followed Knowles.

LONDON, BRITISH LIBRARY, ADD. 17450, 5v

Notatio anniuersariorum in quibus requiritur mandatum

[1] Alwardus abbas .xiiii. kl. Ianuarii.

Abbot Ælfweard (*ca* 975–?1009), obit 19 December. He was not omitted by William, as Knowles suggested (*The Heads of Religious Houses*, p. 51), but rather misplaced in the *De antiquitate* before Sigegar, where he appeared receiving the privilege of Pope John. See *DA*, ch. 61 (ed. Scott, pp. 128–9).

[2] Beorthedus abbas .vi. idus Februarii.

Abbot Brihtred (1009?–1016x1019), obit 8 February. He was Ælfweard's successor and according to an interpolation in *DA*, ch. 23 (ed. Scott, pp. 72–4), he was involved in an attempt to translate the bones of Dunstan to Glastonbury. On this subject see R. Sharpe, 'Eadmer's Letter to the Monks of Glastonbury Concerning St Dunstan's Disputed Remains', in this volume.

[3] Turstinus abbas .v. idus Martii.

Abbot Thurstan (*ca* 1077x1078–1096), obit 11 March. This date is also given in London, British Library, Cotton Vitellius C. xii (a martyrology from St Augustine's, s. xi/xii), at fol. 122. On Thurstan see further *DA*, ch. 78 (ed. Scott, pp. 156–9).

[4] Liuerigus episcopus .xiiii. kl. Aprilis.

Bishop Lyfing (1027–46), obit 19 March. This same obit appears in a marginal note to the Trinity text of ch. 67 of the *De antiquitate* (ed. Scott, p. 138), for Bishop *Liuingus*, stating also that he was a monk of Glastonbury. He is likely to have been the bishop of Crediton, Cornwall and Worcester who died 20 or 23 March 1046 (ASC CD) rather than the bishop of Wells and archbishop of

---

[33] For the abbatial list in the *De antiquitate*, see ch. 71 (ed. Scott, pp. 146–9), and for that reconstructed by Knowles *et al.*, see *The Heads of Religious Houses*, pp. 50–2.

Canterbury (998x999–1013 and 1013–20), who died 12 June. See Keynes, 'Episcopal Succession', p. 215. The Leofric Missal records the death of Lyfing on 19 February (ed. Warren, p. l).

[5] Sigefridus episcopus non. Aprilis.

Sigefrith, bishop of Norway (*ca* 960), obit 5 April. The date of his death agrees with that in the *DA*, ch. 67 (ed. Scott, pp. 139 and 206), where he is also said to have given four copes to the abbey; see Birkeli, 'The Earliest Missionary Activities', pp. 28–9. This obit confirms the distinction between the two tenth-century bishops called Sigefrith. The other, bishop of Sweden, was commemorated on 15 February. See *Acta Sanctorum Bollandi, Februarii* II (Antwerp, 1658), pp. 847–51.

[6] Brithwius episcopus et abbas Glaston. .iii. idus Aprilis.

Brihtwig, abbot of Glastonbury (*ca* 1019–24) and bishop of Wells (1024?x1033), obit 11 April. The same obit also appears as a mid-eleventh-century Abingdon addition in Cambridge, Corpus Christi College 57, fols 41–94, printed by M. R. James, *A Descriptive Catalogue of the Manuscripts in the Library of Corpus Christi College, Cambridge*, 2 vols (Cambridge, 1909–12) I, 115–18. See also Keynes, *The Diplomas of King Æthelred 'the Unready'*, p. 239, n. 22. The 'autobiography' of Giso, bishop of Wells (1061–88), however, records Brihtwig's death on 12 April; see *Historiola Primordiis Episcopatus Somersetensis*, in *Ecclesiastical Documents*, ed. J. Hunter, Camden Society 8 (London, 1840), pp. 15–20, at 15. The year of his death is recorded in ASC 1033 E under the name Merehwit, where it is stated that he was bishop of Somerset (Wells) and was buried at Glastonbury. It was noted in the *De antiquitate* that he was buried in the northern portico of the chapel of St John the Baptist (chs 31 and 67; ed. Scott, pp. 84–5 and 138–9). His gifts to the abbey included an altarfrontal and a cross, on which see *DA*, ch. 63 (ed. Scott, pp. 130–1).

[7] Cilnothus abbas Glaston. idus Aprilis.

Cilnoth, abbot of Glastonbury, obit 13 April. This is probably Abbot Æthelnoth (1053–1077x1078), whose charter setting aside land for the support of the poor is preserved in the Great Cartulary. Was this part of an arrangement for Æthelnoth's anniversary? See *The Great Chartulary of Glastonbury*, ed. A. Watkin, 3 vols, SRS 59, 63–4 (1947–56) III, 701–2. D. Whitelock suggested that he was deposed on Whitsun (28 May) 1078; *Councils and Synods with other Documents relating to the English Church I. A.D. 871–1204*, ed. D. Whitelock *et al.*, 2 vols (Oxford, 1981) II, 624–5. The problem was discussed further by F. Harmer, *Anglo-Saxon Writs* (Manchester, 1952), pp. 553–4, but neither Harmer nor Whitelock took account of the Glastonbury charter, which is dated to Easter Day 1079.

[8] Brithgyua benefactrix Glaston. .iiii. non. Aprilis.

Brihtgifu, *benefactrix* of Glastonbury, obit 2 April. No such woman appears in the *De antiquitate*, in the contents-list of the lost Glastonbury cartulary (the *Liber terrarum*), or in the Great Cartulary. A *Bricteva* is named in DB, I, 97rb (*Somerset*, 35.4) as holding land in Somerset, but with no obvious relationship to Glastonbury.

[9]   Brithwoldus episcopus et monachus Glast. .x. kl. Maii.

Brihtwold, bishop of Ramsbury (1005–45) and monk of Glastonbury, obit 22 April. His death, but not the day, and his benefactions to Glastonbury were recorded in *DA*, ch. 68 (ed. Scott, pp. 138–41), where he was also described as a monk of Glastonbury. His obit is recorded in ASC 1045 C and possibly in CCCC 57 where part of the name is given.

[10]   Ealpheagus dux .xiiii. kl. Maii.

Ælfheah, ealdorman of Central Wessex (959–970x971), obit 18 April. His death was recorded by John of Worcester, who stated that he was buried at Glastonbury in 971; see *Florentii Wigorniensis Monachi Chronicon ex Chronicis*, ed. B. Thorpe (London, 1848), p. 142, s.a. 971. See also the new edition of the *Chronicon* by P. McGurk, forthcoming. It would be interesting to know where John found his information: his record of this obit is unique in that it gives the year of Ælfheah's death, where our list does not. John also preserves the unique obit of Wulfstan, deacon of Glastonbury, in 981; see the *Chronicon*, ed. Thorpe, pp. 146–7. Could he have had access to a now lost *liber uitae* of Glastonbury? He was certainly interested in collecting such information and knew William of Malmesbury's *Gesta pontificum* at least. See R. Darlington and P. McGurk 'The *Chronicon ex Chronicis* of "Florence" of Worcester and its Use of Sources for English History before 1066', *Anglo-Norman Studies* 5 (1982), 185–96. Ælfheah signed one charter of 972 (S.784). However, Whitelock noted (*Wills*, p. 121) the text of this was from a thirteenth-century cartulary and could be corrupt. Apart from S.784, the last charter that Ælfheah witnessed is dated 970 (S.779). If the widow who received a charter (S.775) in that year was his wife then this would confirm 970 and not 971 as the date of his death (see Ælfswith below, no. 15). Ælfheah was the elder brother of ealdormen Ælfhere and Ælfwine; see A. Williams, '*Princeps Merciorum gentis*: The Family, Career and Connections of Ælfhere, Ealdorman of Mercia, 956–83', *Anglo-Saxon England* 10 (1982), 143–72. A number of his charters are recorded as having been at Glastonbury: they appear in the *Liber terrarum* contents-list as nos. 69, 96, 109 and 113 (S.747). In his will, S.1485, he left Batcombe to his wife and after her death to his son or brother, with reversion to Glastonbury 'for the sake of our father and our mother and all of us'. This suggests a strong connection between his family and Glastonbury.

[11]   Edelfleda benefactris Glast. .xiiii. kl. Iunii.

Æthelflæd, *benefactrix* of Glastonbury, obit 19 May. This name is a common one and hence identification is uncertain. She is unlikely to be the Æthelflæd *matrona* who lived at Glastonbury – on whom see B., *Vita S. Dunstani*, chs 9–11, in *Memorials of St Dunstan*, ed. W. Stubbs, RS 63 (London, 1874), pp. 3–52, at 16–20, and whose obit is given as 13 April by M. Alfordus (otherwise known as M. Griffith), in *Fides Regia Anglicana*, in *Annales Ecclesiastici et Civiles Britannorum, Saxonum, Anglorum*, ed. M. Alford, 4 vols (Liège, 1663) III, 262; and see *Acta Sanctorum Bollandi, Maii* IV (Antwerp, 1685), pp. 349–50. She could be Æthelflæd of Damerham, the second wife of Edmund I and daughter of Ealdorman Ælfgar (ASC 946 D). The latter left Damerham to Glastonbury in her will, datable to 962x991 (S.1494), for the souls of herself, Edgar and Edmund. An Ely calendar commemorates on 20 May Ealdorman Byrhtnoth's wife, Ælfflæd, and his wife's sister, Æthelflæd of Damerham; it is printed in B. Dickins, 'The Day of Byrhtnoth's Death and Other Obits from a Twelfth-Century Ely Kalendar', *Leeds Studies in English* 6 (1935), 14–24, at 17–23. The calendar in G preserves the obit of one Ælfflæd *mulier Ælfgari* on 26 May. Robinson suggested that this Ælfgar might have been the ealdorman so named and that Ælfflæd *mulier* could be the mother of Æthelflæd of Damerham and her sister Ælfflæd; see his 'The Mediaeval Calendars', p. 177.

[12] Eadmundus senior rex Anglie .vii. kl. Iunii.

King Edmund I (939–46), obit 26 May. ASC 946 gives St Augustine's Day, 26 May. According to the *DA*, ch. 31 (ed. Scott, pp. 84–5), and John of Worcester's *Chronicon*, s.a. 946 (ed. Thorpe, p. 134), he was buried at Glastonbury. See further *DA*, chs 55–6 (ed. Scott, pp. 114–19), and Æthelflæd's will, as above (no. 11). He was said to lie in the tower of the larger church. The calendar G also preserves this obit.

[13] Eadgarus rex .viii. idus Iulii.

King Edgar (957x959–975), obit 8 July. The same date is in ASC 975 CAB. His burial and what may have been a later attempt to create a royal cult at Glastonbury are recorded in the *DA*, chs 62, 66 (ed. Scott, pp. 128–31, 134–5); for his numerous gifts see chs 60–2 (ed. Scott, pp. 122–31). Note that John of Worcester also recorded that Edgar was buried at Glastonbury 'according to kingly custom' (*Chronicon*, s.a. 975; ed. Thorpe, p. 143).

[14] Ini rex .xi. kl. Augusti.

King Ine of Wessex (688–726), obit 22 July. He abdicated, leaving for Rome in 726; see D. Dumville, 'The West Saxon Genealogical Regnal List and the Chronology of Early Wessex', *Peritia* 4 (1985), 21–66, at 41. His obit was recorded in the calendar G for the same day (*[D]epositio Ine regis Occidentalium [Saxonum]*) and again in the Muchelney calendar, but for 20 July (*Ine rex qui dedit Ilymynster*); see Robinson, 'The Mediaeval Calendars', pp. 134 and 174, and Gerchow, *Die Gedenküberlieferung*, pp. 330–1. See also *Acta Sanctorum Bollandi, Februarii* I (Antwerp, 1658), pp. 905–14, where Ine's obit is recorded for 7 February. His benefactions to Glastonbury were recorded in *DA*, chs 39–43 (ed. Scott, pp. 92–102).

[15] Elsuyy benefactrix Glast. .ii. idus Augusti.

Ælfswith, *benefactrix* of Glastonbury, obit 12 August. One Ælfswith is recorded in a number of charters in the Glastonbury archives: nos. 103, 110, 111, 114 and 127 in the *Liber terrarum*, and S.462, 747, 775. The *De antiquitate* adds that she gave a stole with maniple and a chasuble (ch. 62; ed. Scott, pp. 128–31). In the latter she is called *regina*, which may be an error since no such queen is elsewhere recorded for the tenth century. Moreover, in the list in the *De antiquitate* of estates given by this 'queen' is a grant for which the text has survived, S.775. In this Ælfswith is called nun and widow. The estate granted was at Idmiston, which was one of a number of estates previously given to one Wulfric, others of which were acquired by Ealdorman Ælfheah and possibly his brother Æthelwine. This might reinforce the impression that Ælfswith, nun and widow, was the wife of Ælfheah and that this entry is her obit. S.747 and S.462 both refer to Ælfswith, wife of Ælfheah (see above, no. 10). Of the estates she received, five were owned by the abbey in 1066.

[16] Eilwardus abbas Glast. .v. idus Nouembris.

Æthelweard, abbot of Glastonbury (*ca* 1024–53), obit 9 November. His obit agrees with that in Vitellius C. xii, 148v. ASC D records his death before All Saints' Day, 1053. He was noted for his translation of Edgar; see *DA*, ch. 66 (ed. Scott, pp. 134–5), and also *The Register of Malmesbury Abbey*, ed. J. Brewer, 2 vols, RS 72 (London, 1879–80) I, 57.

[17] Elfere dux .xi. kl. Nouembris.

Ealdorman Ælfhere, obit 22 October. He was the brother of Ælfheah, and is mentioned together with Ælfswith in Ælfheah's will, S.1485. See Williams, '*Princeps Merciorum*', pp. 166–7. John of Worcester recorded his death s.a. 983 (ed. Thorpe, p. 147), but his burial at Glastonbury is only noted in the interpolated ch. 31 of the *De antiquitate* (ed. Scott, pp. 84–5). He received a number of estates recorded in the Glastonbury archive: nos. 89/90, 116, 117 in the *Liber terrarum*, and S.555. According to the *DA*, ch. 62 (ed. Scott, pp. 128–31), Ælfhere gave all these to Glastonbury, together with Batcombe, mentioned in his brother's will. Only Batcombe was held by the abbey in 1066. Thus either the lands were lost before that date or they were never given. In the latter case it is interesting that these charters should survive in the Glastonbury archive: possibly some, at least, of the charters of Ælfhere and his family were deposited at the abbey for safe-keeping. Mention of one further charter, which might have belonged to this Ælfhere, is preserved in a list of charters under the heading *Cartae de diuersis reddituous uel rebus datis ecclesiae Glaston*, separate from that of the *Liber terrarum* contents-list, in Cambridge, Trinity College R. 5. 33, 81r: *Carta Elfere de quadam domo in Bristolt*. The list is printed in *JG*, ed. Hearne, II, 389–92, at 392.

[18] Eilwinus dux et monachus Glast. .vi. kl. Decembris.

Æthelwine, ealdorman and monk of Glastonbury, obit 26 November. *DA*, ch. 31 (ed. Scott, pp. 83–5), recorded that Ealdorman Æthelwine was buried at Glastonbury. The only Æthelwine who witnessed as ealdorman was the son of Æthelstan 'Half King' and Ealdorman of East Anglia (962–92), on whom see C. Hart, 'Æthelstan "Half King" and his Family', *Anglo-Saxon England* 2 (1973), 115–44, at 133. His obit, however, was recorded for 24 April at his foundation of Ramsey; see the Ramsey obit-list recorded by J. Leland, *De Rebus Britannicis Collectanea*, ed. T. Hearne, 2nd ed., 6 vols (London, 1774) II, 587–8. Since no other Æthelwine witnessed as ealdorman it is likely that an error has been made in this entry, or its exemplar, either in describing Æthelwine as an ealdorman or in the form of his name.

[19] Herlewinus abbas Glast. .x. kl. Nouembris.

Herluin, abbot of Glastonbury (1100–18), obit 23 October. Vitellius C. xii, fol. 147, has 24 October. For his deeds see *DA*, ch. 79 (ed. Scott, pp. 158–61). He was buried next to Thurstan *ad sanctum Andream*.

[20] Eadmundus rex iunior .iii. kl. Decembris.

King Edmund Ironside (April – November 1016), obit 29 November. According to the Anglo-Saxon Chronicle he died in 1016 on St Andrew's Day, 30 November, and was buried at Glastonbury. A gift of land made by Edmund to the abbey is recorded in the *DA*, chs 64, 69 (ed. Scott, pp. 132–3, 144–5). However, the account given in ch. 64 may not be William's work (see *The Early History*, ed. Scott, p. 205); it described Cnut's visit to Glastonbury on St Andrew's feast to honour Edmund, and provided a convenient explanation for the charter of privileges made by Cnut to Glastonbury (recorded in *DA*, ch. 65; ed. Scott, pp. 132–3).

[21] Sigericus archiepiscopus et monachus Glast. .iii. kl. Nouembris.

Sigeric, archbishop of Canterbury (990–4) and monk of Glastonbury, obit 30 October. He was translated from Ramsbury to Canterbury in 990 and died in 994. *English Historical Documents c. 500–1042*, ed. D. Whitelock, English Historical Documents I, 2nd ed. (London, 1979), no. 1 (p. 236, n. 3), gives 28 October; see further N. Brooks, *The Early History*, pp. 278–87. Sigeric gave seven altar-cloths to Glastonbury, with which the church was decorated on his anniversary; see *DA*, ch. 67 (ed. Scott, pp. 136–9). The *De antiquitate* provides the only evidence other than this list that Sigeric was a monk of Glastonbury.

[22] Aelstanus dux .vi. kl. Iunii.

Ealdorman Æthelstan, obit 27 May. His burial is noted in *DA*, ch. 31 (ed. Scott, pp. 82–5). The obvious candidate is Æthelstan 'Half King' who retired to become a monk at Glastonbury in or after 956. Hart, 'Æthelstan "Half King"', pp. 125–6, suggested on the basis of charter witness-lists that he retired in mid-summer, 956. Although, for the possibility that he witnessed charters in the autumn of 956, see the discussion of Eadwig's charters by Keynes, *The Diplomas of King Æthelred 'the Unready'*, pp. 48–68, at 59–61. For evidence of grants that he received, see nos. 40, 41, 42, 55, 101 in the *Liber terrarum* contents-list and S.371, 442, 498. It is not, however, clear that all these estates were made over to Glastonbury or that they formed part of Glastonbury's early endowment (*contra* Hart, 'Æthelstan "Half King"', p. 126). Dunstan's biographer, B., noted Æthelstan's association with Dunstan before the death of Edmund; see *Vita S. Dunstani*, ch. 31, in *Memorials*, ed. Stubbs, pp. 44–5.

[23] Henricus Winton. episcopus et abbas Glaston. .vi. idus Augusti.

Henry, bishop of Winchester (1129–71) and abbot of Glastonbury (1126–71), obit 8 August. The year of his death was discussed in *Registrum Johannis de Pontissara*, ed. C. Deedes, Canterbury and York Society 30 (Oxford, 1924), p. 628. His 'autobiography' is recorded in *AD*, ed. Hearne, II, 304 ff. His anniversary was observed by Abbot Robert (*AD*, ed. Hearne, II, 331–2).

[24] Sefridus Cicestrensis episcopus et abbas Glaston. .iii. idus Augusti.

Seffrid, abbot of Glastonbury (1120x1121–1125) and bishop of Chichester (1125–45), obit 11 August 1150. His obit is similarly recorded in Paris, Bibliothèque Nationale, fr. 18953 (a seventeenth-century history of the abbey of Séez), and quoted in *Chronicles of the Reigns of Stephen, Henry II and Richard I*, ed. R. Howlett, 4 vols, RS 82 (London, 1885–9) IV, 110, n. 6. He was bishop of Chichester until his deposition in 1145. H. Mayr-Harting in *The Bishops of Chichester 1075–1207*, Chichester Papers 40 (Chichester, 1963), 4–7, suggested that after this he retired to Glastonbury; see also J. Carley, *Glastonbury Abbey* (Woodbridge, 1988), p. 18, n. 4, where C. A. R. Radford's opinion to the same effect was noted. An excavated twelfth-century burial might have been that of Seffrid; C. A. R. Radford, 'The Excavations at Glastonbury Abbey 1956–7', *SDNQ* 27 (1955–60), 165–9, at 169. Seffrid gave a pall, chasuble and alb to the monastery and received a privilege from Pope Calixtus; see *DA*, chs 81–2 (ed. Scott, pp. 162–5).

[25] Hugo laicus et soror Mabilia pater et mater Roberti abbati .iii. kl. Maii.

Hugo, layman, and Mabel, sister, the father and mother of Abbot Robert of Winchester, obit 29 April. This entry is the only source known to me that supplies the names of Robert's parents. His brother, Herbert, was mentioned in the Glastonbury survey of 1189 as holding land at Glastonbury, and may be the same as Herbert, son of Hugh, one of the jurors for the Glastonbury return; see *Liber Henrici*, ed. Jackson, pp. 3–4, 21–3 and 83.

[26] Robertus abbas Glast. Vitalis festo deus illi proximus esto.

Robert, abbot of Glastonbury (1173–80), obit 28 April (the feast of Vitalis). Robert's obit is also given as 28 April (1180) by *AD*, ed. Hearne, II, 331. It is also preserved in Vitellius C. xii, 126v, and London, British Library, Cotton Nero C. ix (Christ Church, Canterbury, s. xiii), 10v. Robert was the only abbot whose name was copied into the Christ Church martyrology together with the names of thirty-one monks of Glastonbury. It is possible that he entered into some confraternal agreement with Christ Church and that the names represent the members of the community at the time. See also the St Augustine's calendar (Vitellius C. xii) which records the obits of abbots Æthelweard, Thurstan, Herluin and Robert together with eighty-four monks of Glastonbury. Again such information could only have come from a *liber uitae* and one that was kept at least from the time of Æthelweard's death.

[27] Henricus rex secundus .ii. non. Iulii.

King Henry II (1154–89), obit 6 July. This agrees with the day recorded elsewhere; see J. Dart, *The History and Antiquities of the Cathedral Church of Canterbury* (London, 1726), Appendix, p. xxiv, and *Gesta Regis Henrici Secundi*, ed. W. Stubbs, 2 vols, RS 49 (London, 1867) II, 67–71, at 71.

III

INTERPRETATIONS

Fraud and its Consequences:
Savaric of Bath and the Reform of Glastonbury

CHARLES T. WOOD

In medieval England, few monasteries achieved the stature of Glastonbury. Although its location in Somerset meant that it was far removed from the wealth of urban centres, its holdings in land were extensive; its church was to become one of the largest in Western Christendom; and by the start of the fifteenth century its abbots had achieved such prominence that one of them, John Chinnock, was to head the English delegation at the Council of Constance, 1414–18. Nor, in medieval terms, was this success difficult to explain, for Glastonbury traced its foundation back to Joseph of Arimathea, uncle of the Blessed Virgin and that noble decurion who for three days had loaned Christ the use of his tomb. Moreover, it was also true that in 1191 the monks had discovered the bones of King Arthur in their graveyard,[1] and that discovery had in turn led to the further recognition that Arthur had been the direct descendant of Joseph, albeit on the maternal side.

Though compelling in the Middle Ages, these claims are often viewed with less favour today. As a result, in most accounts they emerge as little more than charming tales, legends that give an added air of enchantment to a lovely place. Yet, if the associations of Joseph and Arthur with Glastonbury are purely legendary – no more than pious frauds – it may be worth asking just why these claims were made, just why those responsible decided that it would be desirable to link the fortunes of a Benedictine monastery to those of Britain's most famous king, not to mention those of a man who became its foremost apostle only as result of Glastonbury's claims. Curiously, because things Arthurian are so much a province of literature, and because Joseph of Arimathea (at least in his British phase) is so much a province of High Anglicanism as well as of literature, these issues have received scant attention from historians, a neglect this paper proposes to end.

The evidence suggests that Glastonbury became aware of its Arthurian legacy long before it recognized that Joseph of Arimathea had been its founder and Arthur's ancestor. Since that awareness came only in 1191, with the discovery of the royal bones, it may prove instructive to review the most contemporaneous (though not necessarily the most accurate) account of the

---

[1] The vagueness and variety of Glastonbury's own evidence allows a date of either 1190 or 1191 here, possibly even 1189, but the argument to be presented at notes 8 and 9 below suggests that 1191 is to be preferred.

dig, a passage from Giraldus Cambrensis's *De principis instructione*, a work probably written in 1193:

> Now the body of King Arthur, which legend asserts was exempt from death and hence was transferred by spirits to a distant place, was found in our own days at Glastonbury, deep in the earth and placed in a hollow oak log between two stone pyramids erected long ago in the consecrated graveyard, the site being revealed by strange and almost miraculous signs; and it was afterwards transported with honour to the church and decently consigned to a marble tomb.[2]

To the modern mind, a 'site . . . revealed by strange and almost miraculous signs' will inevitably have certain doubts attached to it, and that such was also the case with at least some medieval minds is suggested by other parts of Giraldus's account, ones in which he offers somewhat more substantial explanations for why the monks began their dig and how they knew just whose bones they had found:

> Now although there were certain indications in their writings that the body would be found there . . . it was above all King Henry II of England who most clearly informed the monks, as he himself had heard from an ancient Welsh bard, a singer of the past, that they would find the body at least sixteen feet beneath the earth, not in a tomb of stone, but in a hollow oak. . . . Now in the grave there was found a cross of lead, placed on a stone [about eight feet above the log] and . . . fixed on the under side. This cross I myself have seen, for I have felt the letters engraved thereon. . . . They run as follows:
> Here lies the famous King Arthur,
> Buried with Guinevere his second wife,
> In the Isle of Avalon.[3]

In spite of Giraldus's assurances that he himself has seen and touched the cross, its reported words fail to inspire confidence. Moreover, even though this passage goes on to explain that Arthur's body was placed so deep, with the cross fixed letter-side-in to the bottom of the stone, so that it 'might not by any means be discovered by the Saxons, who occupied the island after his death', it remains difficult to understand why the stone and its inscription should have been found so far above the oaken sepulchre – or why the stone itself should have been buried at such great depth. Here, however, C. A.

---

[2]   Giraldus Cambrensis, *De principis instructione*, Distinctio I, ch. 20, in *Giraldi Cambrensis Opera*, ed. J. S. Brewer, J. F. Dimock and George F. Warner, 8 vols, RS 21 (London, 1861–91) VIII, 126 (my translation). For a brief review of the range that other accounts could take, see Richard Barber, 'Was Mordred Buried at Glastonbury? An Arthurian Tradition at Glastonbury in the Middle Ages', *Arthurian Literature* 4 (1985), 37–69. I use Giraldus because, as an outsider who visited soon after the discovery, he strikes me as the person who is most apt to be reporting accurately the kinds of explanations offered by the monks at the time.

[3]   Giraldus Cambrensis, *De principis instructione*, Distinctio I, ch. 20, in *Giraldi Cambrensis Opera*, ed. Brewer *et al.*, VIII, 127. For clarity in my own argument, I have reversed Giraldus's order here; in the original, the passage beginning 'Now in the grave . . .' comes first.

Ralegh Radford has offered the most plausible explanation. His own excavations have demonstrated that a deep hole was indeed dug in the right place around 1190 (chips of Doulting stone, first used at Glastonbury to face the Lady Chapel built in the period 1184–9, were found at its bottom), and they further demonstrated that the level of the whole graveyard was significantly raised before the beginning of the twelfth century. It follows, then, that the first dig was genuine, and it may well be that the stone with its concealed identifying cross once lay flush with the original surface, before new layers of concealing clay were added.[4]

On the other hand, probably the most suspicious aspect of this whole affair is the simple fact that the discovery of Arthur's bones was no more than the last in a series of similar discoveries that had been taking place with astonishing regularity at least since 1184. Among them, for example, were the bones of SS Patrick, Indract, Brigit, Gildas, and Dunstan, the last of which would give rise to vigorous disputes with Christ Church, Canterbury, where, as archbishop, Dunstan indisputably had been buried, former abbot of Glastonbury though he had been. And if one asks why 1184 should have seen the beginnings of these archaeological triumphs, the answer is very clear, for it was on St Urban's Day, 25 May, of that year that fire had almost totally destroyed the abbey, thereby necessitating its reconstruction. That being the case, it seems reasonable to suppose that these new-found relics were no more than one aspect of the complex capital fund drive needed to support the monks' rebuilding efforts.[5]

Nevertheless, such an hypothesis – logically satisfying though it may be – serves only to raise further questions. For example, why was Arthur somewhat tardily added to what was otherwise a group consisting purely of saints? And why was it alleged that it had been Henry II specifically who had informed the monks about the bones' precise location? Lastly, though also most puzzlingly, if Henry had indeed been responsible, why had the monks waited for two years after his death before beginning their search? Slow as the mills of God may grind, this delay seems incomprehensible unless it be granted that Arthur's discovery was somehow related to a crisis

---

[4]   C. A. Ralegh Radford, 'Glastonbury Abbey', *The Quest for Arthur's Britain*, ed. Geoffrey Ashe *et al.* (New York, 1969), pp. 126–37. In purely archaeological terms, Radford's argument about the added layer of clay can explain how a cross bearing what he judges to be eleventh-century lettering came to be buried so deeply, but it fails to address the curious way in which the cross was affixed to the stone, an issue to which Giraldus does speak, and presumably on the basis of what the monks had told him. Also, in terms of the literary and historical evidence as we now have it, the Radford hypothesis would appear to require an Arthur who was rather better known in the eleventh century than appears to have been the case.

[5]   I do not mean to imply here that none of the saints thus discovered had had previous associations with Glastonbury, for such was not the case. Rather, what happened in most instances was simply that previously unsubstantiated tradition was given concrete form after the fire through the miraculous survival and discovery of these saints' relics. For details on this development, see Antonia Gransden, 'The Growth of the Glastonbury Traditions and Legends in the Twelfth Century', *Journal of Ecclesiastical History* 27 (1976), 337–58, at 339, 342–9.

in fundraising, a crisis closely related to Henry II, and yet one the severity of which was not fully felt – or the solution to which was not fully found – until long after Henry, too, had been placed in his grave.

The known facts surely support this further hypothesis, though not always directly. In the aftermath of the fire of St Urban's Day, Abbot Robert of Winchester turned almost immediately to the challenge of reconstruction. Funds generated by the saintly relics so miraculously discovered were doubtless a part of his plan from the very beginning, but of much greater importance was the pledged assistance of Henry II. Still labouring under the cloud created by Becket's unfortunate fate, his fear of the wrath of God intensified in 1183 by the death of the Young Henry his heir, this first of the Plantagenet kings was in no position to turn a deaf ear to ecclesiastical appeals. As a result, after 1183 he responded willingly to clerical requests for aid for projects ranging from the refounded expansion of Amesbury to our present concern, the rebuilding of Glastonbury. Indeed, for the completion of this latter project he is variously reported to have promised either the total annual revenues of his West Country demesne or, more stunningly, the surplus revenues of the entire realm of England.[6]

Whatever the case, the sums envisaged were clearly large, and it was their anticipated magnitude, one suspects, that encouraged Robert of Winchester to favour a grandiose scale in his plans. For in the absence of this royal munificence it is difficult to believe that he would have undertaken a reconstruction the contemplated size of which threatened to rival Old St Peter's in its magnitude. If so, though, disaster struck with the death of Henry II since the accession of his son Richard the Lionheart meant that England was now ruled by a king determined to use his every resource not for the benefit of abbeys like Glastonbury, but for the liberation of the Holy Land itself.

In other words, with Richard's accession the royal funding of Glastonbury came to an end, and that this stoppage provoked a real financial crisis is suggested by the frequency with which its monks now took to the road, bearing their relics to the far corners of the realm in a desperate attempt to encourage gifts from the faithful that would at least partially compensate for the loss of Henry's generosity.[7] Still, if the funds thus generated remained insufficient, the same year that had brought crisis in the form of Richard's accession was also to bring what proved to be the ultimate solution, the investiture of a new abbot, Richard's cousin Henry of Sully.

One can speculate, of course, that Henry's membership in the Anglo-French nobility had made him familiar with the exploits of Arthur, and these both in the form set forth by Geoffrey of Monmouth and, rather more problematically, in that recently created by Chrétien de Troyes. Moreover, at Glas-

---

[6]   See *Cronica*, chs 95–6 (ed. Carley, pp. 174–9), for the preferably cautious view, one based on Adam of Damerham: *AD*, ed. Hearne, II, 333–4.

[7]   *Cronica*, chs 97, 100 (ed. Carley, pp. 178–81, 184–5). Adam of Damerham's version of the crisis is that Richard the Lionheart 'turned his mind to matters of war and took no interest in our new church, and so work on the building came to a standstill because there was no one to pay the labourers': *AD*, ed. Hearne, II, 341, as translated in Gransden, 'Glastonbury Traditions', p. 355.

tonbury itself there appears to have been more than a little knowledge of the Welsh versions. Nevertheless, that Arthur had emerged as *the* hero for people of Henry's station in life (and potentially for his monks as well) would have had little importance for the abbey if it had not been for the fact that on 29 March 1187 the widow of Richard's younger brother Geoffrey, Constance of Brittany, had given birth to a son and, with the consent of Henry II, had named him Arthur.[8] In turn, this fact alone, while indicative of the high place that Arthur had attained in royal circles, would not have had significance except for the fact that on 11 November 1190 Richard the Lionheart – unmarried, childless, and about to undergo all the life-threatening dangers of a Crusade – decided formally to designate his nephew Arthur as heir to the crown.[9]

Given these facts, then, it rather looks as though Henry of Sully and his monks may well have been moved to look for Arthur's bones in their graveyard not because Henry II had so counselled them, but only because Richard the Lionheart's designation of his nephew as royal heir had created a context within which it was logical to assume that the very discovery of those bones, and at Henry II's inspiration at that, would make it awkward indeed for the crusading son if he were stubbornly to refuse to renew the financial generosity of his father. Whatever Richard's difficulties with Henry had been – and the record shows that they had been many – the truth was that their shared dynastic commitment to Arthur united them in ways that made it difficult to believe that the new king would long continue his indifference to Glastonbury's financial plight after he had been brought to recognize that Arthur's bones had come to light there largely as a result of Henry's intervention. In short, even the loose ends of Giraldus Cambrensis's tale start to make sense once one appreciates that its specifics took shape only a year and a half after Henry's death and in response to Richard's solution for his own succession problems.

Be that as it may, fraud has its consequences both for good and for ill. On the positive side, it seems clear in the present instance that the financial prospects created by Glastonbury's new-found Arthurian presence enabled it not just to continue its rebuilding, but also to provide its monks with a standard of living well in excess of that envisaged in the Rule of St Benedict. In turn, though, because wealth and prosperity always have their detractors, Glastonbury was soon to find that it was not without its critics, the most outspoken of whom proved to be Savaric of Bath, the bishop in whose diocese Glastonbury lay.

---

[8]   Charles T. Wood, *Joan of Arc and Richard III* (New York, 1988), p. 24 and n. 62.

[9]   *Foedera, conventiones, literae, et cuiuscunque generis acta publica . . .*, ed. Thomas Rymer, 20 vols (London, 1704–35) I, 53. Since this letter to Pope Clement III was written from Sicily, its date of 11 November means that news of it would not have reached England until 1191, thereby lending support to my dating in note 1 above. For discussion of Plantagenet dynasticism crucial to the argument of the paragraph that now follows, see Wood, *Joan and Richard*, pp. 23–5 and notes, and also Charles T. Wood, 'Les gisants de Fontevraud et la politique dynastique des Plantagenêts', *La Figuration des morts dans la chrétienté médiévale* (Fontevraud, 1989), pp. 195–208.

Without exception, abbey chroniclers are unremittingly hostile to Savaric, John of Glastonbury first among them. As he reports it in his *Cronica siue antiquitates Glastoniensis ecclesie*, in 1192 Savaric had been so attracted by the prospects of Glastonbury's wealth that he used his imperial connections and promises of money to persuade Richard the Lionheart, then a German captive, to nominate him not just as bishop of Bath, but as abbot of Glastonbury as well. Conflict began immediately, but true crisis came only with the accession of John, at which point Savaric decided fully to make good on his claims to the abbey, the wealth of which was becoming ever more apparent:

> Bishop Savaric . . . came on Pentecost with a strong and hostile troop, not as a shepherd entering through the door of the sheepfold, but climbing up through the wall when the doors had been shattered. When he was not received and admitted by the monks of their own will, he brought a workman and had the door-bolts of the church and treasury broken by force, dishonourably seized the church's vestments, [and] had the canons of Wells and other seculars vested in them. . . . When [the monks] who had not wished to be present at his enthronement assembled to perform the divine office, he turned them out of the church in flight, and all that day and the following night he laid siege to the cloister with a band armed with swords and cudgels. . . . Those confined to the infirmary he publicly denounced as excommunicates, afflicted them with hunger and fasting, and denied them their supply of ordinary fluid, even water. The next day . . . they were irreverently beaten in the presence of many, both of clerks and laity. And so, when some of them had been broken by fear of punishment and others by blandishments . . . they submitted to his lordship.[10]

Shocking though this episcopal visitation is meant to appear, there is, perhaps, another side to the story. By 1199 the striking magnificence and scale of Glastonbury's reconstruction had become more than apparent, and as Savaric's own actions were soon to suggest, the monks themselves appear to have been enjoying the excesses of the good life. Not to put too fine a point on the matter, any reasonable bishop would surely have concluded that in Glastonbury he had a monastery thoroughly out of control and in need of reform, so if Savaric responded with steps aimed at eliminating luxurious vestments and overly ostentatious altar plate, following up with a reduction in the daily food and drink allowance to more normal monastic standards, there are grounds for concluding that he was no more than attempting to act as the good shepherd, one determined to reform his flock.[11] And if he had the

---

[10] *Cronica*, ch. 105 (ed. Carley, pp. 192–3). For an explanation of why my translation differs from David Townsend's, printed by Carley, see my review of Carley's edition in *Speculum* 62 (1987), 427–30, at 429.

[11] For further evidence that suggests reforming intent, not rapacious greed, see *Cronica*, chs 100–1 (ed. Carley, pp. 184–9). The record suggests an attempt to reimpose due authority, I think, and in this regard I am also struck by the crisp manner in which Pope Innocent III is reported to have rejected Glastonbury's appeals and its attempt to elect a new abbot (*Cronica*, ch. 106; ed. Carley, pp. 194–7). If the situation had been half as bad as the monks alleged, there is every reason to believe that

worst offenders 'beaten in the presence of many', even though that deed struck our chronicler as 'irreverent', a more accurate term for it would surely be 'penitential'.

Still, as John of Glastonbury points out, 'A suitable bestowal of bodily necessities usually encourages monks in the divine service and to a very great extent eliminates the hateful cause of grumbling'.[12] On the other hand, since the reforming episcopal regime of Savaric and his successor Jocelin of Bath meant that for twenty years, to 1219, no such 'suitable bestowal' took place, grumbling became a way of life. It was, however, to be fully leavened by more imaginative endeavours. If fraud has its consequences, one of them is likely to be further frauds combined with the creative reuse of earlier ones, and so it proved here. If the prosperity associated with the discovery of Arthur's bones had led to the disastrous reforms of Savaric, then the obvious solution was to free Glastonbury from Bath's episcopal jurisdiction, thereby also freeing it from the nightmare of rigorous adherence to the Benedictine Rule.

Here, as it happened, the monks were exceedingly fortunate. In the 1120s William of Malmesbury had written his *De antiquitate Glastonie ecclesie*, a work in which that scrupulous scholar had recorded not just all of Glastonbury's known history, but also those ancient charters that had long guaranteed the abbey its liberties. Since the content of these documents closely resembles that to be found in known Benedictine forgeries of the early twelfth century, their authenticity has long been questioned,[13] but Savaric's intervention had the effect of breathing new life into their strictures. Indeed, so much was this the case that in the thirteenth century Glastonbury hastened to supplement the record through the addition of similar charters and privileges that had either come to light or been issued since William of Malmesbury had completed his labours. Seldom has a pattern been clearer.

In 725, for example, King Ine supposedly stressed that since Glastonbury was 'the mother of saints', its monks 'should have the power of choosing and appointing their own ruler'. Then, as though that were not enough, the charter in his name goes on to specify:

> Moreover I especially do prohibit and forbid, calling on the intercession of Almighty God, the perpetual Virgin Mary, the blessed apostles Peter and Paul and all the saints, any bishop to presume, on any pretext at all, to establish his episcopal seat, or to celebrate solemn mass, or to consecrate altars, or to dedicate churches, or to confer holy orders, or to do anything at all in the church of Glastonbury itself, or in any of the churches subject to it . . . unless he be invited by the abbot or brethren. . . . Moreover let such a bishop make provision for this, that every year he, and his clerks that are at Wells, should acknowledge his mother

Innocent would have done something about it. That he did not demonstrates that he, too, believed that Savaric was merely chastening a wayward flock.

[12] *Cronica*, ch. 90 (ed. Carley, pp. 168–9).
[13] For a discussion of the case for forgery within a comparative Benedictine framework, see the editorial discussion in *The Early History*, ed. Scott, pp. 27–33.

church at Glastonbury with litanies on the second day after the Lord's ascension.[14]

Given Ine's charter, it is perhaps unsurprising to find that in 944 Edmund the Elder should reputedly have cautioned 'lest any mortal, whether bishop or ealdorman, or any servant of theirs, should rashly dare to enter [Glastonbury] in order to hold pleas or plunder or do anything which could be in opposition to those serving God there', adding that these were things that 'I forbid . . . by God's prohibition'.[15] Similarly, in 971 Edgar the Peaceable was made to say that he also confirmed and corroborated 'what had hitherto been scrupulously observed by all my ancestors, that neither the bishop of Wells nor his servants shall have any power at all over this monastery'.[16] Sixty years later, in 1032, Cnut allegedly forbade 'anyone at all to dare to enter that island [of Glastonbury], regardless of his rank or dignity', everyone being enjoined to 'await the judgement of the abbot and the convent alone' as was proper under 'the authority of the omnipotent Father and the Son and the Holy Spirit and by the prohibition of the perpetual Virgin'.[17] If William the Conqueror, understandably ignorant of Glastonbury's unusual freedom from episcopal jurisdiction, is reported to have assumed initially that 'the bishop of Wells ought to determine [matters] in the chapter', his subsequent charter admits the mistake, stressing that 'all jurisdiction there, both in ecclesiastical and secular affairs, was [the abbot's] . . . [w]herefore the bishop of Wells, if he had allegations to make, should come to Glastonbury at his command'.[18] Lastly, if Pope Calixtus II decreed in 1123 'that no one at all be permitted to disturb that monastery internally or to take away its possessions',[19] the Henry II of later chroniclers summed it all up in the 1180s with the simple statement that Glastonbury Abbey and all its possessions 'should be entirely free from all jurisdiction of the bishop of Bath, just as is my own crown'.[20]

Forgeries though these charters undoubtedly are, in the thirteenth century they helped to achieve the desired goal. In 1219, Honorius III dissolved the union of Bath and Glastonbury, and in the same year the monks were able freely to elect an abbot of their own choosing for the first time since 1192. Their choice fell on William Vigor, one of their emissaries to the pope, and from what is recorded of him it appears that their high expectations of his abbacy were not misplaced:

---

[14]   *DA*, ch. 42 (ed. Scott, pp. 100–1). It seems an especially nice touch here to have prohibited 'any bishop', but then to have made clear the identity of the only one the monks feared by having the charter insist that 'he, and his clerks that are at Wells', should yearly 'acknowledge his mother church of Glastonbury'.
[15]   *DA*, ch. 56 (ed. Scott, pp. 118–19).
[16]   *Ibid.* ch. 60 (pp. 124–5).
[17]   *Ibid.* ch. 65 (pp. 132–3).
[18]   *Ibid.* ch. 76 (pp. 154–5).
[19]   *Ibid.* ch. 82 (pp. 164–5).
[20]   *Cronica*, ch. 95 (ed. Carley, pp. 176–7).

When Abbot William had taken up his administration, he was liberal and benevolent to all, bestowing generous alms upon the poor and even larger gifts upon great men. He set tyranny aside and with paternal concern fostered the monks as he would sons, freely conferring many gifts upon them for their bodies' recreation. In order to improve the convent's beer he added half again as much grain and oats to each brew. He also conceded to the convent a second tithe of all the abbey's grain, for the convent's recreation from week to week. Mercy is called down upon him who is merciful: and so he drew up a charter in which he, with all the convent, excommunicated anyone who might contradict or violate this concession.[21]

With the elevation of William Vigor, then, the monks of Glastonbury may well have thought that justice had at last been restored to the world – an outcome in which their own counterfeiting efforts had had at least a modest role. At the same time, though, there remained grounds for concern. The canons of Wells retained properties that more properly belonged to Glastonbury, and there was little reason to suppose that some future bishop of Bath and Wells might not decide, in his ambition, to imitate the reforming zeal of Savaric by attempting to reimpose his episcopal authority. In other words, more still needed to be done, and it was this fact that was ultimately to lead to the recognition of Joseph of Arimathea as Glastonbury's founder.

Strikingly, the original version of William of Malmesbury's *De antiquitate Glastonie ecclesie* knows nothing of Joseph. Rather, it merely reports 'that Lucius, king of the Britons, sent a plea to Eleutherius, the thirteenth in the line from the blessed Peter, that he should illuminate the darkness of Britain with the light of Christian preaching', and that he had sent two missionaries, SS Phagan and Deruvian, to do so. But William then added, apparently at the urging of his monastic patrons, that while Phagan and Deruvian had built the 'old church' of St Mary at Glastonbury, there was some evidence to indicate that it owed its original foundation to disciples of Christ. If so – and the writings of Freculph made William believe that this was not improbable – they must have been sent by Gaul's apostle, St Philip.[22]

There the matter might have rested except for developments in the independent world of literature. Thanks to *The Gospel of Nicodemus*, Joseph of Arimathea was already a popular figure, but by the 1190s Robert de Boron was recounting the westward journey not just of Joseph, but of the whole Grail company. Then, in the first quarter of the thirteenth century the continuators of Chrétien de Troyes and the *Estoire del Saint Graal* had St Philip sending him to Britain where he and his successors guarded the Grail until the time of Arthur.[23] Unsurprisingly, then, the amplified edition of the *De antiquitate* that took shape shortly before 1250 included with its fraudulent

[21]   *Ibid.* ch. 111 (pp. 206–7). Note also that on these same pages the monks under William Vigor regain the sumptuous vestments, etc., that Savaric had taken from them (note 11 above). These changes *do* sound like reforms abandoned!

[22]   *The Early History*, ed. Scott, p. 168.

[23]   Valerie M. Lagorio, 'The Evolving Legend of St Joseph of Glastonbury', *Speculum* 46 (1971), 209–31, at 215.

charters a reassuring account of how St Philip had dispatched 'his very dear friend, Joseph of Arimathea, who . . . came to Britain in 63 AD'. At Glastonbury, he and his companions had built a church 'of twisted wattle, an unsightly construction no doubt but one adorned by God with many miracles'. It was, adds pseudo-William, 'the first one in that territory'.[24] Left unstated, for it needed no stress, was the real point of the passage, that churches first in their foundation take precedence over all others, in this case the ones belonging to that late-comer the bishop of Bath and Wells and his villainous associates, the canons of Wells.

Still, if this paper is right in its readings, it would appear that if fraud had its consequences, it had its limits as well. Thus, for example, Glastonbury's monks did not rush to discover their founder's bones, and even more striking, perhaps, is the equally negative fact that before the abbey's dissolution in 1539, not one person associated with it attempted to claim that it owned, or once owned, the Holy Grail.[25] From a monastery that claimed to possess, among its other relics, four fragments of bread from the five loaves with which Christ had fed the five thousand, this was modesty indeed. It would appear, though, that this modesty was not just a product of the normal forger's caution, a fear of claiming things so outrageous that the whole fabricated structure becomes endangered. Rather, given Joseph's role in the crucifixion, and further given the Holy Grail's somewhat heterodox associations, it seems likely that the monks' failures here may well have arisen from religious scruples, from a recognition that there were some frauds that could endanger the faith.

This is not to say, however, that Joseph of Arimathea lacked usefulness to Glastonbury. Whatever his initial role in helping the abbey to maintain its newly regained independence – and on this issue the record is silent – by the second quarter of the fourteenth century he was to emerge as a helpful figure in Glastonbury's attempts to regain lands from the bishop of Bath and Wells and his canons. With monotonous regularity these battles ended up in the

---

[24]   *DA*, ch. 1 (ed. Scott, pp. 44–5).

[25]   It is difficult to prove negatives, of course, but three points strike me. First, the monks themselves appear never to have searched for Joseph's bones even though both Melkin the Bard and John of Glastonbury claimed that they had indeed been interred in the abbey: James P. Carley, 'Melkin the Bard and Esoteric Tradition at Glastonbury Abbey', *The Downside Review* 99 (1981), 1–17, esp. 17, n. 57. As far as we know, only an outsider, John Blome of London, ever sought to look, and, in so doing, he sought permission not from Glastonbury itself, but only from Edward III: *Foedera*, ed. Rymer, II, 179. Second, when Glastonbury began genuinely to stress its founding by Joseph, roughly from the abbacy of John Chinnock on, its story stressed John of Glastonbury's version, that Joseph had brought the relics of Christ's blood and perspiration not in the Holy Grail, but in two cruets. Lastly, that this avoidance of the Grail was far from accidental is then suggested by the third point, the very late creation of Chalice Well and of the legends surrounding it. As this historian reads the evidence, Joseph's associations with Glastonbury must have led to increased numbers of pilgrims searching for the Holy Grail, but the monks refused to gratify their desires with its production. Instead, they created Chalice Well, into the depths of which the Grail could be shown to have disappeared forever. The very modesty of this fraud is, I think, suggestive, especially when one considers the alternatives.

court of the archbishop of Canterbury, and that Joseph had a leading role to play in them is nowhere more suggestively implied than in the fact that in about 1350 Robert of Avesbury, a registrar for that court, traced the ancestry of King Arthur back to Joseph in his *Historia de mirabilibus gestis Edwardi III*.[26] Since that ancestry had earlier appeared only in John of Glastonbury's *Cronica*,[27] the obvious conclusion is that the abbey must have been relying on it heavily in its litigation, for how else would the registrar have heard of it?

By that point, of course, a century had passed since Glastonbury had first recognized Joseph as its founder, and it may well be that the passing years had given a greater aura of truth to this story than it would have had for the refashioner of the *De antiquitate*. If so, it could for the first time be used with confidence, unhampered by scruple. And there was to be a happy outcome, for as John of Glastonbury reports it, Abbot Adam of Sodbury and his prior John of Breynton brought 'the contests between the lords the bishop of Bath, the deacon of Wells, and the abbot of Glastonbury regarding the moors and boundaries of the church of Glastonbury . . . to a praiseworthy conclusion, after spending over a thousand marks'. After that, John, now abbot, 'governed all things benevolently in the course of his pastoral direction and restored all the manors in the best of fashions.'[28] Thanks to the wealth generated by the discovery of Arthur, these were costs that Glastonbury could well afford, and thanks to the pre-eminent independence now assured by its illustrious founder, the monks could also face the future confident that improvements wrought would always be theirs to enjoy. If this story has a moral, then, it is surely that while reform poses difficulties, fraud had its consequences, some of which may prove benign.

---

[26] See *The Chronicle of Glastonbury Abbey*, ed. Carley, p. xxviii.
[27] On the proper dating of John of Glastonbury, see the introduction in *ibid.* pp. xxv–xxx, and my own further arguments as presented in my review, cited in note 10 above, pp. 427–9. Antonia Gransden remains unconvinced by Carley's redating (in her review in *Albion* 19 [1987], 54–8), but her arguments are less persuasive than polemical.
[28] *Cronica*, ch. 140 (ed. Carley, pp. 264–9).

Glastonbury Abbey and Education

NICHOLAS ORME

That medieval monasteries were centres of education is a piece of popular folklore which, for once, has not been disproved by historical research. Until the end of the nineteenth century, historians imagined them providing virtually all the schooling in medieval and early Tudor England, both for their inmates and for the public.[1] Self-contained grammar schools were thought to have been largely developed by Henry VIII and Edward VI after the monasteries fell. This view received a severe blow from the research of A. F. Leach beginning in the 1880s, which showed that grammar schools were a powerful force alongside the schools of the monasteries as early as the twelfth century. Leach went too far in the opposite direction and denied that monastic education had any real worth, so that for a time its reputation was diminished, but since the late 1920s and the writings of W. A. Pantin and David Knowles, more balanced judgements have been formed. While it is now agreed that medieval England had many other schools, those of the monasteries are recognized as having been an important group. They taught not only monks but other boys, and provided the world as well as the cloister with literate clerics and laymen. The dissolution of the monasteries was a loss to English education.

Glastonbury was the richest house in England in 1086 and the second richest in 1535, with a large complement of monks. There were 72 in 1172, and though this fell to 45 after the Black Death, it rose again to 55 on the eve of the Reformation. There was consequently a frequent intake of novices and good potential resources for training them. By the fourteenth century, some of the monks were being educated to university level within the abbey walls, and a few were sent to Oxford to study theology. There were also non-monastic students within the walls – noble boys, servers and choristers – outnumbering the student monks and equalling the roll of an independent town school of the day. Unfortunately, the internal history of Glastonbury is poorly documented compared with Canterbury, Durham and Westminster, where the abbey records survived the Reformation through the foundations continuing as cathedrals. We are well provided with evidence about education only in the mid-fourteenth and early sixteenth centuries, and there are

---

[1] On the historiography of this topic, see N. Orme, *English Schools in the Middle Ages* (London, 1973), pp. 2–8, and on monastic education in general, pp. 224–51.

many gaps in our knowledge. The institutions by which it was given are often obscure, and its quality is very hard to judge.

From the mid-tenth century onwards Glastonbury observed the Rule of St Benedict which emphasized the training of young monks.[2] The Rule allowed recruits to be admitted as children or as adults. In the latter case, they had to spend a year as novices under the supervision of a senior monk. They learned by heart the psalms and most of the material which they had to recite in the daily services, but they were also expected to be literate. Time was provided for reading every day, and everyone was to study a book from the library every Lent. St Benedict did not specifically mention the schooling of recruits in letters, perhaps because in sixth-century Italy it was not difficult for speakers of the vernacular to learn written Latin. In England, on the other hand, where the spoken language was quite different from Latin, formal schooling was necessary, certainly for the boys. In 745 we find the English synod of *Clofesho* ordering precisely that children in monasteries shall study in schools,[3] and the earliest mention of education at Glastonbury relates to such a child. St Dunstan was born *ca* 909 and placed by his parents in the abbey a few years later, while he was still a boy. According to his first biographer, B., who wrote in 995x1005, Dunstan studied letters, received the tonsure, and was eventually able to read holy books, including volumes belonging to visiting Irish pilgrims. We are not told who did the teaching, but Osbern, a later writer, conjectured that the Irish fulfilled the role.[4]

The ultimate responsibility for education in a monastery belonged to the abbot. At Glastonbury, Michael of Amesbury (1235–52) was remembered as being 'assiduous in the exhortation and instruction of youths',[5] and Walter of Monington (1342–75) wrote letters advising and warning his student monks at Oxford.[6] The very last abbot of all, Richard Whiting (1525–39), was praised in later times for receiving noble boys and sending them to study in the universities.[7] Naturally, the abbot could not carry out the daily supervision and teaching, which had to be deputed (as St Benedict recommended) to other senior monks. An early example of such an arrangement is that of John of Whatelegh, a young recruit in the mid-twelfth century. He was entrusted to a mature brother called John Canan, who is referred to as his 'master' and who eventually told him the site of the alleged tomb of St Dunstan.[8] Later, we hear of a general officer in charge of training recruits: the master of the

[2]   *The Rule of St Benedict*, ed. O. Hunter Blair, 5th ed. (Fort Augustus, 1948), pp. 144–51 (chs 58–9).

[3]   *Councils and Ecclesiastical Documents Relating to Great Britain and Ireland*, ed. A. W. Haddan and W. Stubbs, 3 vols (Oxford, 1869–78) III, 364–5.

[4]   B., *Vita S. Dunstani*, chs 4–5, and Osbern, *Vita S. Dunstani*, chs 6–8 (*Memorials of St Dunstan*, ed. W. Stubbs, RS 63 [London, 1874], pp. 7–11, 74–8).

[5]   *Cronica*, ch. 113 (ed. Carley, pp. 212–13).

[6]   See below, pp. 289–90.

[7]   *De antiquitate Benedictinorum in Anglia*, in *Apostolatus Benedictinorum in Anglia*, ed. C. Reyner (Douai, 1626), Tractatus I, p. 224.

[8]   *DA*, ch. 25 (ed. Scott, pp. 76–7); *Cronica*, ch. 97 (ed. Carley, pp. 178–9).

novices. He is first mentioned at Glastonbury in 1321 when Abbot Geoffrey Fromond granted him and his assistants 20s. a year from the tithes of East Brent. This sum was still being paid in 1539.[9]

The practice of committing boys to monasteries as monks died out in England during the twelfth century. After this, recruits were generally in their late teens and sometimes older. In 1218–19 the general chapter of the English Benedictine monasteries prohibited anyone from becoming a monk until he was nineteen, save in exceptional circumstances, and in 1278 this was clarified as admission on probation at eighteen and full profession at nineteen.[10] On his arrival, the novice had to bring a set of clothes for his use, and bedclothes were eventually required as well. Some houses made inordinate demands in this respect, and the general chapter intervened to limit the expense to £5, and later simply to what was sufficient.[11] Poorer candidates may have been clothed by the abbey, as happened in the case of a man called Popham who entered Glastonbury in 1309.[12] For him the chamberer provided:

	s.	d.
9½ ells of black russet for robes and a sleeveless tunic at 20d. per ell	15	10
Hose of black serge		10
Shoes		8
Maniple		9
One fur lining for a supertunic	3	6
The same for a hood	1	2
	22	9

The novice, once admitted, was supervised by his master in the choir, the cloister and the refectory – in other words in his worship, studies and good manners.[13] His period of probation was a minimum of a year, but seems to have often lasted longer. In 1277 the general chapter laid down that no one should eat or sleep outside the monastery in his first two years,[14] and even when the novice had taken his vows as a monk, he was not usually given full status until he had been ordained priest by the bishop. Glastonbury probably housed about half a dozen novices and recently professed monks at any one time, all of whom would be receiving supervision and training.

---

[9]　For the master of the novices in 1321, see *Cronica*, ch. 136 (ed. Carley, pp. 254–5); the sixteenth-century payment is mentioned in PRO, SC 6 Henry VIII/3118 m. 3.
[10]　*Documents Illustrating the Activities of the General and Provincial Chapters of the English Black Monks, 1215–1540*, ed. W. A. Pantin, 3 vols, Royal Historical Society, Camden 3rd ser. 45, 47, 54 (London, 1931–7) I, 10, 99.
[11]　*Ibid.* II, 49–50, 206.
[12]　I. Keil, 'The Chamberer of Glastonbury Abbey in the Fourteenth Century', *PSANHS* 107 (1962–3), 79–92, at 91.
[13]　*Documents*, ed. Pantin, I, 73.
[14]　*Ibid.* II, 50.

The principal task of the novice was to learn the liturgy. Eight services were recited in church each day, the material differing throughout the week, so that the whole seven-day cycle had to be known, and known by heart. An ordinance of 1277 specified the learning of the psalter, hymns, canticles, invitatories, responsories, antiphons and the common material for saints' days. Only university graduates and other learned recruits were excused this memory work and allowed to read the service from a book. The novice had also to learn the monastic rule and the local customs of his monastery.[15] Some of this material was assimilated 'on the job' in church or refectory, but there were probably also special training sessions with the master of the novices in the cloister. The well-known arrangements at Durham Priory in the early sixteenth century may be a guide in this respect. There, schooling took place in the west alley of the cloisters in

> a fair great stall of wainscot where the novices did sit and learn, and also the master of the novices had a pretty seat or stall of wainscot over against the stall where the novices did sit and look at their books, and there did sit and teach the novices both forenoon and afternoon.[16]

Learning the services by heart did not mean that books were not used, and monks were certainly not illiterate. As we have seen, Benedict expected them to be able to read and study, and the presence of scholars and writers in the Glastonbury community shows that some of the brethren were skilled in this respect. After the entry of child monks was discontinued, the novices being older had probably already acquired a reading knowledge of Latin in a school elsewhere. If they were deficient in this respect, presumably the novice master had to teach them Latin too, or give the task to another monk.

In the thirteenth century the feeling grew among monastic leaders that the academic (as opposed to the liturgical) training of monks might be better organized. This was probably a reaction to the growth of universities. Hitherto monasteries had possessed as good facilities for learning as any institution, but the rise of the universities set higher standards. They offered teaching in all the liberal arts and philosophy, and in the higher faculties of medicine, civil and canon law, and theology. The secular clergy (those not members of religious orders) began to make use of these facilities, so did the friars, and the monks found themselves in danger of being left behind. Accordingly in 1247 the general chapter directed all abbeys and priories with sufficient monks and resources to organize a daily lecture on theology or canon law to be given by a monk or a scholar from outside.[17] As members of the Order could hardly lecture effectively unless they too had studied at a university, the next logical step was to provide a means for them to do so. In 1277 the general chapter (presided over by the abbot of Glastonbury, John of Taunton) agreed to establish a house of studies at Oxford and levied a tax of

---

15   *Ibid*. I, 73–4; II, 38, 50, 84.
16   *The Rites of Durham*, ed. J. T. Fowler, Surtees Society 107 (Durham, 1903), pp. 84–5.
17   *Documents*, ed. Pantin, I, 27–8.

3d. in the pound on all monasteries to pay for it.[18] The house, Gloucester College on the site of the present-day Worcester College, duly opened for Benedictine student monks in about 1291.[19]

We do not know how many monks from Glastonbury (if any) went to the college in its early years,[20] but in 1336 Pope Benedict XII commanded every Benedictine monastery to send one monk to university for every twenty of its brethren.[21] It may have been this that prompted Abbot John of Breynton (1334–42) to build a set of rooms in the college for his monks, consisting of a hall for everyday use and four chambers. The cost was £40.[22] One of the old buildings of Worcester College on the south side of the front quadrangle still displays the coat of arms of Glastonbury (a cross, Virgin and Child), reset from another place – possibly from the ground floor of the present Staircase 14 which has been suggested as the site of the abbey's hall.[23] Breynton's successor Walter of Monington continued and improved the Oxford connection. As president of the general chapter in 1356 he mediated when the prior of the college illegally evicted the monks of St Augustine's, Canterbury, from their accommodation, and in 1360 he suggested new statutes for the better governing of the community.[24] He took seriously his duty of sending monks to Oxford, and corresponded with them, dispensing advice and instructions. His letters show that there were three Glastonbury students at Gloucester College in the summer of 1357, four in 1361 and at least three in the spring of 1366, to whom the abbot proposed to add four more after Easter.[25] If he built up the complement to seven or eight, he did better than either the pope required or the abbots achieved at comparable monasteries like Christ Church, Canterbury, and Westminster.[26]

Sending students to Oxford was expensive for the abbey and a worry for the abbot. Although the site of Gloucester College was outside the city walls away from the main university community, there were still plenty of distractions to tempt the student monks. In about November 1360 Monington ordered Brother William Nye, his senior student at Oxford, to give careful

---

[18] *Ibid.* 59, 75, 100–1.

[19] W. A. Pantin, 'Gloucester College', *Oxoniensia* 10–11 (Oxford, 1946–7), 65–74.

[20] Compare Westminster Abbey, whose monks apparently did not go until the 1330s (Barbara F. Harvey, 'The Monks of Westminster and the University of Oxford', *The Reign of Richard II*, ed. F. R. H. Du Boulay and Caroline Barron [London, 1971], pp. 108–30, at 110–11).

[21] *Bullarum Privilegiorum ac Diplomatum Romanorum Pontificum Amplissima Collectio*, ed. C. Coquelines, 14 vols (Rome, 1739–44) III, pt ii, 214–20.

[22] *Cronica*, ch. 140 (ed. Carley, pp. 266–7).

[23] *An Inventory of the Historical Monuments in the City of Oxford* (London, 1939), p. 124; J. Campbell, 'Gloucester College', *Worcester College Record* (1983), 15–23, at 21. I am grateful to Dr E. Wilson for this reference.

[24] *Documents*, ed. Pantin, III, 25–7.

[25] *Ibid.* pp. 27, 30–2, 55.

[26] Christ Church sent about four and Westminster two at this time (W. A. Pantin, *Canterbury College, Oxford*, 4 vols, Oxford Historical Society, ns 6–8, 30 [Oxford, 1946–85] IV, 16–17; Harvey, 'The Monks of Westminster', pp. 111–13).

supervision to two other Glastonbury monks, John Luccombe and Robert Sambourne, who had evidently gone astray. They were not to go out of the college without Nye's permission and were to be accompanied wherever they went. Even their teachers were to visit them at the college, and in future all their time was to be spent celebrating masses and doing academic work.[27] Nye was ineffective and Monington's next letter complained that Luccombe and Sambourne continued to reject all discipline, practising fishing and hunting in warrens to the scandal of the Order. He summoned them home at once, and made known his displeasure with Nye and another monk, John Lange, accusing them both of disobedience.[28] Luccombe and Sambourne must have made their peace, for both returned to Oxford in due course, but in 1364 Monington was again upset to hear that Sambourne had spent all his allowance, told him to be more careful and sent him only a small sum of 11s. 8d. to keep him going.[29] Later letters in 1365–6 suggest that the monks were behaving themselves better, and that affairs were more satisfactory.[30] Some of the students followed the arts course (including grammar and philosophy) and others studied theology. There are no systematic records of university graduations in the fourteenth century, however, and it is not clear whether any of the monks already mentioned took degrees. A few certainly did so later on. Thomas Coffyn (prior in 1408), Nicholas Faukes (monk in 1377) and Nicholas Frome (abbot from 1420 to 1456) all graduated as doctors of theology, while Richard Hounesworth (monk 1377–1408), Thomas Knight (monk in 1424) and Thomas Wasyn (prior in 1493) rose to be bachelors.[31] But as with monks generally, the graduates were a small minority. Most never achieved a degree because of inadequate schooling in the abbey, lack of a strong vocation for learning, or the very long curriculum involved – some nine years even for the bachelor's degree.[32]

Unlike university studies, the teaching of Latin grammar and other elementary subjects in monasteries was slower to attract the interest of monastic leaders. No doubt the ancient rather informal arrangements for such teaching were felt to be adequate. It was the popes in the fourteenth century who took the initiative in this area. In 1311 Clement V issued the decree *Ne in agro*, ordering all monasteries to maintain a master giving instruction in the elementary branches of learning, provided they had the resources to do so.[33] In 1336 Benedict XII extended the requirement, laying down that every monastery should maintain a teacher of the 'primitive sciences' – grammar, logic and philosophy. The teacher could be a monk or an outsider, and in either

27   *Documents*, ed. Pantin, III, 30–1.
28   *Ibid*. pp. 31–2.
29   *Ibid*. pp. 53–4.
30   *Ibid*. pp. 54–5.
31   A. B. Emden, *A Biographical Register of the University of Oxford to A.D. 1500*, 3 vols (Oxford, 1957–9) I, 455; II, 671, 730, 973–4, 1062; III, 1997.
32   Compare Harvey, 'The Monks of Westminster', p. 115; R. B. Dobson, *Durham Priory, 1400–1450* (Cambridge, 1973), p. 353.
33   *Corpus Juris Canonici*, ed. E. Friedberg, 2 vols (Leipzig, 1879–81) II, cols 1166–8.

case he was to receive a salary: 10 *livres tournois* (about £1 13s. 4d.) for a monk and twice as much for an outsider. External *students*, on the other hand, were not to be taught with the monks, so the novices continued to study on their own.[34] Abbot Monington responded to this legislation as conscientiously as he did with regard to university studies. Books added to the library in his time included Latin dictionaries (there were already Latin grammars and literary texts),[35] and his letters show his concern to provide the abbey with schoolmasters. In 1357 he asked one of his Oxford monks to get the advice of Master Walter Moryng, fellow of Merton College, about appointing an instructor in letters and song.[36] In 1364 he told Robert Sambourne at Oxford that he wished him to 'read' (i.e., lecture on) philosophy during the autumn, apparently at Glastonbury,[37] and in 1366 he ordered Geoffrey Marscall, another of his Oxford students, to get ready to teach the junior brethren in the cloisters.[38] Similar teaching continued (at least intermittently), since John Totford, the seventh monk in seniority, occurs as 'master of the school' in 1456,[39] and there was still a schoolmaster in 1538.[40] The evidence suggests that the teacher, as in some other large Benedictine abbeys, was a monk of the house rather than an outsider, preferably someone who had already studied to a higher level at a university.

But the teaching of monks was not the only instruction that went on in Glastonbury. Despite the disappearance of child oblation in the twelfth century, there went on being boys in monasteries all over England. Some were noble youths, the orphan sons of abbey tenants held in wardship or boarders sent at the expenses of their parents. Boys of this kind lived in the abbot's household, waited on by lay servants in a setting not unlike the household of a lay nobleman. In due course they inherited their property and became noblemen themselves, or went into the higher ranks of the Church as secular clergy.[41] Others were boys of lower rank living in the monastic almonry, maintained out of charity in return for doing useful services. Most monks were priests by the thirteenth century and celebrated a private mass each day at an altar in the abbey church, which required a boy to serve and say the

[34] *Bullarum Privilegiarum . . . Collectio*, ed. Coquelines, III, pt ii, 214–20.
[35] J. P. Carley and J. F. R. Coughlan, 'An Edition of the List of Ninety-Nine Books Acquired at Glastonbury Abbey during the Abbacy of Walter de Monington', *Mediaeval Studies* 43 (1981), 498–515, at 510–11; T. W. Williams, *Somerset Mediaeval Libraries* (Bristol, 1897), pp. 64–5, 67, 71, 73–5, 78 (where the *Doctrinale* and *Grecismus* are the standard Latin grammars of Alexander of Ville-Dieu and Evrard of Béthune).
[36] *Documents*, ed. Pantin, III, 27.
[37] *Ibid.* pp. 53–4.
[38] *Ibid.* p. 55. For Marscall's surname, see J. P. Carley, 'An Annotated Edition of the List of Sixty-Three Monks Who Entered Glastonbury Abbey during the Abbacy of Walter de Monington', *The Downside Review* 95 (1977), 306–15, at 309.
[39] *The Register of Thomas Bekynton, Bishop of Bath and Wells, 1443–1465*, ed. H. C. Maxwell-Lyte and M. C. B. Dawes, 2 vols, SRS 49–50 (1934–5) II, 445–50.
[40] See below, pp. 295–6.
[41] On this topic, see N. Orme, *From Childhood to Chivalry: The Education of the English Kings and Aristocracy, 1066–1530* (London, 1984), pp. 60–3.

responses. A further group were choristers who helped the monks sing in the choir and the secular priests who staffed the Lady Chapel.[42] Glastonbury had a Lady Chapel by the late twelfth century, and under Abbot Adam of Sodbury (1323–34) a body of four chantry priests (secular clergy, not monks) was appointed to sing melodic chant there every day.[43] Similar Lady Chapels were employing boys at Worcester Priory by the 1390s and at Winchester by 1402, and this was certainly the case at Glastonbury by the 1530s.[44] All these boys had to be educated: the noble ones because literacy was part of their life-style, and the lesser ones to do their duties of reading and singing. The monastery also stood to gain from the process, since servers sometimes became novices when they grew up, providing the house with recruits.

The first major reference to the teaching of non-monastic boys at Glastonbury comes from 1377, though the practice was probably older. In that year the abbey was required to pay a clerical poll tax in respect of 45 monks, 13 chaplains, 6 clerks and 39 'clerks of the school' (*clerici scole*), whose names are listed in table 1.[45] 'Clerk' was a common alternative word for 'scholar' in the fourteenth century, and they were 'of the school' to differentiate them from older clerks who acted as sacristans or singing men. What little we know of the school-clerks comes from some injunctions of Archbishop Arundel during his visitation of the abbey in 1408. No monk was to employ a clerk without the abbot's permission; all such clerks and other youths in the monastery under the age of twenty were to keep out of the monks' own accommodation, and they were to go straight from their table to the church or the school.[46] This suggests that many of the clerks in the list were employed as servers in church to the monks, and 39 was close to the number of monks who were priests and celebrating masses. They were evidently fed and probably boarded in the abbey, no doubt in the almonry as was the custom in most large monasteries. Their school must have been separate from that of the novices, in view of the prohibition on monks and non-monks being taught together, and they must have had a teacher of their own, since monks are not known to have instructed lay boys in any English monastery. No records survive of the teachers' names, but they are likely to have been chaplains or professional lay schoolmasters employed by the abbey in return for a salary. Similar arrangements can be traced at several other large Benedictine houses.[47]

42   Orme, *English Schools*, pp. 243–7.
43   *Cronica*, ch. 139 (ed. Carley, pp. 264–5).
44   Orme, *English Schools*, p. 246; see below, p. 295.
45   PRO, E 179/4/1 m. 3.
46   *The Register of Thomas Bekynton*, ed. Maxwell-Lyte and Dawes, II, 555–6.
47   Orme, *English Schools*, pp. 240, 245.

TABLE 1

Clerks of the School (Clerici Scole) at Glastonbury Abbey, 1381

(Public Record Office, E 179/4/1 m.3)

In the original, the names are listed in one column. The Christian names have been modernized.

William Wyrcestr'	John Mille
Nicholas Barwe	Walter Baude
John Leycestr'	John Sokyr
William Modeford	John Paulet
John Sporier	Richard Marel
Richard Geffray	Walter Lipiȝate
John Hore	John Piper
Walter Boghleye	William Sandel
William Hulle	Peter Tourk
Thomas Edward	John Vrye
John Stabler	John Thomas
Richard Hoper	John Corston
Robert Fitziames	Richard Stoke
William Miles	John Rude
John Dunster	John Gatyn
Walter Hostiler	Richard Holcomb
John Vouel	Richard Hopere
John Gaunt	John Lym
Robert Weston	Roger Payn
John Staple	

An alternative possibility is that the school in 1377 was larger than 39, because only 'adults' over the age of 14 were liable to pay the poll tax, and we know that there were younger boys in the abbey in later times. If this is correct, the school may have numbered 60 to 80 boys aged seven and upwards, perhaps including all the eligible scholars: noble boys in the abbot's household, servers, choristers and even fee-paying boys from the town of Glastonbury outside. In short, the abbey school may (at times) have catered for the surrounding district as well. Lists of medieval schoolboys are rare, and this one ought to enable us to trace their origins and later careers. Unhappily, the task is immensely difficult. Parentage and subsequent lay occupations are hard to establish because we can so rarely be sure that people with similar names were truly the same. If the boys became clerics we would normally expect to find them being ordained and instituted to benefices, but the appropriate records are missing in Bath and Wells diocese till 1401, by which time most would have passed through the system. At present we can merely make a few guesses. Almonry boys elsewhere were sometimes monks' relatives, so Robert Fitziames, William Miles and Roger Payn may have belonged to the families of Thomas Fitzjames, John Miles and John Payne, monks of Glastonbury in 1377.[48] Sometimes the boys themselves became monks, so John Staple may be the brother of that name who is mentioned in 1408.[49] Others left their monasteries to pursue careers as secular clergy or laymen, and clergy called John Dunster, Robert Fitzjames, John Leycestr', William Modeford and William Sandel appear in later episcopal records between 1402 and 1421.[50] It is quite possible that these were the former clerks of the school, but it is equally hard to be sure.

The sources for the history of education at Glastonbury become more sparse in the fifteenth century, but increase again in the sixteenth. They show that the structures previously described continued down to the dissolution of the abbey in 1539, though the word 'continue' may need qualifying. Teaching and studies could burgeon or decline from year to year, and as we shall see from evidence from about 1538, the abbey's educational facilities may have been intermittent in the short term. Still, the traditional organizations went on existing in theory and often in practice. An unlikely document – part of a lawsuit over property at Mells in 1568 – attests to the survival of the lay boys.[51] The lawsuit turned on the question whether a certain heiress had been married to Richard Beere, nephew of the abbot of that name who ruled from 1494 to 1525, and three elderly witnesses claimed to remember the younger Beere when he and they were boys in the abbey in the 1510s. Beere, they said, had been brought up with a lay career in mind, his uncle intending him to marry his ward Jane Samuel. In due course the boy was sent to Oxford and to the Inns of Court, but in 1522–3 he decided to become a monk of the London Charterhouse, and the marriage did not take place. Instead he was executed in 1537 with others of his house for refusing to acknowledge Henry VIII as head of the English Church. The evidence is interesting because it suggests a range of ranks and careers among the abbey boys. One of the witnesses in 1568 was a gentleman, one a yeoman and one a husbandman. When the future Carthusian monk is added, all three of the traditional estates of society are represented.

Some of these boys continued to be maintained to serve in the church. In 1538 a monk complained that 'the boys which hath their finding [i.e., support] of the abbey to help the priests at mass, doth not their duty'.[52] We even know one of their names: William Good, who is mentioned in the abbey accounts of 1538–9, went on to graduate at Oxford, became schoolmaster of Wells Cathedral under Mary Tudor and ended his life in Rome as a Jesuit. In later life he remembered serving the altar of St Joseph of Arimathea in the

[48]   Carley, 'An Annotated Edition of the List of Monks', pp. 309–10.

[49]   *Ibid.* p. 310.

[50]   *The Register of Walter Gifford . . . and of Henry Bowett, Bishop of Bath and Wells, 1401–7*, ed. T. S. Holmes, SRS 13 (1899), pp. 26, 37; *The Register of Nicholas Bubwith, Bishop of Bath and Wells, 1407–1424*, ed. T. S. Holmes, 2 vols, SRS 29–30 (1914) I, 107, 140, 315.

[51]   F. A. Gasquet, 'Blessed Richard Beere', *The Downside Review* 9 (1889–90), 158–63.

[52]   *Dean Cosyn and Wells Cathedral Miscellanea*, ed. A. Watkin, SRS 56 (1941), p. 160.

abbey when he was eight years old.[53] Other boys were choristers whose presence is at last confirmed in this period. A stray account roll of 1532–3 mentions a 'Master Fynche', ten fellows (i.e., chaplains or clerks) of the Lady Chapel and ten boys, while a similar roll of 1538–9 lists 'Master Renyger' with identical companions under the same heading.[54] Fynche and 'Renyger' were evidently successive masters of the choristers at Glastonbury, and though nothing is known of Fynche, James Renynger's career has left some traces in records. A former singing man at Eton College,[55] he was appointed to the post at Glastonbury on 10 August 1534 by a document which survives.[56] In it he undertook to sing and play the organ in the Lady Chapel and to play instrumental music at Christmas and other seasons, perhaps at feasts in hall. He was to instruct six choristers of the Lady Chapel in pricksong (harmony) and descant, and teach two of them to play the organ as well. Why only six choristers were mentioned when there were apparently ten is not clear. In return he was to have a salary of £10 a year plus a gown and two loads of firewood worth a further 26s. 8d. There was also a clause that if Renynger were conscripted to serve the king (the Chapel Royal was a notorious poacher of musicians), he could resume his post if he returned within a year. When the abbey was dissolved, Renynger went to London where he served for a time as organist and choirmaster of the church of St Dunstan in the East, and he was still alive in 1570 when he was given a Crown pension as a member of a former abbey.[57]

The monastic community likewise continued to have a master of the novices and a monk-schoolmaster. The first of these posts was held in 1525 by John Verney, who appears as thirtieth (rather junior) in a list of 46 monks.[58] The second is mentioned in the last visitation of Glastonbury Abbey carried out by the bishop of Bath and Wells in July 1538 – an episode which throws a good deal of light on education in the house during its final years. The bishop interviewed the monks in turn, and while the older brothers felt that matters were well on the whole, the younger ones were strongly critical of the arrangements for learning.[59] John Pantalion claimed that the senior monks grudged the younger brethren time to study, and William Joseph said that 'the prior and [Edmund] Cooker are ever against that the young men shall have any learning'. Pantalion claimed that al-

---

[53]   PRO, SC 6 Henry VIII/3118 m. 17; J. Armitage Robinson, *Two Glastonbury Legends* (Cambridge, 1926), pp. 46–7, 66–7.
[54]   PRO, SC 6 Henry VIII/3115, SC 6 Henry VIII/3118 m. 17.
[55]   F. L. Harrison, *Music in Medieval Britain*, 3rd ed. (London, 1967), p. 462.
[56]   PRO, E 135/2/31; printed by A. Watkin in 'Last Glimpses of Glastonbury', *The Downside Review* 67 (1948–9), 76–86, at 76–9.
[57]   *Ibid.*; A. F. Leach, *English Schools at the Reformation, 1546–8* (London, 1896), pt ii, 145.
[58]   *The Registers of Thomas Wolsey, Bishop of Bath and Wells, 1518–23, J. Clerke, Bishop of Bath and Wells, 1523–41, W. Knyght, Bishop of Bath and Wells, 1541–7, and G. Bourne, Bishop of Bath and Wells, 1554–9*, ed. H. C. Maxwell-Lyte, SRS 55 (1940), p. 85.
[59]   *Dean Cosyn and Wells Cathedral Miscellanea*, ed. Watkin, pp. 159–64, discussed by R. W. Dunning, 'Revival at Glastonbury', *Studies in Church History* 14 (Oxford, 1977), 213–22.

though the abbot ought to pay the monks' schoolmaster, the latter received only £2 13s. 4d. and the rest of his salary was provided by the novices themselves from their allowances – some paying 20s. a quarter. Geoffrey Benyng denied that there was an instructor at all, and Joseph said that appointments were made when visitations were pending and rescinded afterwards. In 1535 Thomas Cromwell had issued injunctions to all monasteries, one of which revived the old Benedictine custom of a lecture of one hour on holy scripture every day. Here Joseph alleged that no lectures took place between Easter and Whitsunday 1538, and that a lecturer had only been appointed for the visitation. Two other monks agreed that the injunction about lectures was not observed. Finally, William Kentwyne and John Phagan complained about lack of access to a library or books, an odd remark considering Glastonbury's large resources in this field. The 1538 reports are full of ill-humour, perhaps reflecting a time when monasteries were under great psychological pressure, and they contain some inconsistencies. They warn us, nevertheless, against complacency. Whatever the rules about schoolteaching, lectures and libraries, there could easily be inefficiency and negligence in observing them.

The abbey continued to send students to Oxford until the Dissolution, and thirteen can be traced at Gloucester College between about 1510 and 1539.[60] There may have been more, because we have no systematic records of their presence, and there were definitely three in residence together from 1537 to 1539. We can say more certainly that few of them continued to take degrees, because records of graduations survive after 1505 and these list only four Glastonbury men: one bachelor of canon law (Nicholas London) and three bachelors of divinity (Nicholas Andrew, Thomas Athelstan and John Neot).[61] Here, university regulations were a factor. Monks who had not taken MA degrees had to spend nine years of study for the BD, and although Athelstan and Neot did this successfully, it was a lengthy and expensive process. Some welcome light is thrown on the Glastonbury students of this period by the letter-book of Robert Joseph, monk of Evesham, Oxford scholar and eventually prior in charge of students at Gloucester College.[62] During a spell at Evesham in 1530–2, Joseph amused himself by writing letters to various monks whom he had met at Oxford, including Athelstan and Neot, both of whom wrote letters back which have not been preserved. Joseph wrote good colloquial Latin in the humanist manner and so, apparently, did his Glastonbury friends, which need not surprise us for Abbot Beere had been a humanist scholar and had corresponded with Erasmus himself. Joseph's letters show that both Athelstan and Neot were receptive to new ideas. Neot was reading Erasmus as well as the more traditional Duns Scotus, and Athelstan actually called the theology of Scotus 'dirty puddles'. Neot must have been

[60]   On this topic, see *ibid.* pp. 213–22.
[61]   A. B. Emden, *A Biographical Register of the University of Oxford, A.D. 1501 to 1540* (Oxford, 1974), pp. 9, 16, 360, 414.
[62]   *The Letter Book of Robert Joseph*, ed. H. Aveling and W. A. Pantin, Oxford Historical Society, ns 19 (Oxford, 1967).

one of Joseph's closest friends, for eleven of the latter's letters were written to him and Joseph submitted Latin verses for his approval. Neot himself composed some prayers for St Leonard's day. A picture emerges of monks who were not simply drudging students but fluent Latinists, witty writers, sociable with one another and sedate in their pursuits which included (in Neot's case) fishing, visiting friends and playing bowls. They were quite unaware that the Reformation was about to overtake them.

When Neot had taken his BD in 1535, he was allowed to stay on at Oxford, possibly to study for another four years to get his doctorate. This extension of his privilege aroused resentment in the abbey, and at the bishop's visitation in 1538 eight monks drew attention to Neot's lengthy absence and its allegedly poor results.[63] John Pantalion said that Neot was 'little perfect in his learning' and William Joseph 'that he cannot neither preach nor read [i.e., lecture]'. There seems to have been a feeling that the favour shown to him (attributed to the prior) was depriving someone else of a university place. Roger Wilfred said that Pantalion would be well learned if he might go to Oxford, and the bishop seems to have agreed since Neot was recalled soon afterwards and Pantalion was sent in his stead. When Dr Richard Layton, the king's agent, came to dissolve the abbey in 1539, he too thought poorly of its graduate monks. The house, he said, possessed no university doctor and 'but three bachelors of divinity, meanly learned', i.e., Andrew, Athelstan and Neot.[64] Perhaps there was a little truth in this, as in the complaints about the abbey school. With three monks at Oxford, Glastonbury had fallen behind Bury St Edmunds with four, Christ Church, Canterbury, with about six and Durham with eight – but then Christ Church and Durham had received episcopal help to endow their own university colleges.[65] The monastic life was never easily compatible with university study. There were the constraints of daily prayer and administrative duties, the limited number of strong vocations to study, and the expense involved in sending a monk away. Taking the period 1336–1539 as a whole, Glastonbury's university record was not significantly worse than that of similar houses, even if it was not a brilliant one. It certainly fulfilled the spirit of the papal legislation.

There was another respect in which Glastonbury kept up with the other great Benedictine houses: it became responsible for non-monastic students at university. An individual example of this can be found in Monington's letters, one of which concerns a kinsman of his called Bodenham, evidently a schoolboy, who was sent to Oxford to study and placed under the care of one of the Glastonbury monks there.[66] Another case, that of Abbot Beere and his nephew, has already been mentioned. Meanwhile, benefactors were begin-

[63] *Dean Cosyn and Wells Cathedral Miscellanea*, ed. Watkin, pp. 160–2.

[64] *Letters and Papers, Foreign and Domestic, of the Reign of Henry VIII*, ed. J. Gairdner and R. H. Brodie, 21 vols (London, 1862–1910) XIV, pt ii, pp. 60–1. Compare the remarks of Henry VII about Westminster Abbey in 1504 (*Calendar of Close Rolls, 1500–9* [London, 1963], p. 139).

[65] *The Letter Book of Robert Joseph*, ed. Aveling and Pantin, p. 265; Pantin, *Canterbury College*, IV, 56; Dobson, *Durham Priory*, pp. 347–8.

[66] *Documents*, ed. Pantin, III, 54–5.

ning to endow scholarships to support undergraduates at university, and monasteries were sometimes chosen as trustees of the schemes with power to administer the endowments and select the scholars. Durham Priory was involved in this way from 1380, Christ Church, Canterbury, from a year or two later, and Glastonbury from about 1502.[67] The Glastonbury connection came about through a wealthy knight of the late fifteenth century, Sir John Byconyll of South Perrott, who possessed considerable lands in Somerset and Dorset.[68] Byconyll married twice (his second wife Elizabeth was the widow of John Saintmaur), but he was a childless man and determined to bequeath part of his property to charity. Education had been one of his interests since at least 1485 when he gave some water mills to the Franciscan friary at Dorchester to pay for the training of boy recruits, and by 1490 he was well enough known at Oxford for the university to ask his help in repairing its parish church, St Mary the Virgin.[69] His plan to set up a series of university scholarships first appears in a codicil to his will, dated 1500.[70] It laid down that his wife, during her widowhood, was to maintain from his estates five scholars at Oxford learning 'the law divine for teaching Christian people', each receiving four or five marks a year (£2 13s. 4d. or £3 6s. 8d.). After her death, part of his lands was to be alienated to endow the scholars in perpetuity, and the responsibility for administering the lands was to belong to the head of whichever religious house Sir John should be buried in. This lack of precision is curious, because the knight appears to have planned to be buried at Glastonbury, and suggests that friction had arisen causing him to warn the abbey not to take his patronage for granted.

In the event, when Sir John died in 1501 he was buried at Glastonbury,[71] and in February 1502 eleven of his feoffees got a royal licence to convey his manors of Nunney, Cameley and Lyde in Somerset and other smaller pieces of property, worth £52 per annum, to the abbot of Glastonbury, Richard Beere.[72] The royal valuation of the abbey's possessions in 1535 shows that £33 6s. 8d. a year from the income of these lands was then being applied to the maintenance of ten scholars at Oxford, each receiving five marks (£3 6s. 8d.), plus £7 to a chantry priest saying prayers for the knight.[73] The scholars lived in one of the university halls, Hart Hall on the site of the modern Hertford College, which belonged to Exeter College and specialized like the

[67]   Dobson, *Durham Priory*, p. 348; Pantin, *Canterbury College*, III, 227; IV, 85.
[68]   For biographies of Byconyll, see A. S. Bicknell, 'A Forgotten Chancellor and Canon', *PSANHS* 40 (1894), 208–26, and J. C. Wedgwood and Anne D. Holt, *History of Parliament: Biographies of the Members of the Commons House, 1439–1509* (London, 1936), pp. 74–5.
[69]   J. Hutchins, *The History and Antiquities of the County of Dorset*, ed. W. Shipp and J. W. Hobson, 4 vols (Westminster, 1861–73) II, 364–5; *Epistolae Academicae Oxon*, ed. H. Anstey, 2 vols, Oxford Historical Society 35–6 (Oxford, 1898) II, 407.
[70]   Bicknell, 'A Forgotten Chancellor', pp. 217–21.
[71]   *The Itinerary of John Leland in or about the Years 1535–1543*, ed. Lucy Toulmin Smith, 5 vols (London, 1906–10) I, 289.
[72]   *Calendar of Patent Rolls, 1494–1509*, p. 275.
[73]   *Valor Ecclesiasticus tempore Henrici VIII auctoritate regia institutus*, ed. J. Caley, 6 vols (London, 1810–34) I, 145.

latter in accommodating students from the west of England. When the abbey was dissolved in 1539, the University of Oxford asked Thomas Cromwell to safeguard the scholarships, and a warrant (which does not survive) was issued ordering them to be paid by the receiver-general of Crown lands in Somerset.[74] Lists of the scholars' names duly appear in the receiver-general's accounts, and though the earliest dates from 1546, it appears to be a little-changed copy of the list at about the time of the abbey's dissolution.[75] The seven out of the ten scholars on the list who are known to have taken degrees did so between 1533 and 1544, so they may represent Abbot Whiting's last appointments. One of them, Walter Colmer, had the same surname as the prior of Glastonbury in 1522 and the bailiff of the Byconyll endowment in 1535.[76]

None of the ten is known to have studied divinity. All took the degrees of MA or BA or did not graduate, so one of Byconyll's wishes appears to have been modified early on. Moreover, once the Crown assumed the duty of paying the scholars, its officers (chiefly the lord treasurer and his deputies) took over the right to fill the scholarships, and by 1559 they were promoting their own protégés from England as a whole.[77] Even the Somerset link, therefore, was eventually broken. The Byconyll exhibitions are nevertheless interesting because, up to the Reformation, they completed the abbey's involvement in the gamut of public education from school to university. We expect monasteries to have schooled their own members, but what Leach failed to realize was the extent of the teaching of other people in the great Benedictine houses. Not only monks but future agriculturalists, secular clergy, graduates (including at least one schoolmaster) and gentlemen were taught or assisted to study by Glastonbury. When we are tempted to call the monasteries 'worldly', it is an aspect of their worldliness that ought to be remembered.

[74] Anthony Wood, *The History and Antiquities of the University of Oxford*, ed. J. Gutch, 2 vols (Oxford, 1792–6) II, 642–3.
[75] PRO, LR 6/104/1–4, LR 6/15/2–4.
[76] See above, notes 58 and 73. The scholars' names were: Walter Colmer, John Ashe, William Radbert, Walter Were, Robert Pawlet, Ralph Hunte, John Hodge, John Wetecombe, John Godinge and Richard Attewe.
[77] For the history of these exhibitions, see N. Orme, 'The Byconyll Exhibitions at Oxford, 1502–1664', *Oxoniensia*, forthcoming.

From Ynys Wydrin to Glasynbri: Glastonbury in Welsh Vernacular Tradition

CERIDWEN LLOYD-MORGAN

No history of Glastonbury can ignore the Arthurian traditions localized there, any more than any account of King Arthur, whether scholarly or popular, can be complete without reference to Glastonbury. The identification of Geoffrey of Monmouth's *insula Auallonis* in the *Historia regum Britannie* or the *insula pomorum* of the *Vita Merlini* with Glastonbury certainly took place before the end of the twelfth century. With equal confidence we assume that the Arthurian legend is of Celtic, even specifically Welsh origin, notwithstanding the obscurity surrounding the precise date and details of the process which transformed the apparently historical Arthur into the warrior leader of early Welsh poetic tradition and thence into the courtly creature of twelfth- and thirteenth-century French romance.[1]

Whatever the ultimate origins of the Arthurian legend and the nature of early Welsh tradition in particular, it is clear that from at least the thirteenth century traditions that had evolved elsewhere – notably in France – began to be incorporated into the native Welsh stock concerning Arthur and his entourage. In earlier centuries, of course, Welsh literature was produced and transmitted orally and might only be set down in writing at a comparatively late date. It is salutary to recall that the earliest surviving Welsh manuscripts containing vernacular Arthurian literature were produced as late as the thirteenth century. The three earliest manuscripts of *Brut y Brenhinedd*, the Welsh versions of the *Historia regum Britannie*, have been dated to the thirteenth century, two of them to the beginning of that century,[2] and the Black Book of Carmarthen, whose poetry contains some of our earliest Arthurian references, was probably being copied around 1250.[3] Our total corpus of written vernacular literature is comparatively small compared with that of our near-

---

[1]   R. S. Loomis, *Arthurian Literature in the Middle Ages* (Oxford, 1959); Rachel Bromwich, 'Celtic Elements in Arthurian Romance: A General Survey', in *The Legend of Arthur in the Middle Ages*, ed. P. B. Grout, R. A. Lodge, C. E. Pickford and E. K. C. Varty (Cambridge, 1983), pp. 41–55.

[2]   *Brut y Brenhinedd, Llanstephan MS 1 Version*, ed. Brynley F. Roberts (Dublin, 1971), pp. xxiv, xxix, xxxvii; Brynley F. Roberts, 'Testunau Hanes Cymraeg Canol', in *Y Traddodiad Rhyddiaith yn yr Oesau Canol*, ed. Geraint Bowen (Llandysul, 1974), pp. 274–302, esp. 288 ff.

[3]   E. D. Jones on the manuscript in *Llyfr Du Caerfyrddin*, ed. A. O. H. Jarman (Cardiff, 1982), pp. xiii–xxiv.

est neighbours, Ireland and England, but there is no doubt that much material flourished in oral tradition. In many cases no written copy may have been
made until the advent of antiquarians like John Jones of Gellilyfdy in the
seventeenth century and Gwallter Mechain in the eighteenth, or the only
trace may be an enigmatic reference preserved in the Triads.

It is in this context that we must set the purpose of the present study,
which is to trace the references to Glastonbury in the Welsh vernacular
tradition. Cambro-Latin texts or Latin texts with Welsh associations, from the
Historia regum Britannie to the Welsh saints' lives, will not be included, for
they were produced in very different circumstances, for a different audience
and even for very different purposes. This is not to imply that those involved
in the production of vernacular texts referring to Glastonbury were unfamiliar with the written, Latin sources; indeed, the opposite is generally true, as
we shall see. Nor should it be assumed that the audience for whom the
Welsh texts were intended was unfamiliar with certain popular traditions
which, arguably, lay behind some of those Latin texts. But many of the Latin
texts were consciously designed for a particular purpose which had nothing
to do with popular tradition: much of the chronicle material originating in
Glastonbury Abbey itself would naturally adopt a particular standpoint,
whilst the *uitae* of SS Cadog and Gildas seem intended to demonstrate that
even as powerful a secular lord as Arthur must yield to the authority of the
saint and thus to the spiritual authority. Although the raw material of popular tradition may be present in these cases, it has been consciously reworked
with a specific motive in mind and thus distorted.

It is hoped that the present approach, concentrating on the vernacular
sources, will provide a commentary on the development of Arthurian prose
narrative in Welsh in the later Middle Ages as well as helping to clarify the
status of Glastonbury and its Arthurian associations within the Welsh vernacular tradition. In referring to Glastonbury in legend or history the surviving
vernacular sources use three place-names: Ynys Wydrin, Ynys Afallach, and
Glasynbri or Lasynbri, each of which will be examined in turn.

Ynys Afallach seems to be the earliest to appear in the written sources.
Afallach is first attested as a personal name, not a place-name, in one of the
early Welsh genealogies, where the Northern British dynasty of Coel Hen is
traced back to 'Aballac map Amalech, qui fuit Beli Magni filius, et Anna,
mater eius'.[4] It appears again in the pedigree of the rulers of Powys. Geoffrey
of Monmouth seems to have borrowed the name *Aballac* either from Harleian Genealogy I or a similar source; in the form *Ynys Afallach*, however, it is
ambiguous, for it could be construed as a personal name still ('the island of
Afallach') or as a common noun meaning, perhaps, 'place of apples'.[5] Be that
as it may, the Welsh form *Ynys Afallach* first appears from the thirteenth
century onwards in the Welsh *Brutiau*, the translations of Geoffrey's *Historia
regum Britannie*, where the Welsh redactors use it to translate his *insula Aual-*

4   *Early Welsh Genealogical Tracts*, ed. P. C. Bartrum (Cardiff, 1966), p. 9.
5   *Trioedd Ynys Prydein*, ed. Rachel Bromwich, 2nd ed. (Cardiff, 1978), pp. 266–8
(henceforth *TYP*).

Ionis.[6] The same form occurs in related texts, such as the triad 'Trywyr Gvarth a uu yn Ynys Prydein' ('Three Dishonoured Men who were in the Island of Britain'), which may not be much older than the late fourteenth-century Red Book of Hergest (Oxford, Jesus College 111), the earliest manuscript in which it is preserved.[7] As Rachel Bromwich has shown, this is the one triad in the Red Book group which seems entirely based on Geoffrey of Monmouth, probably immediately derived from one of the *Brutiau* in Welsh. According to the triad, at the battle of Camlan 'brathvyt Arthur yn angheuavl. Ac o hynny y bu uarv. Ac y myvn plas yn Ynys Auallach y cladvyt' ('Arthur was fatally wounded. And from that [wound] he died, and was buried in a hall on the Island of Afallach').

The same form was employed in Galfridian material as late as the seventeenth century, in a Welsh translation of selections from Alanus de Insulis's commentary on Geoffrey's *Prophetie Merlini*, which, according to Brynley F. Roberts, was probably based on the first printed edition of the commentary, produced in Frankfurt in 1603, and it may not predate by many years the dates of the two surviving manuscripts, one, Aberystwyth, National Library of Wales, Llanstephan 173, being early seventeenth century, and the other, National Library of Wales, Panton 68, bearing the date 5 May 1650.[8]

The form *Ynys Afallach* also appears in a short Welsh text based on Giraldus Cambrensis's accounts of the exhumation in Glastonbury Abbey in 1190 or 1191 of the supposed remains of Arthur and Guinevere. This translation, sometimes known as *Claddedigaeth Arthur* ('the Burial of Arthur') is, however, again fairly late.[9] The earliest manuscript in which it survives, Aberystwyth, National Library of Wales, Llanstephan 4, was copied around 1400, by one of the three main scribes of the Red Book of Hergest,[10] and the text itself may belong to the second half of the fourteenth century, an important period for translation activity in Wales. The text opens with a brief account of Arthur's coronation, borrowed from the companion narrative now known for convenience as 'The Birth of Arthur',[11] and ultimately based

---

[6]   See, for example, *Brut Dingestow*, ed. Henry Lewis (Cardiff, 1942), Book IX, ch. 4; Book XI, ch. 2 (pp. 148, 185); also *Brut y Brenhinedd*, ed. Roberts, pp. 49–50, note to line 782. The modern Welsh form, *Ynys Afallon*, now used exclusively in preference to *Ynys Afallach*, seems to have been first used by Theophilus Evans in his *Drych y Prif Oesoedd*, first published in 1716, a late example of devotion to the Galfridian or 'British' history. Evans uses *Ynys Afallon* in translating the inscription on the famous lead cross at Glastonbury, and gives Camden as his source; Theophilus Evans, *Drych y Prif Oesoedd*, ed. Garfield H. Hughes (Cardiff, 1961), p. 94. However, present-day use of this form in Welsh is almost certainly due to the influence of the long poem, *Ymadawiad Arthur*, by T. Gwynn Jones, written in 1902.

[7]   *TYP* no. 51, pp. 131–9; my translation.

[8]   Brynley F. Roberts, 'Cyfieithiad Cymraeg o Esboniad Alanus de Insulis ar y *Prophetiae Merlini*', *Bulletin of the Board of Celtic Studies* 22 (1966–8), 130–49.

[9]   Timothy Lewis and J. D. Bruce, 'The Pretended Exhumation of Arthur and Guinevere. An Unpublished Welsh Account Based on Giraldus Cambrensis', *Revue Celtique* 33 (1912), 432–51; D. Simon Evans, 'Dau gopi o destun', *Trivium* 3 (1968), 30–47.

[10]   Gifford Charles-Edwards, 'The Scribes of the Red Book of Hergest', *The National Library of Wales Journal* 21 (1980), 246–56, esp. 250, 255.

[11]   J. H. Davies, 'A Welsh Version of the Birth of Arthur', *Y Cymmrodor* 24 (1913),

on Geoffrey's *Historia regum Britannie,* one of the Welsh *Brutiau* probably
being the actual source, as the text itself suggests. Since the *Brutiau* do not
provide much detail, the redactor found himself forced to look elsewhere:

> Llyma hyspysrwyd llyfreu eclurach noc chwedyl y brut y wrth diwed
> arthur vrenhin. Ac y adnabot gwirioned am chwedleu dychymygyon
> geuawc adnabydet y darlleawdyr bot yma deu gabidwl gwedi eu
> hyspyssu on llyfyr ni yr hwnn a elwir drych yr eglwys.

> Here is information from books [which are] clearer than the stories of
> the Brut about the end of King Arthur. And in order to know the truth
> about false, imaginary stories, let the reader know that here are two
> chapters set forth from our book which is called the Mirror of the
> Church.[12]

The main source then is the *Speculum ecclesie,* but the account of the exhumation in *De principis instructione* is also used for the description of the sixteen
wounds in Arthur's head, and the discovery of Gwenhwyfar's bones, as well
as for the account of the founding of Glastonbury by Arthur and his setting
the image of the Virgin Mary in his shield. The Welsh redactor retains Giraldus's identification of Glastonbury with Avalon: 'ynys avallach. y lle a elwir
yr awr honn glastynbri' ('the island of Afallach, which is now called Glastonbury').[13]

At about the same time as Llanstephan 4 was being copied, another important Arthurian manuscript, Aberystwyth, National Library of Wales,
Peniarth 11, was produced in Glamorganshire, almost certainly for the same
patron, Hopcyn ap Thomas.[14] Peniarth 11 contains what is named in the
colophon on folio 279 as 'ystoryaeu seint greal' ('the stories of the holy
grail').[15] These comprise a Welsh translation of two early thirteenth-century
French prose romances, *La Queste del Saint Graal*[16] and *Perlesvaus.*[17] In the
second part of the text, based on the *Perlesvaus,* the redactor regularly trans-

---

247–64. It is possible that the two texts, relating the birth and the burial of Arthur,
were compiled by the same redactor and were originally, perhaps, a single text.

12   Llanstephan 4, 505r–v; my translation.

13   Llanstephan 4, 507r.

14   Charles-Edwards, 'The Scribes of the Red Book'; Brynley F. Roberts, 'Un o Lawys-
grifau Hopcyn ap Thomas o Ynys Dawy', *Bulletin of the Board of Celtic Studies* 22
(1966–8), 223–8; Prys Morgan, 'Glamorgan and the Red Book', *Morgannwg* 20 (1976),
42–60.

15   *Selections from the Hengwrt MSS,* ed. Robert Williams, 2 vols (London, 1876–92) I,
433 (henceforth *SG*); *Y Seint Greal* has been adopted as the most convenient title. See
also Ceridwen Lloyd–Morgan, 'A Study of *Y Seint Greal* in relation to *La Queste del
Saint Graal* and *Perlesvaus*' (unpubl. DPhil dissertation, University of Oxford, 1978),
and 'Perceval in Wales: Late Medieval Welsh Grail Traditions', in *The Changing Face of
Arthurian Romance: Essays on Arthurian Prose Romances in Memory of Cedric E. Pickford,*
ed. Alison Adams, Armel H. Diverres, Karen Stern and Kenneth Varty (Cambridge,
1986), pp. 78–91.

16   *La Queste del Saint Graal,* ed. A. Pauphilet (Paris, 1923) (henceforth *Q*).

17   *Le Haut Livre du Graal. Perlesvaus,* ed. W. A. Nitze and T. A. Jenkins, 2 vols
(Chicago, 1932–7).

lates 'Isle d'Avalon' in the French as 'Ynys Auallach', and, furthermore, introduces this same form in the first part where it was not suggested by the French source. The colophon of the *Queste del Saint Graal* refers to the knight Boorz narrating the adventures, which were then 'mises en escrit et gardees en l'almiere de Salebieres' ('set in writing and kept in the Library [or archive] of Salisbury'),[18] but in the Welsh version 'wynt aanuonet y ynys auallach oe cadw' ('they were sent to Ynys Afallach to be kept').[19]

Taken with the consistency with which the redactors of the texts discussed above, derived from Geoffrey of Monmouth, Giraldus Cambrensis and Alanus de Insulis, unhesitatingly refer to Ynys Afallach, this use of it by the translator of the *Seint Greal* may indicate that this name was traditional to the Welsh and was not simply an attempt to give a Welsh form for *insula Auallonis*.[20] Whether or not there had been an indigenous tradition connecting Arthur's death or disappearance with Ynys Afallach is, of course, another question. Had such a tradition once existed, it is still impossible to establish whether it was known to the redactors of these surviving sources, and equally uncertain whether those redactors perceived the element *Afallach* as a personal name still or identified it with the Island of Apples (*insula pomorum*) of the *Vita Merlini*.[21]

References to Ynys Afallach can be found occasionally in the work of the poets, notably in that of Lewis Glyn Cothi in the second half of the fifteenth century, in his poem addressed to another poet, Dafydd Llwyd o Fathafarn:

> Arthur o'i ddolur oedd wan,
> Ac o ymladd Cad Gamlan,
> Felly'n Ynys Afallach
> Y fo a aeth yn fyw iach.
>
> Cawn o feddygon honno
> Yn fy oes, pes cawn efo,
> Dygwn, nis ceisiwn, mewn cudd
> Drwy Ddyfi draw i Ddafydd.[22]

Here Dafydd Llwyd is said to have fallen off his horse, and the poet describes Arthur, weak from his wound after the battle of Camlan, being taken to Ynys Afallach, where he recovered life and health. Lewis then jokingly offers to bring doctors from that island back through the Dyfi river to heal Dafydd. A similar example occurs in Lewis Glyn Cothi's poem to Bedo Coch from Rhaeadr Gwy, where again the reference is to healing.[23]

---

[18] Q 279.33–280.1.
[19] *SG* 170.15–16.
[20] *Brut y Brenhinedd*, ed. Roberts, p. 50; J. E. Lloyd, 'The Death of Arthur', *Bulletin of the Board of Celtic Studies* 11 (1941–4), 158–60, at 160.
[21] *Life of Merlin. Geoffrey of Monmouth, Vita Merlini*, ed. and trans. Basil Clarke (Cardiff, 1973), line 908, p. 100.
[22] *Gwaith Dafydd Llwyd o Fathafarn*, ed. W. Leslie Richards (Cardiff, 1964), no. 96, lines 27–34, p. 187.
[23] 'Velly, val gwaith Avallach/Athrawon nev i'th roi'n iach . . .', see *Gwaith Lewis*

Although the poets undoubtedly had access to a vast store of oral tradition, on which they frequently drew in their highly referential verse, and although they often display familiarity with material which has not survived in written sources, at this date, the late fifteenth century, it is often impossible to tell whether they were reflecting genuine oral traditions or were influenced, directly or indirectly, by written literature. Certainly many Arthurian references in the poetry of this period are ultimately derived from written sources, including some of French origin. It seems unlikely, therefore, that Lewis Glyn Cothi was reflecting a purely indigenous tradition.

Turning now to Ynys Wydrin, one of the earliest authorities – if not *the* earliest – to suggest that this was the old Celtic name for Glastonbury is Giraldus Cambrensis. In his *Speculum ecclesie* he discusses the various names and their origins and this passage is retained in its entirety in the late fourteenth-century *Claddedigaeth Arthur*.[24] Of the name Ynys Wydrin the redactor states:

> Ef a notteit heuyt galw y lle hwnnw ynys wydrin o achaws auon aoed yny damgylchynu a lliw glas gwydrawl ar y dwfyr. ac wrth hynny y gelwis y Saesson hi gwedy y goresgyn glastynbri. kanys glas yn Saesnec yw gwydyr yghymraec.

> Also it was the custom to call that place Ynys Wydrin because of the river which surrounded it, and the glassy blue colour of the water. And for this reason the English after the conquest called it Glastynbri, for *glas* in English is *gwydyr* [glass] in Welsh.

But despite this explanation, and despite the apparently impeccable Welsh form of Ynys Wydrin, this name appears only rarely in the surviving written material. Apart from *Claddedigaeth Arthur*, based on Giraldus, the earliest reference seems to be as late as the fifteenth century, for example in Guto'r Glyn's poem to the house of Sir Richard Herbert, who was executed in 1469, and the reference itself, as often in this type of eulogy, is too cryptic to be illuminating for present purposes.[25]

Ynys Wydrin does appear again in a prose text, *Darogan yr Olew Bendigaid*, probably composed in the first half of the fifteenth century.[26] This short, composite text, linking Arthurian material drawn from a variety of sources with the legend of Thomas Becket and the Holy Oil, opens with an account

---

Glyn Cothi, ed. Gwallter Mechain and Tegid, 2 vols (Oxford and Denbigh, 1837–9) II, 348 (lines 25–6).

[24] Llanstephan 4, 507v.

[25] *Gwaith Guto'r Glyn*, ed. John Llywelyn Williams and Ifor Williams (Cardiff, 1939), no. xlix, lines 59–60, p. 133: 'Awn at organ y Teirgwent,/I Ynys Wydrin, gwin Gwent.'

[26] For the texts, see R. Wallis Evans, 'Darogan yr Olew Bendigaid a Hystdori yr Olew Bendigaid', *Llên Cymru* 14 (1981–2), 86–91; for discussion, see Ceridwen Lloyd-Morgan, 'Darogan yr Olew Bendigaid: chwedl o'r bymthegfed ganrif', *Llên Cymru* 14 (1981–2), 64–85, and 'Prophecy and Welsh Nationhood in the Fifteenth Century', *Transactions of the Honourable Society of Cymmrodorion* (1985), 9–26. Quotations are taken from the earliest manuscript, Aberystwyth, National Library of Wales, Peniarth 50, for which see Evans, 'Darogan yr Olew Bendigaid', pp. 88–9.

of Naciens, a character drawn from the romances of the French Vulgate Cycle, retiring from active service ('gwedy treulaw ohonaw y ieuengtid mewn ragorawl vilwryaeth') to become a hermit 'yr cappel periglus o ynys Wydrin' ('at the Perilous Chapel of Ynys Wydrin'). In view of the fact that the redactor of *Darogan yr Olew Bendigaid* is very heavily dependent on written sources in Welsh, French and Latin, and a written source can be found for virtually every morsel of Arthurian tradition he has crammed into the opening section, it seems likely that he borrowed this reference from a written text. Since many of the other proper names used have been divorced from their original narrative context before being incorporated into *Darogan yr Olew Bendigaid*, it is likely that this was also the case with Ynys Wydrin. One possible source is *Claddedigaeth Arthur*. Not only does the earliest manuscript of that text, Llanstephan 4, predate Peniarth 50, the earliest copy of *Darogan yr Olew Bendigaid*, it may well come from the same area. We have noted that the scribe of Llanstephan 4 was also involved in the production of the Red Book of Hergest for Hopcyn ap Thomas of Glamorgan, and it has been suggested that Peniarth 50 was copied at Neath Abbey, in the same area.[27] Even if there was no direct link between these two manuscripts, it is possible that the redactor of *Darogan yr Olew Bendigaid* had access to another manuscript of the account of the Glastonbury exhumation, for at least four later manuscripts of *Claddedigaeth Arthur* have come to light, none of them, apparently, being direct copies of Llanstephan 4, the evidence of variants indicating a number of lost exemplars.[28]

Since the instances of Ynys Wydrin in Welsh vernacular sources are extremely scarce, and in this last case, may be ultimately derived from Giraldus Cambrensis via the Welsh translation, it seems that those involved in the production of vernacular prose and poetry in the fourteenth and fifteenth centuries were somewhat unfamiliar with this name. Certainly it can no longer have been common in popular tradition about Arthur or Glastonbury, if indeed it ever was: it is possible that Giraldus himself, or a source used by him, invented the Welsh form to 'explain' the English name, and link it with Ynys Afallach.

If Ynys Wydrin appears only rarely, even in the literature of the fourteenth and fifteenth century, the English name, Glastonbury, once borrowed into Welsh rapidly becomes accepted as the name of the abbey and its surrounding settlement. The borrowing and retention of the English form, slightly adjusted to the demands of Welsh phonology as *(G)lastynbri* or *(G)lasymbri*, contrasts with the usual practice of medieval Welsh translators, who tried where possible to find traditional Welsh equivalents for proper names, as when the translator of *La Queste del Saint Graal* replaced 'L'almiere de Sales-

---

[27] First suggested by J. Gwenogvryn Evans in *Report on Manuscripts in the Welsh Language*, 2 vols (Historical Manuscripts Commission, London, 1898–1910) I, pt ii, 389; see also *TYP*, p. xxxviii; unpublished research by my colleague, Graham C. G. Thomas, tends to support this provenance.

[28] Evans, 'Dau gopi o destun', pp. 30–1.

bieres' with 'ynys auallach'.[29] The earliest borrowing of the English name Glastonbury into Welsh occurs in the Welsh redaction of the Life of St David, *Buchedd Dewi*, where the saint is credited with building the first church on the site. Although the original Latin *uita* was composed by Rhigyfarch at the end of the eleventh century, the Welsh version has been shown to belong to the fourteenth century.[30] Here the *Glastonia* of the Latin text has been replaced by the English borrowing:

> Odyna y deuth Dewi hyt yn Glastynburi, ac yno yr adeilawd ef eglwys.

> Dewi went thence to Glastynburi, and there he built a church.[31]

A further fourteenth-century instance, this time from the end of the century, occurs in the *Llyfr Arfau*, attributed to a Siôn Trefor of uncertain identity.[32] This is a treatise on heraldry, and in describing the heraldic arms borne by Uther Pendragon he states:

> A phob un o'r arveu hynn a ddug Arthur i vab, hyt pann welas y gwyrthieu ymynachloc Lasymbri. Ac yna, er moliant i'r Groes Vendigaid, ef a gymyrth arveu eraill, nid amgen no chroes o arian, ac ar y braich deheu iddi delw yr Arglwyddes Vair yn sevyll a'i Mab yn eisteu ar i braich deheu, mewn maes o wyrdd.[33]

> And all these arms were borne by his son Arthur until the time when he saw the miracles in the monastery of Glastonbury. And then, to the glory of the Holy Rood, he assumed other arms, namely, a cross argent, and on the dexter arms of the cross the effigy of the Lady Mary standing and her Son sitting on her right arm, in a field of green [or vert].[34]

At the same period, the Llanstephan 4 text of *Claddedigaeth Arthur*, following Giraldus, describes how Arthur's bones were found 'ym minnwent manachlawc glastynbri' ('in the cemetery of Glastonbury monastery'),[35] the same form, with some slight variation in spelling, occurring in other manuscripts of the same text. Like the redactor of *Buchedd Dewi*, then, that of *Claddedigaeth Arthur*, faced with the Latin *Glastonia* in the manuscript before him, turned to

---

[29]   Similarly the same translator rendered, for example, *Pennevoiseuse* in the *Perlesvaus* as *Penwed* (SG 380.37), *Rome* as *Rhufein* (SG 372.6–7). The same practice was regularly adopted with personal names, where Welsh equivalents were available.

[30]   *Buchedd Dewi*, ed. D. Simon Evans (Cardiff, 1959), p. xxxix: Welsh medium edition, based on Llanstephan 27, the Red Book of Talgarth, again the work of Hywel Vychan, scribe of Peniarth 11 and of substantial parts of the Red Book of Hergest, probably commissioned in this case by Rhys ap Thomas ab Einion, brother of Hopcyn ap Thomas. See also *The Welsh Life of St David*, ed. D. Simon Evans (Cardiff, 1988), pp. liv–lv. For the Latin text see, for example, A. W. Wade-Evans, 'Rhygyvarch's Life of Saint David', *Y Cymmrodor* 24 (1913), 1–73, at 10.

[31]   *The Welsh Life of St David*, ed. Evans, p. 4; *Buchedd Dewi*, ed. Evans, p. 6.

[32]   *Medieval Heraldry. Some Fourteenth-Century Heraldic Works*, ed. Evan J. Jones (Cardiff, 1943), pp. 2–94.

[33]   *Llyfr Arfau*, ibid. pp. 86, 88.

[34]   *Ibid*. pp. 87, 89.

[35]   Llanstephan 4, 505v.

the English name, which, we must therefore conclude, was that most familiar to him. No attempt was made to link the site of the abbey with Ynys Afallach or Ynys Wydrin, except where the source did so.

The English name crops up again in the first half of the fifteenth century, in *Darogan yr Olew Bendigaid*, where it occurs in the context of the tradition relating to Arthur's heraldic arms, just as in the *Llyfr Arfau*. In the earliest manuscript of *Darogan yr Olew Bendigaid*, Peniarth 50, Naciens, in his life as a hermit in the Perilous Chapel at Ynys Wydrin, so pleased God that angels would come down to serve mass: 'mal y gwelas arthur y dydd y danuon-awdd yr arglwyddes veir eiddaw y groes yr honn adewis ef ymanachlawc ynglastynberi a mi ay gwelais yno' ('as Arthur saw on the day that the Lady Mary sent to him the cross which he left in the monastery in Glastonbury and I myself saw it there').[36] As a result of this gift of the cross, Arthur henceforth carried instead of his former heraldic device a shield of green with a white cross with an image of the Virgin in the top right-hand quarter, exactly as described in the *Llyfr Arfau*.

It might seem possible that the *Llyfr Arfau* was the source at this point, albeit that that text seems to be of north-eastern provenance, in contrast to the south-eastern origins of Peniarth 50. However, a more likely source is a Latin text, and a Glastonbury one at that, namely the *Cronica siue antiquitates Glastoniensis ecclesie* compiled by John of Glastonbury shortly after 1340.[37] In his chronicle John gives by far the fullest extant account of the events referred to in the Welsh *Darogan yr Olew Bendigaid*. Arthur, he records, was called by an angel to go to the *heremitorium* of St Mary Magdalene at Beckery, near Glastonbury. Arthur decided to take a squire or knight with him but, the night before, the latter was fatally wounded after dreaming he had gone to the chapel and stolen a candlestick from it. Arthur accordingly sets out alone the next morning, and at the chapel sees an old man saying mass. During the service the Virgin Mary appears and offers up her son. After the service,

> domina et gloriosa mater in signum predictorum dicto regi crucem contulit cristallinam que usque in hunc diem de dono eiusdem regis in thesauraria Glastonie honorifice collocatur et custoditur ac annuatim tempore quadragesimali in processionibus feriis quartis et sextis per conuentum institutis defertur quia feria hoc miraculum factum est, scilicet die cinerum.

> that lady, the glorious Mother, brought to the king, as a token of the events described above, a crystal cross, which to this day is honourably housed and guarded in the treasury of Glastonbury and is carried every year during Lent through the convent, in the processions which are appointed for Wednesdays and Fridays, since this miracle occurred on a ferial day – that is on Ash Wednesday.[38]

---

[36] Peniarth 50, 90r.
[37] On dating, see *The Chronicle of Glastonbury Abbey*, ed. Carley, pp. xxv–xxx.
[38] *Cronica*, ch. 34 (ed. Carley, pp. 78–9).

Having repented of his sins, Arthur subsequently changed his arms to those described in detail in the *Llyfr Arfau*.

John of Glastonbury's chronicle is derived from a variety of written sources, to which he seems to have been fairly faithful, tending if anything to abridge rather than to add creatively further details from his own imagination.[39] We can assume, then, that he was recording a genuine tradition. The same tale of Arthur and the squire, with only minor variation, is included in the French grail romance of *Perlesvaus*.[40] Although W. A. Nitze, in his edition of the *Perlesvaus*, concluded that John of Glastonbury was *not* indebted to the *Perlesvaus* for this narrative,[41] more recently James P. Carley has suggested that the *Perlesvaus* was indeed John's source. This possibility is strengthened by Carley's discovery of a fourteenth-century fragment of the *Perlesvaus* at Wells Cathedral, which, he believes, could have been copied from a French exemplar in the Glastonbury library itself.[42] If both the *Perlesvaus* and a copy of John's own chronicle were kept at the abbey, it is not impossible that the redactor of the Peniarth 50 version of *Darogan yr Olew Bendigaid* had come across this story in a Glastonbury manuscript. It is perfectly credible that a Welshman should travel from Glamorgan to Glastonbury, on pilgrimage perhaps, and the redactor's comment on the famous cross, 'mi ay gwelais yno' ('I saw it there') should perhaps be taken at face value, rather than as a classic authority formula. This comment is omitted in all the other 17 manuscript copies of the Welsh text traced so far, and I have already suggested elsewhere that the redactor of *Darogan yr Olew Bendigaid* was in fact the scribe of Peniarth 50.[43]

It is also possible that the redactor of the *Llyfr Arfau* too was familiar with the same section of John of Glastonbury's chronicle, since the latter provides the explanation for the reference to the 'gwyrthieu ymynachloc Lasymbri', the miracles seen by Arthur in the monastery at Glastonbury. This opens up the interesting perspective of at least two Welsh redactors being familiar with Glastonbury manuscripts. It should not be forgotten, moreover, that Llanstephan 4, only a few decades older than Peniarth 50, derives from two Glastonbury texts: Giraldus Cambrensis's *De principis instructione* and *Speculum ecclesie*. Unfortunately, the Welsh translation of *Perlesvaus*, although contemporary with Llanstephan 4, and possibly produced for the same patron, is definitely *not* based on the version of that French romance found in the fragment discovered by Carley.[44]

---

[39]   See *The Chronicle of Glastonbury Abbey*, ed. Carley, pp. xxxv–xlv; compare *Perlesvaus*, ed. Nitze and Jenkins, II, 114.

[40]   *Ibid.* I, 26–38.

[41]   *Ibid.* II, 105–20.

[42]   James P. Carley, 'A Fragment of *Perlesvaus* at Wells Cathedral Library', *Zeitschrift für romanische Philologie* (forthcoming).

[43]   Lloyd-Morgan, '*Darogan yr Olew Bendigaid*', pp. 79–80.

[44]   A study of the variants in the extant French exemplars indicates that the Welsh version is closest to the early printed editions of the *Perlesvaus*, published in 1516 and 1523; of the manuscripts, its nearest relative is the thirteenth-century manuscript, Oxford, Bodleian Library, Hatton 82. See *Perlesvaus*, ed. Nitze and Jenkins, I, 14; II,

The cymricised forms of the English name Glastonbury remained current into the sixteenth century. The earliest manuscript of *Buchedd Collen*, the Life of St Collen – Cardiff, Central Library, Hafod 19 – which is dated 1536,[45] describes how the saint moved to Glastonbury Abbey, 'i vynachloc glansymbri', and was even made abbot, but rather than take up these duties he chooses the harder task ('drymach a chaledach') of going out to preach amongst the people. After three years he returns to the monastery for another five, but finally retires 'i vynydd glassymbyri' ('to the mountain of Glastonbury', namely the Tor), where he makes himself a hermit cell, from which, in due course, he is invited to dine with Gwyn ap Nudd, king of the underworld or otherworld in Welsh tradition.

A few years later, in the 1540s, Elis Gruffudd, the 'soldier of Calais', was busy compiling his chronicle of the history of the world in Welsh, to send back home from Calais to his native Flintshire.[46] His earliest references to Glastonbury are derived from *Darogan yr Olew Bendigaid* and thus have already been discussed above. However, the name appears again in a rather different context. Whereas the *Historia regum Britannie* – or vernacular versions of it – provides the chief source for Elis's account of Arthur's career, material from a wide variety of other sources has been carefully incorporated to add further detail or add more colour to the narrative. Thus Elis states that Arthur's last battle took place 'ar vaes eang garllaw mynachlog lasenbri' ('on a broad field near the monastery of Glastonbury').[47] Unfortunately, Elis Gruffudd's habit of freely paraphrasing his sources, and his regular use of orally circulating traditions as well as known written texts, make it difficult to pinpoint the precise origin of such a reference.

However, his most interesting reference to Glastonbury occurs not in his Arthurian narrative itself, but in his discussion of the Galfridian history. Here he refers explicitly to the fact that, in his day, it was the English, not the

24–39; Lloyd-Morgan, 'A Study of *Y Seint Greal*', pp. 12–14. In passing it may be noted that Hatton 82 belonged to Brian Fitz Alan, who, despite his family's northern English origins, was based in the Welsh borders in the 1280s (*Perlesvaus*, ed. Nitze and Jenkins, II, 3), and Oswestry and its environs were included in the possessions of the Fitz Alan family (*ibid*. II, 205–7). This not only shows how a copy of the *Perlesvaus* could find its way into a Welsh-speaking area on the borders in the late thirteenth century, it also explains how a verse summary of the story of Cahus and the candlestick, taken from the *Perlesvaus*, came to be included in the closing section of the Anglo-Norman *Fouke le Fitz Waryn*. The surviving prose version of this text, whose narrative is set in the Oswestry area, was probably compiled *ca* 1325–40, and based on an earlier verse redaction. See *Fouke le Fitz Waryn*, ed. E. J. Hathaway *et al.* (Oxford, 1975), pp. xxvii, 60–1.

45 *The Lives of the British Saints*, ed. S. Baring-Gould and John Fisher, 4 vols (London, 1907–13) IV, 375–8. This manuscript also contains the second oldest copy of *Darogan yr Olew Bendigaid*.

46 For biographical details and general surveys of his chronicle, see Thomas Jones, 'A Welsh Chronicler in Tudor England', *Welsh History Review* 1 (1960–3), 1–17; Prys Morgan, 'Elis Gruffudd of Gronant – Tudor Chronicler Extraordinary', *Proceedings of the Flintshire Historical Society* 25 (1971–2), 9–20, and 'Elis Gruffudd yng Nghalais', *Bulletin of the Board of Celtic Studies* 21 (1964–6), 214–18.

47 Aberystwyth, National Library of Wales, 5276D, 340r.

Welsh, who believed most fervently that Arthur was not dead but sleeping, and would return one day. Moreover, he locates this legend at Glastonbury, including the tradition that people had actually seen Arthur there:

> Ac etto J mae yn vwy J son wyntt [sc. y Saeson] am danno ef nonnyni, kanis J maentt twy yn dywedud ac yn koelio yn gadarn J kyuyd ef dracheuyn J vod yn vrenin, yr hrain yn i hoppiniwn a ddywaid J vod ef ynn kysgu mewn googof dan vryn garllaw *glasynbri*. Ac yn wir pe gellid hroddi koel J [r]ai ymrauaelion bobl or ardal hwnnw, yvo ymddangoses ac a ymddiuannodd a llawer o bobyl mewn llawer modd hryuedd erys trychant o vlynyddoedd.

> And yet they [the English] talk much more about him than we do, for they say and strongly believe that he will rise again to be king. In their opinion he is sleeping in a cave under a hill near Glastonbury and indeed if one could give credence to many diverse people from that district he appeared and conversed with many people in many strange ways three hundred years ago.[48]

In view of Elis Gruffudd's use of oral tradition elsewhere in his chronicle, as he himself states quite unambiguously at times, this statement can be accepted with little or no hesitation as a genuine tradition which he had heard.[49]

One striking fact which emerges from a survey of the incidence of the three place-names Ynys Afallach, Ynys Wydrin and Glasynbri, is the absence of the first two in the earlier, native Welsh literature. Apart from the extremely faint possibility that the *Caer Wydyr* ('fortress of glass') in the early Arthurian poem, 'Preiddeu Annwfn', in the Book of Taliesin, might have some vague connection with Ynys Wydrin, there is a deafening silence. None of the early triads include any references, and the only triad which does so is both late (from the end of the fourteenth century) and clearly based on the *Brutiau*. The poetry contains few examples, and those occur mainly in the fifteenth century; whilst the early prose tales are silent on the subject of the death or disappearance of Arthur and the place where he may have been buried or gone to be healed. Virtually all that remains in the earliest strata of written sources is the enigmatic reference to Arthur's grave in *Englynion y Beddau* (The Stanzas of the Graves) in the Black Book of Carmarthen.[50]

Thus all the examples we have of Ynys Afallach and Ynys Wydrin in surviving vernacular sources derive directly or indirectly from chronicle material of one kind or another, or appear – as in the example in the Welsh translation of the *Queste del Saint Graal* – to be suggested by that chronicle

---

[48]   National Library of Wales, 5276D, 342r.
[49]   James P. Carley, *Glastonbury Abbey. The Holy House at the Head of the Moors Adventurous* (Woodbridge, 1988), pp. 98–9, n. 14, suggests that Elis Gruffudd's account may be a variant of the tradition reflected in *Buchedd Collen*, where the castle of Gwyn ap Nudd is located in or on the Tor.
[50]   *Llyfr Du Caerfyrddin*, ed. Jarman, p. 41, line 135, p. 102.

tradition. In this respect, as in so many aspects of surviving Welsh Arthurian material, the influence of Geoffrey of Monmouth seems of crucial importance. Despite the earlier existence of Afallach as a personal name and the possibility that in unanimously and independently adopting Ynys Afallach as a translation of *insula Auallonis*, the redactors of the Welsh *Brutiau* were reflecting a pre-existing tradition, it is almost certainly the *Brutiau* which set the trend for the use of this form in other Welsh texts. This, together with the remarkable scarcity of references to Ynys Wydrin in vernacular sources, suggests that *if* these two names were indeed authentic, and did exist in early Welsh tradition, then there must have been a gap or break in that tradition. This could be a time gap: that is, the original Welsh traditions about a Celtic paradise full of apple trees and associated with a healing female figure or perhaps nine, as reflected in the *insula pomorum* of the *Vita Merlini*, could have been largely forgotten, but were given a new lease of life after the injection of Galfridian vitality. The Welsh storytellers and poets could easily have recognized and remembered the names Ynys Afallach and Ynys Wydrin when something similar was set before them, albeit in a new context. This process can be documented elsewhere, for example, when the redactor of the Welsh translation of *Perlesvaus*, after initial hesitation, recognizes in the French Lohout, the son of Arthur who is killed by Cei, the equivalent of Llacheu, who otherwise appears only in the earliest poetry.[51] In this way the names could be reincorporated into Welsh tradition. Ynys Wydrin, not appearing in so often translated and copied a text as Geoffrey's *Historia regum Britannie*, seems not to have been readopted (or adopted) so enthusiastically, despite its appearance in the Welsh version of Giraldus's account of the Glastonbury exhumation.

However, there may also have been an increasing gap between, on the one hand, those redactors involved in the copying-down of literature, or in the composition or translation of literature in a written form, and on the other hand those storytellers and other transmitters of tradition who were active chiefly or solely in the oral medium. It must be stressed that the sources we now possess are, in their present form, essentially written, literary texts, whatever their ultimate origins might have been. And of course much material which must surely have circulated in the Middle Ages, including some of the Welsh Tristan material, for instance, or the Tegau Eurfron stories,[52] subsists only in very late manuscript copies whose own origins seem to lie in early modern oral tradition.

From the point of view of Arthurian studies in particular, the lack of any indigenous written sources about Ynys Afallach or Ynys Wydrin predating the influential works of Giraldus Cambrensis and Geoffrey of Monmouth demonstrates once again the need for caution when tracing the origins of the Arthurian legend, emphasizing as it does the lack of concrete evidence of

[51]   Lloyd-Morgan, 'Perceval in Wales', p. 88.
[52]   Graham C. G. Thomas, 'Chwedlau Tegau Eurfron a Thristfardd, Bardd Urien Rheged', *Bulletin of the Board of Celtic Studies* 24 (1970–2), 1–9.

any fully developed, native Welsh Arthurian 'saga' or corpus of stories before the advent of the *Historia regum Britannie*.

But if the use of Ynys Afallach and Ynys Wydrin in Welsh seems not only late but indicative of dependence on written rather than oral sources, examples of the name of Glastonbury itself suggest the opposite. Although some of the earliest texts where forms such as *Glasynbri* occur are derived from written sources, the name itself seems to be a direct, oral borrowing from English. But whereas in the earlier sources Ynys Afallach in particular seemed to refer to the legendary resting-place of Arthur, leaving somewhat ambiguous at times the possible identification of that place with Glastonbury, in the texts where forms such as *Glastynbri* appear it is very definitely the abbey which is intended: it is even specified as *'mynachloc* lasynbri' ('the *monastery* of Glastonbury') in many cases. This definite identification and the English-derived form indicate familiarity with the abbey and the traditions conserved in the literature associated with it. And we have the fascinating possibility of at least two Welsh redactors, in the late fourteenth and early fifteenth centuries, not only visiting the abbey but also dipping into its library. These links need not surprise us. The distance involved in travelling to Glastonbury, especially from south-east Wales, is modest, when we consider that in the Middle Ages many Welsh people travelled to Oxford, London, Paris, even Rome. Doubtless there were Welsh pilgrims on the road to Glastonbury, for were not some of our own Welsh saints associated with the abbey? According to *Buchedd Dewi*, St David himself founded the church there, and later in the Middle Ages the monks claimed to have some of his relics (although the Welsh, understandably, preferred to believe they were at St Davids).[53] Again, *Buchedd Collen* asserts that Collen briefly became abbot of Glastonbury and spent many years subsequently in a hermit cell on the Tor.[54]

By the fifteenth and sixteenth centuries, it would seem that Welsh tradition viewed Glastonbury above all as the site of the abbey, the place of pilgrimage perhaps, with Arthurian connections certainly, but more of a Christian holy place than the resting-place of the king, Arthur, who would rise again. Perhaps the Glastonbury exhumation had indeed convinced the Welsh that Arthur was dead and buried rather than asleep, but perhaps popular Welsh tradition preferred its own localizations of the legend in Wales. It is also worth emphasizing that the earliest Arthurian references in

---

[53]   Glanmor Williams, *The Welsh Church from Conquest to Reformation* (Cardiff, 1962), p. 494.
[54]   And if Welsh redactors made use of Glastonbury sources, there is also evidence that Glastonbury chroniclers were themselves, at an earlier period, familiar with Welsh traditions. Leaving aside the uncertain status of the references by Giraldus Cambrensis to Ynys Wydrin, the story of Ider fab Nudd, which precedes the candlestick story in John of Glastonbury's *Cronica*, and which John probably inherited from Adam of Damerham's *Libellus* compiled around 1290 (*AD*, ed. Hearne, I, 47), seems to derive from Welsh tradition. This is suggested by the obviously Welsh name of Ider, and his patronymic, as well as by the localization of his battle with the three giants in North Wales.

Welsh written sources locate Arthur and his associates in the North of Britain or in Cornwall, rather than in Somerset. But in view of the fact that many of the sources discussed above are from the late fourteenth and the fifteenth century, it should be stressed that during this period the name of the true *mab darogan* ('the son of prophecy') or returning saviour-king was not Arthur, but Owein. Yvain de Galles (or 'Owein Lawgoch'), Owain Glyndŵr and Owain Tudur were identified with this Owain, and the legend was consciously manipulated during the fifteenth century with the aim of securing support for the Tudor dynasty.[55] To some Welshmen the battle of Bosworth in 1485 realized the ancient dream of setting a Welshman on the English throne, and the return, therefore, of the *mab darogan*. It is understandable, then, that Elis Gruffudd, writing in the 1540s, should have stressed that it was the English who spoke most about Arthur as the once and future king, and located his sleeping-place as a cave under a hill at Glastonbury.

[55]   R. Wallis Evans, 'Prophetic Poetry', in *A Guide to Welsh Literature*, ed. A. O. H. Jarman and Gwilym Rees Hughes, 2 vols (Swansea, 1976–9) II, 278–97; Glanmor Williams, 'Prophecy, Poetry and Politics in Mediaeval and Tudor Wales', in his *Religion, Language and Nationality in Wales* (Cardiff, 1979), pp. 71–86; *Brut y Brenhinedd*, ed. Roberts, pp. 55–62.

Glastonbury, Joseph of Arimathea and the Grail in John Hardyng's Chronicle

FELICITY RIDDY

Late in life, long after most of us will have given up active research, John Hardyng wrote two versions of his verse Chronicle. He was nearly eighty when he finished the first, which covers the history of England from the creation of the race of giants up to 1437. Hoping for financial reward, he presented it in 1457 to Henry VI. It survives in only one manuscript, London, British Library, Lansdowne 204, which is apparently the presentation copy.[1] About three years later he started the second and much shorter version for Richard, duke of York, who in 1460 laid claim to Henry's throne. York was killed in December of that year, when Hardyng was only part of the way through his new version, but he continued writing for presentation to York's son Edward, earl of March, who became king in May 1461. These events are themselves recorded in the Chronicle, which breaks off in the spring of 1463. Hardyng was still working on the epilogue in the autumn of 1464, and probably died at the age of about eighty-six in the following year.[2] The second version was much more widely read than the first: it survives in twelve more or less complete manuscripts and three fragments, and was printed twice by Grafton in 1543.[3]

These circumstances are worth reiterating because they have a direct bearing on the nature of the texts of the two versions. There has been been an understandable tendency in the past to blur the two, and for literary historians to draw upon them simultaneously as if they were interchangeable. The second version, however, is not merely an abridgement of the first, but a rewriting, under different circumstances and sometimes introducing different material. When Hardyng says to Henry VI in the proem to the Long Chronicle that it is 'Thus newly made for Rememorance/Whiche no man

---

[1] This text has never been printed in full. It is currently being edited by James Simpson, of Girton College, Cambridge. I am editing the life of Arthur from both versions of the Chronicle for Medieval English Texts, Heidelberg.

[2] For biographical details, see C. L. Kingsford, 'The First Version of Hardyng's Chronicle', *English Historical Review* 27 (1912), 462–82, and A. Gransden, *Historical Writing in England II, c. 1307 to the Early Sixteenth Century* (London, 1982), pp. 274–87.

[3] One of the fragments is of a seventeenth-century copy. The manuscripts are listed in E. D. Kennedy, 'John Hardyng and the Holy Grail', *Arthurian Literature* 8 (1989), 185–206, at 191, n. 16. All quotations in this article from the Short Chronicle are taken from London, British Library, Harley 661, unless otherwise stated. The Short Chronicle was edited by H. Ellis, *The Chronicle of Iohn Hardyng* (London, 1812).

hath in world but only ye' (2v), he may be speaking the literal truth. He may have given away in Lansdowne 204 the sole complete copy, never imagining that at his age he would want to do it all over again, and have found himself left with only a draft or a pile of rough notes. When he began the Short Chronicle in 1460, possibly at the instigation of a Lincolnshire Yorkist who saw the use to which it could be put in buttressing the duke of York's claim to the throne, he may have had to work more or less from scratch.[4] The differences between the two texts are at times so great that it seems unlikely that Hardyng could have had a complete copy of the Long Chronicle in front of him when he wrote the later version. The Short Chronicle, moreover, was not finished. A. S. G. Edwards has demonstrated that there are many lines missing from the second halves of the rhyme royal stanzas in which it is composed.[5] Hardyng seems to have had difficulty in thinking up enough 'b' rhymes, and left gaps which he intended to fill when he had completed the Chronicle. Since only a few years before he had been able to think of 'b' rhymes by the score, it looks as if his memory was failing, and this seems to be borne out by various oddities in the text.

All this means that the versions differ in status as well as in content. The Long Chronicle was overseen for presentation by Hardyng himself; he had a direct interest in the Lansdowne manuscript as a means of self-advancement and so there is a strong probability that the marginal glosses added during the final stages of its preparation were authorized by him.[6] The Short

---

[4]   Hardyng was constable of Sir Robert Umfreville's castle at Kyme in Lincolnshire, at least until the latter's death in January 1436/7. There is evidence that Hardyng remained in Lincolnshire thereafter. The Short Chronicle begins with a dedication to the duke of York which includes the 'new' pedigree he adopted in 1460 when he laid claim to Henry VI's throne, and the whole work can be read as a Yorkist genealogy. It seems likely that the reason for the popularity of the Short Chronicle is that it was published as a piece of Yorkist propaganda, and it may have been commissioned as such. A possible patron is the Yorkist Sir Thomas Borough of Gainsborough, sheriff of Lincoln, who is mentioned in several manuscripts of the Short Chronicle. I shall present the detailed evidence for these views in a future article.

[5]   A. S. G. Edwards, 'The Manuscripts and Texts of the Second Version of John Hardyng's *Chronicle*', *England in the Fifteenth Century*, ed. D. Williams (Woodbridge, 1987), pp. 75–84.

[6]   J. Simpson kindly informs me (private communication) that he has tentatively identified six glossing hands in Lansdowne 204 in addition to the hand of the text. Only two are contemporaneous with the production of the manuscript. Hand 2, writing at a late stage in the production of the book, sometimes corrected or added to the glosses written by Hand 1. Hand 2 added the contents-list before the manuscript was bound as well as all the chapter headings. Many of Hand 2's additions cite supposed sources, some wildly inaccurate. Simpson's views have been independently endorsed by J. Withrington, 'The Arthurian Epitaph in Malory's *Morte Darthur*', *Arthurian Literature* 7 (1987), 103–44. I believe that both hands may possibly be the work of one scribe writing at different times and, more importantly, that all the glosses in the parts of the manuscript on which I have worked emanate from Hardyng himself. Whoever was responsible for the last-minute glossing was an obsessive tinkerer who knew the kinds of material that Hardyng had been reading or should have read, and who was forgetful, careless or a manufacturer of evidence. Hardyng seems to have been all three, though since he probably worked on the Long Chronicle

Chronicle, on the other hand, is in this one respect like the *Canterbury Tales*, which was also published after its author's death: there is no authorized text, and although the presumption is that Hardyng composed the glosses,[7] they may well have been added by whoever was responsible for publication. It is in order to emphasize the differences between them that I call the two versions by different names.

Although neither version of the Chronicle has much value as history, Hardyng's understanding of the British past, and the uses to which he puts it, are nevertheless revealing. In particular, his work shows, as Valerie Lagorio and James Carley have both pointed out,[8] how far the Glastonbury version of Britain's early history had come to be accepted elsewhere in England in the century after John of Glastonbury wrote his *Cronica siue antiquitates Glastoniensis ecclesie*. Hardyng was a northerner who had long been resident in Lincolnshire; although he could read French and Latin he was an old soldier, not a university man. He probably did not consult either William of Malmesbury's *De antiquitate Glastonie ecclesie* or John of Glastonbury's *Cronica* directly, as I hope to show; instead, his knowledge of them seems to have been refracted through intermediaries. Kingsford demonstrates that the final section of the Long Chronicle must derive from a Latin or English *Brut*;[9] the legendary part, on the other hand, seems to be based primarily on a version of Geoffrey of Monmouth's *Historia regum Britannie* or a close derivative.[10] The version of the *Historia* which Hardyng consulted may have contained interpolated Glastonbury material; certainly, reading his work helps us to see how Glastonbury's account of its own past has been diffused through various levels of fifteenth-century culture.

It has long been assumed that, whether or not Hardyng knew John of Glastonbury's *Cronica*, he must have encountered the prophecy of Melkin, the earliest surviving occurrence of which is in John's text, and which is held to lie behind Hardyng's mysterious 'Mewynus/The Cronycler in Britayne

---

over several years, it is not surprising that he should have had difficulty in remembering what he had read. In this article I treat all the glosses in both hands as having been composed by Hardyng.

7   Although, in the sections of the text on which I have worked, there is usually broad general agreement among the manuscripts about the general content and positioning of glosses, there is often considerable variation in detail.

8   V. M. Lagorio, 'The Evolving Legend of St Joseph of Glastonbury', *Speculum* 46 (1971), 209–31, at 225; *The Chronicle of Glastonbury Abbey*, ed. Carley, p. liii.

9   Kingsford, 'The First Version', p. 478.

10   Hardyng takes over directly at least one of Geoffrey's seven acknowledgements of Gildas as a source: 'Whose names all also and all thair' werkes / Gyldas dyd wryte as knowen wele these clerkes / Ryght in his boke titled and so hight / De victoria aurelii ambrosii' (41v), which translates Geoffrey's 'eorum nomina et actus in libro repperiuntur quem Gildas de uictoria Aurelii Ambrosii inscripsit'. See *La Légende arthurienne: études et documents*, ed. E. Faral, 3 vols (Paris, 1929) III, 72. (Geoffrey's allusions to Gildas are discussed by N. Wright, 'Geoffrey of Monmouth and Gildas', *Arthurian Literature* 2 [1982], 1–40.) That Hardyng's source was a Latin, not an English, version of Geoffrey seems clear from his statement on 38v: 'As cronycle sayth the sexte and fourty yer' / Oute of latyne as I can hit translate.'

tonge full fyne' (28r). 'Mewynus' is mentioned only in the Short Chronicle.[11] W. W. Skeat, presumably following Leland, conjectured that 'Mewynus' was John of Glastonbury's Melkin, and the identification has been strongly urged by James Carley.[12] 'Mewynus' is certainly a plausible reading of 'Melkynus': an Anglicana *w* can easily be confused with *lk*. We know that Hardyng must have known the Melkin prophecy in some form since in the Long Chronicle he includes information – about Joseph's two phials and his burial at Glastonbury – which derives from it. Nevertheless, since this information occurs in other texts without attribution to Melkin, it is possible that Hardyng came across it elsewhere without being aware of its origins.[13] This would explain why 'Mewynus' is not mentioned in the Long Chronicle where, if he were Melkin, he might be expected to occur. In the Short Chronicle, where he is referred to at least five times, Hardyng does not mention the two phials. Joseph is buried at Glastonbury, to be sure, but since Mordrains, Nascien, and Galaad's heart are all buried there too, quite uncanonically, it looks as if by the time Hardyng was writing Glastonbury was felt to be an appropriate burial ground for any saints with Arthurian connections. This seems to be borne out by the fact that in Henry Lovelich's translation of the Vulgate *Estoire del Saint Graal*, made shortly before the Long Chronicle, Joseph is

---

[11] In the early part of the Long Chronicle, especially the reign of Constantine, Hardyng alludes several times to a source called 'Martyne', 'the Romayne cronycler' (49v) and 'cronycler of Romany' (43v), but he has nothing to do with 'Mewynus'. He is Martinus Polonus, a thirteenth-century Dominican whose *Chronicon pontificum et imperatorum* was used quite frequently by English historians, including Ranulf Higden in his *Polychronicon*. There were copies of Martinus Polonus's work in several Lincolnshire libraries: at the Carmelite convent in Lincoln, at Bardney Abbey, and at the Dominican convent in Boston. (For the first two see J. R. Liddell, ' "Leland's" Lists of Manuscripts in Lincolnshire Monasteries', *English Historical Review* 54 [1939], 88–95, at 90 and 92; for the third see N. R. Ker, *Medieval Libraries of Great Britain* [London, 1964], p. 11.)

[12] *Joseph of Arimathie*, ed. W. W. Skeat, EETS os 44 (1871), p. xli; *The Chronicle of Glastonbury Abbey*, ed. Carley, p. liii. John Leland identifies Hardyng's 'Mewynus' with Melkin in his *Commentarii de scriptoribus Britannicis* (ed. A. Hall, 2 vols [Oxford, 1709] I, 42): 'Certe plausibilius facero, si lectorem admonuero, hunc Melchinum non uno in loco Mevinum vocari a Joanne Hardingo, qui Historiam nostrae gentis, regnante Henrico sexto, rhythmis Anglicis scripsit, publicam fecit.' (See J. Carley, 'Melkin the Bard and Esoteric Tradition at Glastonbury Abbey', *The Downside Review* 99 [1981], 1–17, at 4–5.) Leland's claim that Melkin wrote a *Historiola de rebus Britannicis* may well derive from Hardyng's description of Mewyn/Melkin as 'the Britouns Croniclere'.

[13] It occurs without attribution, for example, in a Latin *Brut* in Oxford, Bodleian Library, Rawlinson C. 398 (*S.C.* 12252), owned by Hardyng's younger contemporary, Sir John Fortescue: 'Ioseph uero ab Armathia ibidem sepultus est [i.e., at Glastonbury] iuxta dictam ecclesiam cum duabus fialis plenis de sudore Christi sanguineo quas secum de terra sancta attulerat' (9r). This manuscript is referred to by Kennedy, 'John Hardyng', p. 187, n. 7. The text is not a standard Latin *Brut*, and a later note in the manuscript attributes it to one Richard Rede who has not been identified. It cannot be Hardyng's source because although it includes Joseph's mission and Arviragus's gift of the Twelve Hides it does not contain the story of Joseph's crucifix or, more importantly, an account of the second founding of Glastonbury by Phagan and Divian or Deruvian in the reign of Lucius.

buried in the 'Abbey of Glaystyngbery' too.[14] Nevertheless the question of who, if not Melkin, the 'Mewynus' of the Short Chronicle might be, remains.

Hardyng's first allusion to 'Mewynus' is as his source for Joseph's conversion of King Arviragus:

> Joseph conuerte this kynge Arviragus
> By his prechynge to knowe the lawe devyne
> And baptised hym as wretyn hath Mewynus
> The Cronycler in Britayne tonge full fyne.   (28r)

This conversion is itself an oddity because Arviragus, who is a good pagan in the *Historia regum Britannie*, quite specifically does not become a Christian in John of Glastonbury's *Cronica* (although he gives Avalon to Joseph), and Hardyng does not make him convert in the Long Chronicle.[15] It looks as if 'Mewynus' at this juncture is only there to provide a rhyme (or what Hardyng thought of as a rhyme) for 'Arviragus'; since the conversion story is Hardyng's own, 'Mewynus' cannot be a genuine source. Nevertheless 'Mewyn' occurs again only two stanzas on, this time in relation to the red-cross shield which Joseph presents to Arviragus:

> The Armes were used in all Britayne
> For comoun signe eche man' to knowe his nacioun
> Fro hys enemyse Which nowe we call certayne
> Seynt Georges armes by Mewyns ynformacioun,
> Which Armes here were hade after Crist passioun,
> Full longe afore seynt George was generate
> Were worshipped here of mekell elder date.   (28r)

All the manuscripts agree in reading 'Mewyns' (or equivalent spelling) in the fourth line, but Grafton prints 'Nennius'. However, all the manuscripts and the printed text also have some version of a marginal gloss at this point in which the 'Mewyns' or 'Nennius' of the text has become 'Marian': 'Marian the Skotte seith these Armys were yeuyn firste to Arviragus longe afore seynt George was bore'. In Princeton University Library, Robert Garrett 142 (47v), in Oxford, Bodleian Library, Douce 345 (*S.C.* 21920) (20v) and in Grafton's print he is called 'Marian the profound cronicler'. The unanimity among the manuscripts in reading 'Marian' in the margin and 'Mewyn' in the text is striking. It suggests that 'Marian' must go back to very early in the textual history of the Short Chronicle, and possibly to Hardyng himself. It is clearly an attempt to make sense of a name that must have sounded peculiar even to a reader of the *Historia regum Britannie*, that repository of strange names. If the gloss is Hardyng's own, it suggests that by the time he came to write it he could not remember any longer whom he had meant by the name 'Mewyn'. Marianus Scotus, the twelfth-century Irish author of a universal chronicle, is

[14] *The History of the Holy Grail by Henry Lovelich*, ed. F. J. Furnivall, 5 vols, EETS es 20, 24, 28, 30, 95 (London, 1874–1965) IV, 324.
[15] Lansdowne 204, 39v. He does not convert in the Latin *Brut* described in n. 13 either.

implausibly referred to much earlier in the text as an authority on how 'Albion' came to be so called and what Brutus's arms were like. Hardyng may well have picked up his name from the *Flores historiarum* of Roger of Wendover and Matthew Paris, mentioned quite frequently as 'Flores' later in the Short Chronicle and in which Marianus Scotus is one of the many authorities cited.

The marginal identification notwithstanding, it seems unlikely that anyone other than Hardyng lies behind this claim for the antiquity of St George's arms, to which I shall return. It looks as if both these references to 'Mewynus' are designed to authenticate his own spurious history. This still does not explain, of course, why Hardyng should have given his mysterious source, however bogus it may be, this particular name. The next occurrences, in his description of the reign of Arviragus's son, Marius, seem to complicate the issue further. Here there are two allusions to 'Mewynus' in relation to the antecedents of the Scots. After giving an account derived from the *Historia regum Britannie* of how the Scots are descended from the intermarriage of the Picts and the Irish, Hardyng clearly turns to another source:

> But Mewynus the Briton Cronyclere
> Saith in his Cronycles other wise.   (29r)

Since in the Long Chronicle he had simply followed Geoffrey of Monmouth, it looks as if he has come across new material in the interim. He goes on to give the alternative account, favoured by fifteenth-century Scottish historians, of the descent of the Scots from the marriage of Gadolus and Pharaoh's daughter, Scota. With his characteristic anti-Scottishness he makes her a bastard daughter: 'This Scota was as Mewyn saith the sage / Doughter and bastarde of kynge Pharao that day'.[16] A brief early version of the story of Gadolus the Scythian and Scota the Egyptian is found in chapter 14 of the *Historia Brittonum* of pseudo-Nennius, but this cannot be Hardyng's source, since he also includes the story of the stone of Scone which is not in the *Historia*. Nevertheless it may well be that 'Mewynus' is a misreading of Nennius, as Grafton (or his copy-text) assumed in the instance I have already discussed. Hardyng could well have known Nennius as the author of a British history,[17] and it may be that the *Historia Brittonum* is intended here as

[16]   This may be a deliberate response to the common contemporary Scottish allegation of Arthur's bastardy. See Kennedy, 'John Hardyng', pp. 199–201, and references.

[17]   The *Historia Brittonum* survives in over thirty manuscripts, and is cited as a source in later histories such as the *Flores historiarum* and *Polychronicon*, from where Hardyng could have picked up the name. There may also be a confused reference to pseudo-Nennius in a gloss in the Long Chronicle, 78r: 'What the Reule of ordour of Saynt Graal was her' is expressed and notifyed as is conteyned in þe book of Josep of arymathie and as it is specified in a dialoge þat Gildas made de gestis Arthur'. (The sources are added by Hand 2.) The *Historia Brittonum* is frequently attributed to Gildas in medieval manuscripts; the dialogue 'de gestis Arthur' is conceivably 'de gestis Britonum', an alternative title for the *Historia Brittonum* (see n. 19 below).

a deliberate attempt to cover (and distort with the bastardy slur) Hardyng's true source, which was most probably a Scottish one.[18]

The last references to 'Mewyns boke' occur much later, during the reign of Arthur, in connection with the Siege Perilous:

> Which Ioseph saide afore that tyme full' longe
> In Mewyns boke the Britouns Cronyclere
> As wretyn' is the Britouns Iestes amonge
> That Galaad the knyght and virgyne clere
> Shuld it escheue.   (49r)

The 'Britouns Iestes' sounds like a translation of 'de gestis Britonum', and the reference may again be to pseudo-Nennius whose *Historia Brittonum* was also known by this name.[19] If Nennius is meant, the allusion is of course entirely without foundation. On the other hand, *De gestis Britonum* was also used for Geoffrey of Monmouth's *Historia regum Britannie*. The Glastonbury copy of Geoffrey's work evidently had this title because this is how John of Glastonbury refers to it, and it is the title William Worcestre uses in his *Itineraria* for the copy which he saw at the abbey.[20] Since 'Mewyns boke' is, according to Hardyng, 'amonge' the 'Britouns Iestes', the reference may be to *Prophetie Merlini* which is included in the *Historia* as a separate book, and 'Mewyns' may be a misreading of 'Merlyns'. A gloss in the Long Chronicle, relating to Arthur's death, refers directly to *Prophetie Merlini*, from which it quotes.[21] *Prophetie Merlini* does not, of course, include any prophecies about Galaad, but in the *Queste del Saint Graal*, which Hardyng certainly drew on for his account of the Grail quest from which this stanza comes, Merlin prophesies that Galaad will achieve the Siege Perilous and the Grail.[22] Although it is very tempting to interpret 'Mewyns' as 'Merlyns', this does not explain why the same mistake is not made in the following stanza:

> But the knyghtes all than' of the Rounde Table
> Conseived well and fully than' beleued
> He was the same person incomperable
> Of whom Merlyne said euer shuld be well cheued.   (49r)

Here Hardyng clearly shows that he knows the Merlin prophecy in the

---

[18] For Scottish historians' use of the story of Gadolus and Scota, see W. Matthews, 'The Egyptians in Scotland: The Political History of a Myth', *Viator* 1 (1970), 289–306. Kennedy, 'John Hardyng', pp. 185–206, argues convincingly that Hardyng uses Joseph and the Grail story as anti-Scottish propaganda.

[19] Higden, for example, lists it as 'Gildas, de Gestis Britonum' in Bk I, ch. 2 of the *Polychronicon* (ed. C. Babington and J. R. Lumby, 9 vols, RS 41 [London, 1865–86] I, 24).

[20] *Cronica*, ch. 22 (ed. Carley, pp. 56 and 278). The *Historia regum Britannie* is more often called 'Historia Britonum' in medieval library catalogues.

[21] 'De quo Merlinus dicit inter prophecias suas quod exitus eius erit dubius' (86v; hand 2). Withrington, 'The Arthurian Epitaph', p. 123, n. 53, identifies the last four words as a direct quotation from *Prophetie Merlini*, probably picked up from elsewhere, however.

[22] *La Queste del Saint Graal*, ed. A. Pauphilet (Paris, 1923), pp. 77–8.

Queste, and is able to get the name right. Nevertheless, since consistency is a virtue he conspicuously lacks, Merlin must remain a possible identification of the source called 'Mewynus', especially since the last reference seems to point, waveringly, in that direction.

After Galaad's death Bors and Percival bring his heart back to England and tell Arthur how he had founded the order of the 'Sanke Roiall' in the Holy Land

in full signyficacioun
Of the Table which Ioseph was the foundoure
At Aualone as Mewyne maketh relacioun
In tokyn' of the Table and refiguracioun
Of the brotherhode at Cristes soper and maunde
Afore his deth of higheste dignyte.   (50v)

Again, Hardyng is drawing on the passage in the *Queste del Saint Graal* in which the three great fellowships are described to Percival: the table of the Last Supper, the table of the Holy Grail instituted 'en semblance et en remembrance de lui'[23] by Joseph of Arimathea, and the Round Table instituted by Merlin, about which he prophesies. The presence of the voice of Merlin in the immediate context of Joseph's table may have been enough to give rise to this factitious attribution. (In the Long Chronicle Hardyng had used this passage at a different point, in describing how Uther Pendragon set up the Round Table at his wedding to Igerne 'by advyse of Merlyns ordynance'. He takes four stanzas on 66r to explain that the Round Table is a 'fygure and remembrance' of Joseph's table of the 'saynte Grale', which is in turn a figure of the table of the supper that Christ made 'in Symounde leprous house'. It is tempting to imagine that when Hardyng came to rewrite the Short Chronicle he could not decipher the reference to Merlin in his own notes.)

It seems, then, that the five passages in which 'Mewynus' is cited as the authority derive from different sources: from Hardyng's own fertile imagination, from a Scottish chronicler and from a conflation of the *Queste del Saint Graal* and *Prophetie Merlini*. 'Mewynus' may be a misreading of Nennius or Merlin or both. The possibility remains, nevertheless, that the name 'Mewynus' itself, though not the material which Hardyng associates with it, derives from 'Melkynus'. The Melkin prophecy was taken over from John of Glastonbury's *Cronica* into other histories; it is included, for example, in a London continuation of the *Flores historiarum*.[24] 'Mewynus' may be to

---

[23] *La Queste*, ed. Pauphilet, p. 74.
[24] London, Lambeth Palace Library, 1106, 10v. (See *Flores historiarum per Matthaeum Westmonasteriensem collecti*, ed H. R. Luard, 3 vols, RS 95 [London, 1890] I, 127.) On the flyleaf of Cambridge, Trinity College, R. 5. 33 (724), a compilation of Glastonbury material written in hands of the thirteenth to sixteenth centuries, there is an excerpt from John of Glastonbury's *Cronica*, beginning 'Issta scriptura inuenitur in libro melkini qui fuit ante merlinum'. (See M. R. James, *The Western Manuscripts in the Library of Trinity College, Cambridge: A Descriptive Catalogue*, 3 vols [Cambridge, 1900–2] II, 199.) See Carley, 'Melkin the Bard and Esoteric Tradition', pp. 2–3, for other occurrences of the prophecy in fifteenth-century manuscripts.

Hardyng what 'Lollius' was to Chaucer: the fictitious source of a writer of unscholarly habits – in Hardyng's case – who composed with fewer resources at his disposal than he cared to admit, and who was anyway an inveterate name-dropper. By the middle of the fifteenth century we may probably assume that Hardyng could have come across Melkin's name in any one of a variety of different contexts. He may have created out of 'Melkynus qui ante Merlinum fuit' a 'Briton cronicler' to lend an authentic-sounding Celtic touch to various features of his history not dealt with by Geoffrey. Nevertheless, even if he did know Melkin's name, it was probably not directly from John of Glastonbury, since there is no clear evidence from Hardyng's version of the Joseph of Arimathea legend that he had read the *Cronica*.

In the Long Chronicle Joseph comes to Britain in A.D. 63 carrying two phials of Christ's sweat as red as blood, and is licensed by King Arviragus to preach the Christian faith. The king also gives him twelve hides of land at 'Mewetryne' (for Yniswitrin), now called Glastonbury, where he is buried (39r). All this must originate in the *Cronica*, but it is unlikely, nevertheless, that John is the immediate source. Hardyng goes on to tell the story of the pagan king Agrestes of North Wales who throws into the sea off Caerleon a life-like crucifix made by Joseph. Agrestes is punished by madness and burns to death in an oven. The crucifix, however, floats ashore at London two generations (and five pages) later, in the time of King Lucius, and is erected at St Paul's as the 'roode of the North Doore'. This episode must derive ultimately from the account in the *Estoire del Saint Graal* of the vicissitudes suffered by Joseph and his son, Josephe, during their conversion of the Britons: Hardyng's Agrestes of North Wales is a conflation of Crudel, King of Norgales (North Wales), and Agrestes, King of Kamaalot. The first imprisons Joseph and Josephe, and is killed by Nascien. The second puts to death twelve of Josephe's followers at a cross erected by Josephe and burns another cross, but later goes mad and commits suicide by leaping into a furnace. The bloody cross of the martyrs turns black and remains so until Arthur's reign.[25] These crosses seem to have given rise to the story of the miraculously surviving crucifix, which is a purely English accretion to the Joseph legend, and which is not Hardyng's own invention. A marginal gloss in Lansdowne 204 summarizes the recovery of the crucifix in the reign of Lucius thus:

How the Roode at north dore whiche Agrestes caste in ...e se in Wales came vp fletynge in Themse at Caerlud now called London in Lucius tyme kyng of Bretayne as is comprised in a table afore the Rode at Northdore and in a story in a wyndow byhynde the sayd Rode.
(42r)

In Hardyng's day there was in fact a famous crucifix in St Paul's known as

---

[25] *The Vulgate Version of the Arthurian Romances*, ed. H. O. Sommer, 8 vols (New York, 1908–16) I, 244–5. John of Glastonbury does not mention Agrestes, but does include the 'perfidus rex Nortwallie' who imprisons Joseph and his companions and is killed by Nascien (*Cronica*, ch. 18; ed. Carley, p. 50).

the Rood at the North Door which was a popular resort of pilgrims, in part, no doubt, because of its association with the cult of Joseph of Arimathea.[26] The 'table' to which the Lansdowne gloss alludes was evidently one of the many which Dugdale describes in Old St Paul's and which, like Glastonbury's own *Magna Tabula*, recorded the history of the building and its contents.[27] Presumably the story of Agrestes and Joseph's crucifix was also depicted in some way in the stained glass of the window. It may be that the 'table' and the window in St Paul's themselves were Hardyng's source for the legend of Joseph's crucifix. It is equally possible that his copy of Geoffrey of Monmouth's *Historia regum Britannie* – which, as I have already suggested, was his main source – contained interpolated material relating to Joseph's mission, perhaps from a Life of Joseph including the story of Agrestes and the crucifix.[28] The St Paul's 'table' and window presumably had a similar source.[29]

Whatever the nature of the text on which Hardyng drew, the material it incorporated – including the story of Joseph's crucifix – must have originated from Glastonbury under the influence of John of Glastonbury's *Cronica*. Joseph's crucifix is a neat device for linking the reigns of Arviragus and Lucius, which only in John's version of history need linking at all. The original text of William of Malmesbury's *De antiquitate Glastonie ecclesie* had awkwardly bequeathed two different accounts of the conversion of Britain

[26]   W. R. Lethaby, 'Old St Paul's – IV', *The Builder* 139 (July–Dec. 1930), 791–3, at 792; W. Dugdale, *The History of St Paul's Cathedral in London* (London, 1658), p. 20. I am indebted to P. Lindley for these references. Skeat (*Joseph of Arimathie*, p. xlvii) quotes Pecock's *Repressor*: 'wherfore it is vein, waast, and idil forto trotte . . . to the rode of the north dore at London rather than to ech other roode in what ever place he be' (*The Repressor of Over Much Blaming of the Clergy*, ed. C. Babington, 2 vols, RS 19 [London, 1860] I, 194).

[27]   Lethaby, 'Old St Paul's', p. 793. For discussion of *tabulae* in churches, see Gransden, *Historical Writing in England II*, p. 495, and C. Richmond, 'Hand and Mouth: Information Gathering and Use in England in the Later Middle Ages', *Journal of Historical Sociology* 1 (1988), 233–53, at 246–7.

[28]   See n. 11 above. Carley (*The Chronicle of Glastonbury Abbey*, pp. 278–9, n. 72) presents evidence suggesting that Glastonbury had a copy of the *Historia regum Britannie* into which Joseph material, including the 'Flos Armathie Ioseph' verses, had been interpolated. Hardyng may have had access to a similar text, but interpolated with post-*Cronica* material. Alternatively, his version of the *Historia regum Britannie* may have been in a manuscript containing other Glastonbury texts which included the story of Agrestes and the crucifix; a parallel would be Oxford, Bodleian Library, Bodley 622 (S.C. 2156), a fourteenth-century historical compilation which contains the *Historia* along with 'Quedam narracio de nobili rege Arthuro in sacramento altaris', also found in John of Glastonbury's *Cronica*. (I am indebted to J. Carley for this reference.)

[29]   In *The Lyfe of Joseph of Armathia* printed by Pynson in 1520 (*Joseph of Arimathie*, ed. Skeat, pp. 35–49), the story of Arviragus's gift of the Twelve Hides of Glastonbury to Joseph and his son Josephes is immediately followed, as in Hardyng, by an account of Joseph's fashioning of 'the rode of north dore of london', though without the tale of Agrestes. This part of the *Lyfe* is largely drawn from John of Glastonbury's *Cronica* or a direct derivative such as Capgrave's *Nova legenda Anglie*, neither of which contains the Rood legend, however. The author of the *Lyfe* has possibly taken this from Hardyng, though it is just as likely to have come from the St Paul's 'table' or its source.

and the foundation of Glastonbury: first, possibly, by missionaries sent by St Philip at an unspecified date and then, more certainly, in the reign of Lucius by missionaries sent by Pope Eleutherius.[30] Later interpolators identified the apostolic mission as that of Joseph of Arimathea in A.D. 63, and took over the names – Phagan and Divian or Deruvian – given to Eleutherius's missionaries by Geoffrey of Monmouth. John of Glastonbury continued the process of reconciling the *De antiquitate* with Geoffrey's scheme of events by placing the arrival of Joseph in the reign of Lucius's great-grandfather, Arviragus; these now become key reigns in the Glastonbury version of history. Hardyng includes the second founding of Glastonbury by Phagan and Divian in both the Long and Short Chronicles as an expansion of his account of the reign of Lucius which derives from the *Historia regum Britannie*. This account begins, as John of Glastonbury does not, with Geoffrey's description of the founding of the archbishoprics of Caerleon, London and York, so that the subsequent grant of the Twelve Hides is assimilated to a wider context and seen as part of a national as well as a local story. William of Malmesbury's originally quite separate foundation stories are unified in both the interpolated versions of the *De antiquitate* and in John of Glastonbury's *Cronica* by having the later missionaries discover the old church at Glastonbury left by their earlier counterparts, along with assorted documents testifying to the church's antiquity. This story does not appear in either the Long or Short Chronicle; instead Hardyng unifies his two accounts of the foundation of Glastonbury by completing in the reign of Lucius the story of Joseph's crucifix, left unfinished in the reign of Arviragus.

But if the legend of Joseph's crucifix can be seen, as I have argued, as a further stage in the process of rationalizing the double foundation story, it is also part of the larger history of the conversion of Britain. Joseph's crucifix in contemporary St Paul's is a tangible reminder of the importance of the reigns of both Arviragus and Lucius in the history of England as a Christian country. The reign of Lucius had had this significance ever since Gildas and, following him, Bede. The Christian mission sent by Eleutherius at Lucius's request is referred to by many later historians. The reign of Arviragus, however, acquired its significance in the history of Christian England only in the fourteenth century, after John of Glastonbury. (The French prose *Brut d'Angleterre*, written before John's *Cronica* in the reign of Edward I and translated into English between 1350 and 1380, calls Arviragus 'Armoger', and his son – who in Geoffrey of Monmouth and Hardyng is Marius – 'Westmere'. Armoger's reign is given no more space than those that surround it and there is, of course, no conversion story. Christianity reaches Britain in the *Brut* only during the reign of 'Lucie'.)[31] The story of Joseph's cross must have developed after the publication of the *Cronica*; whoever made it up presum-

---

[30] William's original text of chs 1–36 of the *De antiquitate* has been reconstructed by Scott: *The Early History*, pp. 168–72; see p. 168 for the conversion of Britain and the foundation of Glastonbury.

[31] *The Brut or The Chronicles of England*, ed. F. Brie, 2 vols, EETS os 131, 136 (London, 1906–8) I, 37–8.

ably turned to the *Estoire del Saint Graal*, on which John himself had already so fruitfully drawn, for further information about events that might plausibly be located in what is now seen as a crucial reign.[32]

Hardyng's narrative of Joseph's mission in the Short Chronicle is more confused than in the Long. It occupies eleven stanzas in all (chapter 47 in Grafton's print), and tells the story of Joseph's arrival and Arviragus's grant of the Twelve Hides twice over, in different words and with slightly different emphases. The dating is not the same as in the Long Chronicle; now Hardyng adopts the chronology of the *Estoire del Saint Graal*, in which Joseph is put in prison for forty-two years after the death of Christ, sustained only by the Holy Grail. John of Glastonbury, summarizing the early parts of the *Estoire* in chapter 18 of the *Cronica*, had omitted this second imprisonment, presumably since it conflicts with the dating in the interpolated *De antiquitate* of Joseph's arrival in Britain in A.D. 63 which John retains, and Hardyng originally followed the Glastonbury version. Now in the Short Chronicle he has Joseph in prison for forty-two years, 'Withoute mete or drynke by any waye/But oonly was comforte by goddes sonde' (27v). His recapitulation five stanzas later does not include the imprisonment but gives Joseph's date of arrival in Britain, not mentioned earlier, as A.D. 76 or 77 (the manuscripts vary on this point). Arviragus's grant of the Twelve Hides is described twice, with 'Insewytryne' being identified as Glastonbury on the first occasion and as Avalon on the second, but thereafter the two accounts diverge. The first goes on to tell the story of Agrestes and the crucifix, followed by Arviragus's death.[33] The narrative then reverts in the next stanza to Joseph's arrival, with Arviragus alive. This time, after being endowed with Avalon, Joseph baptizes Arviragus, shows him 'a figure of Cristes pyne', and gives him a shield bearing a red cross 'Of his own blode whiche from his neck did rynne', which turns up again in the reigns of Lucius, Constantine, Uther Pendragon, and Arthur. The red cross is a national as well as a Christian symbol; it is, apparently, the shield which Galaad will take on the Quest of the Holy

[32]   Hardyng's view of Arviragus as a Christian king was adopted in the sixteenth century by the compilers of two heraldic manuscripts, London, British Library, Harley 1074 (at 163r) and Lansdowne 882 (at 29r). Both were written in the reign of Henry VIII. They include the red-cross arms of Arviragus in lists of the arms of British kings from the earliest times, and quote the Short Chronicle. The compiler of Harley 1074 probably drew on Grafton's print; another item on 197v–198v entitled 'The king*is* titelez to all landes breuely reported' is Hardyng's prologue to the duke of York, written as prose. Lansdowne 882 seems to derive from a manuscript version of the Chronicle. My attention was drawn to these manuscripts by J. Carley, who is in turn indebted to J. Gooddall.

[33]   In Grafton's second 1543 edition of the Chronicle the story of Agrestes and Joseph's crucifix has been omitted from this chapter and from chapter 51, which covers the reign of Lucius, presumably because of the popish implications of the Rood at the North Door of St Paul's. (Grafton dedicated the Chronicle to the duke of Norfolk who, though conservative in religion, had been one of Henry VIII's leading commanders against the Pilgrimage of Grace.) I have not seen Grafton's first edition, published earlier in 1543.

Grail,[34] but Hardyng is more interested in it as the 'comoun signe eche man to knowe his nacioun/Fro hys enemyse'. He is almost defensively concerned to use the story of Joseph's grant of arms to Arviragus in order to prove the antiquity of the badge of St George, a theme to which he returns in both versions of the Chronicle.

The striking thing about all this is that in the short version there is no mention at this point of the Grail, even in its attenuated Glastonbury form as the two phials of blood and sweat.[35] Joseph in the Short Chronicle is not the Grail-bearer at all, but is instead the bearer of the Christian message, and the fashioner of the Rood at the North Door of St Paul's and the red-cross arms. Valerie Lagorio has shown how Joseph's mission was used by the English delegates at four church councils between 1409 and 1434 to buttress their claims for the status and antiquity of the English Church.[36] Hardyng's nationalism is, by comparison, secular and chivalric. Nevertheless he uses Joseph in a similar way, to show that the red cross of St George did not originate with the saint in Cappadocia but in England, at Glastonbury. The Englishness of the symbol was important in a period when St George was increasingly revered not only as the protector of soldiers (and thus as patron saint of the Order of the Garter, founded by Edward III in 1349), but also as

---

[34]   Though there is an inconsistency, since Galaad finds the shield with the red cross drawn in Joseph's blood at Avalon, where Joseph has left it (50r). The accounts of the Grail quest in Arthur's reign in the Long and Short Chronicle draw on the *Queste del Saint Graal* and *Estoire del Saint Graal*, and Hardyng does not, in general, attempt to co-ordinate them with what he has already written about Joseph.

[35]   Harley 661 has the following gloss: 'Nota howe Joseph of Aramathye come into Britayne with Vespasyan and cristeyned a parte of this londe and made the Roode of the North door at Caierlion. Also this Joseph brought into Britayne with hym parte of the blode of Criste whiche is called Seyntgraal the true sayinge is Sank Roiall. Also this Joseph made a Rounde Table for hym and for hys felowes in remembraunce of xii Apostolles which Rounde Table kynge Arthure honoured and held' (27v). The second and third sentences do not occur in any of the other manuscripts and are probably not authorial, especially since neither the Grail nor the Round Table is mentioned at this point in the text. If they are Hardyng's, they represent an unusual attempt to link an earlier part of the Chronicle to a later. Hardyng does not say in his version of the Grail legend (in Arthur's reign) that the 'Sank Roiall' is Christ's blood. It is more likely that these sentences have been added to Harley 661 or its exemplar by a knowledgeable scribe, perhaps the person who filled in the missing fifth line in the first stanza on 27v as follows:

> For fourty yere and two he prisouned laye
> Fro deth of Criste to tyme he hade hym founde
> Withoute mete or drynke be any waye
> But oonly was comfort by goddes sone
> *And of Criste blode he founde in Joseph honde.*

The other manuscripts deal with the gap in a variety of different ways. The knowledgeable scribe may also have corrected Hardyng's 'Mewetryne' to 'Insewetryne'. That the former was Hardyng's spelling seems clear, since this how it appears in the Long Chronicle which was, I believe, written under his supervision. All the manuscripts of the short version except Harley 661 call it 'Mewetryne'.

[36]   Lagorio, 'The Evolving Legend', pp. 219–23.

patron saint of England.[37] In 1415, in the aftermath of Agincourt, the feast of St George was proclaimed a major festival by Archbishop Chichele, and all men were bidden to pray to the saint 'tanquam patrono et protectore dictae nationis speciali'.[38] It looks very much as if Hardyng felt the need to defend the red cross of England against the charge that it had been only recently invented. And so, beyond George, he descries Joseph who validates the antiquity and Englishness of George's red-cross arms.

Hardyng's chivalric nationalism may explain why, in both versions, he includes in the much later reign of Arthur his extraordinary account of the Grail quest, which is not really a quest at all: in one version it lasts four lines and in the other simply drops from the narrative. Galaad goes to Avalon and finds Joseph's shield with the red cross, which he takes to the Holy Land where he sets up his chivalric order of the Holy Grail. In both versions of the Chronicle the Sanke Roiall is thoroughly demystified as the emblem of this order, and Joseph is remembered as the founder of a similar fellowship. When Galaad dies Percival brings his heart home to be buried in Glastonbury, the heart of Christian England:

> And to the kynge his herte in gold preserued
> As Galaad had comaunde he than presente
> Besekyng' hym for that he had hym serued
> It to entere at Aualon anente
> The sepultur and verry monument
> Whare Iosep lyeth of Aramathy so gode
> By syde Nacion that ner' was of his blode
>
> And ther' to sette his sheld that Iosep made
> Which was the armes that we saynt Georges call
> That aftir thar' full many yer' abode
> And worshipt wer' thurgh out this Reme ouer all.   (77r–78v)

John of Glastonbury had, of course, already demystified the Holy Grail, making it a reliquary rather than the cup of the Last Supper. This is hardly surprising, especially given the heterodox implications of the Grail as it is presented in the *Estoire del Saint Graal*. Hardyng's treatment of the Grail seems to derive from a different source: not from the monk's wariness at treading dangerous ground but rather from the indifference of a no more than conventionally pious layman to the theology of the eucharist. We would do well to bear in mind the Hardyngs of a period in which the cult of

---

[37]   The cult of St George, of which the Order of the Garter is an expression, was revived in England during the fourteenth and fifteenth centuries and received particular impetus from the personal devotion of Henry V. (See J. Catto, 'Religious Change under Henry V', in *Henry V: The Practice of Kingship*, ed. G. L. Harriss [Oxford, 1985], pp. 97–115, at 107–8.) A contemporary chronicler reports that after the capture of Rouen in 1419 Henry V had banners set on each of its gates: 'at Porte Martuyle he vp pight / Of Seint George a baner bright' (*The Brut*, ed. Brie, II, 421).
[38]   Quoted by E. C. Williams, 'Mural Paintings of St. George in England', *Journal of the British Archaeological Association*, 3rd ser. 12 (1949), 19–36, at 20. I am indebted to P. Lindley for this reference.

Corpus Christi was so assiduously propagated by the ecclesiastical and civic authorities and when devotion to the Real Presence was a hallmark of orthodoxy; the Hardyngs are the people whose religious views are never recorded. Hardyng seems to have had no interest at all in the Grail as a eucharistic symbol; when he read the *Queste del Saint Graal* he was much more profoundly stirred by the fact that Galaad's shield bore St George's red cross of England than by 'les merveilles de totes autres merveilles' that Galaad finally saw in the Grail.[39] But this is, perhaps, no more than we should expect. Hardyng had, after all, spent over thirty years in the service of a Garter knight and had been with him at Agincourt.[40] Perhaps across half a lifetime he remembered as he read how on that day, according to an English chronicler, the king commanded every man to make ready for the battle 'and said thes wordes: "Sirres! thenkes this day to quyte youe as men, and feightes for þe righte of Englond! and, in the name of Almyghty God, avaunt baner! and Saynt George, this day thyn helpe!" ' And then perhaps he recalled, too, how he and the others had knelt down 'and made a cros on þe grounde, and kissit it, and put hem in the mercy of God'.[41]

[39]   *La Queste*, ed. Pauphilet, p. 278.
[40]   Hardyng entered the service of the Garter knight Sir Robert Umfreville (*ca* 1361–1436/7) in 1403.
[41]   From a fifteenth-century continuation of the *Brut*; see *The Brut*, ed. Brie, II, 555. I am grateful to C. Meale for referring me to this text, and to J. Carley for suggesting improvements to the whole article.

LIST OF CONTRIBUTORS

Philip Rahtz, formerly Professor of Archaeology, University of York

Michael D. Costen, Senior Lecturer in Adult Education and Resident Tutor for the County of Somerset, Department for Continuing Studies, University of Bristol

C. James Bond, freelance field archaeologist and landscape historian, based in Tickenham, Avon; part-time tutor, Department for Continuing Studies, University of Bristol

John B. Weller, chartered architect from Bildeston, Suffolk, with special interest in agricultural buildings

Robert W. Dunning, Editor, Victoria History of Somerset

Lesley Abrams, Research Associate, Department of Anglo-Saxon, Norse, and Celtic, University of Cambridge

James P. Carley, Associate Professor, Department of English, York University, Toronto

Ann Dooley, Co-ordinator of the Celtic Studies Programme, St Michael's College, University of Toronto

Sarah Foot, Research Fellow, Gonville & Caius College, Cambridge

David Ewan Thornton, Research Scholar, School of Celtic Studies, Dublin Institute for Advanced Studies

Richard Sharpe, Reader in Diplomatic, University of Oxford

Julia Crick, Research Fellow, Gonville & Caius College, Cambridge

O. J. Padel, Research Assistant, Department of Welsh History, University College, Aberystwyth

Matthew Blows, formerly of the University of London

Charles T. Wood, Daniel Webster Professor of History, Dartmouth College, Hanover, N.H., U.S.A.

Nicholas Orme, Professor of History, University of Exeter

Ceridwen Lloyd-Morgan, Archivist, National Library of Wales, Aberystwyth

Felicity Riddy, Reader in English, University of York

INDEX

INDEX OF CHARTERS

INDEX OF MANUSCRIPTS

DATE DUE

HIGHSMITH 45-220